2014

the best campsites in Spain & Portugal

over 280 independent reviews

Compiled by: Alan Rogers Travel Ltd

Designed by: Vine Design Ltd

Additional photography: T Lambelin, www.lambelin.com
Maps created by Customised Mapping (01769 540044)
contain background data provided by GisDATA Ltd

Published by: Alan Rogers Travel Ltd,
Spelmonden Old Oast, Goudhurst, Kent TN17 1HE
www.alanrogers.com Tel: 01580 214000

British Library Cataloguing-in-Publication Data:
A catalogue record for this book is available
from the British Library.

ISBN 978-1-909057-46-3

Printed in Great Britain by Stephens & George Print Group

Contents

Alan Rogers - in search of ‘the best’

Alan Rogers Guides were first published over 40 years ago. Since Alan Rogers published the first campsite guide that bore his name, the range has expanded and now covers 27 countries in six separate guides. No fewer than 20 of the campsites selected by Alan for the first guide are still featured in our 2014 editions.

There are many thousands of campsites in Spain and Portugal of varying quality: this guide contains impartially written reports on almost 300, including many of the very finest, each being individually inspected and selected. We aim to provide you with a selection of the best, rather than information on all – in short, a more selective, qualitative approach. New, improved maps and indexes are also included, designed to help you find the choice of campsite that’s right for you.

Finally, in 2013 we launched the new Alan Rogers Travel Card. Free to readers, it offers exclusive online extras, money saving deals and offers on many campsites. Find out more on page 10.

We hope you enjoy some happy and safe travels – and some pleasurable ‘armchair touring’ in the meantime!

“ ...the campsites included in this book have been chosen entirely on merit, and no payment of any sort is made by them for their inclusion.”

Alan Rogers, 1968

How do we find the best?

The criteria we use when inspecting and selecting campsites are numerous, but the most important by far is the question of good quality. People want different things from their choice of site so we try to include a range of campsite ‘styles’ to cater for a wide variety of preferences: from those seeking a small peaceful campsite in the heart of the countryside, to visitors looking for an ‘all singing, all dancing’ site in a popular seaside resort. Those with more specific interests, such as sporting facilities, cultural events or historical attractions, are also catered for.

The size of the site, whether it’s part of a chain or privately owned, makes no difference in terms of it being required to meet our exacting standards in respect of its quality and it being ‘fit for purpose’. In other words, irrespective of the size of the site, or the number of facilities it offers, we consider and evaluate the welcome, the pitches, the sanitary facilities, the cleanliness, the general maintenance and even the location.

Expert opinions

We rely on our dedicated team of Site Assessors, all of whom are experienced campers, caravanners or motorcaravanners, to visit and recommend campsites. Each year they travel some 100,000 miles around Europe inspecting new campsites for the guide and re-inspecting the existing ones. Our thanks are due to them for their enthusiastic efforts, their diligence and integrity.

We also appreciate the feedback we receive from many of our readers and we always make a point of following up complaints, suggestions or recommendations for possible new campsites. Of course we get a few grumbles too – but it really is a few, and those we do receive usually relate to overcrowding or to poor maintenance during the peak school holiday period. Please bear in mind that, although we are interested to hear about any complaints, we have no contractual relationship with the campsites featured in our guides and are therefore not in a position to intervene in any dispute between a reader and a campsite.

Independent and honest

Whilst the content and scope of the Alan Rogers guides have expanded considerably since the early editions, our selection of campsites still employs exactly the same philosophy and criteria as defined by Alan Rogers in 1968.

'telling it how it is'

Firstly, and most importantly, our selection is based entirely on our own rigorous and independent inspection and selection process. Campsites cannot buy their way into our guides – indeed the extensive Site Report which is written by us, not by the site owner, is provided free of charge so we are free to say what we think and to provide an honest, 'warts and all' description. This is written in plain English and without the use of confusing icons or symbols.

Looking for the best

Highly respected by site owners and readers alike, there is no better guide when it comes to forming an independent view of a campsite's quality. When you need to be confident in your choice of campsite, you need the Alan Rogers Guide.

- Sites only included on merit
- Sites cannot pay to be included
- Independently inspected, rigorously assessed
- Impartial reviews
- Over 40 years of expertise

Written in plain English, our guides are exceptionally easy to use, but a few words of explanation regarding the layout and content may be helpful. In Spain we have used the 16 official administrative regions, whilst in Portugal we use the five regions defined by the Portugal Tourist Board. A full page introduction to each region highlights its main areas of interest, places to visit and the local cuisine.

Region

Index town

Site name

Postal address (including area) T: telephone number. E: email address

alanrogers.com web address (including Alan Rogers reference number)

A description of the site in which we try to give an idea of its general features – its size, its situation, its strengths and its weaknesses. This section should provide a picture of the site itself with reference to the facilities that are provided and if they impact on its appearance or character. We include details on pitch numbers, electricity (with amperage), hardstandings etc. in this section as pitch design, planning and terracing affects the site's overall appearance. Similarly we include reference to pitches used for caravan holiday homes, chalets, and the like. Importantly at the end of this column we indicate if there are any restrictions, e.g. no tents, no children, naturist sites.

Facilities

Lists more specific information on the site's facilities and amenities and, where available, the dates when these facilities are open (if not for the whole season). Off site: here we give distances to various local amenities, for example, local shops, the nearest beach, plus our featured activities (bicycle hire, fishing, horse riding, boat launching). Where we have space we list suggestions for activities and local tourist attractions.

Open: Site opening dates.

Directions

Separated from the main text in order that they may be read and assimilated more easily by a navigator en-route. Bear in mind that road improvement schemes can result in road numbers being altered.

GPS: references are provided in decimal format. All latitudes are North. Longitudes are East unless preceeded by a minus sign e.g. 48.71695 is North, 0.31254 is East and -0.31254 is West.

Charges 2014 (or a general guide)

Maps, campsite listings and indexes

For this 2014 guide we have changed the way in which we list our campsites and also the way in which we help you locate the sites within each region.

We now include a map immediately after our Introduction to that region. These maps show the towns near which one (or more) of our featured campsites is located.

Within each regional section of the guide, we list these towns and the site(s) in that vicinity in alphabetical order.

You will certainly need more detailed maps for navigation, for example the Michelin atlas. We provide GPS coordinates for each site to assist you. Our three indexes will also help you to find a site by region and site name, by reference number or by the town where the site is situated.

Understanding the entries

Facilities

Toilet blocks

Unless we comment otherwise, toilet blocks will be equipped with WCs, washbasins with hot and cold water and hot showers with dividers or curtains, and will have all necessary shelves, hooks, plugs and mirrors. We also assume that there will be an identified chemical toilet disposal point, and that the campsite will provide water and waste water drainage points and bin areas. If not the case, we comment. We do mention certain features that some readers find important: washbasins in cubicles, facilities for babies, facilities for those with disabilities and motorcaravan service points. Readers with disabilities are advised to contact the site of their choice to ensure that facilities are appropriate to their needs.

Shop

Basic or fully supplied, and opening dates.

Bars, restaurants, takeaway facilities and entertainment

We try hard to supply opening and closing dates (if other than the campsite opening dates) and to identify if there are discos or other entertainment.

Children's play areas

Fenced and with safety surface (e.g. sand, bark or pea-gravel).

Swimming pools

If particularly special, we cover in detail in our main campsite description but reference is always included under our Facilities listings. We will also indicate the existence of water slides, sunbathing areas and other features. Opening dates, charges and levels of supervision are provided where we have been notified. There is a regulation whereby Bermuda shorts may not be worn in swimming pools (for health and hygiene reasons). It is worth ensuring that you do take 'proper' swimming trunks with you.

Leisure facilities

For example, playing fields, bicycle hire, organised activities and entertainment.

Dogs

If dogs are not accepted or restrictions apply, we state it here. Check the quick reference list at the back of the guide.

Off site

This briefly covers leisure facilities, tourist attractions, restaurants etc. nearby.

Charges

These are the latest provided to us by the sites. In those cases where 2014 prices have not been provided to us by the sites, we try to give a general guide.

Reservations

Necessary for high season (roughly mid-July to mid-August) in popular holiday areas (i.e. beach resorts). You can reserve many sites via our own Alan Rogers Travel Service or through other tour operators. Or be wholly independent and contact the campsite(s) of your choice direct, using the phone or e-mail numbers shown in the site reports, but please bear in mind that many sites are closed all winter.

Telephone Numbers

All numbers assume that you are phoning from within Spain or Portugal. To phone Spain from outside that country, prefix the number shown with the relevant International Code '00 34' and then the number indicated. To phone Portugal prefix the number shown with the International Code '00 351'.

Opening dates

These are advised to us during the early autumn of the previous year – sites can, and sometimes do, alter these dates before the start of the following season, often for good reasons. If you intend to visit shortly after a published opening date, or shortly before the closing date, it is wise to check that it will actually be open at the time required. Similarly some sites operate a restricted service during the low season, only opening some of their facilities (e.g. swimming pools) during the main season; where we know about this, and have the relevant dates, we indicate it – again if you are at all doubtful it is wise to check.

Sometimes, campsite amenities may be dependent on there being enough customers on site to justify their opening and, for this reason, actual opening dates may vary from those indicated.

Some campsite owners are very relaxed when it comes to opening and closing dates. They may not be fully ready by their stated opening dates – grass and hedges may not all be cut or perhaps only limited sanitary facilities open. At the end of the season they also tend to close down some facilities and generally wind down prior to the closing date. Bear this in mind if you are travelling early or late in the season – it is worth phoning ahead.

The Camping Cheque low season touring system goes some way to addressing this in that many participating campsites will have all key facilities open and running by the opening date and these will remain fully operational until the closing date.

Taking a tent?

In recent years, sales of tents have increased dramatically. With very few exceptions, the campsites listed in this guide have pitches suitable for tents, caravans and motorcaravans. Tents, of course, come in a dazzling range of shapes and sizes. Modern family tents with separate sleeping pods are increasingly popular and these invariably require large pitches with electrical connections. Smaller lightweight tents, ideal for cyclists and hikers, are also visible on many sites and naturally require correspondingly smaller pitches. Many (but not all) sites have special tent areas with prices adjusted accordingly. If in any doubt, we recommend contacting the site of your choice beforehand.

Our Accommodation section

182

Over recent years, more and more campsites have added high quality mobile home and chalet accommodation. In response to feedback from many of our readers, and to reflect this evolution in campsites, we have now decided to include a separate section on mobile homes and chalets. If a site offers this accommodation, it is indicated above the site report with a page reference where full details are given. We have chosen a number of sites offering some of the best accommodation available and have included full details of one or two accommodation types at these sites. Please note however that many other campsites listed in this guide may also have a selection of accommodation for rent.

You're on your way!

Whether you're an 'old hand' in terms of camping and caravanning or are contemplating your first trip, a regular reader of our Guides or a new 'convert', we wish you well in your travels and hope we have been able to help in some way.

We are, of course, also out and about ourselves, visiting sites, talking to owners and readers, and generally checking on standards and new developments.

We wish all our readers thoroughly enjoyable Camping and Caravanning in 2014 – favoured by good weather of course! The Alan Rogers Team

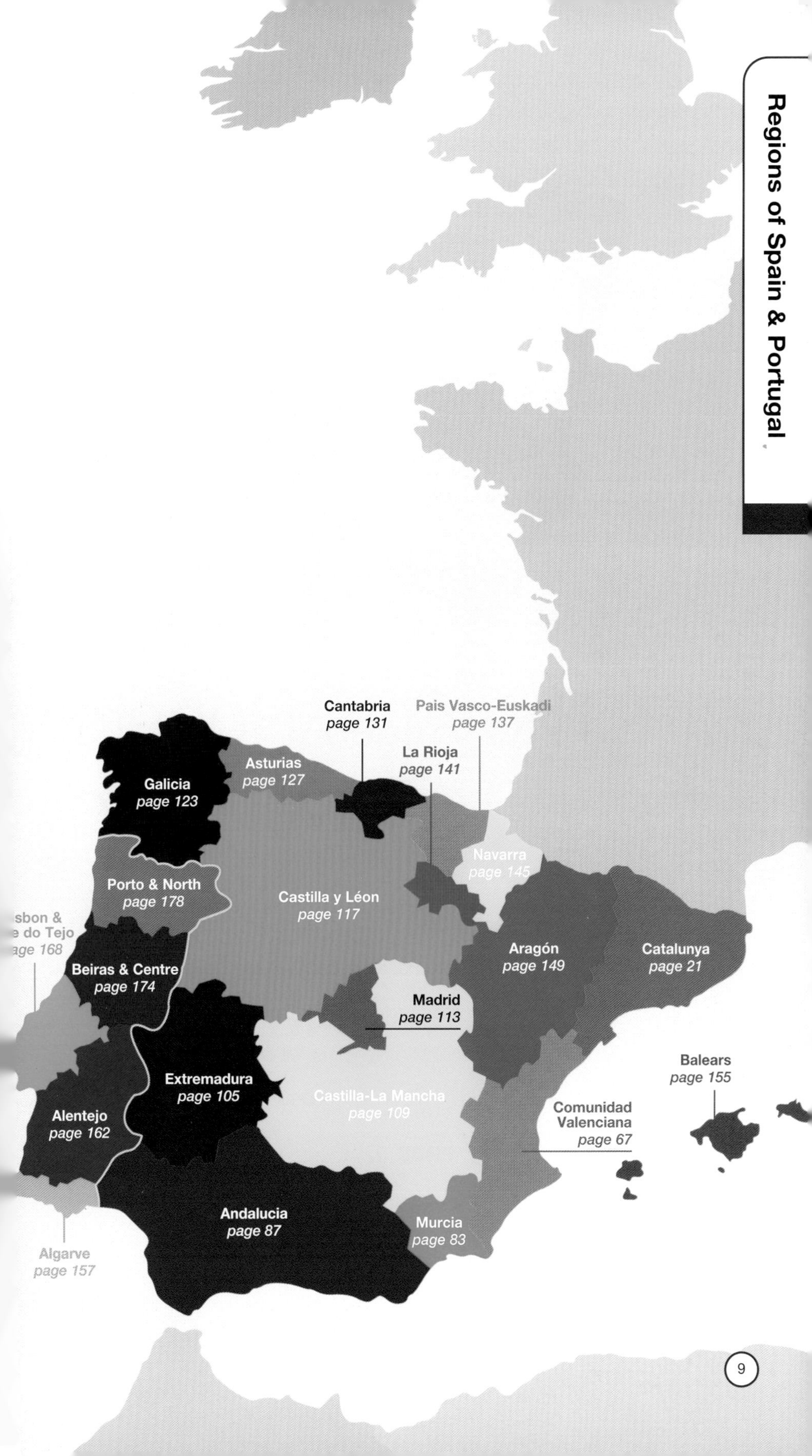
Cantabria
page 131
Pais Vasco-Euskadi
page 137
La Rioja
page 141
Asturias
page 127
Galicia
page 123
Navarra
page 145
Porto & North
page 178
Castilla y Léon
page 117
Aragón
page 149
Catalunya
page 21
Beiras & Centre
page 174
Madrid
page 113
Balears
page 155
Extremadura
page 105
Castilla-La Mancha
page 109
Comunidad
Valenciana
page 67
Alentejo
page 162
Andalucia
page 87
Murcia
page 83
Algarve
page 157

The Alan Rogers Travel Card

At Alan Rogers we have a network of thousands of quality inspected and selected campsites. We also have partnerships with numerous organisations, including ferry operators and tourist attractions, all of whom can bring you benefits and save you money.

Our **FREE** Travel Card binds all this together at

alanrogers.com/travelcard

So register today...and start saving.

The Alan Rogers Awards

The Alan Rogers Campsite Awards were launched in 2004 and have proved a great success.

Our awards have a broad scope and before committing to our winners, we carefully consider more than 2,000 campsites featured in our guides, taking into account comments from our site assessors, our head office team and, of course, our readers.

Our award winners come from the four corners of Europe, from southern Spain to Croatia, and this year we are making awards to campsites in 13 different countries.

Needless to say, it's an extremely difficult task to choose our eventual winners, but we believe that we have identified a number of campsites with truly outstanding characteristics.

In each case, we have selected an outright winner, along with two highly commended runners-up. Listed below are full details of each of our award categories and our winners for 2013.

Alan Rogers Progress Award 2013

This award reflects the hard work and commitment undertaken by particular site owners to improve and upgrade their site.

Winner	
ES87435	Marjal Costa Blanca Eco Camping Resort *Spain*
Runners-up	
DE36720	Camping Elbsee *Germany*
CR6758	Camping Krk *Croatia*

Alan Rogers Welcome Award 2013

This award takes account of sites offering a particularly friendly welcome and maintaining a friendly ambience throughout readers' holidays.

Winner	
NL5970	Camping De Paal *Netherlands*
Runners-up	
FR41100	Camping les Saules *France*
HU5370	Balatontourist Camping Napfény *Hungary*

Our warmest congratulations to all our award winners and our commiserations to all those not having won an award on this occasion.

The Alan Rogers Team

Alan Rogers Active Holiday Award 2013

This award reflects sites in outstanding locations which are ideally suited for active holidays, notably walking or cycling, but which could extend to include such activities as winter sports or watersports.

Winner

DE30700	Südsee-Camp *Germany*

Runners-up

IT62040	Camping Seiser Alm *Italy*
SV4270	Kamp Koren Kobarid *Slovenia*

Alan Rogers Innovation Award 2013

Our Innovation Award acknowledges campsites with creative and original concepts, possibly with features which are unique, and cannot therefore be found elsewhere. We have identified innovation both in campsite amenities and also in rentable accommodation.

Winner

IT60370	Camping Jesolo International *Italy*

Runners-up

ES92120	Camping Monte Holiday *Spain*
NL5985	Vrijetijdspark Beerze Bulten *Netherlands*

Alan Rogers Small Campsite Award 2013

This award acknowledges excellent small campsites (less than 75 pitches) which offer a friendly welcome and top quality amenities throughout the season to their guests.

Winner

ES90960	Camping El Mirador de Cabaneros *Spain*

Runners-up

UK0802	Langstone Manor Holiday Park *England*
SK4955	Camping Lazy *Slovakia*

Alan Rogers Seaside Award 2013

This award is made for sites which we feel are outstandingly suitable for a really excellent seaside holiday.

Winner

IT60200	Camping Union Lido Vacanze *Italy*

Runners-up

FR85000	Camping le Petit Rocher *France*
PO8100	Orbitur Camping São Pedro de Moel *Portugal*

Alan Rogers Country Award 2013

This award contrasts with our former award and acknowledges sites which are attractively located in delightful, rural locations.

Winner

FR32010	Le Camp de Florence *France*

Runners-up

IT62320	Camping Al Sole *Italy*
NL5840	Veluwecamping De Pampel *Netherlands*

Alan Rogers Family Site Award 2013

Many sites claim to be child friendly but this award acknowledges the sites we feel to be the very best in this respect.

Winner

FR83120	Camp du Domaine *France*

Runners-up

FR24350	RCN le Moulin de la Pique *France*
LU7620	Europacamping Nommerlayen *Luxembourg*

Alan Rogers Readers' Award 2013

We believe our Readers' Award to be the most important. We simply invite our readers (by means of an on-line poll at www.alanrogers.com) to nominate the site they enjoyed most.

The outright winner for 2013 is:

Winner

UK0870	Beverley Park *England*

Alan Rogers Special Awards 2013

A Special Award is made to campsites which have suffered a very significant setback, but have coped admirably in very difficult circumstances. In 2013, we wish to acknowledge two very special campsites.

Firstly, this is a highly impressive Austrian campsite badly affected by flooding but which very rapidly returned to its normal very high standard:

AU0265	Park Grubhof *Austria*

Secondly, the owners of FR24180 Saint Avit Loisirs have developed a second top quality site, le Cro Magnon, over a period of 10 years. Very sadly, they have been obliged to close Le Cro Magnon as a result of a possible subsidence risk, and we wish to acknowledge their excellent work at both campsites.

FR24180	Castel Camping Caravaning Saint-Avit Loisirs *France*

Alan Rogers Travel Service

REDUCED BOOKING FEE
NOW ONLY
£25.00

MANY MORE FERRY OPTIONS

essentials

All you need for a fantastic holiday on an Alan Rogers inspected and selected campsite.

Ferry Deals

Crossing the Channel is the start of your holiday and our famous Ferry Deals can offer you the convenience of extraordinary value for money and our widest ever choice of routes. Bear in mind that the flexible pricing of most ferry operators means that you are more likely to get the crossing you want, and at the lowest price, when you book early.

As agents for most cross-Channel operators, we can book all your travel with the minimum of fuss and at great prices. We are able to negotiate very low prices due to the volumes we handle and new offers are regularly being set up. So be sure to check with us before you book!

Routes available

Operator	Route from	Route to	Journey time
Brittany Ferries	Portsmouth	Caen (Ouistreham)	6hrs/9hrs
	Portsmouth	St Malo	9hrs
	Plymouth	Roscoff	6hrs
	Plymouth	Santander	20hrs
	Portsmouth	Santander	24hrs
	Portsmouth	Bilbao	24hrs/32hrs
DFDS SEAWAYS	Newcastle	Ijmuiden(Amsterdam)	15hrs
	Harwich	Esbjerg	17hrs
	Dover	Dunkirk	1.75hrs
	Dover	Calais	1.5hrs
	Newhaven	Dieppe	4.5hrs
	Portsmouth	Le Havre	5.5hrs-8hrs
EURO TUNNEL le shuttle	Folkestone	Coquelles *(between Calais & Boulogne)*	35mins
IrishFerries.com The Low Fares Ferry Company!	Pembroke	Rosslare	3.75hrs
	Holyhead	Dublin	1.75hrs/3.25hrs
P&O Ferries	Dover	Calais	1.5hrs
	Hull	Rotterdam	11hrs
	Hull	Zeebrugge	12.5hrs
P&O Irish	Cairnryan	Larne	1hr-2hrs
	Liverpool	Dublin	8hrs
Stena Line Making good time	Fishguard	Rosslare	3.5hrs
	Harwich	Hook of Holland	6hrs-8hrs
	Holyhead	Dublin	2hrs-3.25hrs
	Cairnryan	Belfast	2.25hrs
	Liverpool	Belfast	8 hrs

Unbeatable Ferry Deals

The Alan Rogers Travel Service offers all routes with all main operators - call us for latest prices and ask us about our famous ferry deals.

Look out for our popular **Caravans go FREE** deals on selected routes at certain times.

Caravans go **FREE** with Brittany Ferries
Portsmouth - Caen
Plymouth - Roscoff
Poole - Cherbourg

Caravans go **FREE** with P&O Ferries
Hull - Zeebrugge/Rotterdam

Don't hesitate to ask our advice on finding the best value for your holiday.

For an instant quote call 01580 214000

alan rogers travel

Getting the most from **off peak touring**

There are many reasons to avoid high season, if you can. Queues are shorter, there's less traffic, a calmer atmosphere and prices are cheaper. And it's usually still nice and sunny!

And when you use Camping Cheques you'll find great quality facilities that are actually open and a welcoming conviviality.

Did you know?

Camping Cheques can be used right into mid-July and from late August on many sites. Over 90 campsites in France alone accept Camping Cheques from 20th August.

Camping Cheque

Save up to 60% with Camping Cheques

Camping Cheque is a fixed price scheme allowing you to go as you please, staying on over 600 campsites across Europe, always paying the same rate and saving you up to 60% on regular pitch fees. One Cheque gives you one night for 2 people + unit on a standard pitch, with electricity. It's as simple as that.

Special offers mean you can stay extra nights free (eg 7 nights for 6 Cheques) or even a month free for a month paid! Especially popular in Spain during the winter, these longer-term offers can effectively halve the nightly rate. See Site Directory for details.

Check out our amazing Ferry Deals!

Why should I use Camping Cheques?

- It's a proven system, recognised by all 600+ participating campsites - so no nasty surprises.
- It's flexible, allowing you to travel between campsites, and also countries, on a whim - so no need to pre-book. (It's low season, so campsites are rarely full, though advance bookings can be made).
- Stay as long as you like, where you like - so you travel in complete freedom.
- Camping Cheques are valid at least 2 years - so no pressure to use them up. (If you have a couple left over after your trip, simply keep them for the following year, or use them up in the UK).

Tell me more... (but keep it brief!)

Camping Cheques was started in 1999 and has since grown in popularity each year (nearly 2 million were used last year). That should speak for itself. There are 'copycat' schemes, but none has the same range of quality campsites that save you up to 60%.

Ask for your **FREE** continental road map, which explains how Camping Cheque works

01580 214002

FREE

downloadable Site Directory

alanrogers.com/directory

campingcheque.co.uk

One of the largest countries in Europe, with glorious beaches, a fantastic sunshine record, vibrant towns and laid back sleepy villages, plus a diversity of landscape, culture and artistic traditions, Spain has all the ingredients for a great holiday.

Tourist Office

Spanish Tourist Office
6th floor, 64 North Row
London W1K 7DE

Tel: 0800 1010 5050
Fax: 0171 629 4257
E-mail: spaininfo@tourspain.es
Internet: www.tourspain.co.uk

Spain has a huge choice of beach resorts to choose from. With charming villages and attractive towns, the Costa Brava boasts spectacular scenery with towering cliffs and sheltered coves. There are plenty of lively resorts, including Lloret, Tossa and Calella, plus several quieter ones. Further along the east coast, the Costa del Azahar stretches from Vinaros to Almanzora, with the great port of Valencia in the middle. Orange groves abound. The central section of the coastline, the Costa Blanca, has 170 miles or so of silvery-white beaches. Benidorm is the most popular resort. The Costa del Sol lies in the south, home to more beaches and brilliant sunshine, whilst in the north the Costa Verde is largely unspoiled, with clean water, sandy beaches and rocky coves against a backdrop of mountains.

Beaches and sunshine aside, Spain also has plenty of great cities and towns to explore, including Barcelona, Valencia, Seville, Madrid, Toledo and Bilbao, all offering an array of sights, galleries and museums.

Population

46.5 million

Capital

Madrid

Climate

Spain has a very varied climate. The north is temperate with most of the rainfall; dry and very hot in the centre; sub-tropical along the Mediterranean.

Language

Castilian Spanish is spoken by most people with Catalan (northeast), Basque (north) and Galician (northwest) used in their respective areas.

Telephone

The country code is 00 34.

Currency

The Euro (€).

Banks

Mon-Fri 09.00-14.00. Sat 09.00-13.00.

Shops

Mon-Sat 09.00-13.00/14.00 and 15.00/16.00-19.30/20.00.
Many close later.

Public Holidays

New Year; Epiphany; Saints Day 19 March; Maundy Thurs; Good Fri; Easter Mon; Labour Day; Saints Day 25 July; Assumption 15 Aug; National Day 12 Oct; All Saints Day 1 Nov; Constitution Day 6 Dec; Immaculate Conception 8 Dec; Christmas Day.

Flanked by the Pyrenees mountains and bathed by the Mediterranean Sea, Catalunya occupies the northeastern part of the Iberian peninsula. It has a strong identity, with a unique culture and language all of its own.

CATALUNYA IS COMPOSED OF FOUR PROVINCES: BARCELONA, TARRAGONA, LLEIDA AND GIRONA

THE REGIONAL CAPITAL IS BARCELONA

Barcelona is the historical capital of Catalunya and Spain's second leading city in both size and importance, after Madrid. The beautiful city has an impressive architectural heritage that includes the Gothic Quarter, with its cathedral, the old City Hall Building, the Episcopal Palace and the splendid Palace of the Generalitat. The city also boasts the work of the incomparable modernist architect Antonio Gaudí. In the centre of the fertile plain of the River Segre sits Lleida, capital of the province of the same name. Prominent atop a hill in the historic quarter of the city is the old cathedral or Seu Vella. The Costa Brava is the coastal zone that begins about 40 km. north of Barcelona and includes the entire shoreline of the province of Girona. It is an area of great natural beauty, formed by a succession of steep cliffs and small coves with finely grained sand. Some of its towns have been massively exploited for tourism but others, such as Tossa de Mar, still maintain their original size and fishing village charm. The principal tourist centres on the coast include Roses, Sant Pere Pescador, L'Escala, L'Estartit, Palamós, Palafrugell, Platja d'Aro, S'Agaro, Sant Feliu de Guíxols, Lloret de Mar and Blanes. There are daily boat services which operate along the coast for most of the year.

Places of interest

Empúries: Greco-Roman city.

Figueres: birthplace of Salvador Dali, museum displaying his finest work.

Girona: one of the oldest and most beautiful Catalan cities, 14th-century cathedral.

La Costa Dorada: stretches south from the Costa Brava to Tarragona, with beautiful, open, well maintained beaches.

Parque Natural de Aigüamolls de L'Empordà: park made up of three reserves, with wildlife and over 320 bird species.

Sitges: attractive beach town, museum of Cau-Ferrat featuring paintings by El Greco.

Tarragona: Roman remains of Tarraco, the original Roman city.

Cuisine of the region

Mediterranean influence with lots of tomatoes, garlic, fresh herbs, olive oil, onions, fish. Wild mushrooms in the autumn. Locally produced wines from Penedés, Conca de Barberá, Pla de Bages and Alella.

Calçots: green onions grilled on a barbecue.

Cod esqueixada: cod soaked in cold water then mixed with tomatoes, olives and onion.

Escalivada: vegetable stew with roasted aubergine and peppers.

Fuet, llonganisa, butifarra: local sausages.

Suquet: seafood casserole.

Recao de binefar: rice cooked with white beans, potatoes and chorizo.

FRANCE
PRADES
BENASQUE
ANDORRA
GUILS DE CERDANYA
PUIGCERDÀ
BELLVER DE CERDANYA
CAMPRODON
ARAGON
N260
SALDES
GUARDIOLA DE BERGUEDÀ
BORREDÀ
BERGA
CATALUNYA
MANRESA
C16/E9
A2
LLEIDA/ LERIDA
BARCELONA
AP7/E15
B10
MONTBLANC
VILANOVA DE PRADES
AP2/E90
POBOLEDA
SITGES
VILANOVA I LA GELTRU
CUBELLES
EL VENDRELL
TARRAGONA
RODA DE BARÀ
MONTROIG
LA PINEDA
SALOU
CAMBRILS
MIAMI-PLAYA
HOSPITALET DEL INFANTE
AMETLLA DE MAR
AP7/E15
AMPOSTA
COMUNIDAD VALENCIANA
0
20
40
60 kms

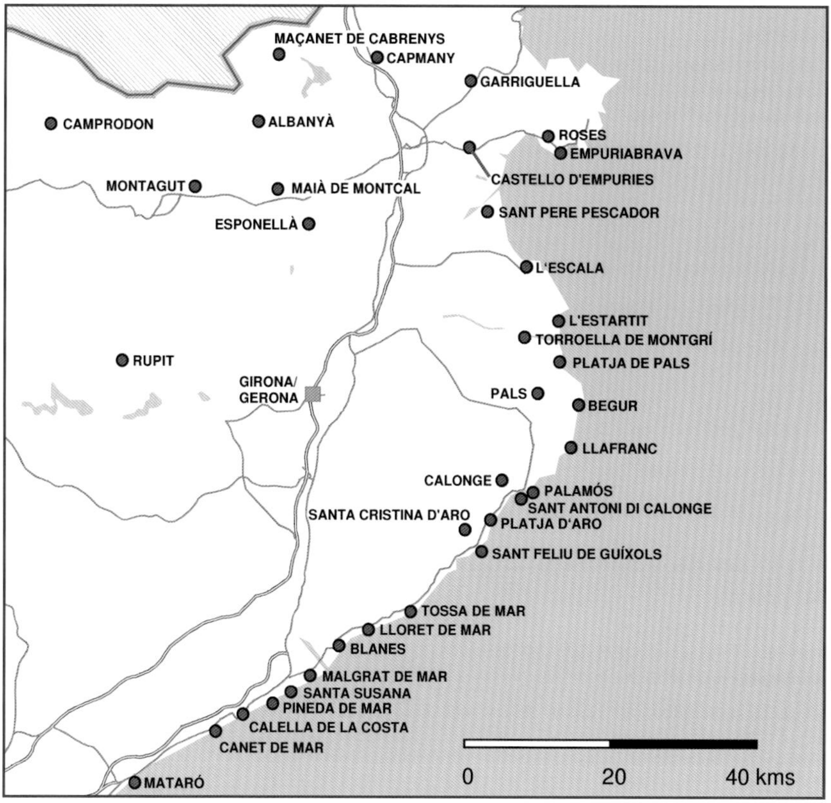

Ametlla de Mar

Camping Caravanning Ametlla Village Platja

Apdo 240, Paraje Santes Creus, E-43860 Ametlla de Mar (Tarragona) T: 977 267 784.
E: info@campingametlla.com **alanrogers.com/ES85360**

Occupying a terraced hillside above colourful shingle coves and two small associated lagoons, this site falls into four areas. The central one with reception and supermarket has a group of 44 touring pitches, below this are chalets for rent and a few touring pitches on ground falling away towards the lagoons and the beach. A second larger touring section also has 54 mobile homes owned by tour operators and finally, the bar/restaurant, pool and other leisure facilities take pride of place on the hilltop, with glimpses of the sea through the trees. There is some train noise, especially in the front section. Nearby is the picturesque fishing village of l'Ametlla de Mar, famous for its fish restaurants, and the site is within the Park Natural del Delta de l'Ebre.

Facilities

Two large toilet blocks, plus a smaller, simpler one. Controllable showers and open-style washbasins. Some private cabins with WC and washbasin and a few also have a shower. En-suite unit for disabled visitors. Baby rooms. Motorcaravan services. Gas. Supermarket (2/4-30/9; small shop incl. bread at other times). Good bar/restaurant with TV and terrace, snack menu and takeaway, new pub/cocktail bar upstairs with balcony and sea views (all 2/4-30/9). Attractive swimming pools (supervised 22/6-15/9). Sub-aqua diving. Kayaking. Fishing. Children's club and play area. Fitness room. Gym. Bicycle hire. Entertainment (July/Aug). Barbecue area. Fishing. WiFi area (charged). Off site: Boat launching 1 km. Village 2 km. Riding 3 km. Golf 17 km. Mature reserve and Port Aventura both an easy drive.

Open: All year.

Directions

Ametlla is 50 km. south of Tarragona. From AP7/E15 (Barcelona-Valencia) at exit 39 (or from N340) follow signs for Ametlla de Mar. Bear right before village following numerous white signs and continue for 2 km. Take care on final steep bend to site.
GPS: 40.8645, 0.7788

Charges guide

Per unit incl. 2 persons and electricity	€ 20.70 - € 36.50
extra person	€ 3.40 - € 6.50
child (under 10 yrs)	€ 2.70 - € 5.20

Less for longer stays in low season.

Albanyá

Camping Bassegoda Park

Camí Camp de l'illa, E-17733 Albanyá (Girona) T: 972 542 020. E: info@bassegodapark.com

alanrogers.com/ES80640

Surrounded by mountains alongside the Muga river, Bassegoda Park is a place to experience Spain in a natural environment but with a touch of luxury. This totally rebuilt site is just beyond Albanyá on the edge of the Alta Garrotxa National Park in an area of great beauty. In their own area, the 60 touring pitches are level and shaded, all on hardstanding and with access to electricity, water and drainage. Tents are dotted informally in the terraced forest areas. Particular care has been taken in the landscaping, layout and design of the attractive pool, bar and restaurant, the hub of the site.

Facilities

A new spacious and well equipped, main toilet building is centrally located and provides controllable showers and facilities for babies and disabled visitors. Two smaller refurbished blocks. Laundry facilities. Gas. Supermarket. Bar, restaurant and takeaway. Swimming pool (1/6-15/9). Playground. New leisure area (5-a-side football, volleyball, basketball). Minigolf. Activities, plus weekend entertainment. Bicycle hire. Barbecue areas. WiFi. Torches useful. Air-conditioned bungalows to rent. Off site: Fishing and river 1 km. Riding 2 km. Sailing 5 km. Golf 20 km.

Open: 14 March - 8 December.

Directions

From Barcelona on AP7/E15 exit 4 take N11 (France), then GI510 to Llers and GI511 to St Llorenc de la Muga and Albanyá. Site beyond village. From France take exit 3 then GI510 to Llers. NO exit 3 northbound on the AP7/E15. GPS: 42.30654, 2.70933

Charges guide

Per unit incl. 2 persons and electricity	€ 29.85 - € 35.40

No credit cards.

Camping Cheques accepted.

Amposta

Camping Eucaliptus

Platja Eucaliptus s/n, E-43870 Amposta (Tarragona) T: 977 479 046. E: eucaliptus@campingeucaliptus.com

alanrogers.com/ES85550

Ideally situated in the Parc Natural del Delta del Ebro, a unique area of wetland and a World Heritage site, Eucaliptus is close to the golden sands of Platja Eucaliptus. Arriving here is like finding an oasis after the extraordinary drive through miles of flat marshland and rice fields. There are 264 small, level, shady grass pitches, 156 for touring, all with electricity (6A). The site is very well maintained and has a pleasant bar/restaurant with a terrace that overlooks both the pool area and the campsite's own lagoon with its variety of wildlife. The pool has an attractive grassy area for sunbathing.

Facilities

The single toilet block is kept very clean and includes open style washbasins and good sized shower cubicles. Baby bath. Good facilities for disabled visitors. Laundry facilities. Dog shower. Shop. Gas. Large bar with satellite TV. Good restaurant and snack bar with takeaway. Play area. Swimming pool with paddling pool (1/6-15/9). Bicycle hire. Barbecue area with covered seating. Large units may require two pitches (no extra charge in low season). Off site: Beach and fishing 300 m. Birdwatching.

Open: 23 March - 30 September.

Directions

Site is 20 km. southeast of Amposta. From the AP7 take exit 41 and follow N340 south. Immediately after crossing River Ebro take exit signed Els Muntells and Sant Jaume, then bear right in 4 km. on TV3405 to Els Muntells. Continue 13.5 km. to site on the right. GPS: 40.65658, 0.77978

Charges guide

Per unit incl. 2 persons and electricity	€ 25.55 - € 33.10
extra person	€ 4.90 - € 6.90

Begur

Camping El Maset

Playa de Sa Riera, E-17255 Begur (Girona) T: 972 623 023. E: info@campingelmaset.com

alanrogers.com/ES81030

El Maset is a delightful and different family owned site in lovely wooded surroundings with views of the sea. There are 107 pitches, of which just 20 are slightly larger for caravans and motorcaravans, the remainder suitable only for tents. The site celebrated its 50th anniversary in 2011. The site entrance is steep and access to the caravan pitches can be quite tricky. However, help is available to tow your caravan to your pitch. Some of the pitches are shaded and all have electricity, 20 also have water and drainage. Tent pitches are more shaded on attractive, steep, rock-walled terraces on the hillside.

Facilities

Good sanitary facilities in three small blocks are kept very clean. Baby facilities. Laundry facilities. Unit for disabled campers but the ground is steep. Fridge hire. Bar/restaurant, takeaway and shop. Swimming pool. Solarium. Play area. Football. Basketball. Games room. Satellite TV. Internet (free) and WiFi (charged). No dogs. No charcoal barbecues. Off site: Beach 300 m.

Open: 13 May - 13 October.

Directions

From the C31 Figueres-Palamos road south of Pals, north of Palafrugell, take GI653 to Begur. Follow signs for Playa de Sa Riera and site is on right (steep entrance). GPS: 41.96860, 3.21002

Charges guide

Per unit incl. 2 persons and electricity	€ 27.70 - € 40.50

Begur

Camping Begur

Ctra d'Esclanya km. 2, E-17255 Begur (Girona) T: 972 623 201. E: info@campingbegur.com

alanrogers.com/ES81040

The choice of pitches on this pleasant, wooded site, just three kilometres from the coast is remarkable; some are on gently sloping grassland, others on hillside terraces or on the hilltop itself, and one steep slope has terraced tent pitches. Two hundred and thirty-two have electricity (10A), water and drainage, 30 are for tents and various corners are occupied by 45 mobile homes and chalets to rent, and by seasonal caravans. At the centre is a swimming pool with grassy terrace and a small paddling pool, overlooked by a bar and snack bar. Begur is an attractive village with a choice of seven beaches.

Facilities

Two modern toilet blocks are fully equipped. Each has open style washbasins, large showers, a good unit for disabled visitors. Baby room. Private bathroom for hire. Laundry facilities. Motorcaravan services. Bar/snack bar. Swimming and paddling pool. Boules. Gym (free). Play area. Large field for family activities (20/6-11/9). Children's 'huerta' (small market garden). Little farm with donkeys, goats, rabbits and chickens. WiFi. Off site: Village 2 km.

Open: 1 April - 26 September.

Directions

From north on AP7 at exit 6 (Girona) take C66 to La Bisbal; before Palafrugell follow signs for Begur. From south on AP7 at exit 9 follow Palamós, Palafrugell, then Begur. Site is 2 km. south of Begur on minor road to Palafrugell. GPS: 41.940216, 3.200079

Charges guide

Per unit incl. 2 persons and electricity € 20.10 - € 41.00

No credit cards.

Bellver de Cerdanya

Camping Solana del Segre

Ctra N260 km. 198, E-25720 Bellver de Cerdanya (Lleida) T: 973 510 310. E: sds@solanadelsegre.com

alanrogers.com/ES91420

The Sierra del Cadi offers some spectacular scenery and the Reserva Cerdanya is very popular with Spanish skiers. This site is situated in an open, sunny lower valley beside the River Segre where the far bank is a National Park (unfenced so children will need supervision). The immediate area is ideal for walkers and offers many opportunities for outdoor activities. The site is in two sections, the lower one nearer the river being for touring units, mainly flat and grassy with 200 pitches of 100 sq.m. or more (100 for touring units), shaded by trees with 15A electricity. The upper area is taken by permanent units.

Facilities

Modern sanitary facilities with extra Portacabin style units (unisex toilets/showers). Facilities for disabled campers are on the upper level (wheelchair users will experience problems). Laundry facilities. Motorcaravan services. Small shop/bar/restaurant (1/7-15/9). Swimming and paddling pools (1/7-5/9). Indoor pool. Play areas. Games room. Outdoor activity centre. Riding. Bicycle hire. River fishing. Dance area. Barbecue areas. Internet. Torches required.

Open: 1 July - 15 September.

Directions

Bellver de Cerdanya is 18 km. southwest of Puigcerdá, which is on the French border opposite Bourg-Madame. Site is on left at the 198 km. marker on the N260 from Puigcerdá to La Seu d'Urgell. GPS: 42.372697, 1.760484

Charges guide

Per unit incl. 2 persons and electricity (5A) € 24.00 - € 33.00

Credit cards not accepted.

Blanes

Camping la Masia

C/Colon 44, E-17300 Blanes (Girona) T: 972 331 013. E: info@campinglamasia.com

alanrogers.com/ES82250

A large resort site, la Masia has 757 pitches with 593 for touring units. These pitches are flat, shaded by trees and in rows with some mobile homes inserted here and there. There is something for everyone at la Masia and the resort town is just outside the gate, as is the fine beach. A large, central building houses the main bar and restaurant. The jewel in the crown of the site is below this complex, where you can enjoy an indoor heated pool, spa, massage, plunge pools and exercise pools, and pamper yourself in luxury in a Roman bath-style setting (extra charge).

Facilities

Five well maintained toilet blocks with facilities for disabled campers. Baby rooms. Motorcaravan services. Laundry facilities. Supermarket and bar (Easter-30/9). Bakery. Restaurants. Snack bars. Swimming pools. All-weather sports complex. Children's climbing wall. Excellent spa centre (charged). Play areas. Boules. Bicycle hire. Communal barbecue areas. Entertainment. Internet. WiFi over site (charged). Torches useful. Off site: Resort town and beach outside the gate. Fishing. Riding 3 km.

Open: 9 January - 9 December.

Directions

From AP7 (Girona-Barcelona) exit 9 follow the N11 to the B600 (Blanes). Entering Blanes look for roundabout with Lidl sign. Take turning for 'campings-Hotels'. Continue following signs, looking for Camping la Masia sign. Avoid Blanes town (narrow roads) GPS: 41.66291, 2.78075

Charges guide

Per unit incl. 2 persons and electricity € 13.50 - € 39.50

Camping Cheques accepted.

Blanes

Camping Blanes

Avenida Villa de Madrid 33, Apdo 72, E-17300 Blanes (Girona) T: 972 331 591. E: info@campingblanes.com

alanrogers.com/ES82280

Camping Blanes is the first of the sites which edge the pedestrian promenade here and probably the smallest. A private gate leads to the beach. Open all year, it is family owned and run and has been in the hands of the Boix family for 50 years. With only 206 pitches and no bungalows or mobile homes, it has a comfortable family atmosphere and is popular with low season visitors. The pitches average between 60-80 sq.m, have 6A electricity, and shade is provided by tall pines. Care must be taken when manoeuvring large units due to low branches and the irregular shape of some of the pitches.

Facilities

Adequate sanitary block with provision for disabled visitors (by key). Baby changing unit. Washing machines and dryers. Motorcaravan service point. Shop (1/6-15/9). Bar (1/4-12/10). Restaurant (7/7-25/8). Takeaway (7/7-25/8). Small swimming pool and sun terrace. Play area. No organised entertainment. Doctor visits. Bicycle hire. Beach alongside site. Car wash. WiFi over site (charged). Off site: Shops in Blanes 500 m. Golf and riding 5 km.

Open: All year.

Directions

Site is south of the town beside the beach before Camping Bella Terra and El Pinar. Follow signs for 'campings/hotel' until individual site sign appears. GPS: 41.65918, 2.77959

Charges guide

Per unit incl. 2 persons and electricity	€ 14.50 - € 37.80

No credit cards in winter season.

Blanes

Beach Camp El Pinar

Avenida Vila de Madrid 39, E-17300 Blanes (Girona) T: 972 331 083. E: camping@elpinarbeach.com

alanrogers.com/ES82300

A long established campsite, El Pinar enjoys an excellent location on the more peaceful, southern edge of Blanes with direct access to the beach. The site is in two halves, arranged on either side of a large road that terminates just past the site entrance gates where it meets the very clean, sandy beach. One side of the site is more modern than the other. The 495 touring pitches are on level sandy grass, most have shade and all have 6A electricity. There is a new mini farm with animals, where children can garden and pick their own vegetables, plus a new games area for children and teenagers.

Facilities

Sanitary facilities in two large blocks (one older but refurbished) include some private washbasins. Facilities for disabled visitors. Baby room. Laundry facilities. Motorcaravan service point. Shop, bar/restaurant and takeaway. Games room. Large swimming pool with adjacent paddling pool on the newer side (1/5-15/9). Multisports area. Bicycle hire. Simple play area. Miniclub (late June-early Sept). Mini farm. WiFi over site (charged). Boat launching can be organised. Beach.

Open: 31 March - 30 September.

Directions

From AP7 or C-32 motorways follow signs for Blanes. Site is the last travelling south from Blanes town centre. Follow camping signs in Blanes until you see the El Pinar sign. GPS: 41.6555, 2.77862

Charges guide

Per unit incl. 2 persons and electricity	€ 29.30 - € 42.00
extra person	€ 5.50 - € 6.50

Blanes

Camping Bella Terra

Avenida Vila de Madrid 35-40, E-17300 Blanes (Girona) T: 972 348 017. E: info@campingbellaterra.com

alanrogers.com/ES82320

Camping Bella Terra is set in a shady pine grove facing a sandy beach on the Mediterranean coast. There are 776 pitches with 700 for touring units, the remainder taken by bungalows to rent. A Spanish caravan club takes 300 pitches between April and June. All pitches have 6A electricity and 195 are fully serviced. The site is in two sections, each with its own reception. The main reception is on the right of the road as you approach, with the swimming and paddling pools, pool bar and restaurant.

Facilities

The newer side of the site has new sanitary blocks with good equipment, including facilities for babies and children. The older side has blocks which are clean, but dated. Provision for disabled visitors and laundry on both sides. Shop, restaurant, bar and takeaway. Outdoor swimming and paddling pools (from May). Playground. Fishing. Bicycle hire. Internet café. WiFi over site (charged). ATM. New sports complex. Miniclub. For dogs, contact site first. Off site: Blanes town 2 km. Road train to the resort (high season). Sailing 1.5 km. Riding 8 km.

Open: 31 March - 30 September.

Directions

Site is on the southwest side of Blanes. From exit 9 on the AP7 Girona-Barcelona follow N11 to the B600 towards Blanes. Before entering Blanes turn southwest following campings/hotels signs at roundabouts, then site signs directing you away from Blanes town, which has narrow roads best avoided by large units. GPS: 41.6616, 2.77612

Charges guide

Per unit incl. 2 persons and electricity	€ 24.50 - € 45.50
extra person	€ 4.50 - € 6.50

Borredá

Camping Campalans

Ctra Sant Jaume de Frontanyá km. 1,5, E-08619 Borredá (Barcelona) T: 938 239 163.
E: campalans@campalans.net **alanrogers.com/ES91380**

With its wonderful location in a quiet river valley with views of the surrounding mountains and reached by a winding road, Camping Campalans is an excellent site for enjoying this beautiful area. It is said that the best wild mushrooms in Catalunya are found here. Combining camping with chalets and a small hotel, the site has 40 mostly grass touring pitches (all with 5-10A electricity) set on terraces beneath a 16th-century building housing reception, a comfortable bar, a good value restaurant and a small shop. The site is 1.5 km. from the nearest village, while the town of Berga with all facilities is 20 km. away.

Facilities

One heated toilet block has well equipped showers, washbasins, en-suite cabins and children's facilities. A further 3 smaller units over the site. Laundry room. Shop, bar and restaurant (all 1/7-31/8, then weekends and PHs). Swimming pool (24/6-15/9). Play area. Football and basketball pitches. Events and activities (Aug). Large adventure trail with three difficulty levels next to site. Mill for group rentals (up to 14 persons). Wooden bungalows and lodges to rent. Off site: Supermarket, bakery, cafés and small shops in Borredá 1.5 km. More comprehensive facilities in Berga 20 km.

Open: 1 July - 31 August, weekends all year.

Directions

From France via Puigcerda on C-16, just before Berga turn left towards Ripoll. After Borredá turn left to Sant Jaume de Frontanyá. Site is east of the village, 1.5 km. on right. GPS: 42.14583, 1.99954

Charges guide

Per unit incl. 2 persons and electricity	€ 30.18
extra person	€ 5.72
child (under 12 yrs)	€ 3.43
dog	€ 2.87

Calella de la Costa

Camping Roca Grossa

Ctra NII km. 665, E-08370 Calella de la Costa (Barcelona) T: 937 691 297. E: rocagrossa@rocagrossa.com
alanrogers.com/ES82420

Roca Grossa's owners, the Bachs family, are very friendly and there is a very happy atmosphere in the campsite. Very steep slopes predominate at this site and there is a challenging 1 in 3, 100 m. climb from reception to the swimming pool set at the top of the site. From June, a road train runs all day to ferry you up to the amenities, but the site is unsuitable for disabled campers. The bonus is some great views over the sea from most of the terraced, but flat and reasonably sized pitches. The site Landrover will be used to position your caravan, whilst short-stay motorcaravans are parked at the bottom of the hill. The beach is just 50 m. across the road and the town is a short walk.

Facilities

An amazing array of clean sanitary blocks means there is not far to walk from any area of the site. Large and small, all blocks are well kept with hot water throughout. Washing machines. Gas. Shop. Pleasant bars and restaurants. Swimming pool (1/5-30/9; with lifeguard). Playground. Road train. Tennis. Sports courts. Recreation programme including children's entertainment (July/Aug). Excursions. WiFi over site (charged). ATM. Torches useful. Off site: Beach, boat launching and fishing 50 m. Town 100 m. Indoor pool and riding 1 km. Golf 2 km. Watersports nearby.

Open: 1 April - 30 September.

Directions

From A7 (Girona-Barcelona) take exit 9 or 10 for Malgrat del Mar on the N11. Turn south towards Calella and site is at 665 km. marker sharing an entrance with another campsite.
GPS: 41.60632, 2.63892

Charges guide

Per unit incl. 2 persons and electricity	€ 41.00
extra person	€ 8.25
child (under 10 yrs)	€ 7.20
dog	€ 4.85

Calonge

Camping Internacional de Calonge

Ctra San Feliu/Guixols - Palamós km 7.6, E-17251 Calonge (Girona) T: 972 651 233.
E: info@intercalonge.com **alanrogers.com/ES81300**

This spacious, well laid out site has access to a fine beach via a footbridge over the coast road. Calonge is a family site with two attractive pools on different levels, a paddling pool and large sunbathing areas. A restaurant, bar and snack bar with great views are by the pool. The 466 touring pitches are on terraces and all have electricity (5A), with 84 being fully serviced. There is good shade from the tall pine trees, and some spectacular coastal views. Some access roads and steps are steep, but a road train operates in high season. There are wonderful views from the upper levels, where there are some larger comfort pitches. The pools are overlooked by the restaurant terraces which have great views over the mountains. A nature area within the site is used for walks and picnics and two separate areas within the site are set aside for visitors with dogs. The beach is accessed over the main road by 100 steps.

Facilities

Generous sanitary provision. One block is heated in winter. Laundry facilities. Motorcaravan services. Gas supplies. Shop (5/4-30/10). Restaurant (1/2-31/12). Bar, patio bar with pizzas and takeaway (5/4-24/10, weekends for the rest of the year). Swimming pools (26/3-16/10). Playground. Electronic games. Disco two nights a week (but not late) in high season. Bicycle hire. Tennis. Hairdresser. ATM. WiFi (free in hotspots). Torches necessary in some areas. Road train in high season.
Off site: Beach and fishing 300 m. Supermarket 500 m. Sailing 1 km. Golf 3 km. Riding 10 km.

Open: All year.

Directions

Site is on the inland side of the coast road between Palamós and Platja d'Aro. Take C31 south to 661 at Calonge. At Calonge follow signs to C253 towards Platja d'Aro and on to site, which is well signed. GPS: 41.83333, 3.08417

Charges guide

Per unit incl. 2 persons and electricity	€ 22.10 - € 51.45
extra person	€ 3.85 - € 8.85
child (3-10 yrs)	€ 1.90 - € 4.80

No credit cards.

Calonge

Camping Cala Gogo

Avenida Andorra 13, E-17251 Calonge (Girona) T: 972 651 564. E: calagogo@calagogo.es
alanrogers.com/ES81600

Cala Gogo is a large traditional campsite with a pleasant situation on a wooded hillside with mature trees giving shade to most pitches. The 578 touring pitches, which vary in size, are in terraced rows, some with artificial shade, all have 10A electricity and water, and 200 have drainage. There may be road noise in eastern parts of the site. A few pitches are now right by the beach, the remainder are up to 800 m. uphill, but a tractor train, almost all season, runs between the centre of the site and the beach.

Facilities

Seven toilet blocks are of a high standard and are continuously cleaned. Some washbasins in private cabins. Two private cabins for hire. Baby rooms. Facilities for disabled visitors. Laundry room. Motorcaravan services. Gas supplies. Supermarket, shop, restaurants/takeaway and bars, two swimming pools (one heated, lifeguards) and a paddling pool. Playground and crèche. Sports centre. Sports and entertainment. Bicycle hire. Kayaks (free). Fishing. WiFi (free in 3 hotspots). Medical service. ATM. No dogs in high season. Photo ID passes issued.

Open: 27 April - 15 September.

Directions

Leave the AP7/E15 at exit 6. Take C66 towards Palamós which becomes the C31. Use the C31 (Girona-Palamós) road to avoid Palamós town. Take the C253 coast road. Site is at km. 46.5, which is 4 km. south of Palamós. GPS: 41.83083, 3.08247

Charges guide

Per unit incl. 2 persons and electricity	€ 23.50 - € 54.50
extra person	€ 3.90 - € 8.40

Discounts for longer stays and for cash payments.

Calonge

Camping Treumal

Ctra 253 km. 47.5, E-17250 Calonge (Girona) T: 972 651 095. E: info@campingtreumal.com

alanrogers.com/ES81400

This very attractive terraced site has been developed on a hillside around the beautiful gardens of a large, spectacular estate house which is close to the sea. The house is the focus of the site's excellent facilities, including a superb restaurant with terraces overlooking two tranquil beaches, protected in pretty coves. The site has 542 pitches on well shaded terraces. Of these, 371 are accessible to touring units and there are some 50 pitches on flat ground alongside the sea – the views are stunning and you wake to the sound of the waves. Electricity (6/10/16A) is available in all parts. Cars must be left on car parks or the site roads. There are 165 pitches occupied by mobile homes and chalets to rent, in addition to studios in the main house. Throughout the seasons, the gardens around the house are a blaze of colour and very appealing. A multi-coloured, flower bedecked and landscaped hillside leads down to the sea from the house with pretty paths and a fishpond. There is a small (10 m) round swimming pool in the lower areas of the gardens. The two beaches are connected by a tunnel carved through the rock.

Facilities

Four well maintained sanitary blocks have free hot water in the washbasins (with some private cabins) and controllable showers, and a tap to draw from for the sinks. No facilities for disabled visitors. New beach block. Washing machines. Motorcaravan services. Gas supplies. Supermarket, bar and takeaway. Restaurant (15/6-15/9). Beach bar. Fishing. Play area. Sports area. Games room. Bicycle hire. Satellite TV. Internet access and WiFi (charged). ATM. Safes. No dogs. Off site: Public transport 300 m. Golf 3 km. Riding 6 km.

Open: 23 March - 30 September.

Directions

Site is southeast of Girona on the coast 3 km. south of Palamós. Avoid the town centre by using C31 (Girona-Palomós) road, leave at km. 321, and take road south to Sant Antoni de Calonge. Take C253 south towards Platja d'Aro. Site is well signed. GPS: 41.836312, 3.08711

Charges guide

Per unit incl. 2 persons and electricity	€ 25.30 - € 51.20
extra person	€ 4.40 - € 8.80

No credit cards.

Salou

La Siesta Salou Camping Resort

Calle Norte 37, E-43840 Salou (Tarragona) T: 977 380 852. E: info@lasiestasalou.com

alanrogers.com/ES84700

La Siesta occupies a remarkable location close to the heart of the thriving resort of Salou, yet only two blocks from the fine sandy beach. The 360 pitches for touring, all with 10A electricity, vary in size, some suitable for larger units, others for tents. There is considerable shade from the trees and shrubs that contribute to the site's attractive appearance. Recent investment has seen the creation of a grassy play area, an impressive new sports provision and an extensive new leisure pool complex.

Facilities

Three clean sanitary blocks include controllable showers and open style washbasins. Unit for disabled visitors. Motorcaravan services. Supermarket. Vending machines. Self-service restaurant and bar with takeaway. New leisure pool complex. Children's club (June-Aug). Playground. Entertainment (July/Aug). Multisports. Short tennis. Torches may be required. WiFi throughout (charged). Off site: Shops, restaurants and bars nearby.

Open: 1 April - 10 October.

Directions

Leave AP7 at exit 35 or A7 (toll-free) motorway at exit for Salou. Follow the Tarragona-Salou road (dual carriageway) until you pass the side of the site on the right. Site is signed (narrow turning). Follow further small signs through the one way system. GPS: 41.0777, 1.1389

Charges guide

Per unit incl. 2 persons and electricity	€ 27.00 - € 47.00

Cambrils

Camping Joan

Passeig Maritim 88, E-43850 Cambrils (Tarragona) T: 977 364 604. E: info@campingjoan.com
alanrogers.com/ES84780

Camping Joan is a very friendly, family run site to the south of the popular resort of Cambrils and with direct access to a fine sandy beach. There are 220 touring pitches, most between 60-90 sq.m. and all with 5A electrical connections. There is good shade. Access can be a little tight and large motorhomes are not accepted. There are 84 chalets to rent and separate areas are devoted to seasonal caravans. This is a lively site in high season with a varied programme of entertainment and activities for all.

Facilities

Three sanitary blocks serve the touring pitches, one refurbished to a high standard. Controllable showers and open style washbasins. Baby rooms and unit for disabled visitors. Motorcaravan service point planned. Bar, restaurant and takeaway (1/3-31/10). Supermarket. Small swimming and paddling pools (1/5-30/9). Playground. Entertainment and children's club (high season). Bicycle and kayak hire. WiFi over site (charged). Direct access to beach, coastal footpath and cycleway.

Open: 23 February - 2 November.

Directions

From north on the AP7, leave at exit 37 (Cambrils) and join the southbound N340. From south on AP7 leave at exit 38 (L'Hospitalet) join motorway A7, leave at first exit and follow signs for Cambrils. Site signed at service station in La Dorada in 2-3 km. Turn right after railway to site. GPS: 41.05789, 1.02669

Charges guide

Per unit incl. 2 persons and electricity	€ 20.00 - € 51.00
extra person	€ 4.00 - € 8.00

Cambrils

Camping Playa Cambrils Don Camilo

Ctra Cambrils-Salou km. 1,5, avenida Oleastrum, E-43850 Cambrils (Tarragona) T: 977 361 490.
E: info@playacambrils.com **alanrogers.com/ES84790**

This is a smart, well kept site with a canopy of mature shading trees, 300 m. from the beach across a busy road. There are 522 small (60 or 80 sq.m) touring pitches on flat ground, divided by hedges, all with 5A electricity. There are many permanent pitches and a quarter of the site is given up to chalet-style accommodation, which is generally separate from the touring pitches. Large units are placed in a dedicated area where the trees are higher. The pool complex includes a smart glassed restaurant and bar with a distinct Spanish flavour reflected in the menu and tapas available throughout the day.

Facilities

Three smart, modern sanitary buildings offer clean facilities with British style WCs and showers in separate buildings. Excellent facilities for disabled campers. Laundry facilities. Supermarket (April-Sept). Bar/snacks and separate restaurant (April-Sept). Swimming pools. Playground. Entertainment in high season. Miniclub. Huge electronic games room. Bicycle hire. Torches useful. WiFi (free).
Off site: Resort town with shops, bars and restaurants.

Open: 15 March - 13 October.

Directions

Leave AP7 autopista at exit 37 and head for Cambrils and then to the beach. Turn left along beach road. Site is 1 km. east of Cambrils Playa (signed from the marina). GPS: 41.06487, 1.08368

Charges guide

Per unit incl. 2 persons and electricity	€ 19.10 - € 55.90

Camping Cheques accepted.

Camprodon

Camping Vall de Camprodon

Ctra C38 Ripoll a Camprodon, E-17867 Camprodon (Girona) T: 972 740 507. E: info@valldecamprodon.net
alanrogers.com/ES91225

This large holiday village is attractively situated in a wooded valley with cows grazing to one side. A stream runs below the site between it and the road. There are 200 grass and gravel pitches, some with shade, others without. Most are occupied by seasonal caravans (some rather scruffy) and private chalets interspersed with just 40 for touring units, all with 4-10A electricity. There are 26 modern chalets for rent. Only 20 km. away is the mountain and ski resort of Vallter 2000.

Facilities

One centrally placed, fully equipped and well maintained toilet block. Large en-suite unit for disabled visitors. Baby/toddler baths. Laundry facilities. Shop and bar/restaurant (July/Aug plus holiday periods and weekends in low season). Swimming and paddling pools (July/Aug). Play area. Adventure play area with zip wire. Fishing and bathing in river. Tennis. Multisports court. Boules. Miniclub (July/Aug). Riding (July/Aug). Free WiFi over site. Separate motorcaravan park outside entrance (€20-26). Off site: Golf (9-holes) and riding 2 km.

Open: All year.

Directions

From south on AP7 take exit 6 (Girona), then C66/A26 to Olot. From north leave AP7 at Figueres, join N11 south and turn west (Olot) to join N260/A26. At exit 84 follow signs for Camprodon on C26 via Valley of Bianya. After tunnels turn on C38 to Camprodon. Site is on the right.
GPS: 42.29033, 2.36242

Charges guide

Per unit incl. 2 persons and electricity	€ 35.60
extra person	€ 7.95

Camping Cheques accepted.

Canet de Mar

Camping Globo Rojo

Ctra NII km. 660.9, E-08360 Canet de Mar (Barcelona) T: 937 941 143. E: camping@globo-rojo.com

alanrogers.com/ES82430

Camping Globo Rojo is cleverly laid out in a relaxed, amphitheatre fashion. Within the various sectors, permanent campers and touring units stay alongside each other. The restaurant, which serves authentic food and tapas, is within a sensitively restored farmhouse. The site is located on the beach road (N11) so is subject to some traffic noise, but the full shading of mature trees also absorbs the noise. The 176 flat, grassy pitches include 135 touring pitches, all with 10A electricity and with an average size of 70 sq.m. An elevated pool and paddling pool are waiting for you to enjoy and the beach is close by.

Facilities

Two sanitary blocks have clean, modern equipment. Baby room. Facilities for disabled campers. Hot water throughout. Washing machines. Motorcaravan service areas. Shop. Bar. Restaurant. Takeaway. Swimming and paddling pools (with lifeguards). Miniclub. Playground. Multisports pitch. Pétanque. Electronic games. Bicycle hire. Free WiFi in restaurant. Dog bath. Car wash. Safes. Off site: Bus to Barcelona and Mataró at gate. Fishing and watersports 100 m.

Open: 1 April - 30 September.

Directions

Site is at the 660.9 km. marker on the N11. Leave the C-32 autoroute at exit 20 (AP7 exit 120) and follow signs to Canet de Mar. Site signed on both carriageways of the N11. GPS: 41.590903, 2.591951

Charges guide

Per unit incl. 2 persons and electricity	€ 23.00 - € 47.00
extra person	€ 4.50 - € 7.50
child (2-10 yrs)	€ 4.00 - € 7.00

Capmany

Camping les Pedres

Ctra Darnius 15, E-17750 Capmany (Girona) T: 972 549 192. E: info@campinglespedres.net

alanrogers.com/ES80240

Camping les Pedres is a quiet site set among cork and pine trees and surrounded by mountain views. In July 2012, this area of the Costa Brava was devastated by fire, but les Pedres is undergoing a remarkable regeneration and now offers 75 touring pitches with 6/10A electricity. The 75 privately owned mobile homes which were destroyed are rapidly being replaced. The pitches are flat and accessible and most have 10A electricity. In high season, there is a family run bar and a restaurant serving a tapas menu, and visitors can cool off in the modest swimming pool.

Facilities

Two clean, well cared for toilet blocks have solar-heated water and good showers. Laundry. Bar and tapas restaurant (high season). Swimming pool (high season). Small area for ball games. WiFi over site (charged). Torches useful. Off site: Wonderful walks from the site. Shopping at le Perthus 20 km. Costa Brava beaches 35 km. Gerona, Barcelona and Figueres (Dalí museum).

Open: All year.

Directions

From N11 which runs parallel to A7 motorway, 7 km. from la Jonquera take GI 602 signed to Capmany. After 2 km. turn left following signs to site and restaurant. GPS: 42.372934, 2.913164

Charges guide

Per unit incl. 2 persons and electricity	€ 19.85 - € 31.40
extra person	€ 3.60 - € 6.70

Castelló d'Empúries

Camping Castell Mar

Platja de la Rubina, E-17486 Castelló d'Empúries (Girona) T: 972 450 822. E: cmar@campingparks.com

alanrogers.com/ES80100

This small site is a 450 m. walk from one of the very attractive Gulf of Roses beaches and within the large Aiguamolls de l'Empordá natural park. Spanish horses are bred in the fields leading to the site. With some 310 pitches (160 for touring), it is smaller than many sites in this part of Spain and has a different, more intimate feel to it. There is a range of separated pitches, most with electricity, and on level ground shaded by trees and some with additional fixed awnings. There is an impressive new swimming pool with views over Roses bay, a restaurant and bar and a large, open-air auditorium.

Facilities

One large, well maintained, clean and modern toilet block. Some washbasins in cabins. Facilities for disabled visitors. Laundry facilities. Bar, restaurant/pizzeria and takeaway. Supermarket. Play areas. New swimming pool. Sports area outside site. Activities and entertainment. Bicycle hire. ATM. Security boxes. Torches required in some areas. WiFi (charged). Off site: Windsurfing school 400 m. Boat launching 500 m. Riding 1 km. Golf 10 km. Discounts at local attractions.

Open: 12 May - 30 September.

Directions

From motorway AP7 take exit 3 south or exit 4 north (there is no exit 3 north). Do not go into Castello d'Empuries or Empuriabrava, but continue on N11 to the C260 towards Roses. At km. 40 La Rubina, turn and pass by La Llar restaurant, site is 1.5 km further. GPS: 42.25517, 3.1366

Charges guide

Per unit incl. 2 persons and electricity	€ 19.00 - € 66.00

No credit cards.

Castelló d'Empúries

Camping Nautic Almata

Ctra GIV-6216 km 2,3, E-17486 Castelló d'Empúries (Girona) T: 972 454 477. E: info@almata.com

alanrogers.com/ES80300

In the Bay of Roses, south of Empuriabrava and beside the Parc Natural dels Aiguamolls de l'Empordá, this is a high quality site of particular interest to nature lovers (especially birdwatchers). A large site, there are 1,109 well kept, large, numbered pitches, all with electricity and on flat, sandy ground. Beautifully laid out, it is arranged around the river and waterways, so will suit those who like to be close to water or who enjoy watersports and boating. It is also a superb beachside site. There are some pitches right on the beach and on the banks of the canal. As you drive through the nature park to the site, enjoy the wild flamingos alongside the road. The name no doubt derives from the fact that boats can be tied up at the small marina within the site and a slipway also gives access to a river and thence to the sea. Throughout the season there is a varied entertainment programme for children and adults, and the facilities are impressive. Tour operators use the site.

Facilities

Toilet blocks of a very high standard include some en-suite showers with basins. Good facilities for disabled visitors. Washing machines. Gas supplies. Excellent supermarket. Restaurants, pizzeria and bar. Two separate bars and snack bar by beach where discos are held in main season. Sailing, diving and windsurfing schools. 300 sq.m. swimming pool. Tennis. Squash. Paddle tennis. Minigolf. Games room. Riding tuition (July/Aug). Play park and miniclub. Fishing (licence required). Car, motorcycle and bicycle hire. Hairdresser. Internet access and WiFi over site (charged). ATM. Torches are useful near beach. Off site: Canal trips 18 km. Aquatic Park 20 km.

Open: 17 May - 21 September.

Directions

Site is signed at 26 km. marker on C252 between Castello d'Empúries and Vildemat, then 7 km. to site. Alternatively, on San Pescador-Castello d'Empúries road (GIV6261) head north and site is well signed. GPS: 42.206077, 3.10389

Charges guide

Per unit incl. 2 persons and electricity	€ 30.70 - € 61.45
extra person (over 3 yrs)	€ 3.15 - € 5.75
dog	€ 5.35 - € 6.90
boat or jet ski	€ 10.30 - € 13.50

Castelló d'Empúries

Camping Mas Nou

Mas Nou no. 7, E-17486 Castelló d'Empúries (Girona) T: 972 454 175. E: info@campingmasnou.com

alanrogers.com/ES80120

Some two kilometres from the sea on the Costa Brava, this is a pristine and surprisingly tranquil site in two parts, split by the access road. One part contains the pitches and toilet blocks, the other houses the impressive leisure complex. There are 450 neat, level and marked pitches on grass, a minimum of 70 sq.m. but most are 80-100 sq.m, and 300 with electricity (10A). The leisure complex is across the road from reception and features a huge L-shaped swimming pool with a children's area. A formal restaurant has an adjoining bar/café, pleasant terrace and rôtisserie under palms. Lots of time and investment goes into the cleanliness, maintenance and appearance of this family owned site.

Facilities

Three absolutely excellent, fully equipped sanitary blocks include baby baths, good facilities for disabled visitors. Washing machines. Motorcaravan services. Supermarket and other shops. Baker in season. Bar/restaurant, rôtisserie and takeaway. Swimming pool with lifeguard (1/5-28/9). Floodlit tennis and basketball. Minigolf. Miniclub (July/Aug). Play areas. Electronic games. Bicycle hire. Internet access and free WiFi over site. Car wash. Off site: Supermarket and shopping facilities 500 m. Public transport 500m. Riding 1.5 km. Beach 2.5 km. Fishing 3 km. Aquatic Park. Golf 12 km.

Open: 12 April - 28 September.

Directions

From A7 use exit 3. Mas Nou is 2 km. east of Castelló d'Empúries, on the Roses road, 10 km. from Figueras. Do not turn left across the main road but continue to the roundabout and return. Site is clearly marked. GPS: 42.26558, 3.1025

Charges guide

Per unit incl. 2 persons and electricity	€ 23.00 - € 44.50
extra person	€ 2.65 - € 5.00
child (4-11 yrs)	free - € 3.55
dog	free - € 2.40

Camping Cheques accepted.

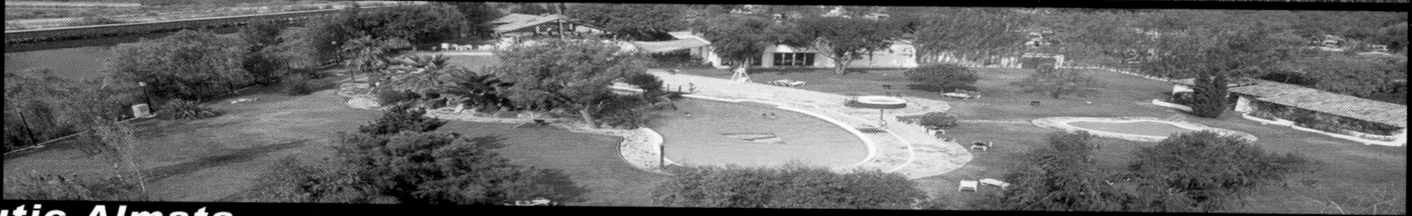

Offers on our
Website

Castelló d'Empúries

Camping Laguna

Platja Can Comes s/n, E-17486 Castelló d'Empúries (Girona) T: 972 450 553. E: info@campinglaguna.com

alanrogers.com/ES80150

Camping Laguna is a relaxed, spacious site on an isthmus within the Catalan National Maritime Park, on the migratory path of many different birds. It has direct access to an excellent sandy beach and the estuary of the River Muga (also a beach). The owners spend much time and effort on improvements. The 756 pitches (50 mobile homes) are shaded and clearly marked on grass and sand, all with 6/10A electricity. There are also 52 fully serviced pitches. A very attractive bar/restaurant and sitting area overlook the impressive lagoons. There are two swimming pools (one is heated in low season). A disco operates across the road from reception, keeping the noise away from the main site. A large riding school operates (May-Sept) and there are many other activities for all ages. The beach frontage is large and has a sailing school. It is said to be possible to cross over to Empuriabrava when the tide is out. There are many pleasant walks in this area and La Laguna is also a good base from which to visit the surrounding towns and countryside. This is an ideal site for family holidays.

Facilities

Five superb toilet blocks have solar heated water, and include facilities for children and disabled visitors. Laundry room. Bar, restaurant and takeaway. Supermarket. Swimming pools (15/5-22/10). Football. Tennis (free in low seasons). ATM. Minigolf. Windsurfing and sailing schools (July/Aug). Fishing. Miniclub. Play areas. Bicycle hire. Riding. Entertainment and competitions. Doctor visits. Satellite TV. Internet access. WiFi over site (charged). Off site: Boat launching. Birdwatching. Golf 15 km.

Open: 27 March - 22 October.

Directions

From AP7/E15 take exit 3 south or exit 4 north (there is no exit 3 north) and then N11 to the C260 towards Roses. At Castelló d'Empúries roundabout (there is only one) follow signs (ignore GPS from here) to Depuradora (2 km) and 'camping' for 4 km. on a hard track road to the site. GPS: 42.2374, 3.121

Charges guide

Per unit incl. 2 persons and electricity	€ 27.80 - € 55.80
extra person	€ 4.25 - € 4.65

Cubelles

Camping la Rueda

Ctra C31 km. 146,2, E-08880 Cubelles (Barcelona) T: 938 950 207. E: larueda@la-rueda.com

alanrogers.com/ES83930

La Rueda is a pleasant, no frills site with 370 pitches, 350 for touring, 167 of these with electricity (4/6/10A). Some pitches are in a small pine wood. The circular central area has flat, grassy pitches set amongst mature trees with bamboo canopies providing extra shade; the final area has grassy pitches without electricity and with little shade. From the far corner, a road takes you under the railway (some noise) to a long sandy beach. An elevated bar and snack bar serving simple, inexpensive fare overlooks the swimming pool. The site is within easy walking distance of shops, bars and restaurants.

Facilities

Two traditional sanitary blocks, one on each side of the site, are clean and have controllable showers and open style washbasins. Baby cubicle. Facilities for disabled visitors in one block (on demand in low season). Laundry facilities. Shop, bar and snack bar with takeaway (15/6-11/9, weekends in low season). Swimming pool (23/6-11/9). Basic playground. Area for ball games. Internet room. WiFi over site (charged). Children's club with occasional family events (July/Aug).

Open: 23 March - 8 September.

Directions

Cubelles is 50 km. southwest of Barcelona. From C32 coastal motorway leave at exit 13 for Cubelles and join C31 west. Site is a short distance on left (at 146.2 km). GPS: 41.19987, 1.64335

Charges guide

Per unit incl. 2 persons and electricity	€ 24.84 - € 45.34
extra person	€ 4.14 - € 6.90

El Vendrell

Camping Vendrell Platja

Avenida del Sanatori s/n, Coma-Ruga, E-43880 El Vendrell (Tarragona) T: 977 694 009.
E: vendrell@camping-vendrellplatja.com **alanrogers.com/ES84020**

In the popular Calafell area, this site is set back from the sea across a beach road. Popular with tourists for many years, the area has apartment buildings, bars and restaurants, and is popular with families. The pitches (70 sq.m) are fairly close together, partially shaded by trees, and all have 6A electricity. Access to all the pitches is through one narrow central avenue of palms which is busy with foot and vehicle traffic. The pleasant pool area with more tall palms and grassy areas, has very wide slides that delight children and adults alike. There is a railway line at the western end of the site.

Facilities

Two modern toilet blocks provide clean facilities with a unit for disabled campers and baby rooms. Washing machines. Car wash. Supermarket. Restaurant. Snack bar. Swimming pools and pool bar. Play areas. Boules. Bicycle hire. Entertainment and activities. ATM. Security boxes. Torches useful. Internet and WiFi. Off site: Resort town and beach nearby. Fishing. Bicycle hire 200 m.

Open: 1 April - 12 October.

Directions

From A7 or A16 take exit 31 for El Vendrell. Then go east to Sant Salvador, and north on coast road towards Platja Calafell. Site is well signed on this road west of the town centre. GPS: 41.1856, 1.5554

Charges guide

Per person	€ 4.50 - € 9.00
pitch incl. electricity	€ 10.50 - € 22.50

Camping Cheques accepted.

Empuriabrava

Camping Rubina Resort

Playa de la Rubina, E-17487 Empuriabrava (Girona) T: 972 450 507. E: info@rubinaresort.com
alanrogers.com/ES80200

Situated in the 'Venice of Spain', Empuriabrava is interlaced with inland waterways and canals, where many residents and holidaymakers moor their boats directly outside their expensive homes on the canal banks. Camping Rubina Resort is a large friendly site 200 m. from the wide, sandy beach, which is bordered on the east and west by the waterway canals. It is a spacious and hospitable site where people seem to make friends easily. There are 500 touring pitches of varying sizes, most enjoying some shade. All have 10A electricity and water connections. Access throughout the site is very good.

Facilities

Toilet facilities are in five fully equipped blocks with facilities for disabled campers (key in reception). Washing machines. Motorcaravan services. Supermarket, bakery and shop, bar and takeaway. Restaurant (1/5-30/9) Internet café. Swimming pool (1/4-10/10). Multisports court. Table tennis. Watersports with windsurfing school. Organised sports activities, children's programmes and entertainment. Playgrounds. Pétanque. Bicycle hire. WiFi over site (charged). Dog shower. Apartments.

Open: 1 April - 15 October.

Directions

Empuriabrava is north of Girona and east of Figueres on the coast. From AP7/E15 take exit 3 south or exit 4 north (note there is no exit 3 north) and then N11 to the C260 towards Roses. At Empuriabrava follow 'camping area' signs to site. GPS: 42.25267, 3.1317

Charges guide

Per unit incl. 2 persons and electricity	€ 20.00 - € 56.00

No credit cards.

Esponellá

Camping Caravaning Esponellá

Ctra de Banyoles-Figueres km. 8, E-17832 Esponellá (Girona) T: 972 597 074.
E: informa@campingesponella.com **alanrogers.com/ES80360**

This large campsite has a lovely setting alongside a slow flowing river. There are 240 small to medium sized pitches, 140 for touring, all with 5A electricity and shaded by trees. Many are fully serviced. The older part of the campsite houses a well stocked shop and a bar/restaurant adjacent to the swimming pools. One smaller pool is heated and partly covered. A small stream runs along the lower side which can be seen from the pool and restaurant area, which faces the swimming pool complex. In summer, children's club activities are run from here and this is the part of the campsite with a lot going on.

Facilities

Two old toilet blocks, a smaller one with only toilets and washbasins near the rental accommodation, and a newer one at the front part of the site. Some washbasins with only cold water. Small shop (Easter-Sept). Restaurant with terrace. Bar and takeaway. Three heated swimming pools. Play area. Boules. Minigolf. Tennis. Children's activities. Small disco. Fishing, swimming and kayaking in the river. Bicycle and kayak hire. Free WiFi in bar area. Communal barbecue area (not allowed on pitches).

Open: All year.

Directions

Esponellá is 20 km. southwest of Figueres. From the N260 Figueres-Olot road, 4 km. west of Navata turn south on Gip512 to Esponellá. After factory on left, cross river and on left-hand bend turn sharp right to site (yellow sign). GPS: 42.18166, 2.79499

Charges guide

Per unit incl. 2 persons and electricity	€ 25.55 - € 33.85
extra person	€ 5.35 - € 6.95

Garriguella

Camping Vell Empordá

Ctra Roses-Jonquera s/n, E-17780 Garriguella (Girona) T: 972 530 200. E: vellemporda@vellemporda.com
alanrogers.com/ES80140

Camping Vell Empordá is a friendly, family site close to the resort of Roses on the northern Costa Brava and on the outskirts of the small town of Garriguella. There are 210 touring pitches, all with 6A or 10A (extra) electricity connections. Smaller pitches are available for campers with tents. Additionally, a range of fully equipped wooden chalets are for rent. The site is terraced and well shaded. On-site amenities include a good restaurant and a well stocked supermarket. There is a convivial bar with a large terrace. The swimming pool is large and attractive and has a separate children's pool adjacent. The site has both a strong Spanish presence and also a loyal European clientèle, including some British tourists, who have been visiting for many years. Close by Garriguella is a typical small Spanish town with an interesting church, Santa Eulalia de Noves. Roses, some 7 km. away, is a smart and lively resort with a wealth of shops, cafés, restaurants and entertainment. The town is also home to a fine citadel, built by the Greeks, and from where there are stunning views over the Bay of Roses. This site is ideal for those who want a welcoming and authentic country location but within easy reach of local beaches.

Facilities

Two large, clean sanitary blocks have facilities for children and disabled visitors. Laundry. Motorcaravan service point. Supermarket and bar (15/5-15/9), restaurant and takeaway (1/6-25/9). Large outdoor swimming pool (15/5-15/9). Children's pool. Play area. Multisports area. Fronton court. Bicycle hire. Free WiFi over site. Tourist information. Chalets for rent. Off site: Cycle and walking tracks 50 m. Riding and golf 5 km. Beach 7 km.

Open: 1 February - 22 December.

Directions

Approaching from the west (Figueres) take eastbound N260, then C252 to Garriguella then follow signs to site. GPS: 42.33888, 3.06726

Charges guide

Per unit incl. 2 persons and electricity	€ 18.35 - € 37.10
extra person	€ 5.10 - € 7.55
child (2-16 yrs)	€ 4.10 - € 6.15

Guardiola de Bergueda

Camping El Bergueda

Ctra B400 a Saldes km. 3,5, E-08694 Guardiola de Berguedá (Barcelona) T: 938 227 432.
E: info@campingbergueda.com **alanrogers.com/ES91390**

The short scenic drive through the mountains to reach this site is breathtakingly beautiful. This attractively terraced campsite next to the Cadi-Moixer Natural Park, is not far from the majestic Pedraforca mountain, and the area is a favourite for Catalan climbers and walkers. Access on the site is quite easy for large units, although the road from Guardiola de Berguedá is twisting. Of the 73 grass or gravel pitches there are 40 for touring, all with 6A electricity. The welcoming and helpful campsite owners will do all in their power to make your stay enjoyable.

Facilities

Two well maintained and well equipped modern toilet blocks are heated and clean. Facilities for disabled campers. Three private cabins with washbasin, toilet and bidet. Washing machines. Small shop, restaurant, bar and takeaway (w/ends only then 1/6-1/11). Outdoor pools (24/6-31/8). Play areas. Free WiFi by reception. Communal barbecues on each terrace (individual ones not permitted). Off site: Mountain biking. Walking and hiking. Snow hiking. Mountain guide service.

Open: Easter - 30 October (and weekends).

Directions

From the C16 Manresa-Berga road 2 km. south of Guardiola de Berguedá turn west towards Saldes. Site is on right after 3.5 km. From France via Puigcerdá take the C16 (Berga/Manresa) to Guardiola de Berguedá, then as above.
GPS: 42.21642, 1.83692

Charges guide

Per unit incl. 2 persons and electricity	€ 27.68 - € 30.00
extra person	€ 5.72 - € 6.30

Guils de Cerdanya

Camping Pirineus

Ctra Guils de Cerdanya km. 2, E-17528 Guils de Cerdanya (Girona) T: 972 881 062. E: guils@stel.es

alanrogers.com/ES91430

On entering this well organised site close to the French border, high in the Pyrenees, you gain an immediate impression of space, green trees and grass – there is always someone watering and clearing up to maintain the high standards here. The pitches are neat, marked, of average size and organised in rows. Generally flat with some on a gentle incline, a proportion have water at their own sink on the pitch. Many trees offer shade but watch for overhanging branches if you have a high unit.

Facilities

One new, central and well equipped sanitary block of top quality and decorated with boxes of bright flowers, is kept spotlessly clean and can be heated. Laundry facilities. Motorcaravan service point. Shop, bar and restaurant. Heated swimming pool and circular paddling pool. Boules. Tennis. Outdoor sports. TV and games room. Snooker. Play area and supervised clubhouse for youngsters. Excursions. Entertainment (high season). WiFi. No dogs. Off site: Bicycle hire 2 km. Riding 4 km.

Open: 21 June - 11 September.

Directions

From Perpignan take N116 to Prades and Andorra. Exit at Piugcerdá taking N250 signed Le Seu d'Urgell and almost immediately take second right for Guils de Cerdanya. Follow for 2 km. to site on right. From the south the best road is the C25/C16/N260 from Manresa to Piugcerdá, turning left for Guils de Cerdanya. GPS: 42.44312, 1.90583

Charges guide

Per unit incl. 2 persons and electricity	€ 36.20 - € 43.90

Hospitalet del Infante

Camping-Pension Cala d'Oques

Via Augusta s/n, E-43890 Hospitalet del Infante (Tarragona) T: 977 823 254. E: info@caladoques.com

alanrogers.com/ES85350

This peaceful and delightful, family run site has a lot going for it: its situation beside the sea with a wide beach of sand and pebbles, its amazing mountain backdrop, the views across the bay to the town and the friendly, relaxed atmosphere created by its owner of 40 years, Elisa Roller, her family and her staff. There are 152 mostly level pitches, some beside the beach, others on wide, informal terracing. Electricity (10A) is available throughout (long leads may be needed in places). Pine and olive trees are an attractive feature and provide some shade. Mobile homes and apartments available to rent.

Facilities

Toilet facilities are clean, neat and recently refurbished with a number of en-suite units (shower, washbasin and WC). Hot water to showers. Heated unit with toilets and washbasins for winter use. Unit for disabled visitors. Additional small block with toilets and washbasins at the far end of the site. Motorcaravan service point. Gas. Restaurant/bar and shop (1/3-30/11). Play area. Kim's kids' club and family entertainment (high season). Fishing. Sailing. Internet and WiFi. Torches required in some areas.

Open: All year.

Directions

Hospitalet del Infante is 35 km. southwest of Tarragona, accessed from the A7 (exit 38) or from the N340. From the north take first exit to Hospitalet del Infante at the 1128 km. marker. Follow 'Campings' signs, then signs to site. GPS: 40.97777, 0.90338

Charges guide

Per unit incl. 2 persons and electricity	€ 24.75 - € 42.95
extra person	€ 4.95 - € 9.50

No credit cards.

Hospitalet del Infante

Camping Naturista El Templo del Sol

E-43890 Hospitalet del Infante (Tarragona) T: 977 823 434. E: info@eltemplodelsol.com

alanrogers.com/ES85370

El Templo del Sol is a large, luxurious terraced naturist site with a distinctly Arabesque style and superb buildings in Moorish style. The owner has designed the magnificent main turreted building at the entrance with fountains and elaborate Moorish arches. The site has over 400 pitches of two different sizes, some with car parking alongside and 85 with full services. There is shade and the pitches are on terraces giving rewarding views over the sea. Steps give ready access to the sandy beach. There is some daytime rail noise especially in the lower areas of the site where the larger pitches are located.

Facilities

The sanitary blocks provide everything you could require. Extensive facilities for disabled campers. Washing machines. Supermarket. Health shop. Souvenir shop. Bars. Restaurant and snack bar (1/4-10/10). Swimming pools (20/3-15/10). Jacuzzi. Cinema. Games area. Boules. Separate children's pool and play area. Miniclub. Library. Entertainment. Hairdresser. Bicycle hire. ATM. No dogs. No jet skis. WiFi over site (charged).

Open: 22 March - 22 October.

Directions

From N340 south of Tarragona, exit at km. 1126 towards L'Hopitalet Plaja and follow signs. Heading north, near km. 1124, turn right immediately after a modern railway bridge and site is just 400 m. on the right. GPS: 40.97723, 0.90093

Charges guide

Per unit incl. 2 persons and electricity	€ 19.25 - € 54.10
extra person	€ 3.40 - € 9.40

L'Escala

Camping Lodge Neus

Cala Montgó, E-17130 L'Escala (Girona) T: 638 652 712. E: info@campingneus.com

alanrogers.com/ES80690

Camping Neus is set on the edge of the Montgri & Illes Medes Natural Park, under mature pines. There are 246 pitches arranged on sets of low terraces, all with 6/10A electricity, 40 are fully serviced. The site is peaceful at all times, especially in summer when the road beyond the site is closed to traffic. A small pool with a circular paddling pool is welcome after a hot day's sightseeing. Other amenities include a tennis court and small bar/restaurant. A new play area and a volleyball court have been added recently and gardens planted, and there is a 'wild camping' area to one side of the site.

Facilities

Renovated sanitary blocks offer clean facilities with baby rooms and facilities for disabled campers. Motorcaravan service point. Shop. Bar. Restaurant. Takeaway. Swimming pool. Paddling pool. Tennis. Volleyball. Play area. TV room. Entertainment and activities in peak season. Club for children. WiFi over site (charged). Bicycle hire. Fully furnished tents to rent. Only electric barbecues are permitted. Off site: Cala Montgó with beach 850 m. Fishing, kayaking, diving 850 m. L'Escala 2 km.

Open: 25 May - 16 September.

Directions

Take exit 5 from the AP7 and the GI623 to L'Escala. Continue to Cala Montgó. Site is on the right 1 km. before beach at Cala Montgó.
GPS: 42.1049, 3.15816

Charges guide

Per unit incl. 2 persons and electricity	€ 21.70 - € 45.20
extra person	€ 3.00 - € 5.00
child (4-12 yrs)	€ 1.00 - € 3.50

L'Escala

Camping l'Escala

Camí Ample, E-17130 L'Escala (Girona) T: 972 770 084. E: info@campinglescala.com

alanrogers.com/ES80700

Camping l'Escala has been on this site for over 50 years and was visited by Alan Rogers. It is a small town site, and all the amenities of the town are within easy reach. The beach is 400 m. away, a canopy of fir trees gives excellent shade, and the sanitary facilities are fabulous. There are 140 pitches (35-80 sq.m) of which 90 are for touring units. In high season there is a bar, snack bar and pizza oven. There is some road noise from the adjacent busy roads, despite the walls that surround the site.

Facilities

New central toilet block of the highest quality with underfloor heating for cooler seasons and sliding glass doors. Wonderful facilities for children featuring tiled pirate ships. Laundry sinks with hot water. Shop, bar, snack bar and pizza oven (all July/Aug). Satellite TV. WiFi over site (charged). No pets allowed. Modern bungalow apartments to rent. Off site: Beach 400 m. Bicycle hire and public transport 500 m. Riding 3 km. Golf 15 km.

Open: 12 April - 21 September.

Directions

From A7/E15 take exit 5 towards L'Escala on GI623. Turn north 2 km. before reaching L'Escala towards Sant Marti d'Ampurias. Site well signed on north side of town and beach. Watch for site name on wall.
GPS: 42.121, 3.13478

Charges guide

Per person	€ 3.00 - € 5.00
pitch incl. electricity	€ 18.75 - € 34.50

No credit cards.

L'Escala

Camping Illa Mateua

Avenida de Montgó 260, E-17130 L'Escala (Girona) T: 972 770 200. E: info@campingillamateua.com

alanrogers.com/ES80740

If you prefer a quieter site, out of the very busy resort of L'Escala, then Illa Mateua is an excellent option. This large, family run site has a dynamic owner Marti, who speaks excellent English. The site is divided by the beach access road and has its own private accesses to the contrasting beaches - one a rocky cove and the other gentle, sandy and sloping. There are 350 pitches across both parts of the site, all with 6A electricity, some on sloping ground, although the pitches in the second part are flat. Established pine trees provide shade for most places with more coverage on the western side. A new purpose-built diving centre and club opened on the site in 2013.

Facilities

Modern and heated sanitary blocks are kept spotlessly clean by omnipresent cleaners. Baby baths and brilliant facilities for children. Laundry facilities. Shop, extensive modern complex of restaurants, bars and takeaways. Infinity pool (June onwards, lifeguard). Pool bar. Play areas. Kayak hire. Bicycle hire. Organised activities for children in high season. Diving school. Sports centre. WiFi over site (charged). ATM. Private access to beach.

Open: 11 March - 20 October.

Directions

From north on A7 take exit 3 to N11, then C31 and GI 623 signed l'Escala. From south take exit 5 from A7 signed l'Escala. Site is clearly marked from town.
GPS: 42.11051, 3.16542

Charges guide

Per unit incl. 2 persons and electricity	€ 24.30 - € 51.25
extra person	€ 3.50 - € 6.90

No credit cards.

L'Estartit

Camping les Medes

Paratge Camp de l'Arbre, E-17258 l'Estartit (Girona) T: 972 751 805. E: info@campinglesmedes.com
alanrogers.com/ES80720

Les Medes is different from some of the 'all singing, all dancing' sites so popular along this coast. The friendly family of Pla-Coll are rightly proud of their innovative and award-winning site, which they have owned for almost 30 years. With just 170 pitches, the site is small enough for the owners and their staff to know their visitors, some of whom have been coming for many years. The top class facilities, along with the personal attention and activities available, make this a year-round home in the sun. The level, grassy pitches range in size from 70-80 sq.m. and are shaded. All have electricity (5/10A) and 155 also have water and drainage. The pool is ringed by palms and is part of an interestingly landscaped area, including an outdoor chess board, producing a relaxing environment in front of the old farmhouse buildings. The open-air dance floor has music twice weekly (in season). A heated indoor pool with sauna and solarium and good access for disabled campers is a great option out of high season. Set back from busy L'Estartit itself (2 km), it is 800 m. to the beach.

Facilities

Two modern spacious sanitary blocks can be heated and are extremely well maintained. Washbasins in cabins, top class facilities for disabled visitors. Baby baths. Laundry facilities. Motorcaravan services. Shop. Bar with snacks and pizza. Good restaurant (1/4-31/10). Swimming and paddling pools (1/5-15/9). Indoor pool with sauna, solarium and massage (15/9-15/6). Play area. TV room. Entertainment, activities and excursions (July/Aug). Diving activities. Multisports area. Boules. Bicycle hire and self-repair shop. Internet access and WiFi. Torches are useful. Dogs are not accepted in July/Aug. Off site: Riding 400 m. Nearest beach and fishing 800 m.

Open: All year.

Directions

Site is signed from the main Torroella de Montgri-L'Estartit road GE641. Turn right after Camping Castel Montgri, at Joc's hamburger/pizzeria and follow signs. GPS: 42.048, 3.1881

Charges guide

Per unit incl. 2 persons and electricity	€ 23.90 - € 43.90
extra person	€ 4.50 - € 9.10
child (2-10 yrs)	€ 2.70 - € 6.20

No credit cards.

L'Estartit

Camping Castell Montgri

Ctra de Torroella-l'Estartit km. 4,7, E-17258 L'Estartit (Girona) T: 972 751 630.
E: cmontgri@campingparks.com **alanrogers.com/ES80070**

This is a very large, bustling site with all the modern paraphernalia of holiday making. A large proportion of this site is reserved for tour operators, but there are three designated areas for independent campers. These provide 590 terraced, shaded and flat pitches, all with electricity (6/10A). There are three excellent swimming complexes and a wide range of amenities and attractions. Whilst large, the site is well organised and, unlike some in this area, offers an active holiday experience for all the family.

Facilities

Toilet facilities are good and are being gradually upgraded. Cleaning is continual but with the numbers on site in high season, queuing and litter may be a problem. Bars and restaurants. Supermarket. Pizzeria. Crêperie. Takeaway. Swimming pools. Tennis. Minigolf. Playground. Large screen TV. Disco. Entertainment. Excursions. Bicycle hire. WiFi over part of site (charged). Torches required.

Open: 11 May - 29 September.

Directions

Leave AP7/E15 at exit 6 and take C66 towards Palamós. Take GI642 towards Parlava and GI643 towards Torroella de Montgri, then GI641 to L'Estartit Site is well signed just north of the town on the left. GPS: 42.0511, 3.1827

Charges guide

Per person	€ 5.00 - € 5.50
pitch incl. car and electricity	€ 10.00 - € 61.00

L'Estartit

Camping Emporda

Ctra Toroella km. 4,8, E-17258 L'Estartit (Girona) T: 972 750 649. E: info@campingemporda.com

alanrogers.com/ES80730

Emporda is just 1 km. from the busy town and superb beach of L'Estartit. It has an open and friendly feel and is surrounded by some delightful views. There are just 250 pitches and a family atmosphere which Francesc, the director, encourages. The level, grassy pitches are 80 sq.m. in size. One area of the site is very shaded and the rest is attractively and adequately shaded by young trees. The great swimming and paddling pools are at the heart of the campsite, which has placed all the facilities neatly together. Varied entertainment is provided in high season. Chalets available to rent.

Facilities

Two very clean sanitary blocks, one with facilities for disabled campers and a baby bath. Cabins with hot and cold water, cold water at other basins. Laundry facilities. Bar. Restaurant, pizzas and takeaway. Supermarket. Large swimming pool (lifeguard in high season) and paddling pool. Entertainment and disco in high season. Miniclub. Aerobics. Electronic games. Two play areas. TV. Aqua gym. Bicycle hire. WiFi over site (charged).

Open: Easter - 12 October.

Directions

From the AP7 take exit 6 and follow C66 (Palamós). Then take GI642 (Parlava) and the GI643 (Torroella de Montgri). Finally, take GI641 towards L'Estartit and the site is well signed on the right shortly before entering the town. GPS: 42.04907, 3.18385

Charges guide

Per unit incl. 2 persons and electricity	€ 18.80 - € 34.80

No credit cards.

La Pineda

Camping La Pineda de Salou

Ctra Costa Tarragona-Salou km. 5, E-43481 La Pineda (Tarragona) T: 977 373 080.
E: info@campinglapineda.com **alanrogers.com/ES84820**

La Pineda is a clean, neat site north of Salou, just 300 m. from an aquapark and 2.5 km. from Port Aventura, to which there is an hourly bus service from outside the site entrance. There is some noise from the road. The site has two swimming pools; the smaller is heated. A paddling pool and outdoor spa are also here, behind tall hedges close to the entrance. A large terrace has sun loungers, and various entertainment aimed at young people is provided in season. The 366 flat pitches (all with 5A electricity) are shaded by mature trees in attractive gardens. La Pineda is a cut above other city sites.

Facilities

Sanitary facilities have been completely refurbished and are excellent. Baby bath. Facilities for disabled visitors. Washing machines. Gas. Shop, restaurant and snacks (July/Aug). Swimming pools, paddling pool and outdoor spa (July/Aug). Small wellness centre with spa in private rooms. Bar. New community room with TV. Bicycle and road cart hire. Games room. Playground. Entertainment (July/Aug). Torches may be required. No pets in August. WiFi. Off site: Aquapark 300 m. Beach and fishing 400 m.

Open: All year.

Directions

From A7 just southwest of Tarragona take exit 35 and follow signs to La Pineda and Port Aventura then campsite signs appear. GPS: 41.08921, 1.1837

Charges guide

Per unit incl. 2 persons and electricity (6A)	€ 30.90 - € 52.30
extra person	€ 5.70 - € 8.60
child (1-10 yrs)	€ 3.90 - € 6.40
dog	€ 3.90

Llafranc

Kim's Camping

Font d'en Xeco 1, E-17211 Llafranc-Palafrugell (Girona) T: 972 301 156. E: info@campingkims.com

alanrogers.com/ES81200

This attractive, terraced site, where the owner and his family have been welcoming guests for over 50 years, is arranged on the wooded slopes of a narrow valley leading to the sea. There is a strong family ethos and the site benefits from many repeat visitors. There are 325 grassy, shaded pitches (70-120 sq.m) for touring units, all with electricity (5A). Many of the larger pitches are on a plateau from which great views can be enjoyed. The terraces are connected by winding drives, which are narrow in places. The village of Llafranc and the beach are a ten minute walk.

Facilities

All sanitary facilities are spotlessly clean and include a small new block and excellent toilet facilities for disabled visitors. Laundry facilities. Gas supplies. Shop. Bar. Bakery and croissanterie. Café/restaurant (15/6-30/9). Swimming pools. Play areas. Children's club. TV room. Excursions. Visits arranged to sub-aqua schools (high season). Bicycle hire. Torches required. WiFi over site (charged). Gas only barbecues. Communal (low season). On-site doctor. Accommodation to rent. Off site: Beach 500 m.

Open: Easter - 30 September.

Directions

Llafranc is southeast of Palafrugell. Turn off the Palafrugell-Tamariu road at turn (GIV 6542) signed Llafranc. Site is on right 1 km. further on. GPS: 41.90053, 3.18935

Charges guide

Per unit incl. 2 persons and electricity	€ 17.00 - € 46.70
extra person	€ 4.20 - € 7.15
child (3-10 yrs)	€ 2.05 - € 3.55

Lloret de Mar

Camping Tucan

Ctra de Blanes-Lloret, E-17310 Lloret de Mar (Girona) T: 972 369 965. E: info@campingtucan.com

alanrogers.com/ES82100

Situated on the busy Costa Brava at Lloret de Mar, Camping Tucan is well placed to access all the attractions of the area and the town itself. The site has a friendly, family oriented approach, with a new children's multisports pitch, new water slides in the attractive pool area and an all season children's activity programme. It is laid out in a herringbone pattern, with 209 accessible, level touring pitches in three different sizes. They are terraced and separated by hedges, all with electricity (3/6/10A) and shade.

Facilities

Two modern toilet blocks include washbasins and facilities for children and disabled visitors, although access can be difficult. Washing machines. Gas. Shop. Bar and good restaurant. Takeaway. Swimming pool, children's pool, water slides and jacuzzi. Playground and fenced play area for toddlers. Children's multisports pitch. TV in bar. Bicycle hire. Entertainment. Miniclub. Internet and WiFi (charged). Charcoal and gas barbecues only. Off site: Town 500 m.

Open: 1 April - 25 September.

Directions

From A7/E4, A19 or N11 Girona-Barcelona roads take an exit for Lloret de Mar. Site is 1 km. west of the town, well signed and is at the base of the hill off the roundabout. The entrance can get congested in busy periods. GPS: 41.6972, 2.8217

Charges guide

Per unit incl. 2 persons and electricity	€ 26.90 - € 56.00
extra person	€ 5.50 - € 9.90

Maçanet de Cabrenys

Camping Maçanet de Cabrenys

Mas Roquet s/n, E-17720 Maçanet de Cabrenys (Girona) T: 667 776 648. E: info@campingmassanet.com

alanrogers.com/ES80650

Hidden away in the foothills of the Pyrenees, Camping Maçanet de Cabrenys is tranquil, calm and well ordered. The enthusiastic owner, Sergi, and his family established the site four years ago in a clearing created in the pine forest by felling 1,000 trees. Twenty-five touring pitches occupy the lower slopes of the clearing and more are being created on the edge of the woods below. There are 25 electricity connections (5/10A), including some to the 25 tent pitches which are among the trees, on terraces. The reception, bar and snack bar are in a wooden chalet above the pool and playing field.

Facilities

Heated sanitary block built in traditional style. Controllable showers, open style washbasins. En-suite unit for disabled visitors. Washing machine. Motorcaravan service point. Pleasant bar and snack bar. Swimming pool (unheated, May-Sept). Bicycle hire. Three barbecue stations (no private barbecues allowed). Wooden chalets to rent. Swimming/fishing in river. WiFi on upper part of site. Off site: Village 3 km. Riding 13 km. Golf 15 km.

Open: 1 March - 31 December.

Directions

Maçanet de Cabrenys is 30 km. northwest of Figueres. From AP7/E15 take exit 3 or 4 onto N11. At km 766 turn west on Gi502 through Maçanet de Cabrenys. Turn left at site sign on narrow, winding road with steep sections, then dirt track to site – unsuitable for large units. GPS: 42.373617, 2.75305

Charges guide

Per unit incl. 2 persons and electricity	€ 28.00 - € 32.40
extra person	€ 5.00 - € 6.20

Camping Cheques accepted.

Maiá de Montcal

Camping Can Coromines

Ctra Figueres-Olot (N-260), km. 60, E-17851 Maiá de Montcal (Girona) T: 972 591 108. E: coromines@grn.es

alanrogers.com/ES80620

Can Coromines is a converted farm behind which the owners (Sally is British and Marc French) have created a delightful little campsite in an orchard-like setting. A track curves in a loop around the site with landscaped, grassy and level pitches on either side, the first 38 are small to medium and without electricity, beyond that are 18 very large pitches with electricity (10A) and some with individual water taps. A variety of trees, some tall, others more recently planted, provide shade to many pitches. Reception and a pleasant bar/restaurant are housed in a wooden lean-to on the back of the farmhouse.

Facilities

One simple, modern toilet block provides controllable showers (charged), open style washbasins and en-suite facility for disabled visitors. Laundry facilities. Pool with paddling area (1/6-15/9). Bar (Easter-Sept) and restaurant (July/Aug). Bread, milk and eggs to order. Communal barbecues; gas/electric barbecues only on pitches. Play areas with zip wire. Bicycle hire. WiFi. Torches useful. Off site: Riding 1 km. Shop, bar and restaurant 1.5 km.

Open: 1 April - 1 November.

Directions

Maiá de Montcal is 20 km. west of Figueres on N260 Figueres-Olot road between kms 59 and 60. Watch out for a small low sign for site. TAKE CARE as entrance is very narrow. Site is 400 m. along narrow farm track. Unsuitable for large units. GPS: 42.209101, 2.737275

Charges guide

Per unit incl. 2 persons and electricity	€ 22.90 - € 30.00

Malgrat de Mar

Camping la Tordera

Camí de la Tordera s/n, E-08380 Malgrat de Mar (Barcelona) T: 937 612 778. E: camping@latordera.com

alanrogers.com/ES82330

With direct access to a beach and to a small nature reserve on the nearby river delta of la Tordera, the site is between Malgrat and Blanes. At present there are about 60 touring pitches, all with electricity (10A), either close to the beach in an open area, or in a new section with 30 larger serviced pitches. There are many more under the trees scattered among the seasonal pitches which dominate this site and give it a very Spanish feel. Note: access to the central pitches can be difficult, with narrow roads and high kerbs; staff will assist.

Facilities

Large sanitary block with controllable showers, open style washbasins (cold water), baby baths and en-suite units for disabled visitors. Smaller block with showers and washbasins. Washing machines. Motorcaravan services. Supermarket. Bar/restaurant with takeaway (1/6-15/9, weekends in low season). Swimming pool with children's section (15/6-15/9). Play areas. Sports field. Activity and entertainment (high season and weekends). Bicycle hire. Games/Internet room. WiFi (charged). Chalets for rent.

Open: 22 February - 10 November.

Directions

Malgrat de Mar is 60 km. northeast of Barcelona and site is 3 km. northeast of town. From Barcelona on C32 motorway, leave at Malgrat de Mar exit and join N11 from Girona. Take right fork (town centre) until you pick up signs 'Zona de Campings', then signs for site. GPS: 41.652304, 2.775483

Charges guide

Per unit incl. 2 persons and electricity	€ 16.00 - € 37.75
extra person	€ 4.20 - € 6.70

Malgrat de Mar

Camping del Mar

Avenida Pomareda s/n, E-08380 Malgrat de Mar (Barcelona) T: 937 653 767. E: info@campingdelmar.com

alanrogers.com/ES82340

Camping del Mar is situated on a quieter part of this coast, some three kilometres from the much larger resort of Blanes. Across the quiet road from the site is a long sandy beach with a lifeguard in high season. Carefully manicured lawns and a well designed site help to create a relaxed atmosphere. All the facilities are kept clean, and the 96 flat, grassy pitches all have electricity (6A) and easy access to a water point. The site is surrounded by a high hedge providing privacy and some shade to those pitches alongside, whilst most of the site has young trees and shrubs providing shade.

Facilities

Two clean sanitary blocks have showers in large cubicles, open style washbasins and controllable hot water. Laundry room. Small shop and bakery. Bar with TV. Restaurant with varied menu. Games room. Swimming pool with safe separate children's pool. Multisports area. Tennis. Large play area. Minigolf. Children's club and entertainment (July/Aug). Fishing. ATM. Communal barbecue. Bicycle hire. Internet. WiFi over site (charged).

Open: 22 March - 13 October.

Directions

From Blanes take GI682. Do NOT go into Malgrat de Mar town (one way system and low bridge 2.5m). Take BV6001, Av. De la Costa Brava instead. At roundabout to north of town follow yellow 'campings' sign to beach. Turn right and site is 2nd on right. GPS: 41.64726, 2.76378

Charges guide

Per unit incl. 2 persons and electricity	€ 22.10 - € 40.40

Mataró

Camping Barcelona

Ctra NII km. 650, E-08304 Mataró (Barcelona) T: 937 904 720. E: info@campingbarcelona.com

alanrogers.com/ES82450

The great advantage of Camping Barcelona is the regular shuttle bus to and from Barcelona (45 mins), which is free in low season. Like other sites in this area, it is on the beach road (N11) which means it is subject to train and traffic noise. However, the 344 touring pitches, which are separated from the permanent areas, do allow you to avoid the problem. Pitches vary in size and most have electricity (6/10/16A Europlug). Reception will assist in arranging many off site activities. There is a rocky coastline 100 m. away, but we recommend you to use the free shuttle to Mataró for serious sunning.

Facilities

Three clean sanitary blocks provide fine facilities; the one nearest the farm will be busy at peak periods. Baby room. Facilities for disabled campers. Washing machines. Freezer. Motorcaravan service areas. Supermarket. Bar. Restaurant. Takeaway. Pool bar. Swimming pool with lifeguard (18/5-29/9). Pétanque. Small playground. Children's farm. Miniclub and entertainment (high season). Disco. Internet. WiFi (charged). Electronic games. Tours booked. Night bus from Barcelona. Bicycle hire.

Open: 1 March - 10 November.

Directions

Site is east of Mataró at the 650 km. marker on the N11. Leave the C-32 autoroute at exits 104 or 108 and follow signs for the sea and Mataró. Site is well signed. GPS: 41.55055, 2.48338

Charges guide

Per unit incl. 2 persons and electricity	€ 24.85 - € 56.20
extra person	€ 4.95 - € 8.95
child (4-12 yrs)	€ 3.75 - € 6.50

Miami-Playa

Els Prats Village Beach & Camping Park

Ctra N340 km. 1137, E-43892 Miami-Playa (Tarragona) T: 977 810 027. E: info@campingelsprats.com

alanrogers.com/ES85330

This Costa Daurada beach resort is constantly developing with excellent facilities and many more improvements planned. This is a very popular area, not far from Tarragona and the Port Aventura theme park. There are 415 touring pitches, all with 5A electricity. They are fairly close together, mostly flat and shaded, and a few are next to the pleasant narrow, white sand/shingle beach. There is a separate area of bungalows to rent and an apartment block in one corner. A feature is the tropical-style beach bar, and tropical plants adorn the site. There is some road and rail noise on the western side of the site.

Facilities

Three blocks provide clean facilities with controllable showers and some washbasins in cubicles. A fourth unit has WCs and open style washbasins. En-suite unit for disabled visitors. Baby rooms. Washing machines. Motorcaravan services. Supermarket. Restaurant, takeaway and three bars. Swimming pool (3/4-17/10). Play area. Bicycle hire. Sailing, windsurfing, canoeing and diving. Activities and some evening entertainment. Dogs accepted in one area. Torches useful. WiFi (free for 5 hrs).

Open: 21 March - 2 November.

Directions

Miami-Playa is 35 km. southwest of Tarragona. Site is between the town and Cambrils on N340. Take exit at 1138 from A7 (Mont-roig del Camp), then turn south on N340. Site on left. GPS: 41.03611, 0.975

Charges guide

Per unit incl. 2 persons and electricity	€ 24.70 - € 47.10
extra person	€ 6.50 - € 7.50
child (1-10 yrs)	€ 1.60 - € 5.50

Montagut

Camping Montagut

Ctra Montagut-Sadernes km. 2, E-17855 Montagut (Girona) T: 972 287 202. E: info@campingmontagut.com

alanrogers.com/ES91220

This is a delightful, small family site where everything is kept in pristine condition. Jordi and Nuria, a brother and sister team, work hard to make you welcome and maintain the superb appearance of the site. Flowers and shrubs abound, with 90 pitches on attractively landscaped and carefully constructed terraces or on flat areas overlooking the pool. All but ten are for touring units with 6A electricity available throughout. A tranquil atmosphere pervades the site and it is a delight to enjoy drinks on the pleasant restaurant terrace, or to sample the authentic menu as you enjoy the views over the Alta Garrotxa.

Facilities

The clean, modern sanitary block has controllable hot showers, open style washbasins, a baby room and an en-suite unit for disabled visitors. Laundry facilities. Motorcaravan services. Supermarket. Restaurant and bar (28/6-31/8, snacks and bar at weekends in low season). Swimming pool and children's pool (1/5-30/9). Sports field. Playground. Pétanque. Barbecue area. Free WiFi over part of site. Torches are useful in some areas.

Open: 11 April - 12 October.

Directions

From south on AP7 leave at exit 6 (Girona), take the C66/A26 towards Olot. From north leave AP7 at Figueres, join N11 south and turn west signed Olot to join N260/A26. Take exit 75, turn right towards Montagut. At end of village turn left (Sadernes) and site is on the left in 2 km. GPS: 42.2469, 2.5971

Charges guide

Per unit incl. 2 persons and electricity	€ 19.00 - € 34.70

Montblanc

Camping Caravaning Montblanc Park

Ctra Prenafeta km. 1,8, E-43400 Montblanc (Tarragona) T: 977 862 544. E: montblancpark@franceloc.fr

alanrogers.com/ES85020

A purpose designed site, Montblanc Park has 280 terraced pitches of which 160 are ostensibly for touring units, although well over 100 are occupied by permanently installed seasonal caravans. They are grassless, all have electricity (20A) and vary in size, with hedging and young trees (so little shade). Water taps are scarce. The upper terraces are taken up by 130 wooden chalets for rent. The bar/restaurant and terrace overlook a large, lagoon-style pool with views across the valley, beyond the busy railway line and the autopista, to the town of Montblanc and the mountains of the Serra del Prades.

Facilities

Two toilet blocks have en-suite units (WC, washbasin and shower) but no separate WCs or showers, so probably under considerable pressure in high season. Baby room. Unit for disabled visitors. Laundry facilities. Supermarket (June-Oct). Bar/restaurant and snack bar with takeaway (weekends only in low season). Swimming pool and paddling pool. Play areas. Games room. Gym. Bicycle hire. Entertainment for children (weekends and high season). Electric barbecues only. Free WiFi in leisure area.

Open: 1 April - 30 November.

Directions

Montblanc is between Barcelona and Lleida on the AP2 motorway. Leave at exit 9 and join N240 (Reus-Tarragona); take first exit towards Prenafeta and site stands out on the hillside ahead.
GPS: 41.3787, 1.1826

Charges guide

Per unit incl. 2 persons and electricity	€ 19.00 - € 34.00
extra person	€ 4.00 - € 6.00
child (0-10 yrs)	free

Montroig

Camping La Torre del Sol

185

Ctra N340 km. 1136, E-43300 Montroig (Tarragona) T: 977 810 486. E: info@latorredelsol.com

alanrogers.com/ES85400

A pleasant banana tree-lined approach road gives way to avenues of palms as you arrive at Torre del Sol. This is a very large, well designed site occupying a good position in the south of Catalunya with direct access to the soft sand beach. The site is exceptionally well maintained by a large workforce. There is good shade on a high proportion of the 1,500 individual, numbered pitches (700 for touring). All have electricity and are mostly of about 90 sq.m. Strong features are 800 m. of clean beachfront, three attractive pools with two jacuzzis in the bar and restaurant area. A new seawater jacuzzi and Turkish sauna were opened in 2012. Occasional train noise on some pitches. The cinema doubles as a theatre to stage shows all season. The complex of three pools, thoughtfully laid out with grass sunbathing areas and palms, has a lifeguard. There is wireless Internet access throughout the site. There is usually space for odd nights but for good places between 10/7-16/8 it is best to reserve (only taken for a stay of seven nights or more). We were impressed with the provision of season-long entertainment, giving parents a break whilst children were in the safe hands of the activities team, who ensure they enjoy the novel Happy Camp and various workshops. There is a separate area where the team will take your children to camp overnight in the Indian reservation.

Facilities

Five very well maintained, fully equipped, toilet blocks include units for disabled visitors and babies and new facilities for children. Washing machines. Gas supplies. Large supermarket, bakery and souvenir shops at entrance, open to public. Full restaurant. Takeaway. Bar with large terrace where entertainment is held daily. Beach bar. Coffee bar and ice cream bar. Pizzeria. Open-roof cinema with permanent seating for 520. 3 TV lounges. Soundproofed disco. Swimming pools (two heated). Solarium. Sauna. Two large jacuzzis. Seawater jacuzzi and Turkish sauna. Sports areas. Tennis. Squash. Language school (Spanish). Minigolf. Sub-aqua diving (first dive free). Bicycle hire. Fishing. Windsurfing school. Sailboards and pedaloes for hire. Playground, crèche and Happy Camp. Fridge hire. Library. Hairdresser. Business centre. WiFi. Car repair and car wash (pressure wash). No animals permitted. No jet skis accepted. Off site: Buses on N340 close to site. Port Aventura. Beach fishing. Riding 3 km. Golf 4 km.

Open: 15 March - 31 October.

Directions

Entrance is off main N340 road by 1136 km. marker, 30 km. from Tarragona towards Valencia. From motorway take Cambrils exit and turn west on N340. GPS: 41.03707, 0.97478

Charges guide

Per unit incl. 2 persons and electricity	€ 20.30 - € 66.55
extra person	€ 3.35 - € 9.90
child (0-10 yrs)	free - € 7.85

Discounts in low season for longer stays.

Camping Cheques accepted.

Palamós

Internacional de Palamós

E-17230 Palamós (Girona) T: 972 314 736. E: info@internacionalpalamos.com

alanrogers.com/ES81500

This is a large, uncomplicated, comfortable site which is clean, welcoming and useful for exploring the local area from a peaceful base. Traditional in style, it is open for a long season and has a range of facilities. It might have space when others are full and has over 453 moderate sized pitches, 355 for touring. The majority are level and terraced with some less defined under pine trees on a gentle slope. Two hundred and eighteen have access to electricity (6A), and 104 have water and drainage. The sanitary facilities are excellent. The pretty beach at La Fosca is a 300 m. walk.

Facilities

Two refurbished toilet blocks and one smart new one are fully equipped with some washbasins in cabins. Facilities for disabled campers. Laundry room. Small shop. Bar and snack bar serving simple food and takeaways (all season). Swimming pool (36x16 m) with paddling pool (1/6-29/9). Small play area. Car wash. ATM. Bicycle hire. Torches necessary. WiFi over site (charged). Off site: Nearest beach and fishing 300 m. Town 1 km. with hourly bus service. Riding 1.5 km.

Open: 23 March - 30 September.

Directions

From C31 road (direction Palamós) take exit 326 and follow signs for La Fosca and Camping Internacional Palamós (not those for another site close by called Camping Palamós). GPS: 41.85722, 3.13805

Charges guide

Per unit incl. 2 persons and electricity	€ 31.20 - € 50.60
extra person	€ 3.50 - € 5.30
child (under 10 yrs)	€ 2.55 - € 3.45

No credit cards.

Camping Cheques accepted.

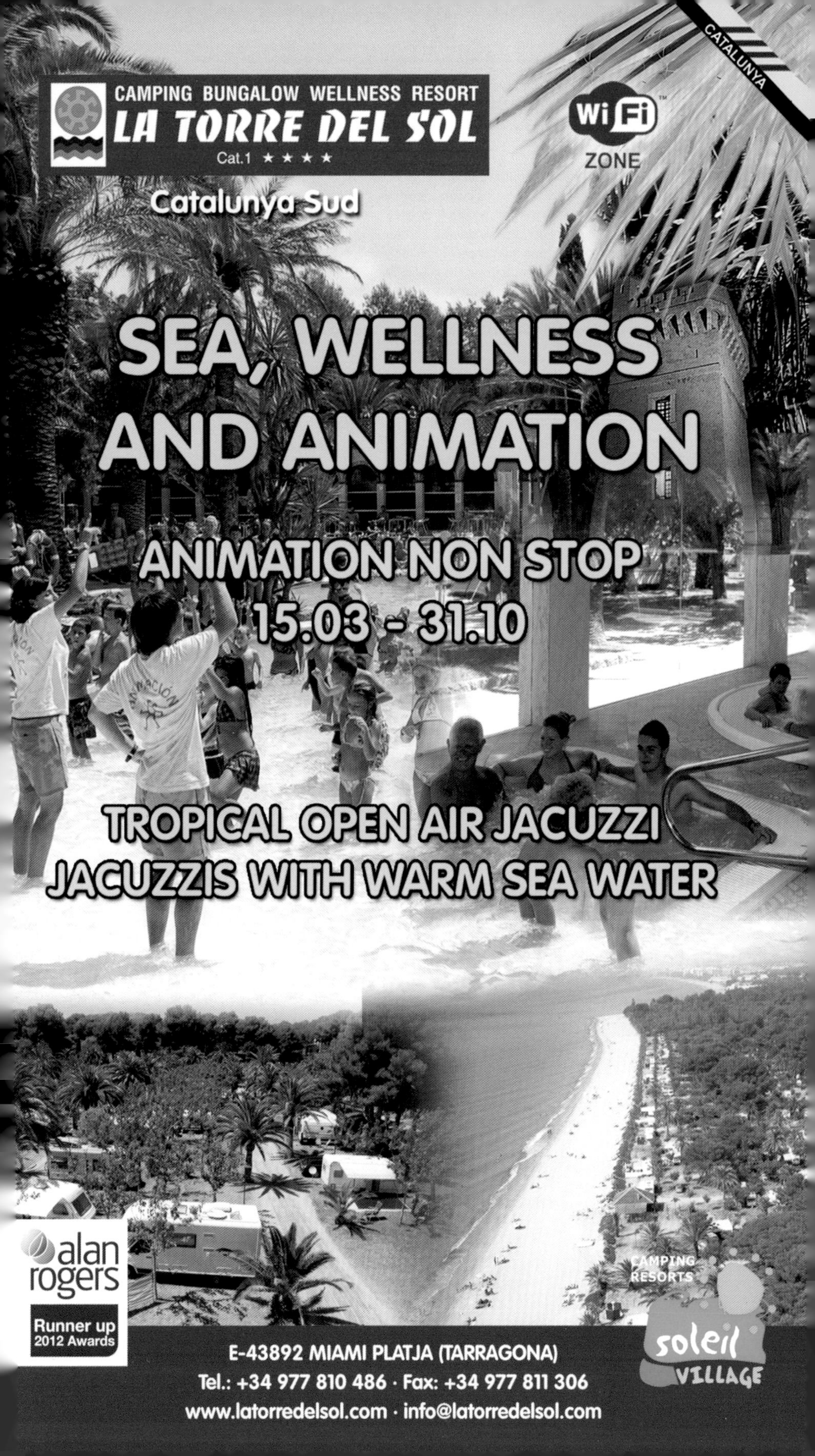
CATALUNYA
CAMPING BUNGALOW WELLNESS RESORT
LA TORRE DEL SOL
Cat.1 ★★★★
Wi Fi ZONE
Catalunya Sud
SEA, WELLNESS AND ANIMATION
ANIMATION NON STOP
15.03 - 31.10
TROPICAL OPEN AIR JACUZZI
JACUZZIS WITH WARM SEA WATER
alan rogers
Runner up 2012 Awards
CAMPING RESORTS
soleil VILLAGE
E-43892 MIAMI PLATJA (TARRAGONA)
Tel.: +34 977 810 486 · Fax: +34 977 811 306
www.latorredelsol.com · info@latorredelsol.com

Montroig

Playa Montroig Camping Resort

Ctra N340 km. 1136, E-43300 Montroig (Tarragona) T: 977 810 637. E: info@playamontroig.com

alanrogers.com/ES85300

What a superb site! Playa Montroig is about 30 kilometres beyond Tarragona set in its own tropical gardens with direct access to a very long, narrow, soft sand beach. The main part of the site lies between the sea, road and railway (as at other sites on this coast, there is some train noise) with a huge underpass. The site is divided into spacious, marked pitches with excellent shade provided by a variety of lush vegetation including very impressive palms set in wide avenues. There are 1,050 pitches, all with electricity (10A) and 564 with water and drainage. Some 47 pitches are directly alongside the beach. This is an excellent site and there is insufficient space here to describe all the available activities. We recommend it for families with children of all ages, and there is much emphasis on providing activities outside the high season. A member of Leading Campings group.

Facilities

Very good quality sanitary buildings with washbasins in private cabins and separate WCs. Facilities for babies and disabled campers. Several launderettes. Motorcaravan services. Gas. Good shopping centre. Restaurants and bars. Fitness suite. Hairdresser. TV lounges. Beach bar. Playground. Jogging track. Sports area. Tennis. Minigolf. Organised activities including pottery. Pedalo hire. Boat mooring. Bicycle hire. Internet café. WiFi over site (charged). Dogs are not accepted. Off site: Public transport 100 m. from gate. Riding, golf and boat launching 3 km.

Open: 4 April - 26 October.

Directions

Site entrance is off main N340 nearly 30 km. southwest from Tarragona. From motorway take Cambrils exit and turn west on N340 at 1136 km. marker. GPS: 41.03292, 0.96921

Charges guide

Per unit incl. 2 persons and electricity	€ 19.00 - € 56.00
extra person	€ 6.50 - € 8.00
child (3-10 yrs)	free - € 6.00

Discounts for longer stays and for pensioners.

Pineda de Mar

Camping Caballo de Mar

Passeig Maritim 52-54, E-08397 Pineda de Mar (Barcelona) T: 937 671 706. E: info@caballodemar.com

alanrogers.com/ES82380

This is definitely a site for lovers of the seaside, with direct access to a lovely, sandy beach. It is divided into two parts by the railway and dual-carriageway. The main part of the site is arranged off a central access road with plenty of shrubs and trees providing shade. In total there are 480 pitches, 380 for tourers. On the beach side of the site, the pitches are generally smaller (60-70 sq.m), all with shade; there is a bar/snack bar and a toilet block, and direct access to the beach. There are attractive new play and sports facilities for young children. There is some road and rail noise.

Facilities

Three toilet blocks are well maintained. En-suite units for hire (main side) with units for disabled visitors. Facilities for babies. Laundry facilities. Motorcaravan services. Shop and baker (15/6-12/9). Main bar and restaurant. Bar and snacks at the beach in high season. Swimming pool, jacuzzi and children's pool. Play area. Paddle court. Bicycle hire. Entertainment organised. Miniclub. Fitness room, massage and UVA machines. Internet. Fishing.

Open: 1 April - 30 September.

Directions

Site is off the N11 coast road, southwest of Pineda de Mar. Then leave N11 at km 669. Follow camping signs to road beside sea. Site signed off the beach road. Ask at reception for directions to beach side of site to avoid low bridges. GPS: 41.61664, 2.64997

Charges guide

Per unit incl. 2 persons and electricity	€ 25.35 - € 42.95

Camping Cheques accepted.

Pals

Camping-Resort Mas Patoxas Bungalow-Park

Ctra C31 Palafrugell-Pals km. 339, E-17256 Pals (Girona) T: 972 636 928. E: info@campingmaspatoxas.com

alanrogers.com/ES81020

This is a mature, friendly and well laid out site for those who prefer to be apart from, but within easy travelling distance of, the beaches (5 km) and town (1 km). It has a very easy access and is set on a slight slope with wide avenues on level terraces providing 376 grassy pitches (minimum 72 sq.m). All have shared 6A electricity and water points. There are a variety of mature trees throughout the site providing welcome shade. On-site amenities include an attractive swimming pool complex with a large terrace, an air-conditioned restaurant, an ice cream parlour and a children's play area. Entertainment takes place on a stage below the terraces during high season. The restaurant menu is varied and very reasonable. There is a large, supervised swimming pool with triple flume, a separate children's pool and a generous sunbathing area at the poolside and on the surrounding grass. A wide range of indoor and outdoor games for all can be found throughout the site. There is a miniclub in high season.

Facilities

Three modern sanitary blocks provide controllable hot showers, some washbasins with hot water. Baby bath. Cabins for children. Facilities for disabled campers. Laundry facilities. Fridges for rent. Gas. Supermarket, restaurant/bar, ice cream parlour, pizzeria and takeaway (limited opening in low season). Swimming pool with bar (1/5-29/9). Tennis. Entertainment and children's club (high season). Fitness area. Games areas. Massage. Disco. Bicycle hire. Internet access. WiFi over site (charged). Torches useful in some areas. Off site: Bicycle hire and riding 2 km. Fishing, watersports and golf 4 km.

Open: 17 January - 14 December.

Directions

Site is east of Girona and 1.5 km. south of Pals at km. 339 on the C31 Figueres-Palamós road, just north of Palafugel. GPS: 41.9568, 3.1573

Charges guide

Per unit incl. 2 persons and electricity	€ 19.00 - € 52.00
extra person	€ 4.30 - € 7.00
child (1-7 yrs)	€ 3.70 - € 5.00

FREE Alan Rogers Travel Card

Extra benefits and savings - see page 10

Platja d'Aro

Camping Valldaro

Cami Vell, 63, E-17250 Platja d'Aro (Girona) T: 972 817 515. E: info@valldaro.com

alanrogers.com/ES81700

Valldaro is a family run site, which is celebrating fifty years and is managed by the three Mestres sisters who remember Alan Rogers visiting when they were young children. It is situated some 1,500 m. back from the sea at Platja d'Aro. It is a multi-national site and popular with British visitors, some of whom have been coming for many years. The site, which resembles a small village, is very well equipped with its own facilities and has been extended. Many of the 544 flat and shaded touring pitches have been made larger, bringing them up to 120 sq.m. There are 400 permanent Spanish pitches and 160 mobile homes and chalets to rent, but these are in separate areas and do not impinge on the touring pitches.

Facilities

Four sanitary blocks are of a good standard and are well maintained. Child size toilets. Washbasins (no cabins) and adjustable showers. Two supermarkets and general shops. Gas supplies. Two restaurants. Large bar. Swimming pools. Outdoor jacuzzi. Tennis. Minigolf with snack bar. Playgrounds. Sports ground. Children's club. New play area with football pitch. Entertainment in season. Hairdresser. Bicycle hire. Barbecue rental. WiFi over site (charged). Satellite TV. Off site: Fishing 1 km. Beach and amenities at Platja d'Aro 1.5 km. Riding 4 km. Golf 5 km.

Open: 22 March - 25 September.

Directions

From Girona on the AP7/E15 take exit 7 to Sant Feliu on C65. On C65 at km. 314 exit to Platja d'Aro (road number changes to C31). In 200 m. at roundabout take GI662 towards Platja d'Aro. Site is at km. 4. Approaching from Palamós, access via Platja d'Aro centre, and the GI662.
GPS: 41.81427, 3.0437

Charges guide

Per unit incl. 2 persons and electricity	€ 21.60 - € 52.00
extra person	€ 4.60 - € 8.00
child (3-12 yrs)	€ 3.00 - € 4.60
dog	€ 3.90

Camping Cheques accepted.

Platja de Pals

Camping Cypsela

Ctra de Pals-Platja de Pals, E-17256 Platja de Pals (Girona) T: 972 667 696. E: info@cypsela.com

alanrogers.com/ES80900

This large and impressive, deluxe site is very efficiently run. The main part of the camping area is pinewood, with 688 clearly marked touring pitches of varying categories on sandy gravel, all with electricity and 552 with full facilities. The 267 élite pitches of 120 sq.m. are impressive. Cypsela is a busy, well administered site, only 2 km. from the sea, which we can thoroughly recommend, especially for families. The site has good quality fixtures and fittings, all kept clean and maintained to a high standard. The site has many striking features, one of which is the sumptuous complex of sports facilities and amenities near the entrance. The gates are closed at night. Several tour operators use the site.

Facilities

Four sanitary blocks are of excellent quality with comprehensive cleaning schedules and solar heating. Three have washbasins in cabins and three have amazing children's rooms. Private sanitary facilities to rent. Superb facilities for disabled visitors. Serviced launderette. Supermarket and other shops. Restaurant, cafeteria and takeaway. Bar. Hairdresser. Swimming pools. Tennis. Squash. Minigolf. Skating rink. Fitness room. Solarium. Air-conditioned social/TV room. Barbecue and party area. Comprehensive entertainment programme in season. Bicycle hire. Business centre. First aid room. WiFi (charged). ATM. Dogs are not accepted. Off site: Shuttle bus. Golf 1 km. Beach and fishing 2 km. Riding 6 km.

Open: 17 May - 14 September.

Directions

From AP7/E15 at Girona take exit 6 towards Palamós on the C66. Road changes number to the C31 near La Bisbal. 7.5 km. past La Bisbal, exit to Pals on the GI652. Follow signs for Platja de Pals. At El Masos take 6502 for 1 km. Main entrance is on the left. GPS: 41.98608, 3.18105

Charges guide

Per unit incl. 2 persons and electricity	€ 53.00 - € 80.00
extra person	€ 6.50
child (1-10 yrs)	€ 4.50

Platja de Pals

Camping Playa Brava

Avenida del Grau 1, E-17256 Platja de Pals (Girona) T: 972 636 894. E: info@playabrava.com

alanrogers.com/ES81010

This is an attractive and efficiently run site with an open feel, having direct access to an excellent soft sand beach and a freshwater lagoon where you can enjoy watersports and launch your own boat (charged). The ground is level and grassy with shade provided for many of the 745 spacious touring pitches by a mixture of conifer and broadleaf trees. All the pitches have 10A electricity and 160 have water and drainage. The large swimming pool has an extensive grass sunbathing area and is overlooked by the terrace of the restaurant and bar. This is a clean, secure and pleasant family site, suitable for sightseeing and for those who enjoy beach and water activities. The restaurant is very pleasant and offers a most reasonable menu of the day including wine. The new inside/outside bar is open to the public. There is also a new reception building, a supermarket and a performance area. An energetic entertainment programme runs during July and August, and there is a full programme of excursions. Playa Brava is a good base from which to explore the area and see a wide variety of places.

Facilities

Five modern toilet blocks include facilities for disabled visitors. Laundry facilities. Motorcaravan service point. Supermarket. Bar/restaurant. Takeaway. Swimming pool. Tennis. Minigolf. Beach volleyball. Play area. Bicycle hire. Watersports on river and beach, including sheltered lagoon for windsurfing novices. Stage show. Internet. WiFi over site (charged). Satellite TV. Torches required in some areas. No dogs. Off site: One 18-hole golf courses (50% discount online via Playa Brava) 500 m. Fishing and sailing 300 m. Riding 6 km. Coastal paths from site.

Open: 18 May - 8 September.

Directions

From the AP7/E15 at Girona take exit 6 (Palamós) on the C66. 7.5 km. past La Bisbal, exit to Pals on the GIV-6502. Follow signs for Platja de Pals-Golf Platja de Pals. Site is on left just before road ends at beach car park. GPS: 42.001130, 3.193800

Charges guide

Per unit incl. 2 persons and electricity	€ 33.50 - € 58.00
extra person	€ 2.50 - € 3.50

No credit cards.

Platja de Pals

Camping Inter-Pals

Avenida Mediterrania, E-17256 Platja de Pals (Girona) T: 972 636 179. E: interpals@interpals.com

alanrogers.com/ES81000

Alan Rogers visited this site in the 1970s, using it as his base in this area of the Costa Brava. Luis, the long-standing manager, still remembers his visit with affection. At that time it was described as a 'site shaded by an umbrella of pines' and it retains a very authentic Costa Brava atmosphere of tranquillity with its local stone terraces and sea views. There are 450 level, terraced pitches, most with shade and some with sea views through the trees. On-site amenities include recently renovated toilet blocks and a new supermarket. A formal restaurant and a bar overlooks the new swimming pool.

Facilities

Three well maintained toilet blocks include facilities for disabled campers. Motorcaravan service point. Laundry facilities. Shops. Restaurant/bar. Pizzeria. Supermarket by entrance. Swimming pool. Jacuzzi. Playground. Bicycle hire. Activities and entertainment in high season. Excursions. Watersports arranged. Mini-adventure park. Medical centre. Internet access. WiFi. Some breeds of dog are excluded (check with site). Torch useful.

Open: 31 March - 25 September.

Directions

Site is on the road leading off the Torroella de Montgri-Bagur road north of Pals and going to Platja de Pals. Follow signs to Gran Platja. Site on right after supermarket. GPS: 41.97533, 3.19317

Charges guide

Per unit incl. 2 persons and electricity	€ 29.80 - € 51.80

Camping Cheques accepted.

Poboleda

Camping Poboleda

Placa de les Casetes s/n, E-43376 Poboleda (Tarragona) T: 977 827 197. E: poboleda@campingsonline.com

alanrogers.com/ES85080

Time stands still at this unique site, watched over by La Morera de Montsant, a peak of the Serra del Montsant. Situated among olive groves, on the edge of the lovely old village of Poboleda, it is an idyllic site for tents, small caravans and motorcaravans. Large units would have problems negotiating the narrow village streets and even small caravans might find it tricky. The 151 average sized pitches (70 with electricity) are set on broad grassy terraces under olive and almond trees in a peaceful haven.

Facilities

One small block, open all year, is fully equipped, as is a larger block open for high season. Shower for children. Facilities for disabled visitors (key). Laundry service. Breakfast can be ordered. Bar. Swimming pool (24/6-11/9). Tennis. Boules. Reception sells basics. WiFi area (free). Off site: Bars, restaurants and shops in village. Bicycle hire 10 km. Fishing and boat launching 12 km. Gaudí Centre in Reus 30 km. Beach and Port Aventura theme park 40 km.

Open: All year.

Directions

Poboleda is best approached from the south. From AP7 at exit 34, take T11 (Reus then Falset) and continue on N420. After Borges del Camp turn north on C242 for 18 km over Coll d'Alforja. Take T702 west for 6 km to Poboleda. Watch for tent signs and follow through narrow streets. Not recommended for large units. GPS: 41.23231, 0.84316

Charges guide

Per unit incl. 2 persons and electricity (4A)	€ 32.32
extra person	€ 6.48

Puigcerdá

Camping Stel

Ctra N152 Ramal-Llivia s/n, E-17520 Puigcerdá (Girona) T: 972 882 361. E: puigcerda@stel.es

alanrogers.com/ES91440

High in the Pyrenees, right on the French border, this is an extremely efficient site. Part of a large, attractive building, the spacious entrance houses a modern reception (English is spoken). From here you will quickly be on your way to one of the flat, terraced pitches. Many of the pitches have shade and all are marked, clean and organised in rows with a water tap for each row. There is some road noise so, in order to avoid this and have views of the Cerdanya valley and the eastern Pyrenees, take one of the pitches on the upper terraces - it is worth the trouble.

Facilities

Sanitary facilities in the main building are of very high standard and kept very clean. A small block serves the upper terraces. Separate unit with facilities for disabled campers. Laundry facilities. Shop. Bar/restaurant. Swimming pool (20/6-14/9). Boules. Adventure style play frame (supervision needed). Adventure club (watersports and outdoor activities). Bicycle hire. Entertainment (high season). Barbecues are not permitted. Large motorcaravans and twin-axle caravans are not accepted.

Open: 30 May - 14 September.

Directions

From Perpignan take N116 to Prades and Andorra. At roundabout at the border crossing at Puigcerdá take first right for Llivia. Site on left after 1 km. From south, the best road is the C25/C16 from Manresa to Puigcerdá then head for the French border and turn left towards Llivia. GPS: 42.44153, 1.94128

Charges guide

Per unit incl. 2 persons and electricity	€ 35.30 - € 42.80

Camping Cheques accepted.

Roda de Bará

Camping Stel

Ctra N340 km. 1182, E-43883 Roda de Bará (Tarragona) T: 977 802 002. E: rodadebara@stel.es

alanrogers.com/ES84200

Camping Stel is situated between mountains and the sea with direct access to an excellent beach via a passage under the railway, which runs along the entire coast (so expect some rail noise, especially on the lower pitches). The 800 pitches are generally in rows separated by hedges, all have electricity (5A) and many have individual sinks. In one area, radios and TVs are not allowed. The central area contains a large bar/restaurant with terrace and snack bar overlooking the attractive pool complex, which includes a wonderful fun pool for children, a flume and a pleasant grass area carefully set out with palms.

Facilities

Three clean sanitary blocks provide showers, washbasins in cabins, facilities for children and disabled visitors and four high-quality private bathrooms for rent. Baby baths. Launderette. Motorcaravan service area. Tourist shop. Supermarket. Bar/restaurant and snack bar. Swimming pool with children's section, flume and jacuzzi. Sports complex. Tennis. Padel court. Gym. Bicycle hire. Activities. Miniclub. Internet room with free WiFi. WiFi over site (charged). Chalets for rent. No dogs. Torches useful.

Open: Easter - 28 September.

Directions

From east on AP7 leave at exit 31 and take motorway link to join N340 west. From west take exit 32 onto N340 east. Site is at 1182 km. marker on the N340 near Arc de Bará, between Tarragona and Vilanova. GPS: 41.16969, 1.46469

Charges guide

Per unit incl. 2 persons and electricity	€ 24.10 - € 32.85
extra person	€ 7.65 - € 9.00

Roses

Camping Salatá

Port Reig s/n, Platja Salatá, E-17480 Roses (Girona) T: 972 256 086. E: info@campingsalata.com

alanrogers.com/ES80090

Situated in the heart of Roses, in one of the most attractive areas of the Costa Brava, Salatá is a short walk from the magnificent seafront promenade with its bars, restaurants and shops. There are 233 grass touring pitches, all with 16A electricity and some shade (80-110 sq.m). Buildings and amenities are very well maintained. The campsite is part of a complex that includes apartments and the Hotel Terraza where a spa centre, indoor pool and other amenities can be enjoyed by campers in low season.

Facilities

Very clean toilet blocks have British style toilets and very good showers. Facilities for disabled visitors. Facilities for babies and children. Washing machines. Gas. Bar with snacks. Swimming pool. Playground. Entertainment programme for adults and children (15/6-15/9). Internet. WiFi. Barbecue area. Bicycle hire. Minigolf. No dogs from 29/6-23/08. Off site: Extra facilities at hotel nearby.

Open: 1 March - 30 November.

Directions

From the AP7/E15, take exit 3 south or exit 4 north (there is no exit 3 northbound) and then the N11 to the C260 and on to Roses. Site is well signed before you enter the town. GPS: 42.26588, 3.15762

Charges guide

Per unit incl. 2 persons and electricity	€ 25.30 - € 53.00
extra person	€ 5.15 - € 8.65

Rupit

Camping Rupit

Ctra de Vic-Olot km. 31,5, E-08569 Rupit (Barcelona) T: 938 522 153. E: info@rupit.com

alanrogers.com/ES83400

The last 15 kilometres of the approach road to this site are not for the faint hearted, but if a remote rural setting is what you are looking for, then this could be the site for you. The main area is attractive: on the right is a beautiful stone building housing reception, a bar and a restaurant, to the left an avenue of modern chalets for rent. There are 60 touring pitches, all with electricity (3/7A), most at the far end of the site, on level grass but with no shade and rather featureless. This is a quiet and relaxing site.

Facilities

The central toilet block provides open-style washbasins, some with hot water. Private shower cubicles (but no door to the changing area). Baby baths. WCs for disabled visitors (no showers). Washing machine. No shop (bar sells essentials). Bar with takeaway and separate restaurant (restricted opening in low season). Swimming pool (June-Aug). Games room. Play area. Communal barbecue area. Chalets and tents for hire. Site unsuitable for long vehicles. Off site: Rupit town 1 km. Riding 5 km. Fishing and bicycle hire 15 km.

Open: 27 March - 8 December.

Directions

Rupit is 30 km. south of Olot. From Olot head south on C152, then C153 for 31.5 km. This road climbs steadily and is very winding in places. Site is 1 km. before the town of Rupit. The site entrance is on a sharp bend where extra care is required. GPS: 42.02516, 2.45883

Charges guide

Per unit incl. 2 persons and electricity	€ 24.80 - € 33.20
extra person	€ 5.15 - € 7.25

Camping Cheques accepted.

Saldes

Camping Repos del Pedraforca

Ctra B400 km. 13.5, E-08697 Saldes (Barcelona) T: 938 258 044. E: pedra@campingpedraforca.com

alanrogers.com/ES91400

Looking up through the trees in this steeply terraced campsite next to the Cadi-Moixero Natural Park, you see the majestic Pedraforca mountain, its amazing rugged peak in the shape of a massive stone fork giving it its name. Access to the site is via a steep, curving road which could challenge some units. There are 200 pitches, including 100 for touring, all with electricity (5/10/16A) and 15 with connection to water and waste water. They vary in size and accessibility, although there are suitable pitches for larger units. The long scenic drive through the mountains to reach the site is breathtakingly beautiful.

Facilities

Two clean sanitary blocks (one updated 2012). At peak periods there may be queues. Facilities for disabled campers. Family room with baby baths. Laundry facilities. Shop and bar (1/4-31/10). Restaurant and takeaway (20/6-10/9). Heated indoor swimming pool, gym and spa. Outdoor pool (15/5-10/9). Play areas. Football and basketball pitches. Entertainment in high season. Games and social rooms. Rooftop relaxation area. Free WiFi on part of site. Charcoal barbecues only. Torches required. Off site: Motorcaravan service point close.

Open: 1 April - 31 October (then holidays and weekends).

Directions

Saldés is west of Guardiola de Bergueda, 125 km. north of Barcelona. From the C16 Manresa-Berga road 2 km. south of Guardiola de Bergueda turn west towards Saldés. Site is in 13.5 km. and is well signed. GPS: 42.23078, 1.75245

Charges guide

Per unit incl. 2 persons and electricity	€ 27.05 - € 36.85
extra person	€ 4.65 - € 5.75

Camping Cheques accepted.

Salou

Camping Resort Sanguli Salou

Passeig Miramar-Plaça Venus, Apdo 123, E-43840 Salou (Tarragona) T: 977 381 641. E: mail@sanguli.es
alanrogers.com/ES84800

Camping Resort Sanguli Salou is a superb site boasting excellent pools and entertainment. Owned, developed and managed by a local Spanish family, it has something for all the family with everything open when the site is open. There are 1,090 pitches of varying sizes (70-100 sq.m) all with electricity (7.5-10A). Mobile homes occupy 58 pitches and there are fully equipped bungalows on 147. A wonderful selection of trees, palms and shrubs provide natural shade and an ideal space for children to play. The good sandy beach is little more than 50 metres across the coast road and a small railway crossing. Although large, Sanguli has a pleasant, open feel and maintains a quality family atmosphere due to the efforts of the very keen and efficient staff. There are three very attractive themed pools, which include water slides and elephants. Amenities include a children's play park, organised activities for adults and children, a miniclub, tennis courts, table tennis, minigolf, a football pitch, volleyball, and a fitness room. Evening shows are presented in the site's magnificent amphitheatre, there is a cinema and the site's Sanguli restaurant serves Mediterranean cuisine. Located on the promenade near the centre of Salou, the site can offer the attractions of a busy resort while still being private and it is only 3 km. from Port Aventura. This is a large, professional site providing something for all the family, but still capable of providing peace and quiet for those looking for it.

Facilities

The six sanitary blocks are constantly cleaned and are always exceptional, including many individual cabins with en-suite facilities. Improvements are made each year. Some blocks have excellent facilities for babies. Launderette with service. Motorcaravan services. Car wash (charged). Gas supplies. Snack bars. Indoor and outdoor restaurants with takeaway. Swimming pools. Fitness centre. Sports complex. Fitness room (charged). Playgrounds including adventure play area. Miniclub. Minigolf. Communal barbecue. Multiple Internet options including WiFi (free). Security bracelets. Well equipped medical centre. Off site: Activities on the beach 50 m. Bus at gate. Bicycle hire 100 m. Fishing 200 m. Riding 3 km. Port Aventura 4 km. Aquopolis and golf 5 km.

Open: 4 April - 2 November.

Directions

On west side of Salou 1 km. from the centre, site is well signed from the coast road to Cambrils and from the other town approaches.
GPS: 41.075, 1.116

Charges guide

Per unit incl. 2 persons and electricity	€ 29.00 - € 78.00
extra person	€ 7.00
child (4-12 yrs)	€ 5.00

Reductions outside high season for longer stays. Special long stay offers for senior citizens.

Sant Antoni di Calonge

Eurocamping

Avinguda Catalunya 15, E-17252 Sant Antoni di Calonge (Girona) T: 972 650 879.
E: info@euro-camping.com **alanrogers.com/ES81350**

This large, welcoming campsite is attractively landscaped, with lawns, flowers and pretty features around the site. It has 634 shaded touring pitches of varying sizes, of which 100 are fully serviced. There are two pool complexes, one near the entrance with an unusual feature where one large pool cascades into another at a slightly lower level. Alongside is a paddling pool, an outdoor chess game and a large grassy area. In the centre of the site, there is a larger lagoon-style pool with a huge entertainment, seating and activity area, with a newly redesigned restaurant and terrace. This family orientated site is popular with visitors from the Netherlands and Germany so it is a good idea to book for busy periods.

Facilities

Four clean toilet blocks vary in size and are well positioned. Two private cabins for rent. Good facilities for disabled visitors. Family rooms. Washing machines. Gas supplies. Pleasant bars and good restaurant. Swimming and paddling pools. Playgrounds. Tennis. TV in bar. Fitness suite. Activities programme including children's entertainment. Minigolf. On-site doctor. Mail boxes. WiFi (charged). ATM. Excursions. Beach train (July/Aug). Torch useful. Off site: Public transport from the gate. Supermarket at entrance. Bicycle hire 300 m. Beach and fishing 300 m. Golf 6 km. Riding 15 km.

Open: 21 April - 23 September.

Directions

Sant Antoni di Calonge is southeast of Girona on the coast. Leave the AP7/E15 at exit 6. Take the C66 towards Palamós which becomes the C31. Use the C31 (Girona-Palamós) road to avoid Palamós town. Take the C253 coast road. Site well signed at northern end of Sant Antoni. GPS: 41.8470, 3.0986

Charges guide

Per person	€ 3.00 - € 7.55
pitch	€ 21.00 - € 35.10
child (3-9 yrs)	€ 2.60 - € 5.15
dog	€ 4.10

Salou

La Siesta Salou Camping Resort

185

Calle Norte 37, E-43840 Salou (Tarragona) T: 977 380 852. E: info@lasiestasalou.com

alanrogers.com/ES84700

La Siesta occupies a remarkable location close to the heart of the thriving resort of Salou, yet only two blocks from the fine sandy beach. The 360 pitches for touring, all with 10A electricity, vary in size, some suitable for larger units, others for tents. There is considerable shade from the trees and shrubs that contribute to the site's attractive appearance. Considerable recent investment has seen the creation of a pleasant, grassy play area for children and impressive new sports provision. An extensive new leisure pool complex has been built, overlooked by the existing bar/restaurant offering comprehensive and competitively priced menus, and entertainment in high season. A surprisingly large supermarket caters for most needs in season, and close by are all the shops, bars, restaurants and nightlife of Salou. The town is popular with British and Spanish holidaymakers and has just about all that a highly developed Spanish resort can offer, including miles of sandy beaches. Close by is Port Aventura, an amazing theme park, whilst days out could include a trip by train to Barcelona to see Gaudí's incredible Sagrada Familia cathedral or, in complete contrast, a drive along the coast to the Parc Natural del Delta de l'Ebre, one of Europe's largest wetland habitats and a World Heritage Site.

Facilities

Three bright and clean sanitary blocks provide very reasonable facilities including controllable showers and open style washbasins. Unit for disabled visitors. Motorcaravan services. Supermarket. Various vending machines. Self-service restaurant and bar with takeaway. Extensive new leisure pool complex. Children's club (June-Aug). Entertainment (July/Aug). Playground. Multisports and short tennis courts. Medical service daily in season. ATM point. Torches may be required. WiFi over site (charged). Off site: Many shops, restaurants and bars nearby. Port Aventura is close. Bicycle hire 200 m. Fishing 500 m. Riding and golf 6 km.

Open: 1 April - 10 October.

Directions

Leave AP7 at exit 35 or A7 (toll-free) motorway at exit for Salou. Follow the Tarragona-Salou road (dual carriageway) until you pass the side of the site on the right. Site is signed (narrow turning). Follow further small signs through the one way system.
GPS: 41.0777, 1.1389

Charges guide

Per unit incl. 2 persons and electricity	€ 27.00 - € 47.00
extra person	€ 5.00 - € 10.00
child (4-9 yrs)	€ 3.60 - € 5.00

Sant Feliu de Guíxols

Camping Sant Pol

Carrer del Doctor Fleming 118-134, E-17220 Sant Feliu de Guíxols (Girona) T: 972 327 269.
E: info@campingsantpol.cat **alanrogers.com/ES81800**

Sant Pol is a small, family owned site set on a pretty hillside on the edge of Sant Feliu, 350 m. from the beach and town. An attractive solar-heated pool and a paddling pool, bar and restaurant are the central focus of the site with shaded terraces and pitches of differing sizes curving down the slope. There are 29 pitches for touring units (all fully serviced) including 13 smaller pitches for tents. The on-site restaurant features regional á la carte dishes based on the best local produce. The cosiness of this site is in marked contrast to the majority of sites in the area. San Feliu is an attractive seaside town with lots of cafés, restaurants and two crescent shaped, white sandy beaches and a marina. The local area has museums and archaeological sites. Dali's house is within driving distance (book ahead). A great small family site for exploring the area or just to relax and enjoy the delightful ambience among the terraced gardens. Unusually, dogs are accepted in the bungalows.

Facilities

One excellent toilet block. Washing machines and dryer. Small supermarket. Intimate restaurant/bar and terrace. Solar heated swimming pools. Play area. Entertainment for children in high season. Minigolf. WiFi over site (charged). Excursions. Barbecue loan service. Bicycle hire. Half and full board available. Torches needed in some areas. Off site: Large supermarket, restaurants 300 m. Beach 350 m. Riding 1 km. Golf 5 km. Regular bus service into town.

Open: 30 March - 4 November.

Directions

Sant Pol between Sant Felieu de Guíxols and Girona. Take the C65 (Girona-Palamós) road. Leave at km. 312 (S'Agaró) to outskirts of Sant Feliu. Site signed from 1st roundabout and directly off 3rd roundabout. Steep entrance. GPS: 41.786504, 3.041274

Charges guide

Per unit incl. 2 persons and electricity (6A)	€ 18.00 - € 45.00
extra person	€ 4.00 - € 7.00
child (5-10 yrs)	€ 2.00 - € 4.00

Sant Pere Pescador

Camping la Gaviota

Ctra de la Platja s/n, E-17470 Sant Pere Pescador (Girona) T: 972 520 569. E: info@lagaviota.com
alanrogers.com/ES80310

La Gaviota is a delightful, small, family run site at the end of a cul-de-sac with direct beach access. This ensures a peaceful situation with a choice of the pleasant L-shaped pool or the fine clean beach with slowly shelving access to the water. Everything here is clean and colourful and the Gil family are very keen that you enjoy your time here. There are 157 touring pitches on flat ground with shade and 8A electricity supply. A lush green feel is given to the site by many palms and other semi-tropical trees and shrubs. The restaurant and bar are very pleasant indeed and have a distinct Spanish flavour.

Facilities

One clean, smart toilet block with British style WCs and excellent facilities. Superb facilities for disabled visitors. Two great family rooms plus two baby rooms. Washing machine. Gas supplies. Supermarket (fresh bread), pleasant bar, terrace and delightful restaurant (all Mar-Oct). Swimming pool (May-Oct). New playground. Games room. Organised activities for adults and children. Beach sports, kayaking, kite- and windsurfing. Torches useful. ATM. WiFi over site (charged). Off site: Riding 4 km.

Open: 23 March - 28 October.

Directions

From the AP7/E15 take exit 3 onto the N11 north towards Figueres and then the C260 towards Roses. At Castello d'Empúries take the GIV 6216 and continue to Sant Pere Pescador. Site is well signed in the town. GPS: 42.18901, 3.10843

Charges guide

Per unit incl. 2 persons and electricity	€ 31.90 - € 54.90
extra person	€ 3.90 - € 4.90

No credit cards.

Sant Pere Pescador

Camping Las Dunas

Ctra San Marti-Sant Pere, E-17470 Sant Pere Pescador (Girona) T: 972 521 717.
E: info@campinglasdunas.com **alanrogers.com/ES80400**

Las Dunas is an extremely large, impressive and well organised resort-style site with many on-site activities and an ongoing programme of improvements. It has direct access to a superb sandy beach that stretches along the site for nearly a kilometre with a windsurfing school and beach bar. There is also a much used, huge swimming pool, plus a large double pool for children. Las Dunas is very large, with 1,700 individual hedged pitches (1,500 for touring units) of around 100 sq.m. laid out on flat ground in long, regular parallel rows. All have electricity (6/10A) and 180 also have water and drainage. Shade is available in some parts of the site. Pitches are usually available, even in the main season. Much effort has gone into planting palms and new trees here and the results are very attractive. The large restaurant and bar have spacious terraces overlooking the swimming pools or you can enjoy a very pleasant, more secluded, cavern-style pub. A magnificent disco club is close by in a soundproofed building (although people returning from this during the night can be a problem for pitches in the central area of the site). With free, quality entertainment of all types in season and positive security arrangements, this is a great site for families with teenagers. Everything is provided on site so you don't need to leave it during your stay. A popular site for British rallies. A member of Leading Campings group.

Facilities

Five excellent large toilet blocks with electronic sliding glass doors (resident cleaners 07.00-21.00). British style toilets but no seats, controllable hot showers and washbasins in cabins. Excellent facilities for youngsters, babies and disabled campers. Laundry facilities. Motorcaravan services. Extensive supermarket, boutique and other shops. Large bar with terrace. Large restaurant. New takeaway and terrace in 2012. Ice cream parlour. Beach bar in main season. Disco club. Swimming pools. Playgrounds. Tennis. Archery. Minigolf. Sailing/windsurfing school and other watersports. Programme of sports, games, excursions and entertainment, partly in English (15/6-31/8). Exchange facilities. ATM. Safety deposit. Internet café. WiFi over site (charged). Dogs taken in one section. Torches required in some areas. Off site: Resort of L'Escala 5 km. Riding and boat launching 5 km. Water park 10 km. Golf 30 km.

Open: 17 May - 19 September.

Directions

L'Escala is northeast of Girona on coast between Palamós and Roses. From A7/E15 autostrada take exit 5 towards L'Escala on GI623. Turn north 2 km. before L'Escala towards Sant Marti d'Ampúrias. Site well signed. GPS: 42.16098, 3.107774

Charges guide

Per unit incl. 2 persons and electricity	€ 22.50 - € 68.00
extra person	€ 3.50 - € 6.00
child (3-10 yrs)	€ 3.00 - € 3.50
dog	€ 3.20 - € 5.00

Sant Pere Pescador

Camping Riu

Ctra de la Platja s/n, E-17470 Sant Pere Pescador (Girona) T: 972 520 216. E: info@campingriu.com
alanrogers.com/ES80320

Camping Riu is an established campsite which runs alongside the Fluvia river and is owned by the Senia group. There are 200 pitches, of which 190 are for touring units, all with electricity (5/10A mostly Europlug), on flat ground and shaded by mature trees. The bungalows are in a separate area away from the touring pitches and there are six innovative camping shelters for cyclists and walkers. The pleasant bar/restaurant and terrace overlooks the floodlit pool and children's area, where some entertainment is held in high season. Children's activities run throughout the season, and the site has an attractive new multisports and play area. The friendly director, Rosa, and her staff are very keen that you enjoy their family campsite, which has an ongoing programme of updating and improvement.

Facilities

Two toilet blocks are clean and well positioned with good showers. Facilities for disabled visitors. Baby rooms. Washing machines. Motorcaravan service point. Gas supplies. Small supermarket, restaurant and takeaway (all open in high season). Attractive swimming pool and children's pool. New playground and multisports area. Gym. Bicycle hire. Activities including entertainment for children. Kayaking (rental at reception). Tennis. Fishing. Excursions. Torches useful. WiFi over site (charged). Off site: Public transport 400 m. Road train to beach (1.5 km) from site in high season. Golf 20 km.

Open: 31 March - 16 September.

Directions

Sant Pere Pescador is on the coast between Roses and L'Escala. From AP7/E15 exit 4 take N11 north towards Figueres, then C31 towards Torroella de Fluvia. Take Vilamacolum road east and continue to Sant Pere Pescador. Site is well signed in town. GPS: 42.18757, 3.08914

Charges guide

Per unit incl. 2 persons and electricity	€ 25.20 - € 51.25
extra person	€ 3.15 - € 5.20
child (3-12 yrs)	free - € 4.10
dog	€ 1.80 - € 3.95

CAMPING LAS DUNAS

BEST 2013

AMPING
JNGALOWPARK

it Pere Pescador - Costa Brava

e holiday paradise
' the whole family!

mpsite and Bungalow park
ated at an endless sandy
ach. A holiday paradise for the
ole family. Immense variety
eisure activities and animation
gramme for all ages.
te-of-the-art sanitary facilities
l outstanding shopping centre.

LAS Dunas
CAMPING
BUNGALOW PARK

Camping Las Dunas
Tel. **(+34) 972 521 717**
Fax **(+ 34) 972 550 046**
info@campinglasdunas.com
GPS N 42º 09' 43" E 03º 06' 32"

w.campinglasdunas.com

ADAC Super-Platz 2012 · EUROPA-PREIS · ANWB 'CAMPING VAN HET JAAR' · LeadingCampings

Sant Pere Pescador

Camping Las Palmeras

Ctra de la Platja, E-17470 Sant Pere Pescador (Girona) T: 972 520 506. E: info@campinglaspalmeras.com

alanrogers.com/ES80330

A very welcoming, open site, which is attractively laid out and cared for. The 230 grass pitches are flat and well maintained, with some shade and 10A electricity. Ten pitches also have water and drainage. Thirty smart mobile homes are placed unobtrusively at one end of the site. A very pleasant pool complex has a lifeguard and the brightly coloured play areas are clean and safe. A great beach, noted for watersports, is a 200 m. walk through a gate at the rear of the site. A full activities programme for children allows parents a break during the day and there is organised fun in the evenings in high season. Full recreational facilities include a gym. The very Spanish-style restaurant serves high quality food. The owner, Juan Carlos Alcantara, and his wife have many years experience in the campsite business which is clearly demonstrated. You will enjoy your stay here as there is a very happy atmosphere. The beach is a magnet for kite- and windsurfers, and lessons and equipment are available nearby.

Facilities

Two excellent, very clean, solar powered toilet blocks include first class facilities for disabled campers. Baby rooms. Facilities may become a little busy at peak periods. Washing machines. Motorcaravan services. Supermarket, restaurant/bar/takeaway open all season (children's menu). Swimming pools (heated). Play areas. Tennis. Five-a-side. Fronton. Boules. Gym. Barbecue. Bicycle hire. Miniclub. Entertainment. Satellite TV. Internet. WiFi over site (charged). ATM. Torches useful. Off site: Beach and fishing 200 m. Sailing and boat launching 2 km. Riding 4 km. Golf 7 km.

Open: 12 April - 18 October.

Directions

Sant Pere Pescador is south of Perpignan on coast between Roses and L'Escala. From the AP7/E15 take exit 4 onto N11 north towards Figueres and then C31 towards Torroella de Fluvia. Take the Vilamacolum road east and continue to Sant Pere Pescador. Site well signed in town.
GPS: 42.18805, 3.1027

Charges guide

Per unit incl. 2 persons and electricity	€ 25.30 - € 54.26
extra person	€ 3.40 - € 4.80
child (3-9 yrs)	€ 1.70 - € 2.90
dog	€ 4.80

No credit cards.
Discounts in low season and for pensioners.

Sant Pere Pescador

Kawan Village l'Amfora

Avenida Josep Tarradellas, 2, E-17470 Sant Pere Pescador (Girona) T: 972 520 540.
E: info@campingamfora.com **alanrogers.com/ES80350**

This spacious site is family run and friendly. It is spotlessly clean and well maintained and the owner operates in an environmentally friendly way. There are 830 level, grass pitches (741 for touring units) laid out in a grid system, all with 10A electricity. Attractive trees and shrubs have been planted around each pitch. There is good shade in the more mature areas, which include 64 large pitches (180 sq.m), each with an individual sanitary unit (toilet, shower and washbasin). The newer area is more open with less shade and you can choose which you would prefer. Three excellent sanitary blocks (one heated) are fully equipped and offer free hot water, each with staff on almost permanent duty to ensure very high standards. Access around the site is generally good for disabled visitors. At the entrance, which is hard surfaced with car parking, a terraced bar and two restaurants overlook a smart pool complex with three pools for children, one with two water slides. In high season (from July) there is evening entertainment (pub, disco, shows) and an activity programme for children. Alongside the site, the magnificent sandy beach on the Bay of Roses offers good conditions for children and a choice of watersports. A bicycle is useful. Dogs are welcome and owners will appreciate the informal exercise areas.

Facilities

Three main toilet blocks, one heated, provide washbasins in cabins and roomy free showers. Baby rooms. Laundry facilities and service. Motorcaravan services. Supermarket. Terraced bar, self-service and waiter-service restaurants. Pizzeria/takeaway. Restaurant and bar on the beach with limited menu (high season). Disco bar. Swimming pools (1/5-27/9). Pétanque. Tennis. Bicycle hire. Minigolf. Play area. Miniclub. Entertainment and activities. Windsurfing. Kite surfing (low season). Boat launching and sailing. Fishing. Exchange facilities. Games and TV rooms. Internet room and WiFi over site (charged). Car wash. Torches required in beach areas. Off site: Riding 4 km. Golf 15 km.

Open: 14 April - 27 September.

Directions

From north on A17/E15 take exit 3 on N11 towards Figueres and then shortly on C260 towards Roses. At Castello d'Empúries turn right on GIV6216 to Sant Pere. From south on A17 use exit 5 (L'Escala) and turn to Sant Pere in Viladamat. Site is well signed in town. GPS: 42.18147, 3.10405

Charges guide

Per unit incl. 2 persons and electricity	€ 26.00 - € 60.00
extra person	€ 4.50 - € 6.20
child (2-9 yrs)	€ 2.50 - € 4.20
dog	€ 2.70 - € 5.20

Senior citizen specials. No credit cards.

Camping Cheques accepted.

FREE Alan Rogers Travel Card

Extra benefits and savings - see page 10

Sant Pere Pescador

Camping Aquarius

Playa s/n, E-17470 Sant Pere Pescador (Girona) T: 972 520 003. E: camping@aquarius.es

alanrogers.com/ES80500

This is a welcoming and organised family site approached by an attractive road flanked by orchards. Aquarius has direct access to a quiet, sandy beach that slopes gently and provides good bathing. Watersports are popular, particularly windsurfing (a school is provided). One third of the site has good shade with a park-like atmosphere. There are 430 touring pitches, all with electricity (6/15A). Markus Rupp and his wife are keen to make every visitor's experience a happy one. The site is ideal for those who really like sun and sea, with a quiet situation. Mr Rupp has a background in architecture and a wealth of knowledge on the whole Catalan area and culture. He has written a booklet of suggested tours (available from reception). The family is justifiably proud of their most attractive and absolutely pristine site which they continually upgrade and improve. The excellent facilities are elegant, tiled and frescoed. A small stage is used for live entertainment in season. The spotless beach bar complex with shaded terraces, satellite TV and evening entertainment, has marvellous views over the Bay of Roses. The Surf Center with rentals, school and shop is ideal for enthusiasts and beginners alike.

Facilities

Large toilet blocks provide some cabins for each sex. Excellent facilities for disabled visitors, plus baths for children. One block has family cabins with showers and basins. Laundry facilities. Gas supplies. Motorcaravan services. Supermarket. Restaurant and bar with terrace. Takeaway. Play centre. Playground and separate play area for toddlers. TV room. Surf Center. Fishing, sailing and boat launching. Minigolf. Bicycle hire. Barbecue and dance once weekly when numbers justify. ATM. Internet. WiFi over site (charged). Dogs are accepted in one section. (Note: no pool). Off site: Riding 6 km. Golf 15 km.

Open: 15 March - 2 November.

Directions

Attention: sat nav takes you on a different route, but easier to drive is from AP7 exit 3 (Figueres Nord) direction Roses on C-68. At roundabout Castello d'Empuries take second right to St Pere Pescador, cross town and river bridge. From there site is well signed. GPS: 42.18092, 3.09425

Charges guide

Per person	€ 3.15 - € 4.35
pitch	€ 9.40 - € 46.90
electricity	€ 3.80

No credit cards.

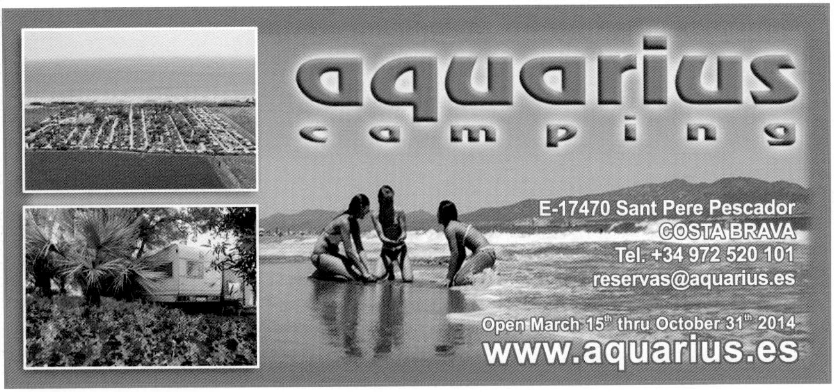

Santa Cristina d'Aro

Yelloh! Village Mas Sant Josep

Ctra Santa Cristina-Platja d'Aro km. 2, E-17246 Santa Cristina d'Aro (Girona) T: 972 835 108.
E: info@campingmassantjosep.com **alanrogers.com/ES81750**

This is a very large, well appointed, open site in two parts. There are 1,023 level pitches (100 sq.m) with 327 for touring units in a separate area, with shade from established trees. All have 10A electricity connections. There are wide access roads and long avenues between the zones. The main side of the site is centred around historic buildings. There is a huge, lagoon-style pool with a bridge to a palm decorated island (lifeguards), overlooked by a large complex including a bar, restaurant and takeaway.

Facilities

Two adequate toilet blocks for touring units (ignore the block for permanent pitches). Facilities for disabled visitors. Baby rooms. Laundry facilities. Supermarket, bars, restaurant, snack bar and takeaway. Swimming pools. Playgrounds. Games room. Tennis. Squash. Minigolf. Spa room and gym. Entertainment. WiFi over part of site (charged). ATM. Bicycle hire. Torches useful.

Open: 17 April - 14 September.

Directions

From AP7 E15 (Girona-Barcelona) take exit 7 and C65 San Filiu road. At entrance to Sant Christina d'Aro take GI662 (right), then first right (Ctra. De Sta Cristina). Site is 1 km. from village. GPS: 41.811167, 3.018217

Charges guide

Per unit incl. 2 persons and electricity	€ 18.00 - € 51.00

Sant Pere Pescador

Camping la Ballena Alegre

Ctra Sant Marti d'Empuries s/n, E-17470 Sant Pere Pescador (Girona) T: 972 520 302.
E: info@ballena-alegre.com **alanrogers.com/ES80600**

La Ballena Alegre is a spacious site with almost 2 km. of frontage directly onto an excellent beach of soft golden sand (which is cleaned daily). They claim that none of the 966 touring pitches is more than 100 m. from the beach. The grass pitches are individually numbered, many separated by hedges, and there is a choice of size (up to 120 sq.m). Electrical connections (5/10A) are available in all areas and there are 670 fully serviced pitches. There are several bungalow areas within the site with their own small pools and play areas, and some have shared jacuzzis. There are restaurant and bar areas beside the pleasant terraced pool complex. For those who wish to drink and snack late there is a pub open until 03.00. The well managed, soundproofed disco is popular with youngsters. A little train ferries people along the length of the site and a road train runs to local villages. Plenty of entertainment and activities are offered, including a well managed watersports centre, with sub-aqua, windsurfing and kite-surfing, where equipment can be hired and lessons taken. You can also use a comprehensive open-air fitness centre near the beach. An overflow area across the road provides additional parking and sports activities. The site has won Spanish tourist board awards and the owners are keen to promote an ecological approach through recycling, use of solar energy and the design of new buildings.

Facilities

Seven toilet blocks are of a very high standard. Facilities for children, babies and disabled campers. Launderette. Motorcaravan services. A range of restaurants, snack bars and takeaways. Swimming pool complex. Jacuzzi. Tennis. Watersports centre. Fitness centre. Bicycle hire. Playgrounds. Soundproofed disco. Dancing. Activities, sports, entertainment, etc. ATM. Dogs only allowed in one zone. Internet and WiFi (charged). Torches useful.

Open: 17 May - 21 September.

Directions

From A7 Figueres-Girona autopista take exit 5 to L'Escala GI623 for 18.5 km. At roundabout take sign to Sant Marti d'Empúries and follow site signs. GPS: 42.15323, 3.11248

Charges guide

Per unit incl. 2 persons and electricity € 26.50 - € 57.00

No credit cards.

Santa Susana

Camping Bon Repos

Malgrat de Mar, E-08398 Santa Susana (Barcelona) T: 937 678 475. E: info@campingbonrepos.com
alanrogers.com/ES82350

If you enjoy the hustle and bustle of the Costa Brava, then Bon Repos is ideal, if a little expensive. It is a long, narrow coastal site with many pitches along the length of the attractive fine sandy beach with direct access and no fence. The 500 touring pitches are of a reasonable size, flat with a sand surface and most with shade, and all have 10A electricity. The railway runs close along one side of the site, which is good for train spotters but does create a noise problem.

Facilities

Two sanitary blocks are dated but clean. The number of showers is low and probably extremely busy at peak periods. Cold water at washbasins. Baby room. Limited units for disabled campers. Laundry facilities. Restaurant. Supermarket. Motorcaravan services. Swimming pools (outdoor March-Oct). Play area. Tennis. Bicycle hire. Entertainment. Free WiFi over site. Torches useful.

Open: All year.

Directions

From A7 exit 9 (A19 exit 22) take road to Malgrat de Mar, then N11 to km 674. On to coast road and turn right by sea and railway line. Follow camp signs to site under railway line. Avoid Malgret de Mar town (narrow with low bridges). GPS: 41.6314, 2.7199

Charges guide

Per unit incl. 2 persons and electricity € 18.90 - € 54.00

FREE Alan Rogers Travel Card
Extra benefits and savings - see page 10

Sitges

Camping El Garrofer

Ctra. C-246a km. 39, E-08870 Sitges (Barcelona) T: 938 941 780. E: info@garroferpark.com

alanrogers.com/ES83920

This large, pine-covered site beside fields of vines is 900 m. from the beach, close to the pleasant town of Sitges. This is an attractive resort with seaside entertainments and is well worth exploring. The site has 526 pitches, many of which are occupied by seasonal caravans or chalets. A central area on dusty, baked earth beneath the trees is devoted to touring caravans and a corner of the site has 28 pitches with water mainly used for large motorcaravans. All have 6A electricity. There is an open field for tents. A cosy restaurant with a small terrace offers a varied menu.

Facilities

One of the three sanitary blocks has been refurbished and provides roomy showers and special bright facilities for children. Separate baby room with bath. Good facilities for disabled campers. Laundry. Bar/restaurant and small supermarket (all season). Saltwater swimming and paddling pools (1/6-31/9). Football pitch. Tennis. Play area for older children and fenced play area for toddlers. Bicycle hire. Boules. WiFi (charged). Off site: Golf 500 m. Beach and fishing 900 m. Sailing 2 km. Riding 4 km.

Open: 28 February - 14 December.

Directions

From north on AP7 leave at exit 29 and take C15/C158 (Sitges) to join C32 motorway east. Leave at exit 26 (Sitges). From Tarragona on AP7 leave at exit 31 to join C32 motorway; continue to exit 26. Follow signs for Sitges and site along C246a to km. 39; site is on right. GPS: 41.23352, 1.78112

Charges guide

Per unit incl. 2 persons and electricity	€ 23.75 - € 35.40
extra person	€ 3.30 - € 5.80

Tarragona

Camping Tamarit Park Resort

N340a km. 1172, Tamarit, E-43008 Tarragona (Tarragona) T: 977 650 128. E: resort@tamarit.com

alanrogers.com/ES84830

This is a marvellous, beach-side site, attractively situated at the foot of Tamarit Castle at one end of a superb one kilometre long beach of fine sand. It is landscaped with lush Mediterranean shrubs, studded with pines and palms, and home to mischievous red squirrels. The 470 good sized pitches have 10A electricity (most with water) and 50 are virtually on the beach, so are very popular. On hard sand and grass, some are attractively separated by hedging and shaded by trees. The management and staff here are very keen to please and standards are very high.

Facilities

The high quality sanitary blocks (two heated) are modern. Private bathrooms to rent. Laundry facilities. Motorcaravan services. Fridge hire. Gas supplies. Bakery. Supermarket, boutique, bars, restaurant and takeaway. Wellness area. Swimming pool. Tennis. Pétanque. Bicycle hire. Minigolf. Playground. Sports zone. Club room with bar. Miniclub. Entertainment programme all season. Fishing. Internet access and WiFi (code). Gas barbecues only permitted. Off site: Village 1.5 km. along beach. Golf 8 km.

Open: 15 April - 16 October.

Directions

From A7 take exit 32 (Tarragona) for 4.5 km. At roundabout (km. 1172) turn back (Atafulla/Tamarit) and after 200 m. turn right to Tamarit (beside Caledonia Bungalow Park). Take care over railway bridge, then immediately sharp left. Site on left after another site (Trillas Tamarit). GPS: 41.1316, 1.3610

Charges guide

Per unit incl. 2 persons and electricity	€ 13.00 - € 49.00

Minimum stay 7 nights 1/7-29/8.

Tarragona

Camping Las Palmeras

Ctra N340 km. 1168, E-43080 Tarragona (Tarragona) T: 977 208 081. E: laspalmeras@laspalmeras.com

alanrogers.com/ES84850

Situated amongst pine, poplar and palm trees, running parallel to a fine, white sandy beach, Camping Las Palmeras is in a wonderful location. The final approach is under the railway (3.5 m) with a sharp turn into the parking area. The site is very long and thin (1.5 km. so bicycles are handy) along the shore. Most of the 700 pitches are on grass with plenty of shade. All have access to 5A electricity, although long leads may be necessary in places. For its beachside location alone, Las Palmeras is worthy of a visit. There is some noise from the frequent trains, which run 24 hours.

Facilities

Four large toilet blocks are maintained to a high standard. Open style washbasins and good sized shower cubicles. Baby rooms. Laundry in each block. Shop, bar and beach restaurant. Smaller bar and snack bar (high season only). Two swimming pools (15/6-15/9). Tennis. Two play areas. Children's club in high season. Gas barbecues only (from 15/6). Internet and WiFi (code). Off site: Town 4 km.

Open: 1 April - 12 October.

Directions

Las Palmeras is easily accessed from the N340 (Barcelona-Tarragona) and is signed after the 1169 km. marker. Beware of the sharp bend at the entrance. GPS: 41.13019, 1.3117

Charges guide

Per unit incl. electricity	€ 13.00 - € 25.00
person	€ 3.00 - € 11.00

Camping Cheques accepted.

Tarragona

Camping Torre de la Mora

Ctra N340 km. 1171, E-43080 Tarragona (Tarragona) T: 977 650 277. E: campmora@tinet.fut.es
alanrogers.com/ES84860

Located on a promontory in a pleasant corner of the Costa Daurada with a village like atmosphere, Torre de la Mora takes advantage of its wonderful location, offering some pitches with beautiful views over the white sandy beaches and rocky promontories of the coastline. The hinterland is pine forest and there are areas where you can pitch a tent, access 6A electricity and feel close to nature. The 200 touring pitches vary in just about every way, some are on the lower flat area, including a few with beach frontage, others are on steep terraces around the promontory. Many of the higher pitches around the old coastal defence fort and building have amazing views.

Facilities

Two large and three small sanitary blocks have been refurbished and are kept clean. There is a mixture of washing facilities, which have hot water, but this fades at peak periods. Facilities for disabled campers (careful selection of pitch is required). Washing machine. Motorcaravan services. Supermarket. Restaurant. Swimming pool and sports area. Play area. Entertainment. WiFi (code). Torches useful. Barbecues are not permitted. Off site: Beach town outside the gate. Fishing. Bicycle hire 1 km. Golf 2 km. Riding 3 km. Boat launching 8 km.

Open: 18 March - 31 October.

Directions

From A7 (Barcelona-Tarragona) exit 32 take N340 towards Tarragona. Turn off for Punta del la Mora and site is well signed approaching the village. The final approach is via some narrow streets so watch for one way signs. Unusual entrance through a high wire fence alongside road. GPS: 41.128, 1.344

Charges guide

Per unit incl. 1 person and electricity	€ 17.75 - € 39.70
extra person	€ 5.20 - € 10.95
child (3-11 yrs)	€ 3.75 - € 6.25
dog	€ 2.10 - € 3.65

Torroella de Montgri

Camping El Delfin Verde

Ctra de Torroella de Montgri, E-17257 Torroella de Montgri (Girona) T: 972 758 454.
E: info@eldelfinverde.com **alanrogers.com/ES80800**

A popular, self-contained and high quality site in a quiet location, El Delfin Verde has its own long beach stretching along its frontage, where activities such as scuba diving are organised. There is an attractive large pool in the shape of a dolphin with a total area of 1,800 sq.m. This is a large site with 917 touring pitches and around 6,000 visitors at peak times. It is well managed by friendly staff. Level grass pitches are 100-110 sq.m. and marked, with many separated by small fences and hedging. All have electricity (6A) and access to water points. Used by British tour operators (38 tents and 122 mobile homes).

Facilities

Six excellent large and refurbished toilet blocks plus a seventh smaller block, all with resident cleaners, have showers using desalinated water and some washbasins in cabins. Facilities for disabled visitors. Laundry facilities. Motorcaravan services. Supermarket, shops, two restaurants, grills and pizzerias (all 28/4-23/9). Three bars. 'La Vela' barbecue and party area. Swimming pools with lifeguard (from 1/5). Large sports area. 2 km. exercise track. Dancing and entertainment weekly in season. Excursions and organised activities. Bicycle hire. Minigolf. Extensive new playground. Trampolines. Beach access. Scuba diving. Fishing. Hairdresser. ATM. Car servicing. Gas supplies. Internet café. WiFi over site (charged). Dogs are not accepted in high season (11/7-14/8). Off site: Golf (20% discount) and riding 4 km. Cycling and walking tracks.

Open: 28 April - 23 September.

Directions

From A7/E15 take exit 6 and C66 (Palafrugell). Then the GI642 east to Parlava and turn north on C31 (L'Escala). Cross River Ter and turn east on C31 (Ulla and Torroella de Montgri). Site signed off the C31 and has a long approach road. Watch for white dolphin marker and flags on the left.
GPS: 42.01197, 3.18807

Charges guide

Per unit incl. 2 persons and electricity	€ 22.75 - € 58.00
extra person	€ 4.75 - € 6.00
child (0-10 yrs)	€ 4.00 - € 5.00
dog (excl. 18/7-21/8)	€ 4.00 - € 5.00

Special offers on long stays in low season.

Tossa de Mar

Camping Cala Llevadó

Ctra GI-682 de Tossa-Lloret km. 18,9, E-17320 Tossa de Mar (Girona) T: 972 340 314.
E: info@calallevado.com **alanrogers.com/ES82000**

Cala Llevadó is a beautifully situated and quiet (although popular), cliff-side site, enjoying fine views of the sea and coast below. It is shaped around a wooded valley with steep access roads and terracing. High up on the site with a superb aspect is the attractive restaurant/bar with a large terrace overlooking the pleasant swimming pool directly below. There are 560 terraced, level touring pitches (489 with 10/16A electricity) on the upper levels of the two slopes, with a great many individual pitches for tents scattered around the site. Many of these pitches have fantastic settings and views. The site is unsuitable for campers with disabilities. In some areas cars may be required to park separately. There are 45 tour operator pitches, 34 bungalows and six new glamping cabins.

Facilities

Four very well equipped toilet blocks are immaculately maintained and well spaced around the site. Baby baths. Laundry facilities. Motorcaravan services. Gas supplies. Fridge hire. Large supermarket. Restaurant/bar, swimming and paddling pools (all season). Three play areas. Small botanical garden. Entertainment for children and adults (July/Aug). Sports courts. Sailing, water skiing, windsurfing, diving, canoe hire. Fishing. Bicycle hire. Excursions. ATM. Internet access and WiFi over part of site (charged). Torches required in some areas. Doctor service in high season. Off site: Tossa de Mar 3 km.

Open: 14 April - 28 September.

Directions

Leave the AP7/E15 at exit 7 to the C65 Sant Feliu road and then take C35 southeast to the GI681 to Tossa de Mar. Site is signed off the GI682 Lloret-Tossa road at km. 18.9, 3 km. from Tossa. Route avoids difficult coastal road.
GPS: 41.71292, 2.906465

Charges guide

Per unit incl. 2 persons and electricity (6A)	€ 26.05 - € 52.00
extra person	€ 6.35 - € 9.25
child (4-12 yrs)	€ 3.65 - € 5.75
dog	€ 5.10 - € 5.45

Less 10% with current Alan Rogers guide.

Vilanova de Prades

Camping & Bungalow Park Serra de Prades

Sant Antoni s/n, E-43439 Vilanova de Prades (Tarragona) T: 977 869 050. E: info@serradeprades.com
alanrogers.com/ES85060

On the edge of the village of Vilanova, nestling in granite foothills with superb views from its elevation of 950 m, this is a welcoming and peaceful site. The 215 pitches are on terraces formed with natural stone and with good access. With 120 for touring units (all with 6A electricity), the remainder are occupied by seasonal caravans. The upper tent pitches have wonderful views. Hedges and trees separate pitches providing a pleasant green environment and some shade. The site has won awards for its approach to ecology. From here it is possible to enjoy the Prades mountains or a day on the beach, an hour's drive away. One of the strengths of this site is the range of adventure and outdoor activities on offer.

Facilities

The modern, heated, well equipped toilet block has washbasins in cabins and is well maintained. Facilities for babies and disabled visitors. Laundry facilities. Motorcaravan services. Shop. Bar and good quality restaurant with takeaway (all year). Heated outdoor swimming pool (24/6-15/9). Gym. Archery. Quad bike and 4x4 hire. Paintball. Tennis. Riding with guided treks. Bicycle hire. Activities. Sports area. Entertainment in season. Safety deposit. Exchange facilities. Gas supplies. Chalets for rent. Torches required in some areas. WiFi over site (charged). Off site: Bar, restaurant and shops in village. Fishing, sailing and boat launching 20 km. Beaches 50 km.

Open: All year.

Directions

From east, leave AP2 (Barcelona/Lleida) at exit 9 (Montblanc) and join N240 towards Lleida. At km. 48 just west of Vimbod', turn south towards Vallclara and then Vilanova de Prades. Site on right after roundabout at entrance to village. From west leave the AP2 at exit 8 towards Tarragona on N240, then as above. GPS: 41.3497, 0.95852

Charges guide

Per unit incl. 2 persons and electricity	€ 33.00
extra person	€ 6.80
child (under 10 yrs)	€ 5.85

Camping Cheques accepted.

Vilanova i la Geltru

Vilanova Park

Ctra de l'Arboc km. 2.5, E-08800 Vilanova i la Geltru (Barcelona) T: 938 933 402. E: info@vilanovapark.com

alanrogers.com/ES83900

Sitting on the terrace in front of the restaurant – a beautifully converted Catalan farmhouse dating from 1908 – it is difficult to believe that in 1982 this was still a farm with few trees and known as Mas Roque (Rock Farm). Since then, imaginative planting has led to there being literally thousands of trees and gloriously colourful shrubs making this large campsite most attractive. It has an impressive range of high quality amenities and facilities open all year. There are 336 marked pitches for touring units in separate areas, all with 6/10A electricity, 168 larger pitches also have water and, in some cases, drainage. They are on hard surfaces, on gently sloping ground and with plenty of shade. A further 1,000 or so pitches are mostly occupied by chalets to rent, and by tour operators. The amenities include an excellent pool with water jets and at night time a coloured, floodlit fountain, which complements the dancing and entertainment taking place in the courtyard above. Nearby is a pleasant nature park with picnic tables. A second pool higher up the site has marvellous views across the town to the sea; here also is an indoor pool and wellness complex and in high season a second, more intimate restaurant, for a special romantic dinner overlooking the twinkling evening lights.

Facilities

Excellent toilet blocks can be heated and have controllable showers and many washbasins in cabins. Baby rooms. Units for disabled visitors. Serviced and self-service laundry. Motorcaravan services. Supermarket. Souvenir shop. Restaurants. Bar with simple meals and tapas. Outdoor pools (1/4-15/10), indoor pool (all year, charged). Wellness centre including sauna, jacuzzi and gym. Play areas. Sports field. Games room. Excursions. Activity and entertainment for all ages. Bicycle hire. Tennis. ATM and exchange facilities. WiFi (charged). Caravan storage. Off site: Golf and riding 1 km. Fishing, sailing and boat launching 3 km. Shops, restaurants and bars in Vilanova 3 km. (local buses). Excursions arranged to Barcelona, Monserrat and Bodegas Torres (wine tasting).

Open: All year.

Directions

Site is 3 km. northwest of Vilanova i la Geltru towards L'Arboc (BV2115). From Tarragona on AP7 take exit 31 onto C32, then exit 16 for Vilanova. Site is on left in 2 km. From Barcelona take AP7 exit 29, C15 Vilanova, then C31 west to km. 153, and turn north on BV2115. Site is on right.
GPS: 41.23237, 1.69092

Charges guide

Per unit incl. 2 persons and electricity	€ 29.90 - € 50.50
extra person	€ 6.20 - € 10.90
child (4-11 yrs)	€ 3.50 - € 6.60
dog	€ 6.50 - € 13.00

Camping Cheques accepted.

FREE Alan Rogers Travel Card

Extra benefits and savings - see page 10

This Mediterranean region is famous for its magnificent orange groves and beautiful long, sandy beaches. Centuries of Moorish presence have resulted in a profound Hispano-Moorish heritage.

VALENCIANA IS MADE UP OF THE PROVINCES OF CASTELLON, VALENCIA AND ALICANTE

THE CAPITAL OF THE REGION IS VALENCIA

La Costa del Azahar (Orange-blossom Coast) stretches from Vinaros to Almanzora, with the great port of Valencia in the centre. Orange groves grow right down to the coast, particularly in the northern section. Good beaches can be found around Benicassim and Peñíscola. South of Valencia, the Costa Blanca derives its name from its 170 miles or so of silvery-white beaches – some of the best beaches are to be found on this coast, especially between Gandía and Benidorm. As a result, it is one of the most popular tourist areas in Spain. The capital city of Valencia boasts a great nightlife and plays host to numerous festivals held throughout the year, including the unique fiesta of Las Fallas de Saint Joseph, when huge papier-mâché sculptures are set ablaze. Throughout it all are bullfights, music and fireworks. Alicante, the capital of the province of the same name, is dominated by the great Moorish castle of Santa Barbara, which offers marvellous views of the entire city. It also has several beaches in and around the town.

Places of interest

Castellón de la Plana: Santa Maria cathedral.

El Puig: monastery, Museum of Print and Graphics (world's smallest book).

La Albufera: vast lagoon, home to 250 species of bird.

Morella: medieval fortress town, dinosaur museum.

Oropesa: 16th-century Tower of the King.

Peñiscola: medieval castle.

Cuisine of the region

Rice is the dominant ingredient, grown locally in paddy fields; the most famous dish is the *Paella Valenciana*. Soups and stews known locally as *ollas* are popular and seafood is readily available. Tiger nut milk is a soft drink exclusive to this region, usually accompanied by *fartons* (local pastries).

Arnadí: dessert with pumpkin and sweet potato.

Arroz al horno: rice baked with chickpeas.

Arroz con costra: meat based paella topped with baked egg crust.

Arroz negro: rice cooked with squid ink.

Bajoques farcides: stuffed peppers.

Olla recapte: with potatoes and pork.

Turrón: made of nuts and honey, either soft and flaky or hard like nougat.

0
25
50
75
100 kms
CATALUNYA
ARAGON
MORELLA
VINAROS
TERUEL
A7/E15
ALCOSSEBRE
RIBERA DE CABANES
OROPESA DEL MAR
BENICASIM
CASTELLON DE LA PLANA
NAVAJAS
MONCOFA
CASTILLA-
LA-MANCHA
COMUNIDAD
VALENCIANA
VILLARGORDO DEL CABRIEL
VALENCIA
A3/E901
CULLERA
A7/E15
ALBACETE
GANDIA
OLIVA
CAMPELL
JÁVEA
BOCAIRENT
MORAIRA
BENIDORM
VILLAJOYOSA
EL CAMPELLO
ALICANTE
MURCIA
A7/E15
CREVILLENTE
LA MARINA
CARAVACA DE LE CRUZ
MURCIA
A37
GUARDAMAR DEL SEGURA
SAN MIGUEL DE SALINAS
SAN PEDRO DEL PINATAR

Alcossebre

Camping Ribamar

Partida Ribamar s/n, E-12579 Alcossebre (Castelló) T: 964 761 163. E: info@campingribamar.com

alanrogers.com/ES85610

Camping Ribamar is tucked away within the National Park of the Sierra de Irta, to the north of Alcossebre, and with direct access to a rugged beach. There are two grades of pitches on offer here. A number of standard pitches (30 sq.m) are available for small tents, and all have electrical connections (10A). The majority of pitches are larger (90-100 sq.m) and are classed as premium, with electricity and a water supply. A number of chalets (with air conditioning) are available for rent. Leisure facilities here include a large swimming pool plus delightful children's pool and a paddling pool. A main amenities building is adjacent and houses the site's slightly sterile bar/restaurant and shop. The Sierra de Irta is a magnificent landscape of intense colours. Although little over two hours' drive south of Barcelona, this is a very under populated region with some excellent long distance footpaths and cycle paths. Alcossebre is a delightful resort town which has retained its Spanish identity unlike some of the larger resorts to the north. The town has three Blue Flag beaches and a wealth of cafés and restaurants.

Facilities

One spotlessly clean toilet block with facilities for babies and campers with disabilities. Laundry facilities. Bar. Restaurant. Shop. Swimming pool. Paddling pool. Multisports terrain. Tennis. Five-a-side football. Boules. Paddle court. Bicycle hire. Play area. Library/social room. Tourist information. Chalets for rent. Direct access to rocky beach. Fishing. WiFi. Charcoal barbecues are not allowed. Off site: Beach 2 km. Alcossebre 3 km. Riding 10 km. Golf 35 km. Coastal walks.

Open: All year.

Directions

Leave AP7 motorway at exit 44 and follow signs to Alcossebre using N340 and CV142. The site can be found to the north of the town. Follow signs to Sierra de Irta and then the site, which is 2.5 km. along a dusty, gravel track. GPS: 40.270282, 0.306729

Charges guide

Per unit incl. 2 persons and electricity	€ 22.20 - € 47.00
extra person	€ 3.70 - € 5.25
child (3-12 yrs)	€ 2.90 - € 4.50

Alcossebre

Camping Playa Tropicana

Playa Tropicana, E-12579 Alcossebre (Castelló) T: 964 412 463. E: info@playatropicana.com

alanrogers.com/ES85600

Playa Tropicana is a unique site which will immediately strike visitors as being very different. It has been given a tropical theme with scores of Romanesque white statues around the site, including in the sanitary blocks. The site has 380 marked pitches separated by lines of flowering bushes under mature trees. The pitches vary in size (50-90 sq.m), most are shaded and there are electricity connections throughout (10A, some need long leads). There are 50 pitches with shared water and drainage on their boundaries. The site is away from the main hub of tourism, alongside a gently shelving sandy beach.

Facilities

Three sanitary blocks delightfully decorated, fully equipped and of excellent standard, include washbasins in private cabins. Baby baths and facilities for disabled visitors. Washing machine. Motorcaravan services. Gas supplies. Large supermarket. Superb restaurant and takeaway (Easter-30/9). Swimming pools (with new indoor facility) and children's pool. Playground. Bicycle hire. Kayak hire. Children's club. Fishing. Torches necessary in some areas. No TVs allowed in July/Aug. WiFi over site (charged).

Open: All year.

Directions

Alcoceber (or Alcossebre) is between Peñiscola and Oropesa. Turn off N340 at 1018 km. marker towards Alcossebre on CV142. Just before town turn right just after two sets of traffic lights. Follow road to coast and site is 2.5 km. Avoid alternative route given by GPS. GPS: 40.222, 0.267

Charges guide

Per unit incl. 2 persons and electricity	€ 24.50 - € 48.00

No credit cards.

Benicasim

Bonterra Park

Avenida de Barcelona 47, E-12560 Benicasim (Castelló) T: 964 300 007. E: info@bonterrapark.com

alanrogers.com/ES85800

A well organised site with extensive facilities, which is popular all year. It is a 300 m. walk to a good beach – and parking is not too difficult. The site has 320 pitches (60-90 sq.m), all with electricity (6/10A), and a variety of bungalows, some attractively built in brick. There are dedicated 'green' pitches for tents. Bonterra has a clean and neat appearance with tarmac roads, gravel covered pitches, palms, grass and trees which give good shade. Overhead sunshades are provided for the more open pitches in summer. There is a little road and rail noise. The site has an attractive pool complex including a covered pool for the winter months. The beach is good for scuba diving or snorkelling – hire facilities are available at Benicasim. This is a well run, Mediterranean-style site with English spoken by reception staff. It is usefully located for visiting attractions such as the Carmelite monastery at Desierto de las Palmas, six kilometres distant, or the historic town of Castellon.

Facilities

Three attractive, well maintained sanitary blocks provide some private cabins, some washbasins with hot water, others with cold. Baby and dog showers. Facilities for disabled campers. Laundry. Motorcaravan services. Restaurant/bar with takeaway. Shop. Swimming pool (heated Sept-June) and paddling pool. Playground (some concrete bases). Tennis. Boules. Multisports court. Small gym (charged). Disco. Bicycle hire. Miniclub. Satellite TV. WiFi over site (charged). Dogs are not accepted in July/Aug. Off site: Town facilities. Supermarket by entrance. Sandy beach and fishing 500 m. Riding 3 km.

Open: All year.

Directions

From E15/AP7 take exit 46 to N340. Site is on the quiet old main road running through Benicasim. Leave N340 at km. 987. At roundabout turn left and travel for 1.5 km. to site on left (white walls). Look for supermarkets, one 200 m. before site and a second directly opposite. GPS: 40.05708, 0.07432

Charges guide

Per unit incl. 2 persons and electricity	€ 28.72 - € 56.26
extra person	€ 4.30 - € 6.26
dog	€ 1.00 - € 2.00

Benidorm

Camping Villasol

Avenida Bernat de Sarria 13., E-03503 Benidorm (Alacant) T: 965 850 422. E: info@camping-villasol.com

alanrogers.com/ES86810

Benidorm is increasingly popular for winter stays and Villasol is a genuinely good, purpose built modern site. Many of the 309 well separated pitches are arranged on wide terraces which afford views of the mountains surrounding Benidorm. All pitches (80-85 sq.m) have electricity and satellite TV connections, with 160 with full services for seasonal use. Shade is mainly artificial. Reservations are only accepted for winter stays of over three months (from 1 October). There is a small indoor pool, heated for winter use, and a very attractive, large outdoor pool complex (summer only) overlooked by the bar/restaurant and attractive, elevated restaurant terrace.

Facilities

Modern toilet blocks provide free, controllable hot water to showers and washbasins and British WCs. Good facilities for disabled campers. Laundry facilities. Good value restaurant. Bar. Shop. Swimming pools, outdoor and indoor. Satellite TV. Playground. Evening entertainment. Safes. Dogs are not accepted. Off site: Beach, fishing and bicycle hire 1.3 km. Riding and sailing 3 km. Golf 8 km.

Open: All year.

Directions

From AP7 take exit 65 (Benidorm) and turn left at second set of traffic lights. After 1 km. at more lights turn right, then right at next lights. Site is on right in 400 m. GPS: 38.538, -0.119

Charges guide

Per person	€ 5.50 - € 7.20
pitch incl. car	€ 11.20 - € 26.40
electricity	€ 4.15

Benidorm

Camping Villamar

Carre del Albir, E-03503 Benidorm (Alacant) T: 966 811 255. E: camping@campingvillamar.com

alanrogers.com/ES86820

An all-year site with a good range of amenities, Villamar operates to high standards and rules. There are 890 pitches for long-term units, with 200 for tourers. The pitches are large and flat, with some shade from young trees. The central pool and amenities complex with its extensive grass areas dotted with palms, is cleverly designed and very smart. Sit on the terraces looking over the tropical scenery as you dine. You will find it difficult to remember that the teeming town of Benidorm is close by.

Facilities

The eight sanitary blocks include open style washbasins (some partitioned), free controllable hot showers, baby areas and units for disabled campers. Well stocked shop. Restaurant. Snack bar. Motorcaravan services. Three outdoor swimming pools (one heated for winter), one indoor pool. Small play area. TV room, games room and leisure area. Boules. ATM. Internet point. Entertainment for children in the summer. WiFi over site (charged). No dogs.

Open: All year.

Directions

Site is northeast of Benidorm at Platja del Abir. From A7 autoroute take exit 65 (Benidorm). After the toll booth continue straight on for 1.5 km. to large roundabout. Go left onto N332 towards Valencia. After 1.5 km. turn right, then take first left to site in 500 m. GPS: 38.555652, -0.097551

Charges guide

Per unit incl. 2 persons and electricity	€ 29.60 - € 41.90
extra person	€ 6.20 - € 8.00

Benidorm

Camping Benisol

Avenida de la Comunidad Valenciana s/n, E-03500 Benidorm (Alacant) T: 965 851 673.

E: campingbenisol@yahoo.es **alanrogers.com/ES86830**

Camping Benisol is a well developed and peaceful site with lush, green vegetation and a mountain backdrop. Mature hedges and trees afford privacy to each pitch and some artificial shade is provided where necessary. There are 298 pitches of which around 115 are for touring units (60-80 sq.m). All have electricity hook-ups (4/6A) and 75 have drainage. All the connecting roads are now surfaced with tarmac. Some daytime road noise should be expected. The site has an excellent restaurant serving traditional Spanish food at great prices, with a pretty, shaded terrace overlooking the pool with its palms and thatched pool bar.

Facilities

Modern sanitary facilities, heated in winter and kept very clean, have free, solar heated water to washbasins, showers and sinks. Laundry facilities. Gas supplies. Restaurant with terrace and bar (all year, closed 1 day a week). Shop. Swimming pool (Easter-Nov). Small, old style play area. Minigolf. Jogging track. Tennis. Golf driving range. ATM. WiFi. Off site: Riding 1 km. Bicycle hire and sea fishing 3 km. Golf 14 km. Bus route.

Open: All year.

Directions

Site is northeast of Benidorm. Exit N332 at 152 km. marker and take turn signed Playa Levant. Site is 100 m. on left off the main road, well signed. GPS: 38.559, -0.097

Charges guide

Per person	€ 3.30 - € 5.25
pitch	€ 9.00 - € 18.10
electricity	€ 3.00

No credit cards.

Benidorm

Camping Caravaning El Raco

Avenida Doctor Severo Ochoa 35, E-03503 Benidorm (Alacant) T: 965 868 552. E: info@campingraco.com

alanrogers.com/ES86850

This purpose built site with good facilities provides about 597 pitches (90 for touring units). There is wide access from the Rincon de Loix road. The site is situated 1.5 km. from the town, Levante beach and promenade. It has wide tarmac roads and pitches of 80 sq.m. or more, separated by low cypress hedging and some trees which provide some shade. Satellite TV connections are provided to each pitch and there are 90 with all services including 10A electricity. The restaurant, bar and elegant pools are all by the entrance, a considerable distance from the touring pitches.

Facilities

Four large toilet blocks are well equipped. Facilities for babies and disabled visitors. Laundry facilities. Gas supplies. Motorcaravan services. Well stocked shop. Busy bar with TV and restaurant (all open to public). Outdoor swimming pool, no slides or diving board (1/4-31/10). Indoor heated pool (1/11-31/3). Playground. ATM. WiFi. Off site: Beach 1 km. Bicycle hire 2 km. Golf 6 km. Theme parks.

Open: All year.

Directions

From north on N332 follow signs for Playa Levante (or Benidorm Palace). At lights turn left (Playa Levante). GPS: 38.5487, -0.0991

Charges guide

Per unit incl. 2 persons and electricity	€ 30.65 - € 38.15
extra person	€ 6.15 - € 7.00
child (3-12 yrs)	€ 4.75 - € 5.75

No credit cards.

Bocairent

Camping Mariola

Ctra Bocairent-Alcoi km 9, E-46880 Bocairent (Valencia) T: 962 135 160. E: info@campingmariola.com
alanrogers.com/ES86450

Situated high in the Sierra Mariola National Park, in a beautiful rural setting but only 12 km. from the old town of Bocairent, this is a real taste of Spain with hilltop views all around. Used mainly by the Spanish, the site is an undiscovered jewel with 170 slightly sloping pitches. These are well spaced and have shade from a mixture of young and mature trees. An orchard area well away from the main site (with no amenities close by) is used for more casual camping. A traditional, stone built restaurant is slightly elevated with views over the site. Accessed by a few steps, this attractive building is covered in roses.

Facilities

Six identical small toilet blocks offer adequate facilities with British style WCs and showers with shared changing area. Open style washbasins. No facilities for disabled visitors. Washing machine. Motorcaravan services. Small shop (weekends only). Bar/restaurant (weekends only in low season). Satellite TV. Outdoor pool with separate paddling pool (June-Sept). Two multisports pitches. Play area. Communal barbecue area. Children's club and entertainment (Aug. only). Off site: Riding and golf 12 km.

Open: All year.

Directions

From the CV40 exit for Ontinyent and follow the CV81. Pass Bocairent and in 2 km. look for camping sign (at textiles factory). Turn south on VV2031 to Alcoy. Turn right at first roundabout and straight on at next through small industrial estate. Persevere onwards and upwards for 10 km. and site is a turn to left. GPS: 38.753317, -0.549402

Charges guide

Per unit incl. 2 persons and electricity	€ 18.00 - € 22.00
extra person	€ 4.50 - € 5.50
child (3-10 yrs)	€ 3.60 - € 4.50

Campell

Camping Vall de Laguar

Calle Sant Antoni 24, la Vall de Laguar, E-03791 Campell (Alacant) T: 965 584 590.
E: info@campinglaguar.com **alanrogers.com/ES86750**

Near the pretty mountain-top village of Campell, this new site is perched high on the side of a mountain with breathtaking views of hilltop villages, the surrounding hills and distant sea. With a wholehearted welcome from the owners, the well maintained site promises a real taste of Spain. The pitches, pool, terrace and restaurant all share the views. The 68 average sized gravel pitches are on terraces and all have 6A electricity and water. Trees and hedges have been planted and now give ample shade. This is a great place to get away from the coastal hustle, bustle and high rise of the beaches.

Facilities

Two new sanitary blocks have excellent clean facilities including some for disabled campers. Washing machines and dryers. Restaurant with pretty terrace (closed Sept). Bar and small pool bar. Outdoor swimming pool (June -Sept). Small entertainment programme in high season. WiFi over site (free). Charcoal barbecues only (communal area). Torches useful. Off site: Attractive town close by. Riding 15 km. Golf and beach 20 km.

Open: All year.

Directions

Site is 20 km. west of Xabia/Javea. From A7/E15 exit 62 head to Ondara/Valencia on the N332 and at the roundabout on the Ondara bypass head to Benidoleig/Orba. At Orba turn right and follow site signs. GPS: 38.7766, -0.105

Charges guide

Per unit incl. 2 persons and electricity	€ 25.55
extra person	€ 5.25
dog	€ 3.00

Crevillente

Marjal Costa Blanca Eco Camping Resort

alan rogers Winner 2013 Awards

Partida de las Casicas, 5, AP7 exit 730 (Catral-Crevillente), E-03330 Crevillente (Alacant)
T: 965 484 945. E: camping@marjalcostablanca.com **alanrogers.com/ES87435**

Marjal Costa Blanca is a new, fully equipped site situated 15 km. inland on the southern Alicante coast, close to the town of Crevillente and the Parque Natural de El Hondo. The 1,432 hardstanding pitches here range in size from 90-180 sq.m, and all have electricity (16A), water, drainage, TV and WiFi connections. On-site amenities include a tropical themed swimming pool complex and a state-of-the-art wellness centre. There is full disabled access, including at the swimming pool and staffed gym. There is accommodation for rent, including 16 Balinese-style bungalows adapted for disabled visitors. The site is a major new initiative and ideal for both family holidays in summer and for winter sun-seekers. The site's principal restaurant, Marjal Plaza, is open all year and, during summer months, features a buffet with fresh, local produce. The site has been developed along very strict environmental guidelines. More than 7,000 mulberry trees have been planted and every effort has been made to conserve resources and use sustainable materials. Activities are organised for all ages - Spanish lessons, tap dancing, quiz night, bingo etc. For younger campers there is a children's club, led by the site's mascot, Marjalita.

Facilities

Six modern, spotlessly clean toilet blocks have washbasins and free showers in cabins. Facilities for children, babies and disabled visitors. Well equipped shop. Bar, restaurant and takeaway (all year). Swimming pool complex with outdoor pool (all year), heated indoor pool (all year), sauna and hammam. Fully equipped gym. Wellness centre. Hairdresser. Play areas. Games rooms. Library. Multisports courts. Minigolf. Tennis. Football. Entertainment and activity programme. Business centre. Bicycle hire. Car hire service. Doctor and vet. Free WiFi.

Open: All year.

Directions

Take the southbound A7 coastal motorway until you reach the fork close to Elche-Crevillente. Continue on AP7 towards Cartagena, take exit 730 (Catral) and follow signs to site. GPS: 38.177901, -0.809504

Charges guide

Per unit incl. 2 persons and all services (plus meter)	€ 26.00 - € 45.00
extra person	€ 4.00 - € 7.00
child (4-12 yrs)	€ 3.00 - € 5.00

Camping Cheques accepted.

Cullera

Camping Santa Marta

Ctra de Faro km. 2, E-46400 Cullera (Alacant) T: 961 721 440. E: info@santamartacamping.com
alanrogers.com/ES86220

Santa Marta is beautifully located on the slopes of a mountain and is shaded by many old Mediterranean umbrella pine trees. Originally a municipal site, it was recently purchased by a group of four campsites and is being fully renovated and modernised. There are 250 small, terraced pitches, 235 for touring with 16A electricity. Access can be difficult due to the many trees. An olive grove has been bought to make 18 motorcaravan pitches. Marta was a local saint and the campsite is named after her shrine which is located high above on the mountain. This shrine is accessible for good hikers by a trail starting at the ancient village bull ring at the entrance to the campsite.

Facilities

Four toilet blocks, which are very well equipped (NB only one hook and no shelf or soap dish in shower cubicles). Separate facilities for women and men. Facilities for disabled campers. Baby room. Small shop. Bar/snack bar with terrace (all season). Swimming and paddling pools (23/6-16/9). Multisports field. No barbecues.

Open: All year excl. 16 December - 14 January.

Directions

From A7/N332 (Valencia-Alicante) take exit for Cullera. Follow signs into Cullera and then signs to Faro or Far, through the centre of town. From the centre follow signs to site. GPS: 39.17694, -0.24333

Charges guide

Per unit incl. 2 persons and electricity (4A)	€ 30.00
extra person	€ 3.50 - € 7.00

El Campello

Camping Costa Blanca

Calle Convento 143, N332 km. 120,5, E-03560 El Campello (Alacant) T: 965 630 670.
E: info@campingcostablanca.com **alanrogers.com/ES86900**

This small site has 80 pitches with 60 for touring units, some with views of the distant hills. Bungalows line three sides of the white-walled, rectangular site with a railway (not too busy) on the final side. Reception is efficient with keen staff members speaking several languages. The flat pitches are on gravel and all have 6A electricity. Some are small (40, 60 or 80 sq.m) and will be a challenge for large units. There is natural shade from trees and some artificial shade. A pleasant pool is the centre-piece with a bright poolside bar and a restaurant with a patio.

Facilities

Four clean refurbished sanitary units offer a variety of facilities including cabins with toilet and basin, toilet and bidet, washbasins with hot water, others with cold. Two baby baths in cabins. Facilities for disabled campers. Washing machines and dryer. Motorcaravan services at entrance (€ 4 per token). Restaurant/bar (all year). Shop (1/7-1/9). Swimming pool. Basic play area (supervision required). Limited live entertainment in season. WiFi. Communal barbecue. Off site: Town facilities. Fishing, sailing, boat launching and watersports 500 m. ATM 1 km. Riding and golf 8 km.

Open: All year.

Directions

From the N332 take exit for El Campello Costa. Go through traffic lights onto the roundabout and take the first exit right. Site is visible from the roundabout although the name is behind the sliding gate!
GPS: 38.43611, -0.38806

Charges guide

Per unit incl. 2 persons and electricity	€ 23.93 - € 44.40
extra person	€ 4.11 - € 5.95
child (1-10 yrs)	€ 3.29 - € 4.75

Gandia

Camping L'Alqueria

Avenida del Grau 142, E-46730 Grau de Gandia (Valencia) T: 962 840 470. E: lalqueria@lalqueria.com
alanrogers.com/ES86200

Camping L'Alqueria is situated on the main Gandia to Grau road and, although in an urban location, it is 1 km. from the beaches of Gandia. The 112 touring pitches are of a good size and on level ground, all with 10A electricity (Europlug) and easy access to one of many water points. Some are separated by dividing hedges and there is plenty of shade from mature trees. There is a football pitch and a large swimming pool (caps required) with a sliding cover and a small paddling pool, adjacent but outside. Below the pools are a steam room, hydro-bath, sauna and jacuzzi. When we visited, a temporary structure provided a small bar and snack bar whilst a new building at the entrance was being completed. A wooden cabin houses a small shop that is reasonably well stocked.

Facilities

Four toilet blocks, three with British style toilets, placed evenly around the site. Mostly combined shower and washbasin cubicles. Laundry facilities (key from reception). Motorcaravan service point. Shop (all year) and snack bar (19/3-15/10). Swimming pool (covered for 1/10-31/5) and outdoor paddling pool (1/6-30/9). Steam room and spa facilities. Fridge hire. WiFi over site (charged).
Off site: Shops, restaurant etc. within 1 km. Beach, fishing, golf, bicycle hire and riding all within 2 km.

Open: All year.

Directions

From A7 (Valencia-Alicante) take exit 60 and follow signs to Gandia on the N332. Through the town follow signs for Grau and Platja de Gandia. Site is northwest of Gandia. GPS: 38.98627, -0.16365

Charges guide

Per unit incl. 2 persons and electricity	€ 23.70 - € 41.85
extra person	€ 3.90 - € 5.75
child (3-10 yrs)	€ 3.20 - € 4.60

Guardamar del Segura

Marjal Guardamar Camping & Bungalows Resort

Ctra N332 km. 73,4, E-03140 Guardamar del Segura (Alacant) T: 966 727 070. E: camping@marjal.com

alanrogers.com/ES87430

Marjal is located beside the estuary of the Segura river, alongside the pine and eucalyptus forests of the Dunas de Guardamar Natural Park. A fine sandy beach can be reached through the forest (800 m). This is a very smart site with a huge tropical lake-style pool with bar and a superb sports complex. There are 212 pitches on this award-winning site, 162 for touring with water, electricity (16A), drainage and satellite TV points. The ground is covered with crushed marble, making the pitches clean and pleasant. There is some shade and the site has an open feel with lots of room for manoeuvring. Reception is housed within a delicately coloured building complete with a towering Mirador, topped by a weather vane depicting the 'garza real' (heron) bird which frequents the local area and forms part of the site logo. The large restaurant overlooks the pools and the river that leads to the sea in the near distance.

Facilities

Three excellent heated toilet blocks have free hot water, elegant separators between sinks, spacious showers and some cabins. Each block has high quality facilities for babies and disabled campers, laundry and dishwashing rooms. Motorcaravan service point. Car wash. Well stocked supermarket. Restaurants. Bar. Large outdoor pool complex (15/4-15/9). Heated indoor pool (all year). Jacuzzi. Sauna. Beauty salon. Well equipped gym. Aerobics. Physiotherapy. All activities discounted for campers. Play room. Minigolf. Floodlit tennis and soccer pitch. Bicycle hire. Car rental. Games room. TV room. Full entertainment programme. Hairdresser. ATM. Free WiFi.

Open: All year.

Directions

On N332 40 km. south of Alicante, site is on the sea side between 73 and 74 km. markers.
GPS: 38.10933, -0.65467

Charges guide

Per unit incl. 2 persons and electricity	€ 38.00 - € 65.00
extra person	€ 7.00 - € 9.00
child (4-12 yrs)	€ 5.00 - € 6.00
dog	€ 2.20 - € 3.20

Low season discounts.

Jávea

Camping Jávea

Ctra Cami de la Fontana 10, Apdo 83, E-03730 Jávea (Alacant) T: 965 791 070. E: info@camping-javea.com

alanrogers.com/ES87540

The final approach to this site emerges from the bustle of the town and is decorated with palms, orange and pine trees, the latter playing host to a colony of parakeets. English is spoken at reception. The neat, boxed hedges and palms within the site, and its backdrop of hills dotted with villas form an attractive setting. Three hectares provide space for 214 numbered pitches with 183 for touring units. Flat, level and rectangular in shape, the pitches vary in size (60-80 sq.m). All pitches have a granite chip surface and 8A electricity. The restaurant provides great food, way above normal campsite standards.

Facilities

Two very clean, fully equipped, sanitary blocks include two children's toilets plus a baby bath. Separate facilities for disabled campers. Two washing machines. Fridge hire. Extensive bar and restaurant with terraces where in high season you purchase bread and milk. Large swimming pool with lifeguard and sunbathing lawns. Play area. Boules. Electronic barriers (deposit for card). Caravan storage. Post. Safes. Five-a-side football. Basketball. Tennis. WiFi. Car rental. Off site: Sandy beach 1.5 km.

Open: All year.

Directions

Exit N332 for Jávea on A134, continue in direction of Port (road number changes to CV734). In town the site is well marked with large orange indicators high on posts. Watch carefully for a sudden slip road sign!
GPS: 38.78333, 0.16983

Charges guide

Per unit incl. 2 persons and electricity	€ 28.81 - € 31.14
extra person	€ 4.88 - € 6.50

FREE Alan Rogers Travel Card

Extra benefits and savings - see page 10

La Marina

Camping Internacional La Marina

Ctra N332 km. 76, E-03194 La Marina (Alacant) T: 965 419 200. E: info@campinglamarina.com

alanrogers.com/ES87420

Very efficiently run by a friendly Belgian family, La Marina has 381 pitches of three different types and sizes ranging from 50 sq.m. to 150 sq.m. with electricity (10/16A), TV, water and drainage. Artificial shade is provided and the pitches are extremely well maintained on level, well drained ground with a special area allocated for tents in a small orchard. The huge lagoon swimming pool complex is absolutely fabulous and has something for everyone (with lifeguards). William Le Metayer, the owner, is passionate about La Marina and it shows in his search for perfection. A magnificent new, modern building which uses the latest architectural technology, houses many superb extra amenities. Facilities include a relaxed business centre with Internet access, a tapas bar decorated with amazing ceramics (handmade by the owner's mother) and a quality restaurant with a water fountain feature and great views of the lagoon. There is also a conference centre and an extensive computerised library. The whole of the lower ground floor is dedicated to children with a Marina Park play area and a 'cyber zone' for teenagers. With a further bar and a new soundproofed disco (Anima2), the building is of an exceptional, eco-friendly standard. A superb fitness centre with attentive personal trainers and a covered, heated pool (14x7 m) are incorporated. A pedestrian gate at the rear of the site gives access to the long sandy beach through the coastal pine forest that is a feature of the area. We recommend this site very highly whatever type of holidaying camper you may be. A member of Leading Campings group.

Facilities

The elegant sanitary blocks offer the very best of modern facilities. Heated in winter, they include private cabins and facilities for disabled visitors and babies. Laundry facilities. Motorcaravan services. Gas. Supermarket. Bars. Restaurant and café (all year). Ice cream kiosk. Swimming pools (1/4-15/10). Indoor pool. Fitness centre. Sauna. Solarium. Jacuzzi. Play rooms. Extensive activity and entertainment programme including barbecues and swimming nights. Sports area. Tennis. Huge playgrounds. Hairdresser. Bicycle hire. Road train to beach. Exclusive area for dogs. Internet café (charged) and free WiFi.

Open: All year.

Directions

Site is 2 km. west of La Marina. Leave N332 Guardamara de Segura - Santa Pola road at 75 km. marker (travelling north), or 78 km. (travelling south). Site is well signed. GPS: 38.129649, -0.649575

Charges guide

Per unit incl. 2 persons and electricity	€ 33.28 - € 62.61
extra person	€ 5.35 - € 8.00
child (1-10 yrs)	€ 3.75 - € 5.50
dog	free - € 2.14

Good discounts for longer stays in low season.

Moncofa

Camping Monmar

Ctra Serratelles s/n, E-12593 Moncofa (Castelló) T: 964 588 592. E: campingmonmar@terra.es

alanrogers.com/ES85900

This very neat, purpose built site is in the small town of Moncofa, just 200 metres from the sea and right beside a water park with pools and slides. There are 170 gravel based pitches arranged in rows off tarmac access roads. The 90 touring pitches all have 6A electricity, water and drainage. Hedges have been planted to separate the pitches but these are still small so there is little shade (canopies can be rented in high season). The site's facilities and amenities are all very modern but small stone reminders of the area's Roman and Arab history are used to decorate corners of the site.

Facilities

Three modern toilet blocks are well placed and provide good, clean facilities. Free hot showers and open style washbasins. Facilities and good access for disabled visitors (key). Laundry facilities. Shop (1/7-31/8). Bar and restaurant (weekends and high season). Swimming pool. Good play area. Boules. Library. Some entertainment in high season. WiFi over site (charged). Animals are not accepted. Off site: Beach 200 m. Water complex.

Open: All year.

Directions

Turn off N340 Castellon-Valencia road on CV2250 signed Moncofa. Follow sign for tourist information office in town and then signs for site. Pass supermarket and turn left to site in 600 m. GPS: 39.80884, -0.1281

Charges guide

Per unit incl. 2 persons and electricity	€ 27.00
extra person	€ 9.00

Moraira

Camping Caravanning Moraira

Camino Paellero 50, E-03724 Moraira-Teulada (Alacant) T: 965 745 249.
E: campingmoraira@campingmoraira.com **alanrogers.com/ES87550**

This neat hillside site with some views over the town and marina is quietly situated in an urban area amongst old pine trees and just 400 metres from a sheltered bay. A striking, stilted and glass-fronted reception building gives great views. Ask about the innovative building features and prepare for pleasant design surprises. Terracing provides shaded pitches of varying sizes, some small (access to some of the upper pitches may be difficult for larger units). There are 17 pitches with full services (6/10A electricity). An attractive irregularly shaped pool with a paved terrace is below the bar/restaurant and terrace.

Facilities

The high quality toilet blocks, with polished granite floors and marble fittings are built to a unique and ultra-modern design. Facilities for disabled campers. Washing machines and dryers. Motorcaravan services. Bar/restaurant and shop (1/6-30/9). Bread and basics at the bar. Small swimming pool (all year). Sub-aqua with instruction. Tennis. Limited children's entertainment in high season. Torches may be required. WiFi. Off site: Shops, bars and restaurants within walking distance. Beach 400 m.

Open: All year.

Directions

Best approach is from Teulada. From A7 exit 63 take N332 and in 3.5 km. turn right (Teulada, Moraira). In Teulada fork right to Moraira. At junction at town entrance turn right signed Calpe and in 1 km. turn right to site on bend immediately after Res. Don Julio. GPS: 38.692, 0.14

Charges guide

Per unit incl. 2 persons and electricity	€ 42.35
extra person	€ 8.80

Navajas

Camping Altomira

Ctra CV-213 Navajas km. 1, E-12470 Navajas (Castelló) T: 964 713 211. E: reservas@campingaltomira.com

alanrogers.com/ES85850

Camping Altomira is a terraced site in a rural, hillside setting on the edge of a quiet village. It offers excellent views across the valleys and hills, a friendly welcome and has both a Spanish and international clientèle. There are 40 touring pitches on the higher levels of the site with some shade (artificial awnings are allowed). Access roads to the gravel pitches are steep with some tight turns. All pitches have shared electricity (6A) and water points, while some have individual sinks, water and waste water disposal. There are three toilet blocks, and two designated children's facilities. In recent years, great efforts have been made to make the site accessible for campers with mobility problems.

Facilities

Three heated toilet blocks have showers in cubicles and open style washbasins. Two laundry areas. Shop. Bar/restaurant with terrace next to play area. Outdoor swimming pool (June-Sept). TV room. Bicycle hire. Kayak hire. Paintball. Zipwire. Communal barbecue areas. New BTT centre. WiFi over site (charged). Off site: Shops, bars and restaurants in the village 500 m. Station 500 m. Small Friday market. Lake beach, fishing and riding 2 km.

Open: All year.

Directions

Site is just off the free autovia (Santander-Valencia). From A23 (Segunto-Teruel) take exit 33 (Navajes), follow CV214 to roundabout, then CV213 to site, 1 km. north of Navajas. GPS: 39.87471, -0.51051

Charges guide

Per unit incl. 2 persons and electricity	€ 20.70 - € 25.90
extra person	€ 4.76 - € 5.95

Camping Cheques accepted.

Oliva

Camping Olé

Partida Aigua Morta s/n, E-46780 Oliva (Valencia) T: 962 857 517. E: campingole@hotmail.com

alanrogers.com/ES86130

Olé is a large, flat, seaside holiday site south of Valencia and close to the modern resort of Oliva. Its entrance is only 250 m. from the pleasant sandy beach. For those who do not want to share the busy beach, a large swimming pool is opened in July and August. There are 308 small pitches of compressed gravel and with 6/10A electricity. Many are separated by hedges with pruned trees giving good shade to those away from the beach. A bar and a restaurant stand on the dunes overlooking the sea, together with a few unmarked pitches that are ideal for larger units. There are small groups of chalets and a few apartments to rent, all within their own areas. The site has a large terrace, part of which is given over to entertainment in high season. The town of Oliva is popular with British and Dutch holidaymakers and has just about all that a smaller Spanish town can offer.

Facilities

Three clean, well maintained sanitary blocks provide very reasonable facilities. The central one serves most of the touring pitches. Laundry facilities. Fridge rental. Well stocked supermarket (1/3-30/9). Various vending machines. Bar with TV and restaurant with daily menu, drinks and snacks (1/3-15/12). Takeaway. Swimming pool (1/7-1/9). Playground. Entertainment (July/Aug). Fishing off the beach. Off site: Golf 800 m. Bicycle hire. Oliva with shops, restaurants and bars.

Open: All year.

Directions

From the north on AP7 (Alicante-Valencia) take exit 61 on N332 through Oliva. From the south take exit 62 and turn left for Oliva. Exit at km. 213 (south) or 210 (north) signed 'urbanisation'. At roundabout take third exit following signs to site.
GPS: 38.8943, -0.0536

Charges guide

Per unit incl. 2 persons and electricity	€ 29.93 - € 42.85
extra person	€ 6.40
child (3-10 yrs)	€ 4.83
dog	€ 3.09

Oliva

Camping Azul

No 1. Apartado 96, E-46780 Oliva (Valencia) T: 962 854 106. E: campingazul@ctv.es

alanrogers.com/ES86115

Found behind the beach and sand dunes, Camping Azul can best be described as rustic and relaxed, ideal for those who prefer a quiet, unregimented site. A barrier at the entrance leads to reception on the left where limited English is spoken. From there, firm sandy roads lead to sandy pitches with many low trees which have been sympathetically pruned to afford partial or full shade. Varying in size, some of the pitches are very compact, and pitching could be difficult. The little trees in and around the bar/café area, with its flower pots and trailing plants hanging from the branches, create a very pleasant Mediterranean atmosphere where food and drinks are served.

Facilities

Modern, heated sanitary block. Facilities for disabled campers. Launderette. Motorcaravan services. Gas supplied. Small shop selling basics. Bar and snack bar. Play area. Bicycle and car hire. Entertainment in high season. Direct beach access. Chalets for rent. WiFi. Off site: Good restaurant providing menu of the day within 500 m. Golf and tennis 1 km. Oliva 3 km. with bars, restaurants, supermarkets and banks.

Open: 1 March - 1 November.

Directions

From north leave AP7 motorway at exit 61 (Oliva) and follow N332 through Oliva. From south take exit 62 onto N332 and turn left for Oliva. At km. 213 (south) or km. 210.8 (north) turn for 'urbanisation' and follow signs to site. GPS: 38.906944, -0.068611

Charges guide

Per unit incl. 2 persons and electricity	€ 26.80 - € 28.80
extra person	€ 4.75

Oliva

Kiko Park Oliva

Ctra Assagador de Carro 2, E-46780 Oliva (Valencia) T: 962 850 905. E: kikopark@kikopark.com

alanrogers.com/ES86150

Kiko Park is a smart site nestling behind protective sand dunes alongside a Blue Flag beach. There are sets of attractively tiled steps over the dunes or a long boardwalk near the beach bar (good for prams and wheelchairs) to take you to the fine white sandy beach and the sea. From the central reception point (where good English is spoken), flat, fine gravel pitches and access roads are divided to the left and right. Backing onto one another, the 180 large pitches all have electricity and the aim is to progressively upgrade all these with full services. There are plenty of flowers, hedging and trees adding shade, privacy and colour. A pleasant, outdoor swimming pool with adjacent children's pool has a paved area with a bar in summer. The restaurant (lunchtimes only out of season) overlooks the marina, beautiful beach and sea. A wide variety of entertainment is provided all year and Spanish lessons are taught along with dance classes and aerobics during the winter. The site is run by the second generation of a family involved in camping for 30 years and their experience shows.

Facilities

Four mature, heated sanitary blocks include facilities for babies and disabled visitors (site is flat and convenient). Laundry facilities. Motorcaravan services. Gas supplies. Supermarket (closed Sundays). Restaurant. Bar with TV (high season). Beach-side bar and restaurant. Swimming pools. Spa with treatments and beauty programmes (charged). Watersports facilities. Diving school in high season (from mid June). Playground. Entertainment for children (from mid June). WiFi (charged). Bicycle hire.

Open: All year.

Directions

From the AP7 take exit 61. From the toll turn right at T-junction and continue to lights. Turn left, then at roundabout turn right. At next roundabout (fountains) take third exit signed Platja and Alicante. Follow one way system to next roundabout then site signs.
GPS: 38.9316, -0.0968

Charges guide

Per unit incl. 2 persons	€ 17.90 - € 40.00
extra person	€ 3.75 - € 7.50
child (under 10 yrs)	€ 3.10 - € 6.80

Oliva

Euro Camping

Partida Rabdells s/n, CN332 km. 210, E-46780 Oliva (Valencia) T: 962 854 098. E: info@eurocamping-es.com

alanrogers.com/ES86120

Approached through a new urbanisation, Euro Camping is a well maintained, British owned site. Spacious and flat, it is set amidst many high trees, mainly eucalyptus, with its own access to a fine sandy beach. From reception, with its helpful English-speaking staff and interesting aviary opposite, wide tarmac or paved roads lead to 315 large, gravel-based pitches which are either marked or hedged (most for touring units). The main site road leads down to a beachside restaurant with superb views and a supermarket.

Facilities

One newly built and two mature sanitary blocks are well maintained. British type WCs, preset hot water in the showers. Toilet facilities for disabled campers. Facilities for babies. Washing machines and dryer. Motorcaravan services. Well stocked supermarket and roast chicken takeaway. Restaurant/bar. Fridge hire. Entertainment in high season. Gas. Bicycle hire. Communal barbecue. WiFi over site (charged). Off site: Golf and riding 1.5 km. Oliva 3 km. with restaurants, cafés and supermarkets. Large street market on Fridays. Ideal area for cycling.

Open: All year.

Directions

From the north and AP7 exit 61 take N332 and drive through Oliva. From the south exit 62 and left for Oliva. Exit at km. 213 (south) or 210 (north) signed 'urbanisation'. At roundabout take fourth exit. Turn right before narrow bridge. Continue and bear right on Carrer de Xeraco. Site is on the left.
GPS: 38.905, -0.066

Charges guide

Per unit incl. 2 persons and electricity	€ 24.02 - € 49.94

Camping Cheques accepted.

FREE Alan Rogers Travel Card

Extra benefits and savings - see page 10

Oropesa del Mar

Camping Didota

Avenida de la Didota s/n, E-12594 Oropesa del Mar (Castelló) T: 964 319 551. E: info@campingdidota.es

alanrogers.com/ES85790

Didota is a family campsite located on the Costa Azahar, slightly to the north of Oropesa del Mar. It is in a holiday area of apartments and campsites, and development of the area continues. The site is next to a sandy and pebbly beach which slopes to the sea. It is small and basic but friendly, with 144 well shaded pitches (90-100 sq.m) with electricity (10/16A), and bungalows to rent. There is an attractive swimming pool with two terraces alongside a restaurant and bar, plus a small, heated, indoor pool. Bicycle and kayak hire are available and there is an outdoor fitness suite, a computer room with satellite TV and a cinema room.

Facilities

One modern, heated toilet block has controllable showers in cubicles and open style washbasins. Facilities for disabled visitors. Washing machine and dryer. Shop for basics. Bar/restaurant and terraces. Takeaway. Heated, indoor swimming pool and outdoor pool. Jacuzzi.
Play areas. Fitness suite. Computer room. Activity and entertainment programmes for adults and children. Bicycle hire. Canoe hire. Tourist information. Bungalows for rent. Off site: Beach (lifeguard in season). Supermarket 500 m.

Open: All year.

Directions

Leave AP7 motorway at Oropesa North exit and follow northbound N340. Leave at the Marina d'Or exit and pass over the railway line. The site is then clearly signed to the right. GPS: 40.12107, 0.15827

Charges guide

Per unit incl. 2 persons and electricity	€ 17.00 - € 42.00

Ribera de Cabanes

Camping Torre la Sal 2

Camí l'Atall, E-12595 Ribera de Cabanes (Castelló) T: 964 319 744. E: camping@torrelasal2.com

alanrogers.com/ES85700

Torre la Sal 2 is a very large site divided into two by a quiet road, with a reception on each side with friendly, helpful staff. There are three pool complexes (one can be covered in cooler weather and is heated) all of which are on the west side, whilst the beach (of shingle and sand) is on the east. Both sides have a restaurant – the one on the beach side has two air-conditioned wooden buildings and a terrace. The 530 flat pitches (all with 10A electricity) vary in size; some have their own sinks, and most have shade, a few have a partial view of the sea. There are 85 bungalows around the two areas. This is a high quality site offering a great choice to campers.

Facilities

Toilet facilities are of a good standard in both sections, with British style WCs, hot water to some sinks, and facilities for disabled campers. Baby rooms. Washing machines. Motorcaravan services. Shop, bars, restaurants and takeaway (all year). Swimming pools – one heated and covered (a large new pool complex should be ready for the season). Jacuzzi and sauna (winter). Play park. Large disco. Sports centre. Tennis. Squash. Outdoor gym. Games room. Bullring. Hairdresser. Entertainment. WiFi.

Open: All year.

Directions

From A7/E15 take exit 45 for Oropesa Del Mar on N340. Follow road to Oropesa and then the many clear signs to the site. GPS: 40.127, 0.158

Charges guide

Per unit incl. 2 persons and electricity	€ 22.08 - € 50.77
extra person	€ 3.96 - € 7.92
child (2-9 yrs)	€ 3.66 - € 7.32

San Miguel de Salinas

Camping Florantilles

Ctra Torrevieja-San Miguel de Salinas, E-03193 San Miguel de Salinas (Alacant) T: 965 720 456.
E: camping@campingflorantilles.com **alanrogers.com/ES87410**

Florantilles is an excellent site situated 6 km. west of Torrevieja, 60 km. south of Alicante and occupying an elevated position overlooking orange groves and the famous salt lake nature reserve, Salinas de la Mata. The site is terraced and well lit, with good sized gravel pitches and tarmac roads. All 262 pitches are separated by hedges and have 10A electricity (metered for long stays), water and waste water drainage. A third of the pitches are for touring, while the others are occupied by privately owned mobile homes or are seasonal pitches, mainly used by retired British owners who spend the winter months here.

Facilities

Two well kept toilet blocks (one heated) with free hot water, plus another smaller block on each level. Good facilities for disabled visitors. Two laundry rooms. Well stocked shop (Mon-Sat), with freshly baked bread. Two unheated swimming pools (15/6-30/9). Bar/café. TV room. Pétanque. Aerobics. Social evenings. WiFi (charged).

Open: All year.

Directions

From north, leave AP7 at exit 758. Take first exit for CV95, then as above. New arrivals park to left of entrance. GPS: 37.97505, -0.75131

Charges guide

Per unit incl. 2 persons and electricity	€ 19.20 - € 38.20
extra person	€ 3.75 - € 8.00

Villajoyosa

Camping Playa Paraiso

Ctra Valencia-Alicante km. 136, Partida Paraiso, 66, E-03570 Villajoyosa (Alacant) T: 966 851 838.

E: jacinto@playaparaiso.com **alanrogers.com/ES86880**

This site has been reopened by new owners who lost one of their other sites to housing developers. Major works are underway to provide modern facilities. When we visited, work was being done on the upper levels of the site to provide serviced pitches and a fully refurbished toilet block. On the lower level, the main site road is of tarmac and the gravel pitches are on shallow terraces as the site slopes gently down to the sea, which provides one of the boundaries. The views are pleasant and trees provide a degree of shade for some pitches, with overhead sunshades on others. Electricity is available (16A).

Facilities

Two toilet blocks are old but well maintained and very clean with spacious showers. Facilities for disabled visitors. Separate wooden building with facilities for babies. Washing machines and dryer. Bar and restaurant with limited menu. Indoor games and TV. Swimming pool (Easter-Oct). Off site: Beach. Bus stop 100 m.

Open: 2 February - 31 December.

Directions

From the N332 take exit at km. 136 to Villajoyosa Playa and site is 100 m. on the right.
GPS: 38.50005, -0.24905

Charges guide

Per unit incl. 2 persons and electricity	€ 26.35 - € 38.55

Discounts of up to 50% in low season.

Villargordo del Cabriel

Kiko Park Rural

Ctra Embalse Contreras km. 3, E-46317 Villargordo del Cabriel (Valencia) T: 962 139 082.

E: info@kikoparkrural.com **alanrogers.com/ES86250**

Approaching Kiko Park Rural, you will see a small hilltop village set in a landscape of mountains, vines and a jewel-like lake. Kiko was a small village and farm, and the village now forms the campsite and accommodation. Amenities are contained within the architecturally authentic buildings, some old and some new. The 76 generous pitches (mainly hardstanding and with 6A electricity and water) have high hedges (as does the site) for privacy. Generous planting has been made, which already affords some privacy, and hundreds of trees planted in 2003 are now providing shade. The restaurant serves extremely good food in a pleasant, spacious setting overlooking the pools and their surrounding lawns.

Facilities

Three toilet blocks are well equipped (but have short timers for lighting and showers), including facilities for disabled campers. Motorcaravan services. Gas supplies. Pleasant bar. Excellent restaurant (1/6-10/9). Takeaway (Easter-Oct). Swimming and paddling pools. Very good playground. Bicycle hire. Entertainment in high season. Many adventure activities can be arranged, including white-water rafting, gorging, orienteering, trekking, bungee jumping and riding. Large families and groups catered for.

Open: All year.

Directions

From autopista A7/E15 on Valencia ring road (near the airport) take A3 (E901) to the west. Villargordo del Cabriel is 80 km. towards Motilla. Take village exit 255 and follow signs through village and over a hill – spot the village on a hill 2 km. away. That is the campsite! GPS: 39.552176, -1.47456

Charges guide

Per unit incl. 2 persons and electricity	€ 22.00 - € 32.30
extra person	€ 5.50 - € 6.80

Vinaros

Camping Vinaros

Ctra N340 km. 1054, E-12500 Vinaros (Castelló) T: 964 402 424. E: info@campingvinaros.com

alanrogers.com/ES85580

This pleasant, spacious, well laid out site has 258 numbered pitches of average size on flat ground. Mature trees provide shade and hedges separate the pitches, all of which have an individual sink. There are shared electrical connections and shared gas connections are scheduled. The site entrance is directly off the N340. There is some traffic noise. The site has an impressive, large social area comprising a bar, swimming pool, jacuzzi, restaurant, large terrace, performance area and small shop. This site is very popular as an all year stopover site and also has long stay British customers enjoying the good discounts in low season.

Facilities

Two clean, fully equipped toilet blocks have some washbasins in cabins and facilities for disabled campers. Laundry facilities. Motorcaravan services. Milk and bread delivered daily. Restaurant (limited opening in low season), and bar with TV. Swimming pool. Pétanque. Musical and other entertainment. Aviary and terrapin pool. Children's club (high season) and activities for adults. Off site: Rail station nearby. Vinaros with bars and restaurants 500 m.

Open: All year.

Directions

Take exit 43 (Ulldecona) from the A7 and head to Vinaros. At the junction with the N340, turn left and head towards Barcelona. Site is at 1054 km. marker directly off the N340, opposite a large garden centre. GPS: 40.4931, 0.4838

Charges guide

Per unit incl. 2 persons and electricity	€ 20.00
extra person	€ 6.00
child (3-10 yrs)	€ 3.00

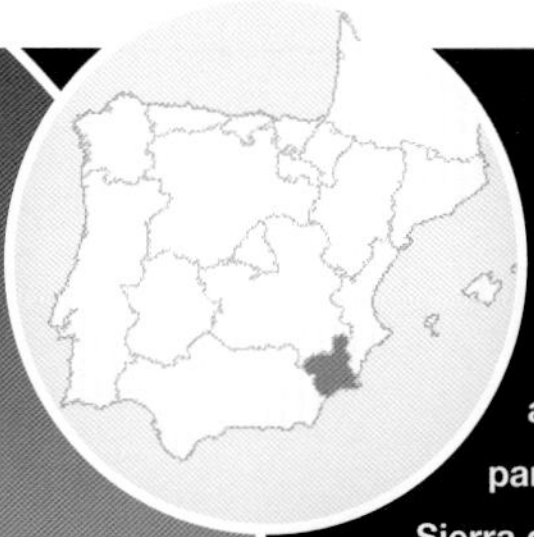

In the province of Murcia you'll find sandy beaches, dunes and unspoilt coves along the coast; inland hills and valleys plus the regional parks of Sierra de Carche, Sierra de la Pila, Sierra de Espuña, and Carrascoy and El Valle.

THE CAPITAL OF THE REGION IS THE CITY OF MURCIA

Murcia, the capital of the region, was founded in the ninth century by the Moors on the banks of the Río Segura. The square of Cardinal Belluga houses two of the town's architectural gems, the Episcopal Palace and the Cathedral, and there is a range of museums and exhibitions to visit. With narrow medieval streets, the characterful town of Cartagena has lots of bars and restaurants plus two nautical museums: the National Museum of Maritime Archaeology and the Naval Museum. Also on a nautical theme, the International Nautical Week is celebrated here in June. Along the coast there are numerous beaches offering a wide range of watersports: sailing, windsurfing, canoeing, water skiing and diving. The area between the coastal towns of Águilas and Mazarrón is a breeding ground for tortoises and eagles. Inland are the historic towns of Lorca and Caravaca de le Cruz. The former is known as the 'baroque city' with its examples of baroque architecture, seen in the parish churches, convents, and houses; the latter too is home to beautiful churches, including El Santuario de Vera Cruz.

Places of interest

Águilas: seaside town with good beaches.

Moratalla: pretty village, castle offering stunning views of the surrounding countryside and forests.

Puerto de Mazarrón: Enchanted City of Bolnuevo - a small area of eroded rocks, nature reserve and lagoon at La Rambla de Moreras.

San Pedro del Pinatar: seaside resort, La Pagan beach is renowned for its therapeutic mud, which reputedly relieves rheumatism and is good for the skin.

Santiago de la Ribera: upmarket resort with sailing club.

Cuisine of the region

Vegetables are important and found in nearly every dish. Fish is also popular, cooked in a salt crust or *a la espalda* (lightly fried and baked), and usually accompanied by rice. Fig bread is a speciality of the region.

Bizcochos borrachos: sponge soaked in wine and syrup.

Cabello de Ángel: pumpkin strands in syrup.

Caldero: made of rice, fish and the hot ñora pepper.

Caldo con pelotas: stew made of turkey with meatballs.

Chuletas de cordero al ajo cabañil: suckling lamb chops served with a dressing of garlic and vinegar.

Tocino de cielo: dessert made with egg yolks and syrup.

Yemas de Caravaca: cake made with egg yolks.

Baños de Fortuna

Camping la Fuente

Camino de la Bocamina, E-30626 Baños de Fortuna (Murcia) T: 968 685 125. E: info@campingfuente.com

alanrogers.com/ES87450

Located in an area known for its thermal waters since Roman and Moorish times, and with just 87 pitches and 14 bungalows, la Fuente is a gem. Unusually, winter is high season here. The main attraction is the huge hydrotherapy centre where the water is a constant 36 degrees all year. The pool can be covered in inclement weather. The site is in two sections, one where pitches are in standard rows and the other where they are in circles around blocks. The hard, flat pitches are on shingle (rock pegs advised), have 10A electricity (Europlug) and 55 have their own mini sanitary unit. Some artificial shade has been added to 22 pitches. There is a very good restaurant with terrace and separate bar.

Facilities

Some pitches have their own facilities, including a unit for disabled campers. Washing machines and dryers. Supermarket. High quality restaurant shared with accommodation guests. Snack bar by pool. Jacuzzi. Bicycle hire. Communal barbecues only. WiFi over site (charged). Off site: Spa town, massage therapies and hot pools 500 m. Fortuna with shops, bars and restaurants 3 km. Golf and riding 20 km.

Open: All year.

Directions

From A7/E15 Alicante-Murcia road take C3223 to Fortuna then follow signs to Baños de Fortuna. The site with its bright yellow walls can be easily seen from the road and is very well signed in the town. GPS: 38.20682, -1.10732

Charges guide

Per unit incl. 2 persons and electricity	€ 17.05
with individual sanitary facility	€ 19.25
extra person	€ 3.57
child (3-12 yrs)	€ 1.38
dog	€ 1.10

Pitch prices discounted after five days.

Cartagena

Camping Naturista El Portus

El Portus, E-30394 Cartagena (Murcia) T: 968 553 052. E: elportus@elportus.com

alanrogers.com/ES87520

Set in a secluded south-facing bay fringed by mountains, El Portus is a fairly large naturist site with magnificent views and direct access to a small sand and pebble beach. This part of Spain enjoys almost all-year-round sunshine. There are some 400 pitches, 300 for touring units, ranging from 60-100 sq.m, all but a few having electricity (6A). They are mostly on fairly level, if somewhat stony and barren ground. El Portus has a reasonable amount of shade from established trees and nearly every pitch has a view. Residential units are situated on the hillside above the site. This is a relaxed site with welcoming, English-speaking reception staff.

Facilities

Five acceptable toilet blocks, all unisex, are of varying styles and fully equipped with hot showers. Opened as required, they are clean and bright. Unit for disabled visitors, key from reception. Washing machines. Motorcaravan services. Well stocked shop. Bar with TV and library. Restaurants. The beach restaurant is closed in low season. Swimming pools (June-Sept). Wellness centre. Play area. Tennis. Pétanque. Yoga. Scuba-diving club (high season). Windsurfing. Spanish lessons. Small boat moorings. Entertainment programme all season. WiFi over site (charged). Off site: Fishing from beach. Golf 28 km. Riding 40 km.

Open: All year.

Directions

Site is on the coast, 10 km. west of Cartagena. Follow signs to Mazarron then take E22 to Canteras. Site is well signed for 4 km. If approaching through Cartagena, exit the town on N332 following signs for Canteras. Site signed on joining the N332. GPS: 37.585, -1.06717

Charges guide

Per unit incl. 2 persons and electricity	€ 22.00 - € 38.00
extra person	€ 5.00 - € 7.00
child (3-9 yrs)	€ 3.50 - € 5.50
dog	€ 3.25

Special discounts for longer stays and in low season.

Isla Plana

Camping Los Madriles

Ctra de la Azohia km. 4,5, E-30868 Isla Plana (Murcia) T: 968 152 151. E: camplosmadriles@forodigital.es

alanrogers.com/ES87480

An exceptional site with super facilities, Los Madriles is run by a hard working team, with constant improvements being made. Twenty kilometres west of Cartagena, the approach to the site and the surrounding area is fairly unremarkable, but the site is not. A fairly steep access road leads to the 313 flat, good to large sized terraced pitches, each having electricity, water and a waste point. Most have shade from large trees with a number benefiting from panoramic views of the sea or behind to the mountains. The site has huge rectangular and lagoon style pools with water sprays and jacuzzis.

Facilities

Four sanitary blocks and one small toilet block provide excellent facilities, including services in one block for disabled campers. Private wash cabins. Washing machines and dryers. Motorcaravan services. Car wash. Supermarket, restaurant/snack bar and bar (all open all season but hours are limited). Swimming pools with jacuzzi. Boules. Play areas. Pets are not accepted. WiFi over site (charged). Off site: Town close by. Beach and fishing (licence required, purchase in Puerto Mazarron) 800 m. Boat launching 3 km. Riding and bicycle hire 6 km. Golf 20 km.

Open: All year.

Directions

From E15/A7 exit 845 follow RM3 towards Cartagena, Fuente Alamo and Mazarron (do not turn into Mazarron). Continue towards Puerto Mazarron and take N332 (Cartagena). On reaching coast continue on N332 (Cartagena, Alicante). At roundabout turn right towards Isla Plana and La Azohia. Site is signed and on the left in 5 km. GPS: 37.57859, -1.19558

Charges guide

Per unit incl. 2 persons and electricity	€ 36.10

Large discounts for longer stays.

La Manga del Mar Menor

Caravaning La Manga

Autovia Cartagena-La Manga, Salida 11, E-30386 La Manga del Mar Menor (Murcia) T: 968 563 014.
E: lamanga@caravaning.es **alanrogers.com/ES87530**

This is a very large, well equipped, holiday-style site with its own beach and both indoor and outdoor pools. With a good number of typical Spanish long stay units, the length of the site is impressive (1 km) and a bicycle is very helpful for getting about. The 1,000 regularly laid out, gravel touring pitches (100 or 110 sq.m) are generally separated by hedges which also provide a degree of shade. Each has a 10A electricity supply, water and the possibility of satellite TV reception. This site's excellent facilities are ideally suited for holidays in the winter when the weather is pleasantly warm. Daytime temperatures in November usually exceed 20 degrees.

Facilities

Nine clean toilet blocks of standard design, well spaced around the site, include washbasins (all with hot water). Laundry. Gas supplies. Large well stocked supermarket. Restaurant. Bar. Snack bar. Swimming pool complex (April-Sept). Indoor pool, gymnasium (April-Oct), sauna, jacuzzi and massage service. New outdoor fitness course for adults. Open-air family cinema (July/Aug). Tennis. Pétanque. Minigolf. Play area. Watersports school. Internet café (also WiFi). Winter activities including Spanish classes. Pet washing area. Off site: Buses to Cartagena and Murcia from outside site. Golf, bicycle hire and riding 5 km.

Open: All year.

Directions

Use exit (Salida) 11 from MU312 dual carriageway towards Cabo de Palos, signed Playa Honda (site signed also). Cross road bridge and double back on yourself. Site entrance is clearly visible beside dual carriageway with many flags flying.
GPS: 37.62445, -0.74442

Charges guide

Per unit incl. 2 persons and electricity	€ 20.00 - € 35.00
extra person	€ 4.10 - € 5.10
child (4-11 yrs)	€ 3.60 - € 4.10
dog	€ 1.25

Camping Cheques accepted.

Moratalla

Camping la Puerta

Ctra de La Puerta s/n, E-30440 Moratalla (Murcia) T: 968 730 008. E: info@campinglapuerta.com
alanrogers.com/ES87440

Camping la Puerta is part of the Camping La Manga group. It is a typical Spanish weekend and holiday site and advance booking is essential for high season and most weekends. Set in the secluded hills above Moratalla, it provides a rural base from which to explore the surrounding countryside. It is a place where you can relax and forget about the hustle and bustle of city life whilst relaxing around the magnificent swimming pool complex. Most of the 159 touring pitches are rather small, so large units could have difficulty in manoeuvring due to randomly growing trees. Limited English is spoken on site.

Facilities

Three fully fitted sanitary blocks provide toilets, washbasins and shower cubicles. Facilities for disabled visitors. Washing machines. Shop. Bar and terrace. Cafeteria and restaurant serving a variety of local dishes. Play area. Tennis. Fishing. Barbecues are not permitted. Off site: Riding 5 km.

Open: All year.

Directions

From the A7 (Murcia-Lorca) exit at 651 km. onto the C415 towards Mula and Caravaca. Follow signs to Moratalla and then on to site which is well signed.
GPS: 38.20555, -1.91975

Charges guide

Per unit incl. 2 persons and electricity	€ 20.20 - € 23.20
extra person	€ 3.60 - € 4.60
child (3-11 yrs)	€ 2.90 - € 3.95
dog	€ 1.20

Famous for its sun, its beautiful traditions, its poets, original folklore, age-old history and magnificent heritage left behind by the Moors, Andalucía is one of the most attractive regions in Spain.

THIS COMPRISES EIGHT PROVINCES: ALMERIA, CADIZ, CORDOBA, GRANADA, HUELVA, MALAGA, JAEN AND SEVILLE

THE REGIONAL CAPITAL IS SEVILLE

With the River Guadalquivir running through it, the charming city of Seville is one of the most visited places in the region. The old city, with its great monuments; the Giralda tower, cathedral and the Alcázar, plus the narrow, winding streets of Santa Cruz, is particularly popular. Also on the Guadalquivir, Cordoba is located northeast of Seville. It too has a picturesque Jewish Quarter along with a rich Moorish heritage. Indeed, the Mezquita is one of the grandest mosques ever built by the Moors in Spain. Located further east on the foothills of the Sierra Nevada mountain range, Granada is home to the impressive Alhambra, a group of distinct buildings including a Royal Palace, splendid gardens, and the fortress of Alcazaba. The Sierra Nevada, Spain's highest range, offers good skiing and trekking. Further south, you'll find the fine beaches and tourist areas of the Costa Tropical and the Costa del Sol, including the developed resort of Malaga. There are more beaches on the west coast plus one of the oldest settlements in Spain, the bustling port of Cádiz.

Places of interest

Almeria: preserved Moorish heritage with greatest purity. Located on a beautiful bay.

Casa-Museo Pablo Ruiz Picasso: art museum including collection of originals by Pablo Picasso.

Jaen: medieval fortress, Renaissance cathedral, 11th-century Moorish baths, Santa Catalina castle.

Jerez de la Frontera: birthplace of sherry and Spanish brandy, site of renowned equestrian school.

Mijas: enchanting village, with narrow streets bordered by brilliantly white-washed houses.

Parque Natural de las Sierras de Cazorla y Segura: largest park in Spain with mountains, river gorges, forests and wildlife.

Ronda: beautiful town on the edge of an abrupt rocky precipice.

Cuisine of the region

Andalucía has more tapas bars than anywhere else in Spain. Seafood in abundance, fresh vegetables and fruit: oranges from Cordoba; persimmons, pomegranates, figs, strawberries from Alpujarra; avocados, mangos, guavas, papayas from the coast of Granada and Malaga. Locally produced wine and sherry.

Alboronía: vegetable stew.

Alfajors: almond and nut pastry.

Gazpacho ajoblanco: cold soup with garlic and almond.

Gazpacho salmorejo: much thicker and made with tomatoes only.

Pestiños: honey coated pastries.

Tocinillo de cielo: pudding made with egg yolks and syrup.

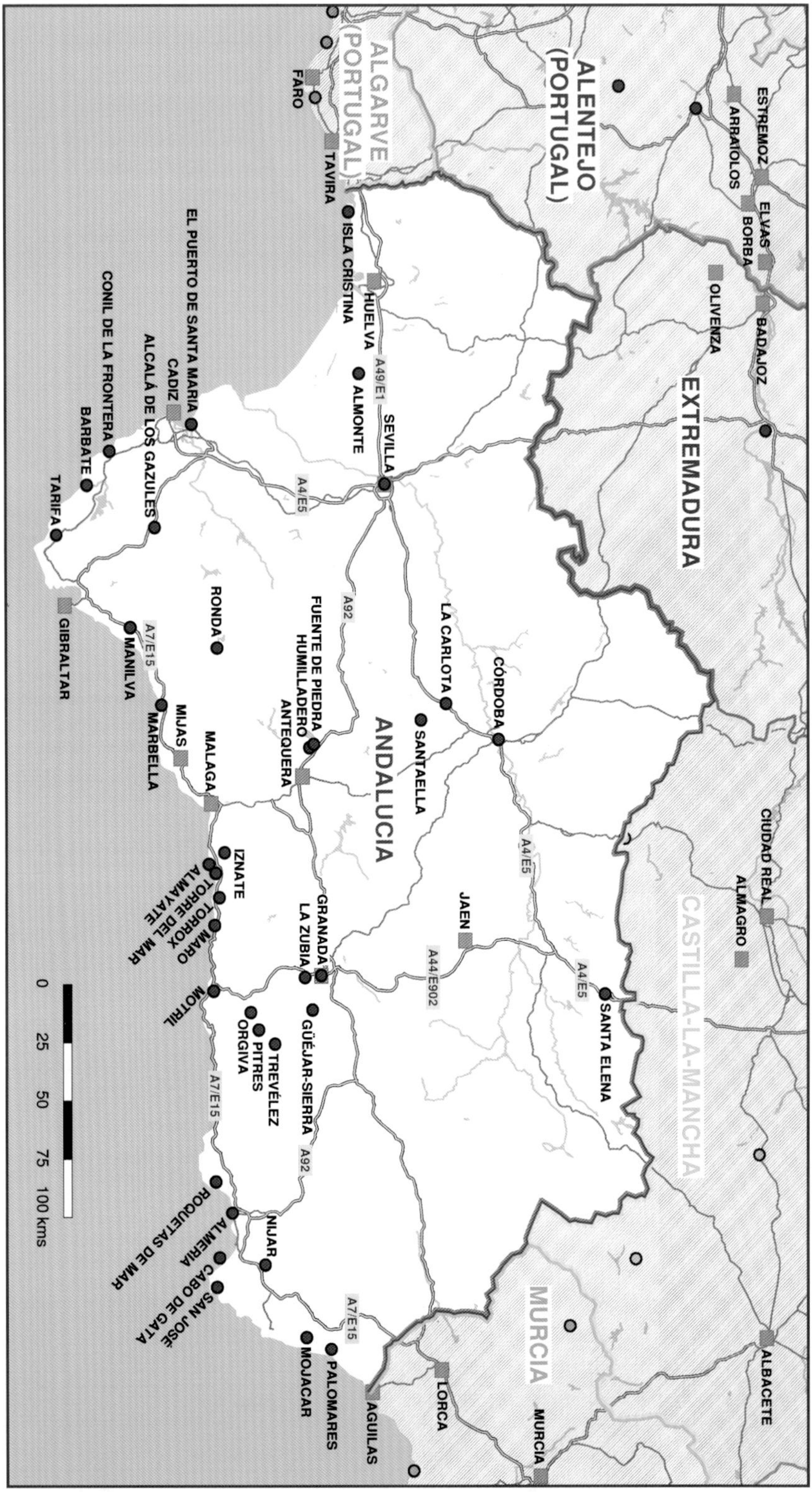
ALENTEJO (PORTUGAL)
ALGARVE (PORTUGAL)
EXTREMADURA
CASTILLA-LA-MANCHA
MURCIA
ANDALUCIA
ESTREMOZ
ARRAIOLOS
ELVAS
BORBA
OLIVENZA
BADAJOZ
FARO
TAVIRA
ISLA CRISTINA
HUELVA
ALMONTE
SEVILLA
EL PUERTO DE SANTA MARIA
CADIZ
ALCALÁ DE LOS GAZULES
CONIL DE LA FRONTERA
BARBATE
TARIFA
GIBRALTAR
MANILVA
RONDA
MARBELLA
MIJAS
MALAGA
FUENTE DE PIEDRA
HUMILLADERO
ANTEQUERA
LA CARLOTA
CÓRDOBA
SANTAELLA
IZNATE
TORRE DEL MAR
ALMAYATE
TORROX
MARO
GRANADA
LA ZUBIA
MOTRIL
JAEN
SANTA ELENA
CIUDAD REAL
ALMAGRO
GÜÉJAR-SIERRA
ORGIVA
PITRES
TREVÉLEZ
ROQUETAS DE MAR
ALMERIA
NIJAR
CABO DE GATA
SAN JOSE
MOJACAR
PALOMARES
AGUILAS
LORCA
MURCIA
ALBACETE
A49/E1
A4/E5
A92
A7/E15
A44/E902
0 25 50 75 100 kms

Alcalá de los Gazules

Camping Los Gazules

Ctra de Patrite km. 4, E-11180 Alcalá de los Gazules (Cádiz) T: 956 420 486.
E: campinglosgazules@hotmail.com **alanrogers.com/ES88900**

The site is set in the beautiful surroundings of the Los Alcornocales Nature Park and has 135 touring pitches with 10A electricity. Although basic, this would make an ideal site for a quiet, relaxing holiday in the countryside. The main building complex, consisting of the shop and restaurant has been newly painted outside and improved, and the well furnished restaurant/bar is a pleasant place to eat. The sanitary facilities have also been improved and there is an inviting swimming pool, open from the end of June.

Facilities

A circular sanitary block offers clean facilities, including those for disabled campers. Washing machine in supervised room. Bar/restaurant. Shop in bar sells basics. Swimming pool (June-Sept). Playground. WiFi over site (charged). Off site: Riding 2 km. Lake beach and fishing 10 km. Golf 20 km. Site is well placed for exploring the local area and for excursions to Cádiz.

Open: All year.

Directions

From A381 Algecieras-Jerez road take exit to Alcalá de los Gazules onto A375 (C440). Continue around village on A375 to Ubrique and proceed to 42 km. marker. Then turn onto the road to Patrite. The site is on the right at the 4 km. marker.
GPS: 36.463, -5.664

Charges guide

Per unit incl. 2 persons and electricity	€ 24.85
extra person	€ 4.90
child (0-10 yrs)	€ 3.90
dog	free

Almayate

Camping Naturista Almanat

Carril de la Torre Alta s/n, E-29749 Almayate (Málaga) T: 952 556 462. E: info@almanat.de
alanrogers.com/ES87830

With direct access to a one kilometre grey sand and shingle naturist beach, this established, all-year naturist site, set amongst agricultural land with a mountain backdrop, is proving a firm favourite with many British seeking winter sun. The facilities on site are to a very high standard. The entire two-hectare site is flat with a fine shingle surface. A large number of mature trees provide much needed shade in the summer months. The 194 touring pitches with 16A electricity, vary in size and shape with the majority demanding physical manoeuvring of a touring caravan.

Facilities

The large, unisex toilet block is fully equipped, regularly cleaned and all under cover. Good facilities for disabled campers near reception. Small shop. Bar/restaurant with terrace. Large unheated swimming pool. New indoor pool with jacuzzi (closed 15/6-15/9). Sauna and gym. Cinema (56 seats). Social room. Play area. Minigolf. Weather permitting, nudity is obligatory in the pool area and bar during the day. Off site: Fishing, riding nearby. Regular bus service 1 km. Torre del Mar is 2 km.

Open: All year.

Directions

From east or west on N340 autovia take exit 265 signed Cajiz Iznate and Costa 340a. Follow Costa direction and on reaching the coast turn left on N340a toward Torre del Mar. Site well signed in 5 km. on right. Turning left from the east (Torre del Mar) is not permitted. GPS: 36.72703, -4.11334

Charges guide

Per unit incl. 2 persons and electricity	€ 32.14 - € 37.00

Almería

Camping la Garrofa

Ctra N340 km. 435,4, direccion a Aguadulce via Litoral, E-04002 Almería (Almería) T: 950 235 770.
E: info@lagarrofa.com **alanrogers.com/ES87650**

One of the earliest sites in Spain (dating back to 1957), la Garrofa nestles in a cove with a virtually private beach accessed only by sea or through the campsite. It is rather dramatic with the tall mountain cliffs behind. Many of the rather small 100 flat and sloping sandy pitches are shaded, with some very close to the beach and sea. Eighty have 6/10A electricity. An old fortress looks down on the campsite – you can walk to it via a valley at the back of the site and across an old Roman bridge. Other walks directly from the site include a Roman road providing fine coastal views.

Facilities

Sanitary facilities are mature but clean. Facilities for disabled campers. Shop. Restaurant/snack bar. Play area. Fishing, boat launching and a beach. Torches useful. WiFi. Off site: Town close by. Walks. Sub-aqua diving. Bicycle hire 2 km. Golf 8 km. Excursions – tickets to attractions sold. Bus stop nearby to Almeria and Aguadulce.

Open: All year.

Directions

Site is west of Almeria. Take 438 exit from the N340 and follow the Almeria/Puerto signs. Then take the Aguadulce direction, from where site is signed.
GPS: 36.8257, -2.5161

Charges guide

Per unit incl. 2 persons and electricity	€ 27.50 - € 30.50
extra person	€ 6.00
child	€ 4.50

Almonte

Camping la Aldea

El Rocio, E-21750 Almonte (Huelva) T: 959 442 677. E: info@campinglaaldea.com

alanrogers.com/ES88730

This impressive site lies just on the edge of the Parque Nacional de Doñana, southwest of Sevilla on the outskirts of El Rocio. The town hosts a fiesta at the end of May with over one million people attending the local shrine. They travel for days in processions with cow-drawn or motorised vehicles to attend. If you want to stay this weekend book well in advance! The well planned, modern site is well set out and the 246 pitches have natural shade from trees or artificial shade and 10A electricity. There are 52 serviced pitches with water and sewerage.

Facilities

Two sanitary blocks provide excellent facilities including provision for disabled visitors. Motorcaravan service point. Swimming pool (May-Oct). Restaurant and bar in separate new complex. Shop. Internet connection. Playground. Off site: Bus stop 5 minutes walk. Beach 15 km. Huelva and Sevilla are about an hour's drive.

Open: All year.

Directions

From main E1/A49 Huelva-Sevilla road take exit 48 and drive south through Almonte to outskirts of El Rocio. Site is on left just past 25 km. marker. Go down to the roundabout and back up to be on the right side of the road to turn in. GPS: 37.1428, -6.491164

Charges guide

Per unit incl. 2 persons and electricity	€ 25.30 - € 27.00
extra person	€ 5.90 - € 6.50

Barbate

Camping Pinar San José

Ctra de Vejer, Los Caños de Meca, km. 10,2, E-11159 Barbate (Cádiz) T: 956 437 030.
E: info@campingpinarsanjose.com **alanrogers.com/ES88570**

Pinar San José first opened in 2008. The site is located in the La Breña Nature Park and has been developed to reflect the natural beauty that surrounds it. The nearest beaches on the Costa de la Luz are around 1 km. distant. On-site amenities are modern and well designed and include two swimming pools, tennis and a sports court. Pitches are grassy and all have electrical connections. There is good provision of water points, and many pitches also have drainage and Internet connections. Several brick built chalets are available for rent. Cabo de Trafalgar (Cape Trafalgar) is nearby and, of course, gave its name to the famous battle several kilometres to the west. The nearest village to the site is Zahora and the great cities of Cádiz and Jerez, as well as Gibraltar, are all accessible in less than an hour. La Breña Nature Park was formerly a massive sand dune and is now a large, forested area criss-crossed by cycle tracks and footpaths. Riding is also possible in the park.

Facilities

Shop. Bar. Restaurant. Two swimming pools. Tennis. Sports court. Play area. Games room. Chalets for rent. Dogs are not accepted in high season. Off site: Nearest beach 1 km. Cádiz 50 km. Fishing. Golf. Watersports.

Open: All year.

Directions

Heading south from Cádiz on the A48 motorway at the Vejer de la Frontera exit and head west on A2230 and then south on A2233 to Zahora. Site is well signed from here. GPS: 36.19998, -6.034627

Charges guide

Per unit incl. 2 persons and electricity	€ 11.10 - € 39.50
extra person	€ 2.50 - € 8.00
child (2-11 yrs)	€ 1.50 - € 5.00
dog	€ 0.50 - € 2.00

Cabo de Gata

Camping Cabo de Gata

Ctra Cabo de Gata s/n, E-04150 Cabo de Gata (Almería) T: 950 160 443. E: info@campingcabodegata.com
alanrogers.com/ES87630

Cabo de Gata is situated on the Gulf of Almería, a pleasant, all-year campsite offering facilities to a good standard. Popular with British visitors through the winter, and within the Cabo de Gata-Nijar Nature Park and set amongst fruit farms, it is only a 1 km. walk to a fine sandy beach. The 250 gravel pitches are level and of a reasonable size, with 6/16A electricity and limited shade from maturing trees or canopies. There are specific areas for very large units with very high canopies for shade and seven chalets for rent.

Facilities

Two, well maintained, clean toilet blocks provide all the necessary sanitary facilities, including British type WCs, washbasins and free hot showers. Facilities for disabled campers. Restaurant, bar and shop (all year). Swimming pool. Football. Pétanque. Tennis. Small playground. Library. Bicycle hire. English spoken. Entertainment programme. Internet access (charged). WiFi over site (charged). Off site: Bus from gate. Nearest beach and fishing 1 km. Golf 10 km. Riding 15 km.

Open: All year.

Directions

From A7-E15 take exit 460 or 467 and follow signs for Retamar via N344 and for Cabo de Gata. Site is on the right before village of Cabo de Gata. The final stretch of road is in a poor state of repair due to restrictions imposed within the natural park.
GPS: 36.808159, -2.232159

Charges guide

Per unit incl. 2 persons and electricity	€ 28.55 - € 32.20
extra person	€ 6.15
child (2-10 yrs)	€ 5.40

Conil de la Frontera

Camping Roche

N340 km. 19,5, Carril de Pilahito, E-11140 Conil de la Frontera (Cádiz) T: 956 442 216.
E: info@campingroche.com **alanrogers.com/ES88590**

Camping Roche is situated in a pine forest near white sandy beaches in the lovely region of Andalucía. It is a clean, tidy and welcoming site. English is spoken but try your Spanish, German or French as the staff are very helpful. A family site, it offers a variety of facilities including a sports area and swimming pools. The restaurant has good food and a pleasant outlook over the pool. Games are organised for children. A recently built extension provides further pitches, a new toilet block and a tennis court. There are 335 pitches which include 104 bungalows to rent. The touring pitches all have electricity (10A), and 76 also have water and waste water. There are pleasant paths in the area for mountain biking and this is an ideal base for visiting the cities of Seville and Cádiz.

Facilities

Three toilet blocks are traditional in style and provide simple, clean facilities. Washbasins have cold water only. Washing machine. Supermarket. Bar and restaurant. Swimming and paddling pools. Sports area. Tennis. Play area. Off site: Bus stops 3 times daily outside gates. Cádiz. Cape Trafalgar. Baelo Claudia archaeological site.

Open: All year.

Directions

From the N340 (Cádiz-Algeciras) turn off to site at km. 19.5 point. From Conil, take El Pradillo road. Keep following signs to site. From CA3208 road turn at km. 1 and site is 1.5 km. down this road on the right. GPS: 36.31089, -6.11268

Charges guide

Per unit incl. 2 persons and electricity	€ 18.81 - € 33.10
extra person	€ 3.71 - € 6.50
child	€ 3.14 - € 5.50
dog	€ 2.14 - € 3.75

Low season discounts.

FREE Alan Rogers Travel Card
Extra benefits and savings - see page 10

Conil de la Frontera

Camping la Rosaleda

Ctra del Pradillo km. 1,3, E-11140 Conil de la Frontera (Cádiz) T: 956 443 327.
E: info@campinglarosaleda.com **alanrogers.com/ES88580**

This excellent site in Andalucía was opened in 1999. Its owner has many years of experience and has listened to what campers want and has then delivered. Much money has been spent and will continue to be spent to make this an even better site. Great care has been taken with the planning to ensure campers have an enjoyable holiday, with many top class facilities and a first class service. There are 335 well kept pitches of three different sizes (70-120 sq.m), the smallest just for tents, the largest with electricity (10A) and water. This is an ideal place to experience the sunshine and culture of Spain.

Facilities

Four modern, fully equipped sanitary blocks have facilities for campers with disabilities and were spotless when seen. Motorcaravan services. Gas supplies. Excellent supermarket (all year). Bar/restaurant (all year). Swimming pool complex (large with stunning views). Large play area. Massage, sauna, gym, yoga room, hairdressing. Wooden bungalows with good facilities and own gardens. Free WiFi over site. No barbecues on pitches 15/6-15/10. Dogs are not accepted in high season.

Open: All year.

Directions

Follow signs to Conil from N340, then signs to site around several roundabouts. Site is 1 km. from centre on Ctra del Pradillo, on the side of this road with a car park in front and a large campsite sign high in the air. GPS: 36.29317, -6.09547

Charges guide

Per unit incl. 2 persons	€ 18.00 - € 37.50
child (3-10 yrs)	€ 2.80 - € 5.60
electricity (per kWh)	free - € 0.20

Conil de la Frontera

Camping Fuente del Gallo

Apdo 48, E-11149 Conil de la Frontera (Cádiz) T: 956 440 137. E: camping@campingfuentedelgallo.com
alanrogers.com/ES88600

Fuente del Gallo is well maintained with 184 pitches allocated to touring units. Each has 6A electricity, and a number of trees provide shade to some pitches. Although the actual pitch areas are generally a good size, the majority are long and narrow. This could, in some cases, prevent the erection of an awning and your neighbour may feel close. In low season it is generally accepted to make additional use of an adjoining pitch. The attractive pool, restaurant and bar complex with its large, shaded terrace, are very welcoming in the height of summer. Good beaches are just 300 m. away

Facilities

Two modernised and very clean sanitary blocks include excellent services for babies and disabled visitors and hot water at all facilities. Laundry room with two washing machines. Motorcaravan services. Gas supplies. Well stocked shop. Attractive bar and restaurant (breakfast served). Swimming pool (1/6-30/9 with lifeguard) with paddling pool. Play area. TV and games machines in bar area. Safety deposit boxes. Excursions. Torches useful. Picnic area with playground and games. WiFi (charged).

Open: 23 March - 30 September.

Directions

From the Cádiz-Algeciras road (N340) at km. 23.00, follow signs to Conil de la Frontera town centre, then shortly right to Fuente del Gallo and playas, following signs. GPS: 36.2961, -6.1102

Charges guide

Per unit incl. 2 persons and electricity	€ 24.50 - € 32.50
extra person	€ 5.50 - € 7.00
child (3-10 yrs)	€ 3.50 - € 5.50

Córdoba

Camping Municipal El Brillante

Avenida del Brillante 50, E-14012 Córdoba (Córdoba) T: 957 403 836. E: elbrillante@campings.net
alanrogers.com/ES90800

Córdoba is one of the hottest places in Europe and the superb pool here is more than welcome. If you really want to stay in the city, then this large site is a good choice. It has 115 neat pitches of gravel and sand, the upper pitches covered by artificial and natural shade but the lower, newer area has little. The site becomes very crowded in high season. The entrance is narrow and may be congested so care must be exercised – there is a lay-by just outside and it is easier to walk in initially. All pitches have electricity (6/10A) plus the newer area has 32 fully serviced pitches and an area for a few large motorcaravans.

Facilities

The toilet blocks include facilities for babies and disabled visitors. Washing machine. Motorcaravan services. Gas supplies. Shop (all year). Bar (1/7-15/9). Swimming pool (1/7-Sept/Oct). Play area. Off site: Bus service to city centre from outside site. Commercial centre 300 m. (left out of site, right at traffic lights). Bicycle hire 2 km. Riding 5 km. Golf 10 km. Fishing 15 km.

Open: All year.

Directions

From Madrid (NIV/E25), take exit at km. 403 and follow signs for Mezquita/Cathedral into city centre. Pass it (on right) and turn right on main avenue. Fork right where road splits, and follow signs for site. GPS: 37.899975, -4.787319

Charges guide

Per unit incl. 2 persons and electricity	€ 26.00 - € 32.00

No credit cards.

El Puerto de Santa Maria

Camping Playa Las Dunas

Paseo Maritimo, Playa de la Puntilla s/n, E-11500 El Puerto de Santa Maria (Cádiz) T: 956 872 210.
E: info@lasdunascamping.com **alanrogers.com/ES88650**

This site lies within the Parque Natural Bahia de Les Dunes and is adjacent to the long and gently sloping golden sands of Puntilla beach. This is a pleasant and peaceful site (though very busy in August) with some 539 separate marked pitches, 260 for touring units, with much natural shade and ample electrical connections (10A). Motorcaravans park in an area called the Oasis, which is very pretty. Tent and caravan pitches, under mature trees, are terraced and separated by low walls. This is a spacious site with a tranquil setting and it is popular with people who wish to 'winter over'. A 2 km. unshaded walk takes you into the bustling heart of Puerto Santa Maria.

Facilities

Immaculate modern sanitary facilities with separate facilities for disabled campers and a baby room. Laundry facilities are excellent. Gas supplies. Bar/restaurant (all year). Supermarket (high season). Very large swimming pool and paddling pool (1/7-31/8). Night security all year. Barbecues are not permitted 15/5-15/10. WiFi throughout (charged). Off site: Beach 100 m. Fishing 500 m.

Open: All year.

Directions

Site is 5 km. north of Cádiz off N443. Take road to Puerto Santa Maria and site is well signed in town (small yellow signs). GPS: 36.5890, -6.2384

Charges guide

Per unit incl. 2 persons and electricity	€ 21.96 - € 27.11
extra person	€ 4.80 - € 5.33
child (3-10 yrs)	€ 4.10 - € 4.56

Fuente de Piedra

Espacios Rurales Fuente de Piedra

Ctra La Rábita s/n, E-29520 Fuente de Piedra (Málaga) T: 952 735 294. E: info@camping-rural.com
alanrogers.com/ES87900

In a remote area of Andalucía, this tiny campsite with just 30 touring pitches looks over the salty lakes and marshes of the Laguna de Fuente. The average sized pitches are on a sloping, terraced hillside, with some having a view of the lake. With a gravel surface and good shade, many pitches slope so chocks would be useful. There is a separate grassy area for tents near the pool and bungalows (cars are not permitted here). Unusually for a site of this size, there is a pool and an excellent bar, snack bar and huge restaurant which serves delicious Spanish food. Try the excellent, inexpensive 'menu del dia'.

Facilities

Sanitary facilities are in one block and are looking a little tired. Facilities for disabled campers. Washing machines. Shop. Restaurant. Bar with TV. Snack bar. Swimming pool. Pool bar. Electronic games. Bicycle hire.
Off site: Lake with flamingos. Bicycle hire 1 km. Fishing 5 km. Riding 10 km. Golf 40 km. Excursions organised in July/Aug.

Open: All year.

Directions

Site is 20 km. northwest of Antequera. From Antequera take A92 and exit at 132 km. point and follow road to the town. Site is well signed from the town but the signs are small. GPS: 37.1292, -4.7334

Charges guide

Per person	€ 3.00 - € 6.00
pitch	€ 5.40 - € 8.00
electricity	€ 5.00

Granada

Camping Suspiro del Moro

Ctra Bailén-Motril km. 144, Puerto Suspiro del Moro, E-18630 Granada (Granada) T: 958 555 411.
E: campingsuspirodelmoro@yahoo.es **alanrogers.com/ES92700**

Suspiro del Moro is a small, family run site with 64 pitches, which packs a big punch with its associated Olympic-size swimming pool and huge bar and restaurant. It is cool and peaceful with great views from the site perimeter. The flat pitches (all with 5A electricity) are shaded by mature trees and there are no statics here. The whole site is neat, clean and well ordered and great for chilling out while visiting the area and the famous Alhambra (connecting buses from the gate). The large restaurant has a most extensive menu with waiter service – a pleasant and very Spanish place to enjoy a meal.

Facilities

Clean and tidy, the small toilet blocks are situated around the camping area with British style WCs and free hot showers. Laundry facilities. Small basic shop. Restaurant/bar (closed Jan). Outdoor swimming pool (15/6-7/9). Small play area. WiFi. Off site: Swimming pool and restaurant adjacent. Public transport 50 m. from gate.

Open: All year.

Directions

Leave Granada to Motril road (E902/A44) at exit 144 (from south) or 139 (from north) and follow unnamed campsite signs. At roundabout go towards Suspiro, then left (signed after turn). Site is 600 m. on right on A4050 beside large restaurant.
GPS: 37.0852, -3.6348

Charges guide

Per person	€ 5.00 - € 5.80
pitch incl. car	€ 9.00 - € 10.50
electricity	€ 3.00 - € 3.50

Granada

Camping Sierra Nevada

Avenida Juan Pablo II no. 23, E-18014 Granada (Granada) T: 958 150 062. E: campingmotel@terra.es

alanrogers.com/ES92800

This is a good site either for a night stop or for a stay of a few days while visiting Granada, especially the Alhambra, and for a city site it is surprisingly pleasant. Quite large, it has an open feel and, to encourage you to stay a little longer, a smart, irregular shape pool with a smaller children's pool open in high season. There is some traffic noise around the pool as it is on the road boundary. With 148 pitches for touring units (10/20A electricity), the site is in two connected parts with more mature trees and facilities to the northern end. Artificial shade is available throughout the site if required (may be quite low).

Facilities

Two modern sanitary blocks, with good facilities, including cabins, very good facilities for disabled campers and babies. Washing machines. Motorcaravan services. Gas supplies. Shop. Swimming pools with lifeguards and charged (15/6-15/9). Bar/restaurant by pool. Tennis. Pétanque. Large playground. Bicycle hire. Free WiFi over part of site. Off site: Supermarket. Bus station 100 m.

Open: 1 March - 31 October.

Directions

From autopista, take Granada North-Almanjayar exit 123 (close to central bus station). Follow road back towards Granada and site is on the right, well signed. From other roads join the motorway to access correct exit. GPS: 37.20402, -3.61703

Charges guide

Per unit incl. 2 persons and electricity	€ 30.00
extra person	€ 6.00

Güéjar-Sierra

Camping Las Lomas

Ctra de Sierra Nevada, E-18160 Güéjar-Sierra (Granada) T: 958 484 742. E: laslomas@campingsonline.com

alanrogers.com/ES92850

This site is high in the Sierra Nevada Natural Park and looks down on the Patano de Canales reservoir. After a scenic drive to Güéjar-Sierra, you are rewarded with a site boasting excellent facilities. It is set on a slope but the pitches have been levelled and are quite private, with high separating hedges and many mature trees giving good shade, (some pitches are fully serviced, with sinks and all but four have electricity). The large bar/restaurant complex and pools have wonderful views over the lake and a grassy sunbathing area runs down to the fence looking over the long drop below.

Facilities

Adequate sanitary blocks (heated in winter) provide clean facilities. First class facilities for disabled campers and well equipped baby room (key at reception). Motorcaravan services. Good supermarket. Restaurant/bar. Swimming pool. Play area. Minigolf. Barbecue. WiFi (charged). Torches useful. A no noise policy (including cars) is strictly enforced midnight-07.00. Off site: Buses to village and Granada (15 km). Bicycle hire 1.5 km. Fishing 3 km. Tours of The Alhambra and Granada organised.

Open: All year.

Directions

From A44/E902 (Jaén-Motril) exit 132 take A395 (Alhamba-Sierra Nevada). At 4 km, exit 5B (Sierra Nevada). At 7 km. exit right onto slip road. At junction (Cenes de la Vega-Güejar-Sierra) turn left. In 200 m. turn right on A4026. In 1.6 km. turn left (Güejar-Sierra) to site. GPS: 37.16073, -3.45388

Charges guide

Per person	€ 4.00 - € 6.00
pitch	€ 12.00 - € 14.00
electricity	€ 3.50

Humilladero

Camping la Sierrecilla

Avenida de Blas Infante, E-29531 Humilladero (Málaga) T: 693 828 199. E: campinglasierrecilla@gmail.com

alanrogers.com/ES87905

La Sierrecilla is a new site situated in the heart of Andalucía on the edge of a pine-covered natural park. It is one of the few areas where eagles, falcons and vultures can still be seen. The 120 good sized touring pitches are on level ground and all have electricity. There is little shade from the young trees, and being on a plain the pitches could become extremely hot during summer. There is a beautiful pool with access for visitors with disabilities, and a good value restaurant with magnificent views of the surrounding countryside. Paths lead through the site to a viewpoint and picnic area, which are extremely popular at weekends. It is an ideal site for exploring Andalucía; it is just 40 minutes from the beaches at Malaga.

Facilities

Two modern sanitary units have some British and some Turkish style toilets, open style washbasins and free hot showers. En-suite unit for disabled visitors. Washing machine. Swimming pool (15/6-15/9). Excellent bar (all year) and charming restaurant (12/3-20/10). Takeaway. Play area. Tennis. Climbing wall. Aerial runway. Caravan storage. WiFi. No barbecues in summer. Mobile homes and bungalows to rent.

Open: All year.

Directions

Travelling north towards Madrid on A4 (E5) take exit 259 (Santa Elena). Drive through town and site is on right up a steep slope. For tall vehicles ask at reception for alternative entrance. Travelling south towards Bailén, take exit 257 then proceed as above. GPS: 37.108094, -4.687117

Charges guide

Per unit incl. 2 persons and electricity	€ 22.00
extra person	€ 3.00

Isla Cristina

Camping Giralda

Ctra Provincial 4117, E-21410 Isla Cristina (Huelva) T: 959 343 318. E: recepcion@campinggiralda.com
alanrogers.com/ES88710

The fountains at the entrance and the circular, thatched reception building set the tone for this very large site. The 587 pitches are quite spacious on sand, most benefiting from the attractive mature trees which abound on the site. Most pitches have electricity (142 are for tents). Access to the excellent beach is gained by a short stroll, crossing the minor road alongside the site and passing through attractive pine trees. This is a quiet site out of the main tourist areas, with good leisure and adventure facilities. The many additional activities are listed below.

Facilities

Four large, modern, semi-circular thatched sanitary blocks are clean and fully equipped. Laundry. Shop and bar (all year). Restaurant and snacks (June-Sept). Swimming pools. Archery. Pétanque. Mountain biking. Beach games. Watersports school. Play area. Organised activity area for groups low season. Excursions booked. Off site: Beach and fishing 200 m. Bicycle hire 1.5 km. Golf 4 km. Riding 7 km.

Open: All year.

Directions

Leave E1/A49 at exit 113 signed Lepe on N444. Turn right on N431, use Lepe bypass, then left to Le Antilla and then on to Isla Cristina. Site is on right (signed) just as you reach Isla Christina (this route avoids speed bumps). GPS: 37.19998, -7.30087

Charges guide

Per person	€ 6.90
caravan and car	€ 10.70
electricity	€ 6.30

Iznate

Camping Iznate

Ctra Benamocarra-Iznate km. 2,7, E-29792 Iznate (Málaga) T: 952 535 613. E: info@campingiznate.com
alanrogers.com/ES87850

This new site is situated amid beautiful scenery 1 km. away from the picturesque village of Iznate. It is surrounded by avocado and olive trees and is on the wine route – the region is the centre of Spain's Muscadet production. The site is well thought out and immaculately maintained. The large swimming pool is an ideal spot for cooling off after a walk and the next door restaurant serves excellent food at very reasonable prices. This is a small, new site and we would recommend booking during high season. There are wonderful views all round the site and eagles, wild boar and black squirrels can be seen in the surrounding countryside.

Facilities

The modern toilet block has hot showers and facilities for disabled visitors. Laundry facilities under a covered area. Fridge hire. Small shop. Bar/restaurant with terrace adjoining the site. Swimming pool (15/5-15/9). Summer entertainment. Pétanque. Play area. TV room. WiFi. Barbecues not permitted in high season. Off site: Beach 20 minutes drive. Towns of Vélez-Málaga, Rincón de la Victoria, Nerja, Torrox, Frigiliana and Sayalonga nearby.

Open: All year.

Directions

From A7/E15 take exit 265 and head towards Cajiz and Iznate. Site is on left after Iznate.
GPS: 36.784486, -4.174556

Charges guide

Per person	€ 3.79 - € 4.74
pitch incl. car	€ 13.24 - € 19.81
electricity	€ 4.07

Discounts in low season (15/9-15/6) depending on length of stay.

La Carlota

Camping Carlos III

Ctra Madrid-Cadiz km. 430, E-14100 La Carlota (Córdoba) T: 957 300 338.
E: camping@campingcarlosiii.com **alanrogers.com/ES90850**

This rural site lies 25 km. south of Córdoba, just off the main Córdoba - Sevilla road and may be a good alternative to staying in the city. A very large, busy site, especially at weekends, it has many supporting facilities including a good swimming pool and a pool, play area and animal corner for children. With the catering services open all year, the site has a more open feel than the bustling municipal site in Córdoba. The touring areas are canopied by trees which offer considerable shade for the 331 separated pitches. On sandy, gently sloping ground, around two-thirds have 5/10A electricity.

Facilities

Modern toilet blocks provide a mix of British and Turkish WCs, with hot showers in the block near reception. Laundry service. Motorcaravan services. Bar/restaurant, shop (all year). Swimming pools (1/6-15/9). Aviary. Boules. Minigolf. Paintball. Play area. Hairdresser. WiFi (charged). Accommodation to rent. Charcoal barbecues not allowed. Off site: Bus service by gate. Village 1 km. Riding 15 km. Fishing and golf 30 km.

Open: All year.

Directions

From NIV Córdoba-Seville motorway take La Carlota exit (at km. 429 point northbound or exit 432 southbound). Site is 500 m. and well signed.
GPS: 37.67664, -4.93329

Charges guide

Per unit incl. 2 persons and electricity	€ 21.85 - € 24.85
extra person	€ 5.35
child (3-12 yrs)	€ 5.00

La Zubia

Camping Reina Isabel

Laurel de la Reina 15, E-18140 La Zubia (Granada) T: 958 590 041. E: info@reinaisabelcamping.com

alanrogers.com/ES92760

Reina Isabel can be found just 3 km. from the centre of Granada and just 1 km. from the entrance to the spectacular Sierra Nevada National Park. The site is open for an extended season and is well located for winter sports holidays in the Sierra Nevada. There are 51 shady touring pitches here (each around 70 sq.m), all with electrical connections. There are also 11 bungalows available for rent. A regular bus service operates to the city centre and to other places of interest, notably the Alhambra Palace.

Facilities

The single toilet block is clean but the toilet and shower cubicles have large frosted glass panels which are revealing at night. Used paper goes into baskets and not into the toilet. Shop in reception, bar/restaurant with takeaway (all season). Outdoor swimming pool (15/5-30/9). Play area. Bungalows for rent. Excursions available. WiFi. Off site: Bus stop with regular service to the city centre. Sierra Nevada ski resort 29 km.

Open: All year.

Directions

Site is south of Granada. Leave A44 motorway at exit 132 and head east on A395. Follow signs to La Zubia, joining the southbound Calle de Laurel de la Reina. Site is clearly signed from here. GPS: 37.12456, -3.58625

Charges guide

Per unit incl. 2 persons and electricity	€ 29.00
extra person	€ 5.90
child	€ 4.35

Manilva

Camping la Bella Vista

CN 340, km. 142,8, E-29691 Manilva (Málaga) T: 952 890 020. E: camping@campinglabellavista.com

alanrogers.com/ES88100

Camping la Bella Vista is a very modern campsite that uses sustainable technology. It enjoys a beach front location in San Luis de Sabanillas, a suburb of Manilva, situated in the nearby hills. The beaches are extensive with clean sand and the site boasts uninterrupted views of the sea. The pitches have water, waste, electricity (16/32A), TV and WiFi connections, and are bounded by developing trees and hedges, which as yet provide little shade or privacy. The coastline's eight kilometres of sandy beaches have reefs and coves to explore, in addition to two urban areas offering varied entertainment. The Costa del Sol enjoys 320 days of sunshine each year with an annual average temperature of 18 degrees. Manilva's history dates from the Stone Age. During the Roman period it had a thriving fishing industry, exporting products back to Rome; well preserved Roman sulphur baths and an aqueduct can be seen in the area. The main industries of the area have been fishing, agriculture and viticulture. The wine industry is currently thriving within the village and guided tours of the vineyards and wine production process are available.

Facilities

One new sanitary block has family bathrooms and facilities for disabled visitors. All areas including pool and sanitary units are accessed by stairs, lift or ramp. Washing machines and dryers. Supermarket. Restaurant with Spanish and international cuisine, with views of the Mediterranean and capable of catering for functions. Bar and lounge. Beach bar with food and drink. Feature pool, children's pool and large terrace with sea view. Play area. Medical facilities and 24-hour security patrols. Sunbed and parasols for hire on beach. Free WiFi over site. Off site: Golf. Scuba diving. Fishing. Tennis. Paragliding. Cycling. Riding. Visits to Ronda, Casares, Antequera, Mijas, Gibraltar 35 km. and the capital Malaga 97 km. Day trips to Africa from Algerciras 30 km.

Open: All year.

Directions

From Malaga and Estepona direction take N340/E5 coast road. After Sabinillas, cross the roundabout after Duquesa golf course, continue to next roundabout, double back on dual carriageway and approach La Bella Vista from the direction of Gibraltar. GPS: 36.347211, -5.235988

Charges guide

Per unit incl. 2 persons, electricity, water and waste water	€ 24.00 - € 48.00
extra person (over 3 yrs)	€ 6.00
dog	€ 3.00

Marbella

Camping Marbella Playa

Ctra N340 km. 192,8, Eluiria, E-29600 Marbella (Málaga) T: 952 833 998.
E: recepcion@campingmarbella.com **alanrogers.com/ES88000**

This large site is 12 kilometres east of the internationally famous resort of Marbella with public transport available to the town centre and local attractions. A sandy beach is about 150 metres away with direct access. There are 430 individual pitches of up to 70 sq.m. with natural shade (additional artificial shade is provided to some), and electricity (10/20A) available throughout. Long leads may be required for some pitches, and those next to the road can experience some noise from 6 am onwards. The site is busy throughout the high season but the high staff/customer ratio and the friendly staff approach ensures a comfortable stay.

Facilities

The four rather dated sanitary blocks are fully equipped and well maintained. Three modern units for disabled visitors. Laundry service. Fridge hire. Large supermarket with butcher and fresh vegetable counter. Bar, restaurant and café (all open all year). Supervised swimming pool (free April-Sept). Playground. Children's activities. Bicycles delivered to site. WiFi over site (charged). Car wash. No charcoal barbecues (June-Oct). Torches advised.

Open: All year.

Directions

Site is 12 km. east of Marbella with access close to the 193 km. point on the main N340 road. Signed Elviria, then follow signs. GPS: 36.49127, -4.76325

Charges guide

Per unit incl. 2 persons and electricity	€ 17.90 - € 35.85
extra person	€ 3.40 - € 6.00
child (1-10 yrs)	€ 2.65 - € 5.26

Marbella

Kawan Village Cabopino

Ctra N340 km. 194,7, E-29604 Marbella (Málaga) T: 952 834 373. E: info@campingcabopino.com
alanrogers.com/ES88020

This large, mature site is alongside the main N340/A7 Costa del Sol coast road, 12 km. east of Marbella and 15 km. from Fuengirola. The Costa del Sol is also known as the Costa del Golf and fittingly there is a major golf course alongside the site. The site is set amongst tall pine trees which provide shade for the sandy pitches (there are some huge areas for large units). The 300 touring pitches, a mix of level and sloping (chocks advisable), all have electricity (10A), but long leads may be required for some. There is a separate area on the western side for groups of younger guests.

Facilities

Five mature but very clean sanitary blocks provide hot water throughout (may be under pressure at peak times). Washing machines. Bar/restaurant and takeaway (all year). Shop. Outdoor pool (1/5-15/9) and indoor pool (all year). Play area. Adult exercise equipment. Some evening entertainment. Excursions can be booked. ATM. Torches necessary in the more remote parts of the site. Only gas and electric barbecues permitted. Off site: Beach 200 m.

Open: All year.

Directions

Site is 12 km. from Marbella. Approaching Marbella from the east, leave the N340/A7 at the 194 km. marker (signed Cabopino). Site is off the roundabout at the top of the slip road. GPS: 36.49350, -4.74383

Charges guide

Per unit incl. 2 persons and electricity	€ 24.00 - € 36.00
extra person	€ 4.75 - € 7.20

Camping Cheques accepted.

Marbella

Camping la Buganvilla

Ctra N340 km. 188,8, E-29600 Marbella (Málaga) T: 952 831 973. E: info@campingbuganvilla.com
alanrogers.com/ES88030

La Buganvilla is a large, uncomplicated site with mature trees providing shade to some of the 250 touring pitches. They all have 16A electricity and are mostly on terraces so there are some views across to the mountains and hinterland of this coastal area. The terrain is a little rugged in places and the buildings are older and in need of some attention, but all were clean when we visited. A pool complex near the bar and restaurant is ideal for cooling off after a day's sightseeing. This is an acceptable base from which to explore areas of the Costa del Sol and it is an easy drive to the picturesque Ronda Valley.

Facilities

Three painted sanitary blocks are clean and adequate. Laundry facilities (not all sinks have hot water). Outdoor pool (all year). Bar/restaurant with basic food. Well stocked small supermarket. Play area. Tennis (high season). WiFi (charged). Dogs are not accepted in July/Aug. Off site: Bus service close to site entrance. Fishing and watersports 400 m. Bicycle and scooter hire 1 km. Golf 5 km. Resort type entertainment close.

Open: All year.

Directions

Site is between Marbella and Fuengirola off the N340/A7. Access at 188.8 km. marker only possible when travelling west, (from Fuengirola). From other direction, continue to 'cambio de sentido' (Elviria) and turn back over the dual carriageway. Site is signed. GPS: 36.5023, -4.804

Charges guide

Per unit incl. 2 persons and electricity	€ 22.82 - € 33.82
extra person	€ 5.50 - € 7.50

Maro

Nerja Camping

Ctra N340 km. 297, E-29787 Maro (Málaga) T: 952 529 714. E: info@nerjacamping.com

alanrogers.com/ES87110

This site is set on the lower slopes of the Sierra Almijara, some five kilometres from Nerja and 2 km. from the excellent beaches. Nerja Camping is a small site of 55 pitches with impressive views of the surrounding mountains and the Mediterranean. There are 25 touring pitches (15A electricity) and four new mobile homes to rent. The pitches are on the small side and set on slopes with some terracing along with some artificial shade. The roads, although sloping, should present few problems for siting units.

Facilities

The single sanitary block has been refurbished and tiled; all washbasins and showers have hot water. Laundry facilities. Small restaurant/bar (Mar-Sept). Essentials from the bar. Small swimming pool (Mar-Sept). Accommodation to rent. Free WiFi throughout. Off site: Nerja limestone caves 1 km. Beach 2 km. Fishing 3 km. Bicycle hire and riding 5 km. Sub-aqua diving, parascending and watersports. Day trips to Granada and Gibraltar. Sierra Nevada 100 km. (1.5 hours in winter).

Open: All year excl. October.

Directions

Site signed from main N340 coast road 5 km. east of Nerja after 296 km. marker. If coming from Nerja, go 200 m. past site entrance (opposite radio masts) to cross the main road. GPS: 36.7605, -3.83475

Charges guide

Per unit incl. 2 persons and electricity	€ 26.00 - € 29.50
extra person	€ 5.75
child (2-10 yrs)	€ 4.00

No credit cards.

Mojacar

Camping Sopalmo

Apdo 761, Sopalmo, E-04638 Mojacar (Almería) T: 950 478 413. E: campingsopalmo@gmail.com

alanrogers.com/ES87490

This is a tiny, homely site run by the cheerful Simon and his charming wife Macu (both speaking some English) who are determined that you will enjoy your stay. The site is on three levels (with a slightly steep gravel track to the gates) with space for 29 tents, caravans or medium sized motorcaravans. All the pitches are marked, level and on gravel with electricity (6A). The site is unspoilt and has much rustic charm with the family house providing the focal point. Attractive trees and shrubs around the site include olives, figs, mimosa and cacti. Some pitches near the road may experience a little traffic noise.

Facilities

The small sanitary block is very clean and fully equipped. Hot showers assisted by solar power. Facilities for disabled campers. Basic laundry facilities. Bar. Breakfast available in summer and the baker calls at 10.30 daily. Torch useful. Free WiFi over site. Off site: Bus to Mojacar from site. Golf 500 m. Beach 1.5 km. Nearest serious shops 5 km. Riding 6 km.

Open: All year.

Directions

Exit from main coast road (N340) at exit 520 (northeast of Almeria). Take the AL152 (formerly A150) to Mojacar Playa and continue south towards Carboneras. Site is 6 km. south of Mojacar Playa, signed off the road. GPS: 37.06533, -1.86881

Charges guide

Per unit incl. 2 persons and electricity	€ 29.85 - € 34.25
extra person	€ 4.00 - € 4.75

No credit cards.

Mojacar

Camping Cueva Negra

Camino Lotaza 2, Frenta-Playa Macenas, E-04638 Mojacar (Almería) T: 950 475 855.
E: info@campingcuevanegra.es **alanrogers.com/ES87560**

This tiny jewel of a site, just 9 km. south of Mojacar, is approached by a short, steep and winding road with passing places. There are only 40 pitches, but they are all 100 sq.m. and 30 have electricity, water and drainage, with artificial shade provided in summer. The elevated site is attractively laid out with views to the nearby sea. The superb covered swimming pool has four jacuzzis and a large, partly covered terrace with an open-air shower for disabled campers. There are facilities for tennis and pétanque and a play area for children.

Facilities

Modern toilet block with facilities for disabled visitors. Laundry with washing machine and dryer. Well stocked shop and small bar (all year). Takeaway (high season). Covered swimming pool (1/5-31/10). Tennis. Pétanque. Play area. Accommodation for rent. Off site: Beach 400 m. Five golf courses nearby. The towns of Mojacar, Aguilas Nijar and Almeria within easy reach.

Open: All year.

Directions

Site is 9 km. south of Mojacar on the Mojacar-Carboneras road, on the right when travelling south. There is a small sign at the entry road. GPS: 37.08674, -1.85396

Charges guide

Per unit incl. 2 persons and electricity	€ 20.15 - € 31.87
extra person	€ 3.68 - € 6.01
child	€ 2.78 - € 6.01

Motril

Camping Don Cactus

Ctra N340 km. 343, Carchuna, E-18730 Motril (Granada) T: 958 623 109. E: camping@doncactus.com

alanrogers.com/ES92950

Situated between the main N340 and the beach, this family run campsite is pleasantly surprising with clever planning and ongoing improvements. It is a comfortable site of 320 pitches (280 for touring). The flat pitches vary in size with electricity (5/12A), some providing water and satellite TV connections, and are arranged along avenues with eucalyptus trees for shade. This quieter section of the coast is beautiful with coves and access to larger towns if wished. The friendly reception staff are very helpful with tourist advice and can arrange trips for you if needed.

Facilities

The large toilet block is dated but clean and provides British style WCs, showers and plenty of washbasins. Laundry facilities. Beach showers. Well stocked shop. Bar, restaurant and takeaway (all year). Swimming pool (in high season € 1.50 per day). Tennis. Play area. Summer activities for children. Outdoor fitness centre for adults. Pets corner. ATM. Internet point. WiFi (charged; free in bar). Dogs are not accepted in July/Aug. Barbecues only in special area. Caravan storage. Car wash facility.

Open: All year.

Directions

From Motril-Carchuna road (N340/E15) turn towards the sea at km. 343. (look at roof level for large green tent on the top of the building!). Travel 600 m. then turn east to site. GPS: 36.70066, -3.44032

Charges guide

Per person	€ 7.25
child (4-10 yrs)	€ 6.95
pitch	€ 16.25
electricity (5A)	€ 4.85 - € 6.95

Nijar

Camping Los Escullos

Paraje de los Escullos s/n, San Jose, E-04118 Nijar (Almería) T: 950 389 811.

E: info@losescullossanjose.com **alanrogers.com/ES87620**

This efficient, well maintained, medium sized site has 171 pitches (60-80 sq.m). They are divided by hedges and trees, 100 have 10A electricity, and some have artificial shading. Specific taps about the grounds provide drinking water. The pool has an overlooking bar and restaurant which is kept busy serving excellent typical Spanish 'menu del dia' food at very low prices. It is a popular site with British tourists seeking the sun. The salinas on the approach to Cabo de Gata are famous for bird life (including flocks of pink flamingo).

Facilities

The main sanitary block is large, clean and fully equipped with hot showers and facilities for disabled campers. Second small sanitary block close to reception. Small supermarket. Bar/restaurant. Takeaway (15/6-15/9). Large outdoor pool (15/5-1/10) and jacuzzi (1/7-1/10). Hairdresser. Massage. Well equipped gym. Internet access. Multisports court. Scuba diving. TV room. Bicycle hire. No charcoal barbecues. Entertainment programme in high season. WiFi (free). Off site: Fishing 1 km.

Open: All year.

Directions

From A7/E15 autovia exit at either exit 479 or 471 in direction of San Jose. On approach to San Jose left turn toward Los Escullos. Site is well signed. GPS: 36.80288, -2.07756

Charges guide

Per unit incl. 2 persons and electricity	€ 23.50 - € 35.20
extra person	€ 5.50 - € 7.25

Camping Cheques accepted.

Orgiva

Camping Puerta de La Alpujarra

Ctra Lanjarón-Orgiva (Las Barreras), E-18400 Orgiva (Granada) T: 958 784 450. E: puertalpujarra@yahoo.es

alanrogers.com/ES92920

You will receive a warm welcome from the family who run this site and nothing is too much trouble. The site overlooks the Sierra Nevada with lovely panoramic views. There are 60 touring pitches, terraced and with plenty of shade (all with electricity connections). This is an area that is becoming more popular with tourists and is an ideal spot from which to explore the mountain villages. Orgiva, steeped in history, is just 1.5 km. from the site and there are many interesting walks from here.

Facilities

Three central sanitary blocks are clean and provide open washbasins and roomy shower cubicles. Toilet for disabled visitors (no shower). Laundry facilities. Shop (baker delivers daily). Bar, restaurant and takeaway (all season, closed Mon-Wed). Outdoor swimming and paddling pools (15/5-15/10). Play area. WiFi. Torches useful. Communal barbecues only. Off site: Bicycle hire 1 km. Orgiva 1.5 km. Pampaneria, Bubion and Capileira.

Open: All year.

Directions

Head south from Granada on A44 (E902) and exit 164 signed Lanjaron onto A348. Alpujarra is signed with Orgiva. Site is on right on outskirts of Orgiva (signed). GPS: 36.90375, -3.43891

Charges guide

Per person	€ 4.00 - € 5.00
child	€ 3.00 - € 4.00
pitch	€ 7.50 - € 10.00
electricity	€ 3.00 - € 4.00

Orgiva

Camping Orgiva

Ctra A348 km. 18,9, E-18400 Orgiva (Granada) T: 958 784 307. E: info@campingorgiva.com

alanrogers.com/ES92930

Set in the high slopes of the Sierra Nevada and only 2 km. from Orgiva, this is a small and well managed site that offers the opportunity to escape into rural Spain. It is open all year and is an ideal place to relax. For those who feel more energetic, there are facilities for climbing, horse riding and canoeing, all within close proximity of the site. The 40 touring pitches are well defined and separated by shrubs and small trees and all have views of the surrounding countryside. Access to the site is good but being high in the mountains it is not suitable for large units. Good English is spoken on site.

Facilities

One centrally placed sanitary block provides toilets, washbasins and shower cubicles. Facilities for disabled visitors. Washing machine and dryer. Very good swimming pool with adjacent small pool for children (June-Sept). Shop. Terrace bar. No barbecues allowed on site.
Off site: Fishing 10 km. Golf 35 km.

Open: All year.

Directions

From A44-E902 Granada-Motril road, exit at 164 km. and take A348 east to Lanjaron and Orgiva. Continue past Orgiva and the site is well signed on left. GPS: 36.88708, -3.41754

Charges guide

Per person	€ 5.30
pitch incl. car	€ 9.30
electricity	€ 4.10

Palomares

Camping Cuevas Mar

Cuevas del Almanzora, E-04618 Palomares (Almería) T: 950 467 382. E: cuevasmar@arrakis.es

alanrogers.com/ES87510

This is a popular, well established and traditional campsite, busy during the warm winter months with 180 pleasant pitches with shrubs and trees providing pitch dividers and shade. A few pitches are quite close to the road but it is not busy with traffic. All the pitches are flat and are of an acceptable 80-100 sq.m. with a clean stone chip surface and 6/10A electricity supply. During the hot summer months, overhead shade canopies are erected on several pitches. This is a pleasant and uncomplicated site with a peaceful atmosphere and a spa.

Facilities

The well designed sanitary blocks provide sufficient showers and toilets for all. Washing machines and dryer. Water to the taps is to European standard, however a single tap near reception provides high quality water from a nearby mountain spring source. Daily fresh bread, emergency provisions and gas from reception. Open-air unheated swimming pool and jacuzzi (May-Sept). Caravan storage. WiFi throughout (weekly charge). Off site: Many restaurants in the vicinity. Public transport 100 m. from gate. Fishing 200 m. Beach 300 m. Naturist beach 800 m. Bicycle hire 3 km. Golf 4 km. Riding 12 km.

Open: All year.

Directions

From E15/A7 exit 537 pass under autovia following signs for Cuevas del Almanzora. At T-junction turn right toward Palomares and Vera. In 1 km. on right hand bend turn left (Palomares). Continue to roundabout, take first exit and site is on left in 2 km. Continue 500 m. to next roundabout and return. GPS: 37.237, -1.798

Charges guide

Per unit incl. 1 or 2 persons	€ 22.80
extra person	€ 5.20
electricity (6A)	€ 4.50

No credit cards.

Pitres

Camping El Balcon de Pitres

Ctra Orgiva-Ugijar km. 51, E-18414 Pitres (Granada) T: 958 766 111. E: info@balcondepitres.com

alanrogers.com/ES92900

A simple country site perched high in the mountains of Las Alpujarras, on the south side of the Sierra Nevada, El Balcon de Pitres has its own rustic charm. Hundreds of trees planted around the site provide shade. There are stunning views from some of the 175 level grassy pitches (large units may find pitch access difficult). The garden is kept green by spring waters, which you can hear and sometimes see, tinkling away in places. The Lopez family have built this site from barren mountain top to cool oasis in the mountains in just fifteen years.

Facilities

Two toilet blocks provide adequate facilities including some for disabled campers (but the steeply sloping site is unsuitable for visitors with mobility problems). Bar/snack bar (with TV and pool table). Swimming pools (charged: € 2.40 adult, € 1.50 child). Barbecues are not permitted. Torches useful. WiFi. Off site: Fishing. Canyoning. Trekking. Parascending. Quad bikes. Sports centre.

Open: All year.

Directions

Site is 30 km. northeast of Motril. Heading south on A44 (E902) exit 164 (Lanjaron) onto E348 towards Orgiva. Fork left at sign (A4132) Pampaneira 8 km. Continue to Pitres (7 km). Site signed (steep and winding roads). GPS: 36.9323, -3.3334

Charges guide

Per unit incl. 2 persons and electricity	€ 26.75 - € 32.10
extra person	€ 5.35 - € 6.42

Ronda

Camping El Sur

Ctra Ronda-Algeciras km. 1,5, Apdo 127, E-29400 Ronda (Málaga) T: 952 875 939.
E: info@campingelsur.com **alanrogers.com/ES88090**

The delightfully decorated entrance with generous manoeuvring area is a promise of something different, which is fulfilled in all respects. The friendly family who run the site have worked hard for many years combining innovative thinking with excellent service. The 125 terraced pitches have electricity (6/10A) and water, and are partially shaded by olive and almond trees. Levels vary so chocks are recommended. Most have relaxing views of the surrounding mountains but at an elevation of 850 m. the upper pitches (the very top 45 pitches are for tents only) allow a clear view of the fascinating town of Ronda.

Facilities

The immaculate sanitary block is fully equipped. Laundry facilities in a separate block. Gas supplies. Bar and very large, high quality restaurant (1/2-31/10). Kidney-shaped pool (1/6-30/9). Playground and adventure play area. Separate camping area for groups. Minigolf. Off road bicycle hire. Internet and WiFi (charged). Off site: Riding 1.5 km. Bicycle hire 2.5 km. The famous town of Ronda with all its attractions. The coast is an hour's drive (50 km).

Open: All year.

Directions

Site is on the A369 Ronda-Algerciras road 3 km. south of Ronda and is well signed.
GPS: 36.7211, -5.1716

Charges guide

Per unit incl. 2 persons and electricity	€ 23.00 - € 29.00
extra person	€ 4.95

No credit cards (except in restaurant).

Roquetas de Mar

Camping Roquetas

Ctra Los Parrales s/n, E-04740 Roquetas de Mar (Almería) T: 950 343 809. E: info@campingroquetas.com
alanrogers.com/ES87680

This level, very well maintained site is conveniently situated 9 km. from the A7 motorway within easy reach of Roquetas de Mar and 400 m. from a stony beach. It is a family run site and English is spoken. There are excellent facilities including two swimming pools and the site is within easy reach of the popular resort of Almeria and the Cabo de Gata nature park. There are 731 quite small touring pitches (60 sq.m), although during the winter months two pitches are allocated for the price of one. All have electricity (5-15A), and 65 also have water and drainage (18 of these are for longer units).

Facilities

Five well equipped toilet blocks spread throughout the site. Two units for disabled visitors are close to the pools, as is a baby room. Spanish restaurant with excellent menu and reasonable prices. Shop. Two swimming pools, one with paddling pool. Tennis. Pétanque. WiFi (charged; free by reception). Off site: Beach and fishing 300 m. Bicycle hire 1 km. Golf and riding 3 km. Towns of Roquetas de Mar and Almeria nearby.

Open: All year.

Directions

From A7/E15 exit 429 head towards Roquetas de Mar. Site is well signed and is 9 km. from the main road. GPS: 36.797814, -2.590992

Charges guide

Per unit incl. 2 persons	€ 19.25 - € 20.60
extra person	€ 5.15
child (1-12 yrs)	€ 5.00
dog	€ 2.35

San José

Camping Tau de San José

Cua de Cala Hibuera s/n, E-04118 San José (Almería) T: 950 380 166. E: tau@parquenatural.com
alanrogers.com/ES87580

This attractive and quiet site was originally part of an old farm, typical of this region. It is well shaded and is particularly suitable for tents and low units. There is limited space for caravans and motorcaravans and phoning ahead is strongly advised. Electricity hook-ups are provided (6/16A) but long leads may be required. A level site, it is set in a nature park and is about 300 m. from the beach and the unspoilt village of San José. There is a new toilet block and the small bar/restaurant has a Spanish atmosphere with a large shady terrace outside, ideal for that relaxing drink.

Facilities

Large modern toilet block with extra unisex showers. Facilities for disabled visitors. Laundry. Small, well stocked shop. Covered barbecue area. A further covered area has pool and electronic games. Play area. Dogs are not accepted. Off site: Village of San José (fish restaurants are a speciality), beach and harbour 300 m. Almeria, and the white villages of Nijar and Mojacar are close by and further afield is the Tabernas desert and 'Mini Hollywood'.

Open: Easter - 1 October.

Directions

From E15 exit 471 or 479 follow signs for San José. Site is north of the village on left hand side (keep the white buildings to your right). Follow made up road to site. GPS: 36.76757, -2.10532

Charges guide

Per unit incl. 2 persons and electricity	€ 27.00 - € 43.00
extra person	€ 6.50 - € 7.50
child	€ 5.00 - € 6.00
dog	€ 2.00

Credit cards accepted for a minimum €100.

Santa Elena

Camping Despeñaperros

Ctra Infanta Elena, E-23213 Santa Elena (Jaén) T: 953 664 192. E: info@campingdespenaperros.com
alanrogers.com/ES90890

This site is on the edge of Santa Elena in a natural park with shade from mature pine trees. This is a good place to stay en-route from Madrid to the Costa del Sol or to just explore the surrounding countryside. The 116 pitches are fully serviced including a satellite TV/Internet link. All rubbish must be taken to large bins outside the site gates (a long walk from the other end of the site). The site is run in a very friendly manner where nothing is too much trouble. Reception has a monitor link with tourist information and access to the region's sites of interest.

Facilities

Two traditional, central sanitary blocks have Turkish style WCs and well equipped showers. Facilities for disabled visitors. One washing machine (launderette in town). Shop. Excellent bar (all year) and charming restaurant (May-Oct). Swimming pools (15/6-15/9). Tennis. Caravan storage. Night security. Communal barbecue area. WiFi over part of site. Off site: Walking, riding and mountain sports nearby. The main road gives good access to Jaén and Valdepeñas.

Open: All year.

Directions

Travelling on A4 (E5) take exit 259 (Santa Elena). Drive through town and site is on right up steep slope (alternative entrance for tall vehicles – ask reception). GPS: 38.34307, -3.53528

Charges guide

Per unit incl. 2 persons and electricity	€ 21.35 - € 23.70
extra person	€ 4.20 - € 4.80
child	€ 3.25 - € 4.00

Santaella

Camping la Campiña

Ctra A379 km. 46,2, la Guijarrosa, E-14547 Santaella (Córdoba) T: 957 315 303.
E: info@campinglacampina.es **alanrogers.com/ES90840**

A charming site amongst the olive trees and set high on a hill to catch cool summer breezes. Matilde, the daughter of the Martin-Rodriguez family, and her husband run this site with enthusiasm and hard work, making a visit here a delightful experience. Everything is immaculately kept with excellent amenities and standards. The 35 pitches are level with a gravel surface and most have shade. There is a large pool in a garden setting and the restaurant, with its traditional rustic charm, has a delightful menu of homemade food. Breakfast is included in pitch prices.

Facilities

Two small traditional sanitary blocks (heated in winter) have clean services including facilities for disabled campers (key at reception). Washing machines. Restaurant. Snack bar. Shop. Outdoor swimming pool (Apr-Oct). Bicycle hire. Play area. TV room. Yoga lessons. Torches useful. Walks and excursions arranged. WiFi throughout. Off site: Bus from gate to Córdoba. Town 2 km. Riding 5 km. Golf 40 km.

Open: All year.

Directions

From the NIV/A4 (Sevilla-Córdoba) take exit 441 (La Rambla-Montilla) or 424 (La Victoria). Continue past Santaella towards La Victoria. Site is tucked off this road behind high hedging. From the A92 use exit 109 (Puente-genil) or from A45 (Malaga-Córdoba), exit 27 (La Rambla) and on towards Santaella. GPS: 37.623, -4.8587

Charges guide

Per unit incl. 2 persons and electricity	€ 25.60 - € 29.05
extra person	€ 5.80

Sevilla

Camping Villsom

Ctra Sevilla-Cadiz km. 554,8, E-41700 Sevilla (Sevilla) T: 954 720 828.
alanrogers.com/ES90810

This city site was one of the first to open in Spain and it is still owned by the same friendly family. The administrative building consists of a peaceful and attractive bar with patio and satellite TV (where breakfast is served) and there is a pleasant, small reception area. It is a good site for visiting Seville with a frequent bus service to the centre. Camping Villsom has around 180 pitches which are level and shaded. A huge variety of trees and palms are to be seen around the site and in summer the bright colours of the flowers are very pleasing.

Facilities

Sanitary facilities have been modernised. Some washbasins have cold water only. Laundry facilities. Small shop selling basic provisions. Bar with satellite TV (open July/Aug). Swimming pool (June-Sept). Putting. Drinks machine. Off site: Bus stop close. Most town facilities including restaurant, supermarket, cinema and theatre.

Open: 10 January - 23 December.

Directions

On main Seville-Cádiz NIV road travelling from Seville take exit at km. 555 signed Dos Hermanos-Isla Menor. At the roundabout turn right (SE-3205 Isla Menor) to site in 80 m. GPS: 37.27735, -5.93683

Charges guide

Per unit incl. 2 persons and electricity	€ 24.80 - € 34.10

Tarifa

Camping Paloma

Ctra Cadiz-Malaga km., E-11380 Tarifa (Cádiz) T: 956 684 203.

alanrogers.com/ES88500

This spacious, neat and tidy, family orientated site is popular with Spanish families and young people of all nations in high season. The area is famous for its ideal kite and windsurfing conditions. Paloma is well established and the many tall palms around the site remind one of the proximity of Africa and the romance of Tangier. The site has 337 pitches on mostly flat ground, although the westerly pitches are sloping. They are of average size with some places for extra large units, some are separated by hedges and most are shaded by mature trees; around 150 pitches have 10A electrical connections.

Facilities

Two sanitary blocks, one of a good size, although a long walk from the southern end of the site. The other block is smaller and open plan. British style WCs with some Turkish, washbasins have cold water. Facilities for disabled visitors in the smaller block. Washing machine. Shop. Busy bar and good restaurant. Swimming pool with adjacent bar (high season only). Play area. Excursions (June-Sept). Dogs are not accepted in high season. Off site: Beach 700 m. Bicycle hire 5 km. Riding 10 km. Tarifa 12 km. Golf 25 km.

Open: All year.

Directions

Site is signed off N340 Cádiz road at Punta Paloma, 10 km. northwest of Tarifa, just west of km. 74 marker. Watch for the site sign – no advance notice. Be sure to use the slip road to turn left if coming from Tarifa. Follow signs down the road for 300 m. GPS: 36.0776, -5.694

Charges guide

Per person	€ 3.89 - € 6.48
child	€ 3.24 - € 5.40
pitch	€ 5.00 - € 10.00
electricity	€ 4.32

Tarifa

Camping Tarifa

Ctra N340 km. 78,87, E-11380 Tarifa (Cádiz) T: 956 684 778. E: info@camping-tarifa.com

alanrogers.com/ES88550

The long, golden sandy beach adjacent to this site is a good feature being ideal for windsurfing and also clean and safe for swimming. The site has a pleasant, open feel and is reasonably sheltered from road noise. It has been thoughtfully landscaped and planted out with an amazing variety of shrubs and flowers and is clean. The 265 level pitches are of varying sizes and are surrounded by pine trees, which provide ample shade. All have electricity (5/10A) and there are adequate water points. There is a smart, modern reception area with an attractive water feature close by.

Facilities

Two modern, fully equipped sanitary blocks have facilities for campers with disabilities and baby room. All were spotlessly clean when seen. Motorcaravan services. Gas supplies. Supermarket and excellent bar/restaurant with patio (fast food only, all open as site). Swimming pool complex with bar. Large play area. Dogs are not accepted. No charcoal barbecues. Off site: Fishing 100 m. Riding 300 m. Bicycle hire 5 km. Excursions.

Open: 28 February - 31 October.

Directions

Site is on main N340 Cádiz road at 78.87 km. marker, 7.5 km. northwest of Tarifa. Large modern signs well ahead of the site with a deceleration lane if approaching from the Tarifa direction. GPS: 36.0613, -5.6692

Charges guide

Per unit incl. 2 persons and electricity	€ 26.50 - € 28.00

Camping Cheques accepted.

Torre del Mar

Camping Caravaning Laguna Playa

Prolongacion Paseo Maritimo, E-29740 Torre del Mar (Málaga) T: 952 540 631. E: info@lagunaplaya.com

alanrogers.com/ES87820

Laguna Playa is a pleasant and peaceful site run by a father and son team (the son speaks excellent English) and they give a personal service, alongside one of the Costa del Sol beaches. Trips are organised to the famous Alhambra Palace in Granada on a weekly basis and the site is well placed for visits to Malaga and Nerja. The 142 touring pitches are flat, of average size and with good artificial shade supplementing that provided by the many established trees on site. All pitches have electricity (10A). The busy restaurant with a terrace offers good value for money and many locals use it.

Facilities

Two well equipped, modern, sanitary blocks, both recently refurbished, can be heated. Baby baths. Good facilities for disabled campers. Laundry facilities. Supermarket. Bar and busy restaurant also used by locals (closed for two weeks in May and Oct). Swimming pools (high season). Play area. Children's entertainment. Spanish classes in low season. Dancing classes. WiFi throughout (free).

Open: All year.

Directions

Site is on the seafront (oeste) of the town of Torre del Mar. Heading for the costa, go to the end of the 'paseo'. Site is on right. GPS: 36.72433, -4.10133

Charges guide

Per person	€ 5.55
pitch and car	€ 11.10 - € 11.85
electricity	€ 4.40

Torrox

Camping El Pino

Ctra Nacional 340 km. 285, Urb. Torrox Park s/n, E-29793 Torrox-Costa (Málaga) T: 952 530 006.
E: info@campingelpino.com **alanrogers.com/ES87810**

El Pino is in the Axarquia region of the Costa del Sol, east of Malaga and is surrounded by avocado groves. The site enjoys some fine views of the surrounding countryside. There are now 425 pitches here, mostly well shaded, and a further 47 mobile homes and chalets for rent. Most pitches have electrical connections and vary in size from 60-100 sq.m. The site is open all year and has some impressive facilities including a swimming pool, supermarket and bar/restaurant. The nearest beach is 800 m. distant – a bus service runs there from the site. El Pino can be found close to Torrox Costa, an area claiming to have the best climate in Europe. The old village of Torrox, like many in the area, has traces of its Arabic origins, with narrow, winding streets and whitewashed houses. Torrox Costa is quite different and has been extensively but attractively developed with a lighthouse at one end and a fine sandy beach, the Playa Ferrara.

Facilities

Toilet block with hot showers and individual cabins. Facilities for disabled visitors. Laundry facilities. Bar, restaurant and shop (all year). Takeaway. Swimming pool with new children's pool (1/6-15/9). Play area. Games room. Pétanque. Children's club. Free WiFi over site. Mobile homes and chalets for rent. Communal barbecue – only gas or electric barbecues permitted on pitches. Off site: Nearest beach 800 m. Fishing and boat launching 1 km. Riding 8 km. Golf 9 km. Malaga 45 km.

Open: All year.

Directions

Leave the A7 Autovia del Mediterraneo at exit 285 (Torrox) and follow signs to Torrox Costa. Site is well signed from here. GPS: 36.739245, -3.949713

Charges guide

Per unit incl. 2 persons and electricity	€ 17.00 - € 22.00
extra person	€ 3.00 - € 4.25
child (under 10 yrs)	€ 2.00 - € 3.00
dog	€ 1.50 - € 2.50

Trevélez

Camping Trevélez

Ctra Trevélez-Orgiva km. 1, E-18417 Trevélez (Granada) T: 958 858 735. E: info@campingtrevelez.net
alanrogers.com/ES92890

Set high up in the Alpujarras region of the Sierra Nevada, Camping Trevélez is a super site that was bought in 2005 by the resident owners, Richard and Alexandra. Since taking over they have worked tirelessly to improve the site and each year have made significant progress. The site, which is open all year, is reached via a narrow, winding road and is ideally suited to tents and smaller motorcaravans which are sited on terraced plots, each with spectacular mountain views. Twenty of the 94 touring pitches have 4-6A electricity. Sit outside at night and wonder at the stars above but make sure you have a torch; it gets very dark at night.

Facilities

One sanitary block, recently redecorated, provides toilets, washbasins and shower cubicles. Facilities for disabled visitors. Washing machine and dryer. Shop. Bar and restaurant. Play area. Swimming pool (1/6-15/9). Barbecues only allowed in designated areas and not at all 15/6-15/10. Fishing. Riding. Free WiFi over part of site.

Open: All year.

Directions

From A44 (E902) Granada-Motril road, exit at 164 km. onto A348. At Orgiva take A4132 for 32 km. to Trevelez. Road is winding and very narrow in places so unsuitable for large units.
GPS: 36.99181, -3.27753

Charges guide

Per unit incl. 2 persons and electricity	€ 24.05 - € 26.95
extra person	€ 4.65
child (under 12 yrs)	€ 3.10

This is one of the most beautiful, and perhaps least known, regions of inland Spain. Its beautiful cities, first Roman and Moorish, then medieval and aristocratic, gave birth to many of the conquistadors – conquerors of the New World.

EXTREMADURA HAS TWO PROVINCES: BADAJOZ AND CÁCERES

Extremadura is a large and sparsely populated region in the west of Spain, bordering central Portugal and consisting of two provinces, both of which bear the name of their main town. Cáceres, to the north, has a fascinating old quarter, ringed by old Moorish walls and superb watchtowers. Nearby Plasencia is home to a splendid Gothic cathedral, old medieval walls and beautiful Baroque and Renaissance palaces. And the attractive town of Trujillo, birthplace of Pizzaro, the conqueror of Peru, has palaces, churches and a bustling town square. To the south is Badajoz, the second province and the largest in Spain. With its fortified main town and Alcazaba (citadel), the city of Badajoz is located on the Vía de la Plata (Silver Route), an old pilgrimage route to Santiago de Compostela used during the Middle Ages. Located on this route, Mérida is one of the best preserved archaeological sites in Spain. Indeed, the city boasts more Roman remains than any other city, including a Roman theatre and amphitheatre, a Roman bridge spanning over 800 metres long, with 60 arches, Roman villas and the Museum of Roman Art.

Places of interest

Alcántara: six-arched Roman bridge, castle, mansions.

Corio: quiet old town enclosed by 4th-century Roman walls, cathedral.

Cuacos de Yuste: town with 15th-century Jeronimos Monastery.

Guadalupe: old pilgrimage centre, church and monastery.

Jerez de los Caballeros: birthplace of various conquistadors.

Olivenza: town with strong Portuguese influence, castle, ethnographic museum, 17th-century church.

Pedroso de Acim: Convento del Palancar – said to be the smallest monastery in the world.

Cuisine of the region

Local cuisine includes Iberian cured ham and a variety of cheeses; *Torta del Casar, La Serena, Ibores, Gata* and *Cabra del Tietar*. Game abounds in this region (partridge, pigeon, turtle dove, rabbit, hare, wild boar, deer) served with wild mushrooms, truffles or wild asparagus. Honey, thyme, heather, rosemary, lavender, lime and eucalyptus are used to prepare a great variety of desserts.

Alfeñiques: caramel dessert.

Nuégados: egg yolk and orange buns.

Perrunillas: small round cakes.

Rosquillas: ring-shaped biscuits.

Técula-mécula: cinnamon, almond and tea.

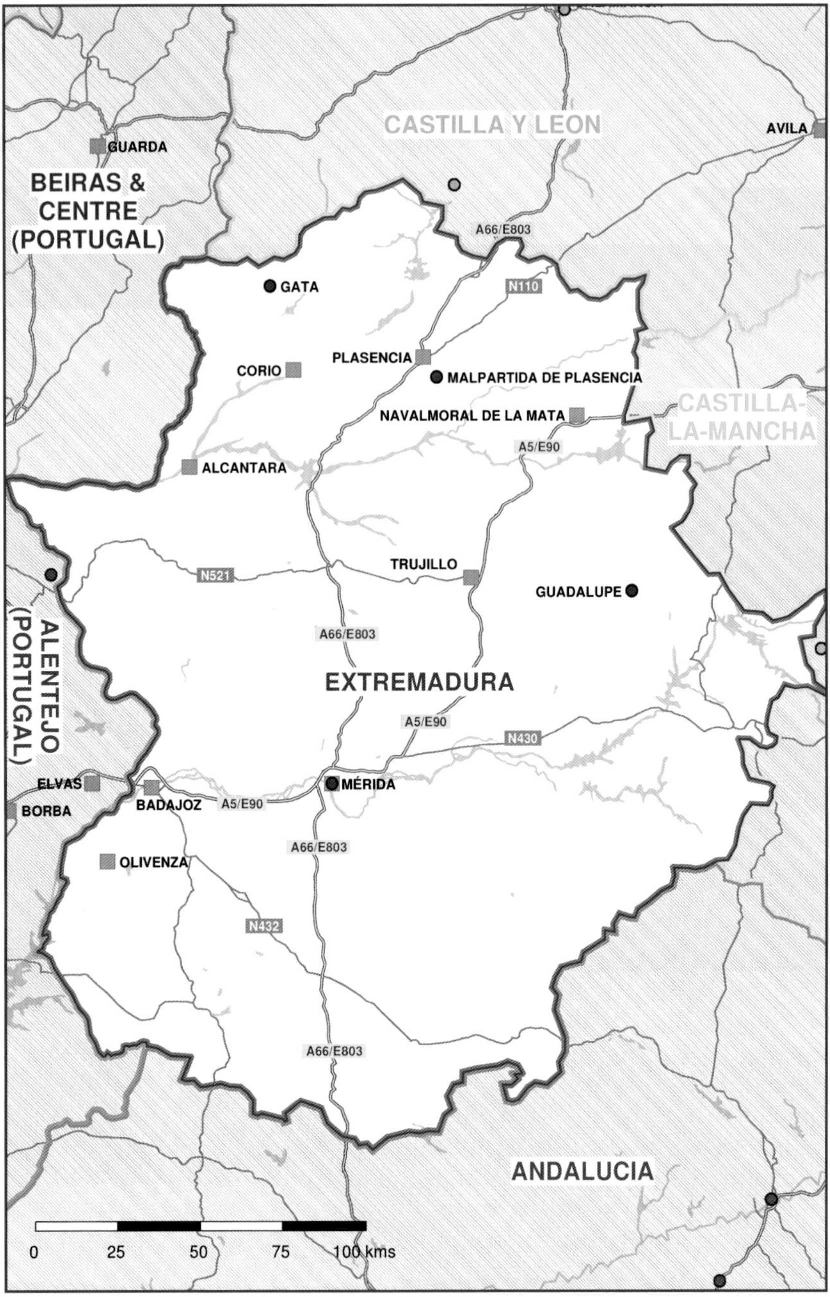
CASTILLA Y LEON
AVILA
GUARDA
BEIRAS &
CENTRE
(PORTUGAL)
A66/E803
GATA
N110
PLASENCIA
CORIO
MALPARTIDA DE PLASENCIA
NAVALMORAL DE LA MATA
CASTILLA-
LA-MANCHA
A5/E90
ALCANTARA
TRUJILLO
N521
GUADALUPE
ALENTEJO
(PORTUGAL)
A66/E803
EXTREMADURA
A5/E90
N430
ELVAS
MÉRIDA
BORBA
BADAJOZ
A5/E90
A66/E803
OLIVENZA
N432
A66/E803
ANDALUCIA
0
25
50
75
100 kms

Gata

Camping Sierra de Gata

Ctra Ex109 a Gata km. 4,1, E-10860 Gata (Cáceres) T: 927 672 168. E: cgata@turiex.com

alanrogers.com/ES94000

For a taste of the real, rural Spain, this very Spanish site (no English was spoken when we visited) is situated just before the tiny village of Sierra de Gata, south of Ciudad Rodrigo and northwest of Plasencia. Situated in beautiful countryside with a small stream alongside the site, the pitches are on grass with plenty of shade from trees. There are 12 bungalows to sleep four to six people. A special area with huts for groups of children to stay is positioned in one corner of the site.

Facilities

Two toilet blocks with British style toilets also include child size toilets, a laundry room and dishwashing facilities. Medium sized shop for necessities in summer. Smart restaurant/bar complex provides good food. Two swimming pools. Tennis. Play area. Fishing. Riding. Bicycle hire. Off site: Restaurant near site entrance.

Open: 15 January - 14 December.

Directions

Approach ONLY from the southwest from the 109 Ciudad Rodrico-Coria road. Where the 205 meets the 109 take turn 20-30 m. north signed Gata 10. Travel along this road until km. 4. Turn left (near restaurant and small bridge) and site is ahead through gate. GPS: 40.21195, -6.64224

Charges guide

Per person	€ 4.00 - € 4.50
child (3-12 yrs)	€ 3.50 - € 4.00
pitch	€ 8.00 - € 8.75
electricity	€ 4.50 - € 5.00

Guadalupe

Camping Las Villuercas

Ctra Villanueva, E-10140 Guadalupe (Cáceres) T: 927 367 139.

alanrogers.com/ES90280

This rural site nestles in an attractive valley northwest of Guadalupe. The 50 pitches (half of them with 10A electricity) are level and of a reasonable size; although large units may experience difficulty in getting into the more central pitches. With an abundance of mature trees most pitches offer some degree of shade. A river runs alongside the site and the ground can be muddy in very wet periods. The site is co-located with hostel accommodation. The restaurant provides excellent food at low prices and leads to a pretty patio with overhead vines and potted plants allowing elevated views of the pools.

Facilities

The single toilet block is older but very clean, with one area for women and one for men, providing British style toilets, washbasins and showers (hot water is from a 40-litre immersion heater which could be overwhelmed in busy periods). Facilities for disabled visitors. Laundry facilities. Restaurant. Bar. Swimming pools. Shop. Tennis. Small playground. Barbecue area. No English spoken. Off site: Riding 2 km. Fishing 3 km.

Open: 1 March - 30 November.

Directions

From NV/E90 (Madrid-Mérida) exit at Navelmoral de la Mata. Follow south to Guadalupe on CC713 (83 km). Site is 2 km. from Guadalupe (near Monastery). From further southwest take exit 102 off E90/NV (northeast of Mérida). Follow signs (Guadalupe). Near 72 km. marker turn left to site in 100 m. GPS: 39.441228, -5.322

Charges guide

Per person	€ 3.50
child (2-12 yrs)	€ 3.00
pitch	€ 9.50
electricity	€ 3.00

No credit cards.

Malpartida de Plasencia

Camping Parque Natural de Monfrague

Ctra Plasencia-Trujillo km. 10, E-10680 Malpartida de Plasencia (Cáceres) T: 927 459 233.
E: contacto@campingmonfrague.com **alanrogers.com/ES90270**

Situated on the edge of the Monfrague National Park, this well managed site owned by the Barrado family, has fine views to the Sierra de Mirabel and delightful surrounding countryside. Many of the 130 good sized grass pitches are on slightly sloping, terraced ground. Scattered trees offer a degree of shade, there are numerous water points and 10A electricity. It would prove difficult to find a more suitable location for those that savour tranquillity. On rare occasions, a goods train travels along the nearby railway line. Created as a national park in 1979, Monfrague is now recognised as one of the best locations in Europe for anyone interested in birdwatching.

Facilities

Large modern toilet blocks, fully equipped, are very clean. Facilities for disabled campers and baby baths. Laundry. Motorcaravan service point. Supermarket/shop. Restaurant, bar and coffee shop. TV room with recreational facilities. Swimming and paddling pools (June-Sept). Play area. Tennis. Entertainment for children in season. Barbecue areas. Free WiFi. Guided safaris into the Park for birdwatching. Off site: Large supermarket at Plasencia. Bicycle hire 2 km. Riding 6 km.

Open: All year.

Directions

On the N630, from the north take EX-208 (previously C524) Plasencia-Trujillo; site on left in 6 km. From the south turn right just south of Plasencia on EX-108 (previously C511) in direction of Malpartida de Plasencia. Right at main exit onto EX-208 to site. GPS: 39.9395, -6.084

Charges guide

Per unit incl. 2 persons and electricity	€ 20.10 - € 20.40
extra person	€ 4.20
child (3-12 yrs)	€ 3.80

Camping Cheques accepted.

Mérida

Camping Mérida

Ctra NV Madrid-Portugal km. 336,6, E-06800 Mérida (Badajoz) T: 924 303 453. E: proexcam@jet.es
alanrogers.com/ES90870

Camping Mérida is situated alongside the main NV road to Madrid, the restaurant, café and pool complex separating the camping area from the road, where there is considerable noise. The site has 80 good sized pitches, most with some shade and on sloping ground, with ample electricity connections (long leads may be needed) and hedges with imaginative topiary. No English is spoken, but try out your Spanish. Reception is open until midnight. Camping Mérida is ideally located to serve both as a base to tour the local area and as an overnight stop en route when travelling either north/south or east/west.

Facilities

The central sanitary facility includes hot and cold showers, British style WCs. Gas supplies. Small shop for essentials. Busy restaurant/cafeteria and bar, also open to the public. Medium sized swimming and paddling pools (May-Sept). Bicycle hire. Play area (unfenced and near road). Caravan storage. Torches useful. Off site: Town 5 km.

Open: All year.

Directions

Site is alongside NV road (Madrid-Lisbon), 5 km. east of Mérida, at km. 336.6. From east take exit 334 and follow camping signs (doubling back). Site is actually on the 630 road that runs alongside the new motorway. GPS: 38.9348, -6.3043

Charges guide

Per person	€ 3.15
child	€ 2.70
pitch incl. car	€ 19.50
electricity	€ 3.15

This region is located south of Madrid and occupies what was the southern part of the ancient kingdom of Castille, including the area known as La Mancha, universally famous as the setting for Miguel de Cervantes great novel 'Don Quijote de la Mancha'.

CASTILLA-LA MANCHA HAS FIVE PROVINCES: ALBACETE, CIUDAD REAL, CUENCA, GUADALAJARA AND TOLEDO

THE CAPITAL OF THE REGION IS TOLEDO

The terrain can be divided into two distinct parts: the plateau, an extensive, flat land with very few mountains, and the mountainous areas, which encircle the plateau around the region's borders, including the foothills along the massifs of the Central mountain range, the Iberian mountain range and the Sierra Morena. Toledo is crammed with monuments and nearly all the different stages of Spanish art are represented with Moorish-Mudejar-Jewish buildings; Gothic structures, such as the splendid cathedral; and Renaissance buildings. Toledo was also home to El Greco and many of his paintings are displayed in the Museum of El Greco. The region of Cuenca is surrounded by mountainous, craggy countryside, with the city itself home to extraordinary houses which hang over the cliff tops of the deep gorges. One of these has been converted into the Museum of Abstract Art. In the heartland of La Mancha, through the region of Ciudad Real, you can follow the Ruta de Don Quijote and see the famous windmills at Campo de Criptana.

Places of interest

Almagro: home of international theatre festival.

Albacete: renowned for its knife-making industry, 16th-century cathedral.

Guadalajara: preserved Moorish walls, 10th-century bridge, Santa Maria la Mayor, 15th-century Duque del Infantado Palace.

Cuisine of the region

Local produce features heavily: aubergines, garlic, peppers, tomatoes, olive oil, meat, including both game and farm animals. Wine from La Mancha, Valdepeñas, Méntrida, Almansa, Dominio de Valdepusa and Finca de Elez.

Alajú: an almond and nut pastry.

Bizcochás de Alcázar: a tart soaked in milk with sugar, vanilla and cinnamon.

Caldereta manchega: lamb stew.

Morteruelo: pâté made of pork and game birds.

Pisto manchego: a type of ratatouille with tomatoes, red and green peppers, courgettes, served either hot or cold.

Tiznao: filleted cod which is flame-grilled in an earthenware dish with pepper, tomatoes, onions and garlic.

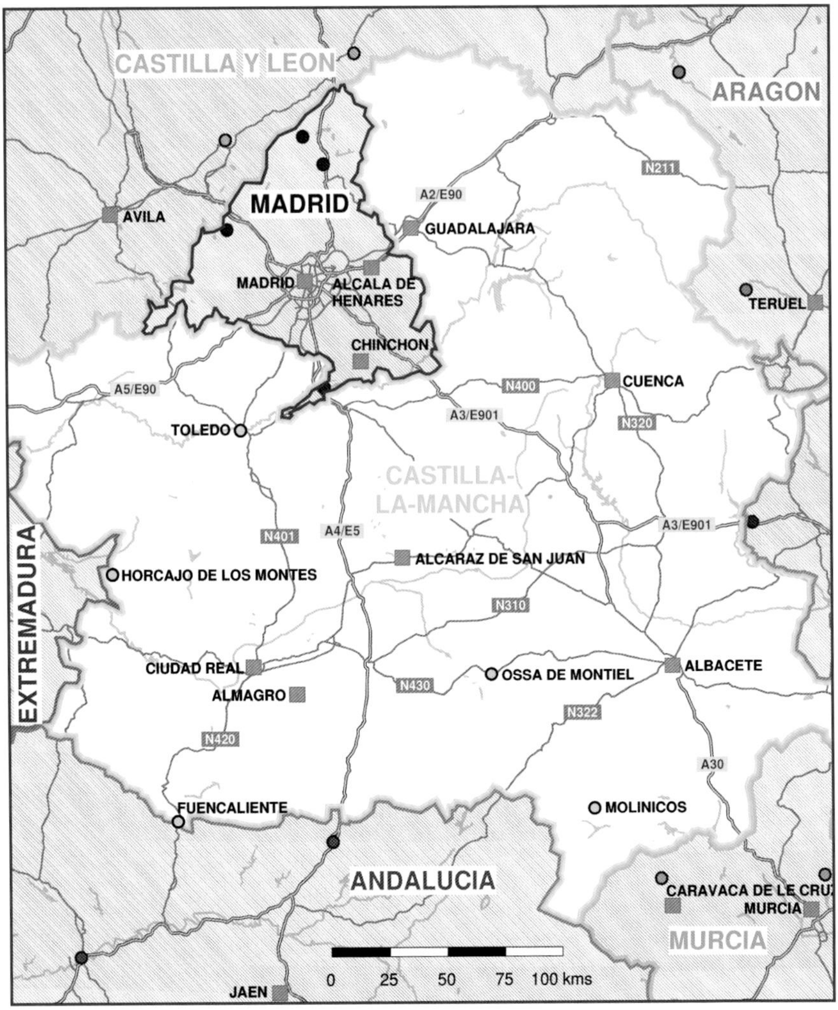

Fuencaliente

Camping de Fuencaliente

Ctra N420 km. 105,8, E-13130 Fuencaliente (Ciudad Real) T: 926 698 170. E: raquel@campingfuencaliente.es

alanrogers.com/ES90880

This quiet site nestles in an attractive valley between the Sierra Modrona and the Sierra Morena. It is ideal for getting away from it all and sampling the peaceful mountain beauty. It could be a useful stopover if crossing Spain coast to coast or if you wish to visit the fascinating historic town of Córdoba. With very few other desirable sites in this region of Castilla - La Mancha, this one is spacious with 91 generously sized pitches (over 100 sq.m) all with electricity (6A) and water. There is natural shade from pine trees and beautiful, restful views.

Facilities

The large, modern toilet block has reasonable facilities. Laundry sinks. Washing machine. Swimming pool (1/6-15/9; free). Restaurant/bar. Supermarket. Playground. Barbecue area with table and benches overlooking the countryside. Off site: Fuencaliente 5 km.

Open: Easter - 30 September.

Directions

From the N420 road (Cuidad Real-Córdoba) turn by 105 km. marker (about 5 km. north of Fuencaliente) onto unmade road signed Camping San Isidro to site. GPS: 38.442, -4.32

Charges guide

Per person	€ 5.00
child (2-10 yrs)	€ 4.50 - € 5.00
pitch incl. electricity	€ 8.00 - € 9.00
dog	€ 4.00 - € 4.50

Horcajo de Los Montes

Camping El Mirador de Cabaneros

alan rogers Winner 2013 Awards

Canada Real Segoviana s/n, E-13110 Horcajo de Los Montes (Ciudad Real) T: 926 775 439.
E: info@campingcabaneros.com **alanrogers.com/ES90960**

With panoramic views all around of the Sierra de Valdefuertes mountains, Camping El Mirador is set in the Cabaneros National Park. This is a well cared for, landscaped site with 80 terraced pitches on gravel and all with electricity. Although level once sited, the approach is via a steep slope which may cause difficulties for larger units. Run by a very helpful and friendly family, this site is in a peaceful location where you can just sit and relax or visit the many attractions that the national park has to offer. It is an ideal base for walking and birdwatching.

Facilities

One spotlessly clean central toilet block with solar heating includes open washbasins and cubicle showers. Facilities for disabled visitors and babies. Laundry facilities. Motorcaravan services. No shop but bread and gas from reception. Bar and restaurant (15/6-15/9, weekends in low season). Outdoor swimming pool. Games room. Basic (unfenced) play area. Off site: Village of Horcajo de los Montes 200 m.

Open: All year.

Directions

From north head towards Toledo. At Toledo, take CM4013 to Cuerva and pick up CM403 to El Molinillo. Turn right on CM4017 to Horcajo de los Montes. Through village onto CM4016 towards Alcoba de los Montes, past garage and up hill for 2 km. Site is on left (narrow approach).
GPS: 39.3219, -4.6495

Charges guide

Per person	€ 4.80 - € 5.20
child	€ 3.70 - € 3.90
pitch	€ 7.70 - € 9.90
electricity	€ 4.20

Molinicos

Campingred Rio Mundo

Ctra Comarcal 412 km. 205, Mesones, E-02449 Molinicos (Albacete) T: 967 433 230.
E: riomundo@campingriomundo.com **alanrogers.com/ES90980**

This uncomplicated and typically Spanish site is situated in the Sierra de Alcaraz (south of Albacete), just off the scenic route 412 between Elche de la Sierra and Valdepenas. The drive to this site is most enjoyable through beautiful scenery and from the west the main road is winding in some places. Shade is provided by mature trees for the 80 pitches and electricity (6/10A) is supplied to 70 (long leads are useful). It is in a beautiful setting with majestic mountains and wonderful countryside which begs to be explored.

Facilities

One toilet block has been upgraded and provides clean modern facilities. Basic toilet facilities for disabled visitors. Washing machine. Small shop for basics. Outside bar serving snacks with covered seating area. Takeaway (all 15/3-12/10). Another bar by the swimming pool. Playground. Pétanque. Free WiFi over part of site. Only gas and electric barbecues permitted. Off site: Riding 7 km.

Open: 15 March - 12 October.

Directions

Site is off the 412 road which runs west to east between the A30 and 322 south of Albacete. Turn at km. 205 on the 412, 5 km. east of Riopar and west of Elche de la Sierra. From here follow signs to site. The road narrows to one lane for a few hundred yards. GPS: 38.48917, -2.34639

Charges guide

Per person	€ 4.50 - € 6.10
child	€ 3.10 - € 4.25
pitch incl. car	€ 11.20 - € 15.30
electricity (6/10A)	€ 3.80 - € 5.35
dog	€ 3.40

Ossa de Montiel

Camping Los Batanes

Ctra Lagunas de Ruidera km. 8, E-02611 Ossa de Montiel (Albacete) T: 926 699 076.

E: camping@losbatanes.com **alanrogers.com/ES90970**

This large campsite is in a lovely setting at the side of one of the many lakes in this area. The route to the site is beautiful and it is well worth the trip, but careful driving was necessary in parts with our large motorcaravan. A smaller, older part of the campsite houses reception, a small shop and a bar/restaurant. Here are medium sized pitches, shaded by pine trees with a small river running through. Over a wooden bridge is the main, newer part of the site with over 200 level, gravel and sand pitches of mixed sizes, shaded again by pine trees.

Facilities

One old toilet block and a newer, more spacious one. If cleaning is maintained they should cope in high season. Small shop. Simple restaurant, snacks and bar. Swimming pools (16/6-9/9). Play area. Children's activities.
Off site: Beautiful walks and many lakes to explore. Watersports in summer. Tourist information either at reception or at nearest village 9 km. Bus stop in village.

Open: All year.

Directions

On E5/NIV Córdoba-Madrid road (south of Madrid) take 430 road towards Albacete. Coming into Ruidera turn right (just after lake on the right) signed Lagunas de Ruideria. Drive 8 km. along this country road to site on right. GPS: 38.93717, -2.84744

Charges guide

Per person	€ 4.25 - € 6.00
child (1-13 yrs)	€ 3.50 - € 5.00
pitch	€ 4.25 - € 6.00
electricity (6A)	€ 3.50 - € 3.80

Discounts for longer stays.

Toledo

Camping El Greco

Ctra CM4000 km. 0,7, Puebla de Montalban, E-45004 Toledo (Toledo) T: 925 220 090.

E: campingelgreco@telefonica.net **alanrogers.com/ES90900**

Toledo was the home of the Grecian painter, El Greco, and the site that bears his name boasts a beautiful view of the ancient city from the restaurant, bar and superb pool. The friendly, family owners make you welcome and are proud of their site, which is the only one in Toledo (it can get crowded). The 150 pitches are of 80 sq.m. with electrical connections (5/10A) and shade from strategically planted trees. Most have separating hedges that give privacy, with others in herringbone layouts that make for interesting parking in some areas. The River Tagus stretches alongside the site which is fenced for safety. There is an attractive, tree-lined approach to the site.

Facilities

Two sanitary blocks, both modernised, one with facilities for disabled campers. Everything is of the highest standard and kept very clean. Laundry. Motorcaravan services. Swimming pool (15/6-15/9, charged). Restaurant/bar (1/4-30/9) with good menu and fair prices. Small shop in reception. Playgrounds. Ice machine.
Off site: Fishing in river. Golf 10 km. Riding 15 km.
An hourly air-conditioned bus service runs from the gates to the city centre, touring the outside of the walls first.

Open: All year.

Directions

Site is on C4000 road on the edge of the town, signed towards Puebla de Montelban; site signs also in city centre. From Madrid on N401, turn off right towards city centre but turn right at the roundabout at the old city gates. Site is signed from the next right turn. GPS: 39.865, -4.047

Charges guide

Per unit incl. 2 persons and electricity	€ 30.60
extra person	€ 6.65
child (3-10 yrs)	€ 5.75

The region of Madrid lies right in the middle of the Spanish mainland bordering Castilla-La Mancha and Castilla and Leon. At the centre lies the city of Madrid, which since the 16th century has been the country's capital.

THE REGION OF MADRID IS A ONE PROVINCE AUTONOMY, ALSO CALLED MADRID

The mountainous region of Madrid can be divided into two areas: the Sierra, in the north and west of the region, which includes part of Somosierra and Guadarrama; and the central and southern parts, where the area is flatter and forms part of the plateau of La Mancha and La Alcarria. Founded by the Moors in the ninth century, Madrid is now a modern, vibrant city offering innumerable attractions to the visitor. Its architectural heritage is immense. Some of the oldest parts of Madrid lie around the Puerta del Sol, a good starting place for exploring the city. Full of outdoor restaurants and bars, Plaza Mayor is considered to be one of the finest in Spain, and in summer becomes an outdoor theatre and music stage. The city also has a large number of parks and gardens, among them El Retiro, the Botanical Gardens, the Parque del Oeste and the Casa de Campo; and numerous museums and art galleries. Outside the capital, the Sierra de Madrid is ideal for winter sports and the beautiful town of Aranjuez, home to the Royal Palace and glorious gardens, is a popular retreat from the city.

Places of interest

Alcala de Henares: university town, birthplace of Cervantes, author of Don Quijote, Cervantes House Museum, Archepiscopal Palace Cathedral.

Chinchón: 15th-century castle, beautiful medieval square, 19th-century church with painting by Goya, home of Alchoholera de Chinchón – aniseed liqueur!

Parque Natural de la Cumbre: mountain park, the highest mountains in the Madrid region.

San Lorenzo de El Escorial: town in heart of Guadarrama Mountains, Monastery of El Escorial, Royal Pantheon.

Cuisine of the region

Tapas is popular with typical dishes including seafood: steamed mussels, anchovies in vinegar and pickled bonito plus croquettes and mini-casseroles. Sea bream and cod are used a lot. Local produce includes beef from the Guadarrama Mountains, olives from Campo Real, aniseed from Chinchón and asparagus from Aranjuez. Madrid is also a good place to experience every regional style of Spanish cooking.

Buñuelos: a type of fritter which is filled with custard, chocolate and cream.

Cocido: meat, potato and chickpea stew.

Con gabardina: prawns cooked in beer.

Torrijas: bread pudding.

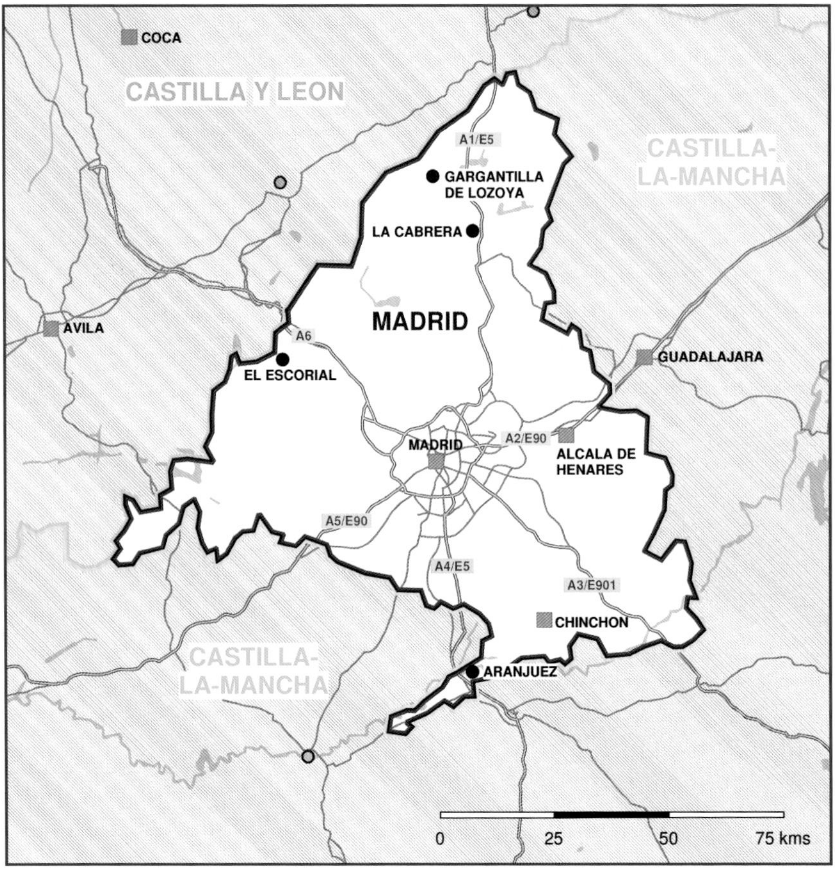
COCA
CASTILLA Y LEON
CASTILLA-
LA-MANCHA
A1/E5
GARGANTILLA
DE LOZOYA
LA CABRERA
MADRID
AVILA
A6
EL ESCORIAL
GUADALAJARA
A2/E90
MADRID
ALCALA DE
HENARES
A5/E90
A4/E5
A3/E901
CHINCHON
CASTILLA-
LA-MANCHA
ARANJUEZ
0
25
50
75 kms

Aranjuez

Camping Internacional Aranjuez

Soto del Rebollo, s/n antigua NIV km 46,8, E-28300 Aranjuez (Madrid) T: 918 911 395.
E: info@campingaranjuez.com **alanrogers.com/ES90910**

Aranjuez, supposedly Spain's version of Versailles, is worthy of a visit with its beautiful palaces, leafy squares, avenues and gardens. This useful, popular and unusually well equipped site is therefore excellent for enjoying the unusual attractions or for an en route stop. It is 47 km. south of Madrid and 46 km. from Toledo. The site is alongside the River Tajo in a park-like situation with mature trees. There are 162 touring pitches, all with electricity (16A), set on flat grass amid tall trees. The site was bought by the owners of la Marina (ES87420) who have worked hard to improve the pitches and the site. Two little tourist road trains run from the site to the palaces daily. You can visit the huge, but slightly decaying, Royal Palace or the Casa del Labrador (translates as farmer's cottage) which is a small neo-classical palace in unusual and differing styles. It has superb gardens commissioned by Charles II. Canoes may be hired from behind the supermarket and there is a lockable moat gate to allow access to the river. There is good security backed up with CCTV around the river perimeter.

Facilities

The largest of three modern, good quality sanitary blocks is heated in winter and well equipped with some washbasins in cabins. Laundry facilities. Gas supplies. Small shop, bar and restaurant (all year) with attractive riverside patio (also open to the public). Takeaway. TV room. Swimming and paddling pools, (1/5-15/10). New play area. Pétanque. Bicycle hire. Canoe hire. WiFi (free). Torch useful. Off site: Within easy walking distance of palace, gardens and museums. Golf 2 km.

Open: All year.

Directions

From the M305 (Madrid-Aranjuez) look for 8 km. marker on the outskirts of town. Then follow campsite signs leading back onto the M305 (going north now). Site is signed right at 300 m. on first left bend. Coming from the south ensure you have the M305 Madrid (other roads are signed to Madrid). GPS: 40.0426, -3.5995

Charges guide

Per unit incl. 2 persons and electricity	€ 25.10 - € 35.10
extra person	€ 4.50 - € 6.00

Gargantilla del Lozoya

Camping Monte Holiday

alan rogers Runner up 2013 Awards

Ctra Rascafria-Lozoya km. 9, Finca El Tercio Nuevo s/n, E-28739 Gargantilla del Lozoya (Madrid)
T: 918 695 278. E: monteholiday@monteholiday.com **alanrogers.com/ES92120**

The Somosierra offers spectacular scenery and is very popular with Spanish skiers. This site is situated in an open, sunny lower valley, in the Madrid area's only beech forest near a large nature reserve. The area is ideal for anglers and walkers and also offers many opportunities for outdoor sports enthusiasts. The site is on terraces and has 308 small pitches with 100 for touring (50 with electricity 5/7A Europlug; long leads required in some areas). These pitches are mainly flat with grass or gravel surfaces and shade from mature trees, but unfortunately are very uneven. The upper area is taken by permanent units.

Facilities

The modern, heated and well equipped toilet block is well maintained. Facilities for disabled visitors and babies. Laundry facilities. Motorcaravan services. Shop. Bar and fair quality restaurant (15/6-15/9, bank holidays and weekends). Swimming pool (mid June-mid Sept). Multisports court. Tennis. Table tennis. Beach volleyball. Play area. Gas supplies. Bicycle hire. WiFi (free).

Open: All year.

Directions

From A1 motorway (Burgos-Madrid) take exit 69 towards Rascafria. Turn right after passing under a railway tunnel and site is on left after 800 m. GPS: 40.949917, -3.729267

Charges guide

Per unit incl. 2 persons and electricity	€ 27.10 - € 29.90

Camping Cheques accepted.

El Escorial

Caravanning El Escorial

Ctra M600 km. 3,5, E-28280 El Escorial (Madrid) T: 902 014 900. E: info@campingelescorial.com

alanrogers.com/ES92000

There is a shortage of good sites in the central regions of Spain, but this is one. El Escorial is very large, there are 1,358 individual pitches of which about 600 are for touring, with the remainder used for permanent or seasonal units, but situated to one side of the site. The pitches are shaded (ask for a pitch without a low tree canopy if you have a 3 m. high motorcaravan). There are another 250 pseudo 'wild' spaces for tourists on open fields, with good shade from mature trees (long cables may be necessary for electricity). The general amenities are good and include three swimming pools (unheated), plus a paddling pool in a central area with a bar/restaurant with a terrace and plenty of grassy sitting out areas. At weekends in high season the site can be noisy. It is well situated for sightseeing visits, especially to the magnificent El Escorial monastery (5 km). Also, the enormous civil war monument of the Valle de los Caidos is very close, while both Madrid and Segovia are 50 km. away.

Facilities

One large toilet block for the touring pitches, plus two smart, small blocks for the 'wild' camping area, are all fully equipped with some washbasins in cabins. Baby baths. Facilities for disabled campers. The blocks can be heated. Large supermarket, restaurant/bar and snack bar/takeaway (all year; w/ends only in low season). Disco-bar. Swimming pools (15/5-15/9). Three tennis courts. Two well equipped playgrounds on sand. ATM.
Off site: Town 3 km. Riding and golf 7 km.

Open: All year.

Directions

From the south go through town of El Escorial, and follow M600 Guadarrama road. Site is between the 2 and 3 km. markers north of the town on the right. From the north use A6 autopista exit 47 to M600 towards El Escorial town. Site is on the left.
GPS: 40.62400, -4.099

Charges guide

Per unit incl. 2 persons and electricity	€ 29.80 - € 36.20
extra person	€ 5.90 - € 7.10
child (3-10 yrs)	€ 4.00 - € 6.50

No credit cards.

La Cabrera

Camping Pico de la Miel

Ctra A1, Salida 57, E-28751 La Cabrera (Madrid) T: 918 688 082. E: info@picodelamiel.com

alanrogers.com/ES92100

Pico de la Miel is a very large site 60 km. north of Madrid. Mainly a long stay site for Madrid, there are a huge number of very well established, fairly old statics. There is a small separate area with its own toilet block for the 80 touring units, all with electricity (8A Europlug). The pitches are on rather poor, sandy grass, but the artificial shade has been removed and trees planted. There are yet more pitches for tents (the ground could be hard for pegs). The noise level from the many Spanish customers is high and you will have a chance to practise your Spanish!

Facilities

Dated but clean tiled toilet block, with some washbasins in cabins. It can be heated. En-suite unit with ramp for disabled visitors. Motorcaravan services. Gas supplies. Shop. Restaurant/bar and takeaway (1/6-30/9 and weekends rest of year). Excellent swimming pool complex (15/6-15/9). Tennis. Playground. WiFi over site.
Off site: Bicycle hire and riding 500 m. Fishing 6 km.

Open: All year.

Directions

Site is well signed from the N1. Going south or north use exit 57 and follow site signs. When at T-junction, facing a hotel, turn left. (Exit 57 is closer to site than exit 60). GPS: 40.85797, -3.6158

Charges guide

Per unit incl. 2 persons and electricity	€ 27.10 - € 29.75
extra person	€ 6.20

The large region of Castilla y León is located inland, bordering Portugal to the west. It has a rich legacy dating back to the Romans, with an extraordinary wealth of castles, cathedrals and mansions, historic cities and towns.

THE REGION IS MADE UP OF THE FOLLOWING PROVINCES: AVILA, BURGOS, LEON, PALENCIA, SALAMANCA, VALLADOLID, ZAMORA, SEGOVIA AND SORIA

Steeped in history and architectural sights, the major towns and cities of the provinces all have something to offer. In the south, the town of Ávila is set on a high plain, surrounded by 11th-century walls; and the graceful city of Salamanca was once home to one of the most prestigious universities in the world. Its grand Plaza Mayor is the finest in Spain. In the east, Segovia is well known for its magnificent Roman aqueduct, with 163 arches and 29 metres at its highest point; the cathedral; and the fairytale Alcazár, complete with turrets and narrow towers. And the attractive city of Soria still retains a Romanesque legacy in its network of medieval streets. Burgos in the north, is the birthplace of El Cid and has a Gothic cathedral of exceptional quality. The lively university city of Leon boasts a Royal Pantheon, decorated by Romanesque wall paintings, and also an impressive Gothic cathedral. There is also a Gothic cathedral in Palencia plus an archaeology museum. South of León, the old walled quarters of Zamora have a retained medieval appearance, with a dozen Romanesque churches. And in the centre of the region, Valladolid is famous for its extravagant and solemn processions during the Holy Week celebrations.

Places of interest

Astorga: city of Roman origin, chocolate museum, cathedral.

Ciudad Rodrigo: Renaissance mansions, cathedral, 12th-century walls.

Coca: impressive Mudejar castle, birthplace of the famous Roman emperor Theodosius the Great.

Pantano de Burgomillodo: reservoir, great for birdwatchers.

Parque Natural del Cañón del Río Lobos: park created around the canyon of the River Lobos with rock formations, cave and good walking tracks.

Parque Natural del Lago de Sanabria y alrededores: mountainous area with deep valleys and glacier lagoons, variety of flora and fauna including 76 types of birds and 17 large mammals.

Cuisine of the region

The region is best known for its roast pork and lamb which has earned it the nickname *España del Asado* (Spain of the Roast). Other local products include trout from León and Zamora, and a variety of pulses: white, red and black beans, Castilian and *Pedrosillano* chickpeas, and various types of lentils. Soups feature a lot in winter: trout soup, typical of Órbigo de León; garlic soup; Zamora soup, a garlic soup with ripe tomatoes and hot chilli peppers.

Bizcochos de San Lorenzo: sponge cakes.

Farinatos: sausages made from breadcrumbs, pork fat and spices.

Hornazos: sausage and egg tarts.

Judias del barco con chorizo: haricot beans with sausage.

Yemas: a sweet made with egg yolks and sugar.

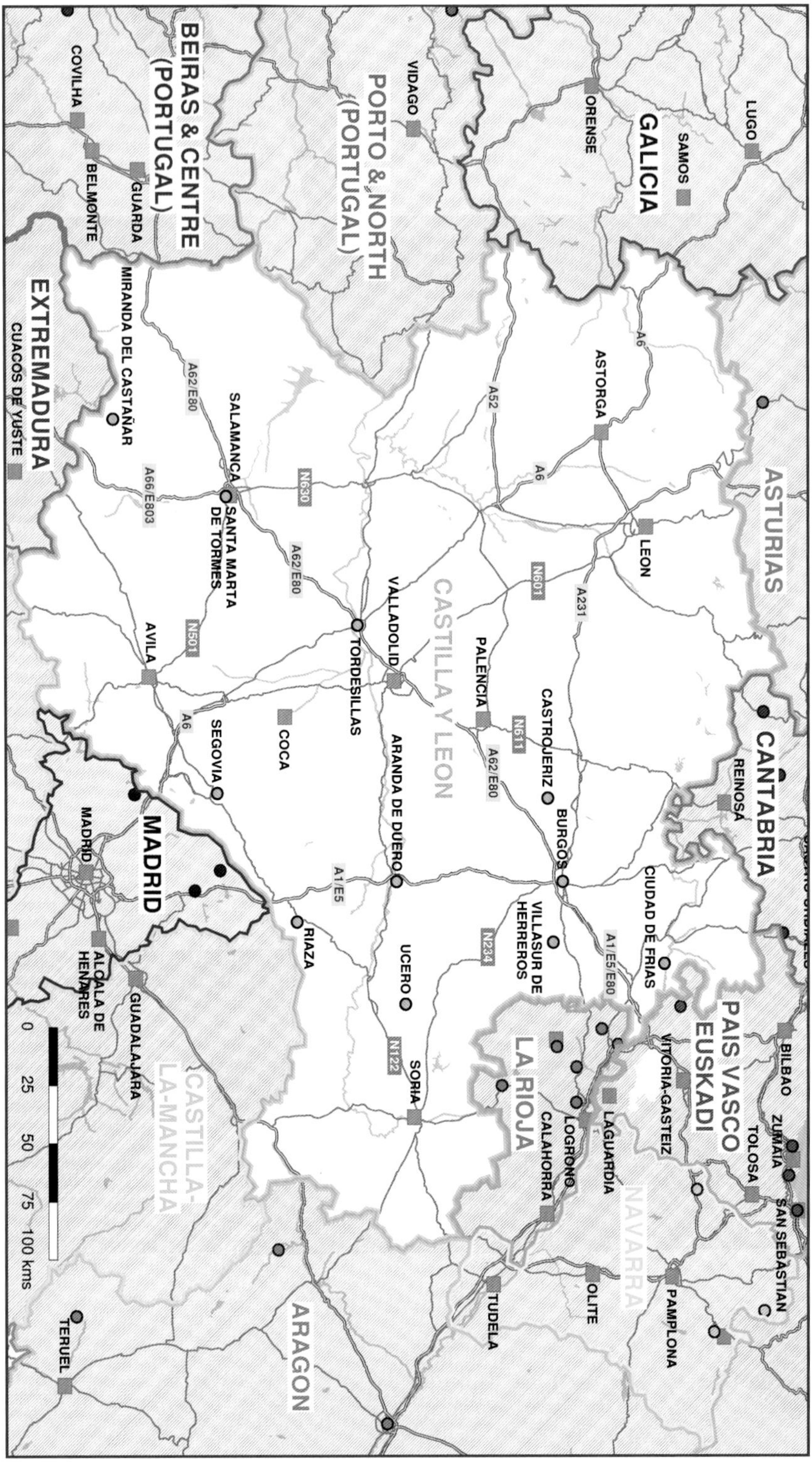
GALICIA
LUGO
SAMOS
ORENSE
VIDAGO
PORTO & NORTH (PORTUGAL)
BEIRAS & CENTRE (PORTUGAL)
COVILHA
BELMONTE
GUARDA
ASTURIAS
CANTABRIA
REINOSA
PAIS VASCO EUSKADI
BILBAO
ZUMAIA
TOLOSA
SAN SEBASTIAN
VITORIA-GASTEIZ
NAVARRA
PAMPLONA
OLITE
TUDELA
LA RIOJA
LAGUARDIA
LOGROÑO
CALAHORRA
ARAGON
TERUEL
CASTILLA-LA-MANCHA
GUADALAJARA
ALCALA DE HENARES
MADRID
EXTREMADURA
CUACOS DE YUSTE
MIRANDA DEL CASTAÑAR
SALAMANCA
SANTA MARTA DE TORMES
AVILA
SEGOVIA
COCA
TORDESILLAS
VALLADOLID
CASTILLA Y LEON
PALENCIA
ASTORGA
LEON
CASTROJERIZ
BURGOS
CIUDAD DE FRIAS
VILLASUR DE HERREROS
ARANDA DE DUERO
RIAZA
UCERO
SORIA
A6
A52
N630
A62/E80
A66/E803
N501
N601
A231
N611
A1/E5
A1/E5/E80
N234
N122
0 25 50 75 100 kms

Aranda de Duero

Camping Costajan

Ctra NI E-5 km. 164-165, E-09400 Aranda de Duero (Burgos) T: 947 502 070.
E: costajan@camping-costajan.com **alanrogers.com/ES92500**

This site is well placed as an en route stop for the ferries, being 80 km. south of Burgos. This is the capital of the Ribera del Duero wine region that produces many fine wines competing with the great Riojas. With 225 unmarked pitches, all with electricity, there are around 100 for all types of touring unit. Large units may find access a bit tricky among dense olive and pine trees and on the slightly undulating sandy ground, but the trees provide good shade. The welcome from Juan Carlos is warm and friendly (in any one of seven languages).

Facilities

Good, heated, modern sanitary facilities have hot and cold water. Facilities for disabled campers. Washing machine. Gas supplies. Shop with essentials (all year). Bar serving simple meals (all year). Free access to adjacent large swimming pool (June-Sept). Tennis. Minigolf. WiFi over site (charged). Torch useful. If reception is unmanned, choose a pitch and book in later.

Open: All year.

Directions

From A1/E5 take exit at 164.5 km. and turn south on N1 towards Aranda de Duero. The site is on the right at the 162 km. mark. GPS: 41.702, -3.68803

Charges guide

Per unit incl. 2 persons and electricity	€ 27.70 - € 29.50
extra person	€ 5.80 - € 6.00

Burgos

Camping Municipal Fuentes Blancas

Ctra Cartuja-Miraflores km. 3,5, E-09193 Burgos (Burgos) T: 947 486 016. E: info@campingburgos.com
alanrogers.com/ES90210

Fuentes Blancas is a comfortable municipal site on the edge of the historical town of Burgos and within easy reach of the Santander ferries. There are around 350 marked pitches of 70 sq.m. on flat ground, 250 with electrical connections (6A) and there is good shade in parts. The site has a fair amount of transit trade and reservations are not possible for August, so arrive early. Burgos is an attractive city, ideally placed for an overnight stop en route to or from the south of Spain. The old part of the city around the cathedral is quite beautiful and there are pleasant walks along the riverbanks outside the site gates.

Facilities

Clean, modern, fully equipped sanitary facilities in five blocks with controllable showers and hot and cold water to sinks (not all are always open). Facilities for babies. Washing machine/dryer. Motorcaravan service point. Small shop (high season). Bar/snack bar and restaurant (high season). Swimming pool (1/7-30/8). Playground. English is spoken. Off site: Fishing and river beach 200 m. Bus service to city or a fairly shaded walk. Golf 30 km.

Open: All year.

Directions

From the north (Santander) continue on N623 through city centre. Follow signs for E5/A1 Madrid. After crossing river take slip road for N120/A231 Leon but then turn left towards Fuentes Blancas and Cartuja de Miraflores for 3 km. Site is well signed on left. GPS: 42.34125, -3.65762

Charges guide

Per person	€ 5.04
pitch incl. electricity	€ 14.39

Castrojeriz

Camping Camino de Santiago

Avenida Virgen del Manzano s/n, E-09110 Castrojeriz (Burgos) T: 947 377 255. E: info@campingcamino.com
alanrogers.com/ES90230

This tranquil site lies to the west of Burgos on the outskirts of Castrojeriz, in a superb location, almost in the shadow of the ruined castle high on the hillside. The 50 marked pitches are level, grassy and divided by hedges, with electricity (10A). Mature trees provide shade and there is a pretty orchard in one corner of the site. This site is a birdwatchers' paradise – large raptors abound. The owner takes visitors out on birdwatching trips currently on an ad hoc basis but he is considering making it a more formal affair. For those who are interested in the pilgrimage to Santiago, the little town is on the ancient Roman road for the pilgrims.

Facilities

Older style sanitary block with hot showers, washbasin with cold water and British and Turkish style WCs. No facilities for disabled visitors. Washing machine. Bar/restaurant and takeaway with traditional cuisine. Bicycle hire. Library. Free WiFi over part of site. Games room. Tennis. Play area. Barbecue area. Ad hoc guided birdwatching. Off site: Fishing and riding 17 km. Nearest beach 100 km.

Open: 1 March - 30 November.

Directions

From N120/A231 (Leon-Burgos), turn on Bu404 (Villasandino, Castrojeriz). Turn left at crossroads on southwest side of town, then left at site sign. From A62 (Burgos-Valladolid) turn north at Vallaquirán on Bu400/401 to Castrojeriz. Turn sharp right at filling station and as above. GPS: 42.2913, -4.1448

Charges guide

Per unit incl. 2 persons and electricity	€ 24.00 - € 26.50

Ciudad de Frias

Camping Frias

E-09211 Ciudad de Frias (Burgos) T: 947 357 198. E: info@campingfrias.com

alanrogers.com/ES92570

Located in a natural park northeast of Burgos, on the edge of the old, small Spanish town of Frias, much of this site is taken up with static units. However, an area at the end is reserved for touring caravans and motorcaravans. A beautiful river runs alongside, about 20 feet below the campsite but with access for fishing, and the level, numbered pitches (30 for touring) have views across the really beautiful scenery surrounding the campsite. A little shade is provided from a few trees. This is a very Spanish site (no English was spoken when we visited). It may be noisy in summer with lively Spanish visitors but it was quiet when we visited in June.

Facilities

One toilet block provides basic facilities with British style WCs, washbasins with cold water only and coin operated showers. Washing machine and dryer. Shop with good range of produce (from 1/6). Bar and restaurant (from 1/6). Two swimming pools (22/6-15/9) and paddling pool. Off site: Transport is needed to visit any interesting places.

Open: 1 April - 30 September.

Directions

Site is on the north side of Frias – approach only from this side. From A1 exit 5 onto A2122 (Quintana Martin Galindez). After 16 km. turn left signed Frias and site is 3 km. GPS: 42.77098, -3.29686

Charges guide

Per person	€ 4.85
pitch	€ 7.50
electricity	€ 4.40

Miranda del Castañar

Camping El Burro Blanco

Camino de las Norias s/n, E-37660 Miranda del Castañar (Salamanca) T: 626 227 646.

E: camping.elburroblanco@gmail.com **alanrogers.com/ES90260**

Set on a hillside, within the Sierra Peña de Francia and with views of the romantic walled village of Miranda del Castañar and its charming, crumbling castle, this site is run by a Dutch couple, Jeff and Yvonne. You are welcomed at the gate and are walked around the facilities. In total, there are 30 level touring pitches, all between 80 to 120 sq.m. and 25 have 6/10A electricity. The pitches are beautifully set in 2.5 hectares of the most attractive natural woodland. Owners of motorcaravans and large caravans should contact the site first, due to the limited number of suitable pitches.

Facilities

One central, modern and fully equipped sanitary facility includes a baby bath. Two washbasins have hot water. Out of season part of the unit is closed and therefore facilities are unisex. Launderette. Gas supplies. Library with book exchange and small bar. Off site: Restaurants, shops and ATM in village 600 m. Municipal swimming pool nearby. Bicycle hire 1 km. River swimming and fishing 1.5 km. Riding 15 km.

Open: 1 May - 1 October.

Directions

The road to Miranda del Castañar is 7 km. northeast of the village of Cepeda. Turn off main SA-225 road (Miranda). After 1.2 km. descending towards town look for left turn onto concrete road. Follow for 1.1 km. to site on right. GPS: 40.4748, -5.99885

Charges guide

Per unit incl. 2 persons and electricity	€ 24.20 - € 26.18

No credit cards.

Riaza

Camping Riaza

Ctra de la Estacion s/n, E-40500 Riaza (Segovia) T: 921 550 580. E: info@camping-riaza.com

alanrogers.com/ES90245

This site is situated in the province of Segovia, a hundred or so kilometres north of Madrid, making it an ideal spot for a few days rest en route north or south. Of the 350 spacious grass pitches 213 are for touring, all with electricity (8A), water, and drainage. The buildings on the site are sympathetically built of local stone and house a large clubroom, bar and welcoming restaurant, a good place to relax and enjoy the excellent menu. The little town of Riaza is typically Castilian and has a few monuments and a very nice 'folksy' restaurant, which offers a daily menu at a low price. It is known for its high quality and people come from afar to savour the Segovian speciality, suckling pig on the spit.

Facilities

Two excellent, centrally located toilet blocks with underfloor heating. Shop. Bar, restaurant and clubroom (all year). Large modern play area. Sports area. Tennis. Archery. Children's club (summer only). WiFi throughout. Off site: Municipal swimming pool adjacent (1/6-31/8). Riding 2 km. Village of Riaza with restaurant and some shopping 2 km. Golf 9 km.

Open: All year.

Directions

From the A1 (Burgos-Madrid) take exit 104 and the N110 towards Soria. Leave the N110 signed Riaza and follow camping signs. At roundabout follow signs for 'Estacion' and site is 50 m. on left. GPS: 41.26944, -3.49749

Charges guide

Per unit incl. 2 persons and electricity	€ 26.90 - € 29.50
extra person	€ 6.10

Santa Marta de Tormes

Camping Regio

Ctra de Madrid km. 4, E-37900 Santa Marta de Tormes (Salamanca) T: 923 138 888.
E: recepcion@campingregio.com **alanrogers.com/ES90250**

Salamanca is one of Europe's oldest university cities, and this beautiful old sandstone city has to be visited. This is also a useful staging post en route to the south of Spain or central Portugal. The site is 7 km. outside the city on the old road to Madrid, behind the Hôtel Regio where campers can take advantage of the hotel facilities. The 129 pitches (with a large area for tents) are clearly marked on slightly sloping ground, with some shade in parts and plentiful electricity points (10A). Access to those pitches not on the wide central road can be difficult for caravans.

Facilities

Very large, fully equipped sanitary block is very clean. Good facilities for disabled campers. Washing machines. Gas supplies. Motorcaravan services. Bar. Supermarket (1/6-30/9). The hotel restaurant, café and swimming pool may be used by campers (discounts at the café and restaurant). Play area. Tennis. Internet and WiFi (both within hotel area). English is spoken.

Open: All year.

Directions

Take main N501 Salamanca-Avila, then to St Marta de Tormes 7 km. east of the city. Hôtel Regio is on the right just outside the town at the 90 km. marker. There are yellow hotel and camping signs in the city and on the roads to the east. GPS: 40.9471, -5.614

Charges guide

Per unit incl. 2 persons and electricity	€ 19.40 - € 21.70

Segovia

Camping El Acueducto

Ctra de San Ildefonso la Granja, km.112, E-40004 Segovia (Segovia) T: 921 425 000.
E: informacion@campingacueducto.com **alanrogers.com/ES92420**

Located right on the edge of the interesting city of Segovia with lovely views across the open plain to the mountains beyond, this is a family run, typically Spanish site. The 200 grass pitches (100 with 6A electricity, water and drainage) are mostly of medium size, although a few pitches near the gate would have room for larger motorcaravans. An uncomplicated site, reception is small but efficient, and the owner is helpful and speaks good English. El Acueducto is about 5 km. from the city. Segovia is deeply and haughtily Castilian, with plenty of squares and mansions from its days of Golden Age grandeur, when it was a royal resort.

Facilities

Two traditional style toilet blocks provide simple, clean facilities. Laundry room. Motorcaravan services. Small shop for essentials. Bar (1/7-31/8). Two swimming pools. Large play area. Bicycle hire. WiFi in reception (charged). Car wash. Gas and electric barbecues only. Off site: Large restaurant nearby. Fishing, golf, riding and boat launching all 5 km. Bus service into city centre. Madrid is within reasonable driving distance.

Open: 1 April - 30 September.

Directions

From the north on N1 (Burgos-Madrid) take exit 99 on N110 towards Segovia. On outskirts of city take third exit onto N603 signed Madrid. Pass one exit to Segovia and take second signed Segovia and La Granja. At roundabout turn right towards Segovia. Site is 500 m. on right. GPS: 40.93125, -4.09243

Charges guide

Per unit incl. 2 persons and electricity	€ 32.30 - € 34.00
extra person	€ 5.60 - € 6.00

Tordesillas

Kawan Village Campingred El Astral

Camino de Pollos 8, E-47100 Tordesillas (Valladolid) T: 983 770 953. E: info@campingelastral.es
alanrogers.com/ES90290

The site is in a prime position alongside the wide River Duero (safely fenced). It is homely and run by a charming man, Eduardo Gutierrez, who speaks excellent English and is ably assisted by brother Gustavo and sister Lola. The site is generally flat with 140 pitches separated by thin hedges. The 133 touring pitches, 132 with electricity (6/10A), six with 10A electricity, water and waste water, vary in size from 60-200 sq.m. with mature trees providing shade. The new toilet block has been designed with environmental sustainability in mind, including solar heated water. This is a friendly site ideal for exploring the area as you move through Spain.

Facilities

One attractive new sanitary block with fully equipped, modern facilities. Showers for children and baby room. Facilities for disabled campers. Washing machines. Motorcaravan services. Supermarket. Bar and restaurant, used by locals, plus a takeaway service (all 1/4-30/9). Swimming pool with new disability lift, plus paddling pools (1/6-15/9). Playground. Minigolf. WiFi over site (charged).

Open: 1 March - 31 October.

Directions

Tordesillas is 28 km. southwest of Valladolid. From all directions, leave the main road towards Tordesillas and follow signs to campsite or 'Parador' (a hotel opposite the campsite). GPS: 41.495305, -5.005222

Charges guide

Per unit incl. 2 persons and electricity	€ 21.40 - € 31.30

Camping Cheques accepted.

Ucero

Camping Cañon del Rio Lobos

Ctra Burgos de Osma-San Leonardo, E-42317 Ucero (Soria) T: 975 363 565.

alanrogers.com/ES92510

This is a delightful site with 83 neat pitches and vast amounts of flowers, set among attractive limestone cliffs of the Burgos canyons. The site is pricey but facilities are excellent and there are few others in the area. Reception is purpose built and control of the security barrier is from within – everything here is very organised. The camp logo depicts a bird of prey and many raptors continuously wheel above the site. The very attractive swimming pool is within a secure walled area, which again has many flowers and shrubs and is private from the road that runs alongside the site (some traffic noise).

Facilities

Two fully equipped toilet blocks (only one opened when site is quiet). Bar serving a 'menu del día' and a smart restaurant. Basic shopping from bar. Swimming pool (charge). Two excellent free tennis courts. Play area. Fishing. Football pitch. Torch useful. Dogs are not accepted. Off site: Local bus service for town (Wed/Sat) 1 km. Walking, climbing, caving, fishing in nearby Parque Natural. Riding 10 km. Golf 35 km.

Open: Easter - 30 September.

Directions

From N234 (Burgos-Soria) turn south in S Leonardo de Yagüe on SO690. Turn left after village on SO920 (El Burgo de Osma). Site is on left in 18 km. just before Ucero. From N122/A11 (Valladolid-Soria) turn north in El Burgo de Osma on SO920 (San Leonardo), 16 km. to Ucero. GPS: 41.7293, -3.0475

Charges guide

Per person	€ 5.00
child	€ 4.00
pitch	€ 13.50
electricity	€ 5.10

Villasur de Herreros

Camping Puerta de la Demanda

Ctra de Pineda km. 2, E-09199 Villasur de Herreros (Burgos) T: 983 796 819.

E: info@puertadelademanda.com **alanrogers.com/ES92540**

This site on flat ground, is overlooked on three sides by the hills and mountains of the Sierra de la Demanda which give the site its name. There is little shade over 50 large, well marked pitches, all of which have electricity (3-6A) and drainage. The modern buildings are of local stone and wood in sympathy with the quiet surroundings, yet providing an excellent set of facilities. The whole site is securely fenced. Just 300 m. away is a dam which may provide non-powered water sports and a river is very close for swimming and fishing. Nearby is the trail of the pilgrims to Santiago de Compostela.

Facilities

Sanitary building with British WCs and free hot showers. Washing machine. Facilities for disabled campers. Shop (April-Sept). Bar serving meals and selling basics (all season). Bicycle hire. Torches useful. Pets are not accepted. Off site: Sailing on nearby reservoir. River fishing 1 km. Shop, restaurants and bars in attractive village 1 km. Superb walking area.

Open: 1 February - 30 November.

Directions

From the N120 (Burgos-Logroño), turn east at Ibeas de Juarros (13 km. east of Burgos) on Bu-P8101/Bu820 through Arlanzon to Villasur de Herreros. Site is beyond village after km. 13. GPS: 42.306, -3.375

Charges guide

Per person	€ 3.70
child (up to 12 yrs)	€ 2.60
pitch incl. car	€ 6.50 - € 7.40
electricity	€ 3.00

With a coastline of inlets and wide, rocky estuaries, sheltering traditional old fishing villages and fine beaches, Galicia is perhaps best known for Santiago de Compostela, the place where the famous pilgrims' route comes to an end.

THIS REGION IS MADE UP OF FOUR PROVINCES: OURENSE, LUGO, A CORUÑA AND PONTEVEDRA

The obvious highlight in the region has to be the beautiful medieval city of Santiago de Compostela, capital of Galicia and world famous centre of the old European pilgrimage. Now a World Heritage Site, the city boasts an impressive Romanesque cathedral with more churches, convents and monasteries dotted around. One of the best times to go to Santiago de Compostela is during the Festival of St James on 25 July, which has also been designated Galicia Day. Following the route into the city, are the towns of Portomarín and Samos. Near Samos, the Lóuzara valley and the Sierra do Oribio are ideal for those interested in hiking and wildlife. The Galician coastline is characterised by high cliffs and estuaries collectively known as the Rías Atlas and Rías Baixas with the Costa da Morte or Coast of Death separating them, so called because of the hundreds of shipwrecks that litter the cliffs and rocks. It was also once considered by the pilgrims to be the 'end of the world'. Along the coast are medieval towns and villages including Noia, Muros, A Coruña and Finisterre. Corcubión, Camariñas and Corme-Laxe are other rias with fishing villages and home to some of the best barnacles in the region.

Places of interest

A Coruña: medieval quarters, Romanesque churches, Roman lighthouse.

Baiona: one of the region's best resorts.

Camariñas: town at the 'end of the world', good barnacle hunting ground, lacemaking traditions.

Lugo: town completely enclosed within preserved Roman walls, along which are 85 towers.

Malpica: seaside harbour, jumping off point for nearby islands.

Pontevedra: picturesque old town with lively atmosphere.

Vigo: fishing port, beaches.

Viveiro: beaches, old town surrounded by Renaissance walls.

Cuisine of the region

Local cuisine features heavily in fiestas and throughout the region are numerous markets. Good quality seafood is found in abundance; *percebes* (barnacles) are a favourite. *Pulpo* (octopus) is also popular and special *pulperías* will cook it in the traditional way. Vegetable dishes include the Galician broth made with green beans, cabbage, parsnip, potatoes and haricot beans. *Aguardiente gallego*, a regional liqueur, is used to make the traditional mulled drink known as *queimada*, where fruit, sugar and coffee grains are added and then set alight.

Caldeirada: fish soup.

Caldo gallego: thick potato and cabbage stew.

Empanada: light-crusted pastries often filled with pork, beef, tuna or cod.

Lacon con grelos: ham boiled with turnip greens.

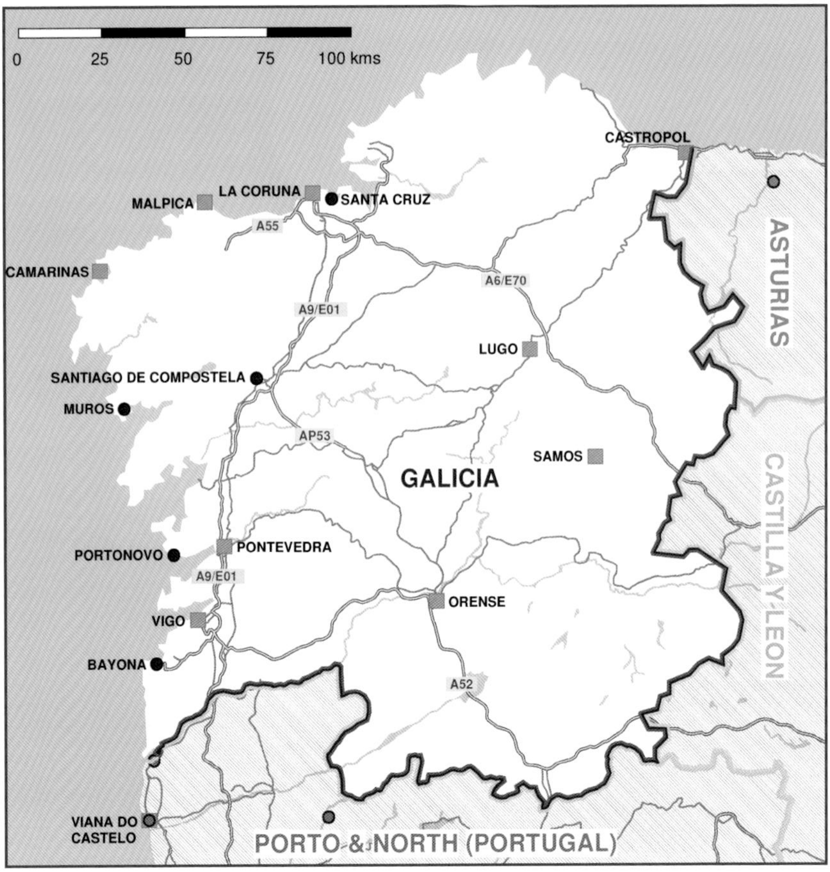

Bayona

Camping Bayona Playa

Ctra Vigo-Bayona km. 19, E-36393 Bayona (Pontevedra) T: 986 350 035.
E: campingbayona@campingbayona.com **alanrogers.com/ES89360**

Situated on a narrow peninsula with the sea and river estuary all around it, this large and well maintained campsite is great for a relaxing break. The 450 pitches, 358 for touring, benefit from the shade of mature trees whilst still maintaining a very open feel. All have 5A electricity and 50 are fully serviced. It is busy here in high season so advance booking is recommended. Sabaris is a short walk away and Bayona is a 20 minute walk along the coast, where you can find a variety of shops, supermarkets, banks, bars and eating places. Maximum unit length is 7.5 m.

Facilities

Three well maintained modern toilet blocks (one open low season), washbasins and shower cubicles. No washing machines but site provides a service wash. Facilities for visitors with disabilities. Well stocked supermarket and gift shop (June-Sept). Terrace bar, cafeteria, restaurant. Excellent pool complex with slide (small charge, redeemable in shop and restaurant). Play area. Organised activities July/Aug. Windsurfing school. Cash machine in reception. WiFi in reception area. Off site: Fishing 100 m. Bicycle hire 5 km. Riding 8 km. Golf 20 km.

Open: All year.

Directions

From Vigo leave AG57, exit 5 (Bayona North). Follow signs to site at Sabaris, 2 km. east of Bayona.
GPS: 42.113978, -8.826013

Charges guide

Per unit incl. 2 persons and electricity	€ 34.00
extra person	€ 7.20
child (3-12 yrs)	€ 4.00

Muros

Camping San Francisco

Camino do Convento 21, Louro, E-15291 Muros (A Coruña) T: 981 826 148. E: ofmlouro@yahoo.es
alanrogers.com/ES89300

Situated 400 m. from the coast, this small and attractive touring site with 104 small pitches occupies a clearing on a hillside that is undoubtedly a magnet for Spanish holidaymakers. Advance booking is recommended. The neatly laid out and numbered pitches are on level grass, divided by trees but with little shade. All have 10A electricity and 74 pitches are fully serviced. The surrounding countryside is scenic and unspoilt by development and the superb white sandy beaches and rocky coves provide endless hours of fun or relaxation for the whole family. Bars and restaurants, together with a few small shops, are all within 300 m. of the site but for everything else, the small town of Muros is only 3.5 km.

Facilities

One modern spotlessly clean toilet block is centrally positioned with all necessary facilities. A family shower room with facilities for disabled visitors is provided in both male and female areas. Washing machines, dryers and a first aid point are housed in separate rooms. Well stocked shop. Café/bar. Restaurant with terrace. Play area. Tennis and multisports court. Off site: Sandy beach and fishing 400 m. Bicycle hire 500 m.

Open: 21 June - 7 September.

Directions

From Santiago de Compostela take AC543 to Noia. Just before Noia turn right onto road signed Muros and continue on AC550. Site well signed 3.5 km. past Muros on right, up a narrow road.
GPS: 42.761975, -9.072701

Charges guide

Per unit incl. 2 persons and electricity	€ 32.85
extra person	€ 5.85
child	€ 4.25

Portonovo

Camping Paxarinas

Ctra San Xenxo-O'Grove, E-36979 Portonovo (A Coruña) T: 986 723 055. E: info@campingpaxarinas.com
alanrogers.com/ES89380

Paxarinas is a family owned and managed coastal site, set on a gently sloping area of hillside overlooking Ria de Pontevedra. Of the 260 very small pitches only 65 are for touring, in the centre of the site. All pitches are numbered and have 5/10A electricity, there is very little shade. It gets very busy in high season and advance booking is recommended. Care is needed with larger units at busy times. The site is situated in a most attractive area of Galicia and with access to two excellent beaches it makes a good stopover whilst visiting the area.

Facilities

Two well maintained modern sanitary blocks. Private cabins. Facilities for disabled visitors. Washing machine and dryer. Play area. Shop, bar and snacks (20/6-15/9). Separate restaurant in adjacent hotel. WiFi. Off site: Two beaches adjacent. Riding 2 km. Golf 8 km.

Open: March - October.

Directions

From AP9 take exit 129 (Pontevedra) and follow signs to Sanxenxo. Take coast road PO308 for 22 km. Site is poorly signed on the left, behind hotel, 3 km. past Sanxenxo and just before a bend.
GPS: 42.392481, -8.844069

Charges guide

Per unit incl. 2 persons and electricity	€ 31.60 - € 35.80
extra person	€ 6.35

Santa Cruz

Camping Los Manzanos

Avenida de Emilia Pardo Bazan, E-15179 Santa Cruz (A Coruña) T: 981 614 825.
E: informacion@campinglosmanzanos.com **alanrogers.com/ES89420**

Los Manzanos has a steep access drive down to the site, which is divided by a stream into two sections linked by a bridge. Pitches for larger units are marked and numbered, 85 with electricity (12A) and, in one section, there is a fairly large, unmarked field for tents. Some aircraft noise should be expected as the site is under the flight path to A Coruña (but no aircraft at night). The site impressed us as being very clean, even when full, which it tends to be in high season. Some interesting huge stone sculptures create focal points and conversation pieces.

Facilities

One good toilet block provides modern facilities including free hot showers. Small shop with fresh produce daily (limited outside June-Sept). High quality restaurant/bar (July/Aug). Swimming pool with lifeguard, free to campers (15/6-30/9). Playground. Barbecue area. Bungalows for rent. WiFi in reception area. Off site: Bus service at end of entrance drive. Beach and fishing 1 km. Bicycle hire 2 km. Golf and riding 8 km.

Open: April - 30 September.

Directions

From the A8/A6 (A Coruña). Take exit 568 onto AP9, then exit 3. Turn left onto NV1 towards Lugo/Madrid and left again on AC173 for Santa Cruz. Site signed from roundabout. Turn right before traffic lights. Site is on the left. GPS: 43.34908, -8.33567

Charges guide

Per unit incl. 2 persons and electricity	€ 25.34 - € 30.40
extra person	€ 5.36 - € 6.30

Santiago de Compostela

Camping As Cancelas

Rue do 25 de Xullo 35, E-15704 Santiago de Compostela (A Coruña) T: 981 580 476.
E: info@campingascancelas.com **alanrogers.com/ES90240**

The beautiful city of Santiago has been the destination for European Christian pilgrims for centuries and they now follow ancient routes to this unique city, the whole of which is a national monument. The As Cancelas campsite is excellent for sharing the experiences of these pilgrims in the city and around the magnificent cathedral. It has 125 marked pitches (60-90 sq.m), arranged in terraces and divided by trees and shrubs. On a hillside overlooking the city, the views are very pleasant. The site has a steep approach road. Electrical hook-ups (5A) are available, the site is lit at night and a security guard patrols. There are many legendary festivals and processions here, the main one being on July 25th, especially in holy years (when the Saint's birthday falls on a Sunday). Examine for yourself the credibility of the fascinating story of the arrival of the bones of St James at Compostela (Compostela translates as 'field of stars'), and also discover why the pilgrims dutifully carry a scallop shell on their long journey. There are many pilgrims' routes, including one commencing from Fowey in Cornwall.

Facilities

Two modern toilet blocks are fully equipped, with ramped access for disabled visitors. The quality and cleanliness of the fittings and tiling is good. Laundry with service wash for a small fee. Small shop. Restaurant. Bar with TV. Well kept, unsupervised swimming pool and children's pool. Small playground. Internet access. WiFi throughout.
Off site: Regular bus service into city from near football ground 200 m. Huge commercial centre (open late and handy for off season use) 20 minutes walk downhill (uphill on the return!). Riding 3.5 km. Golf 8 km.

Open: All year.

Directions

From motorway AP9-E1 take exit 67 and follow signs for 'Casco Historico' and 'Centro Ciudad' then follow site signs. GPS: 42.88939, -8.52418

Charges guide

Per unit incl. 2 persons and electricity	€ 25.60 - € 32.60
extra person	€ 5.20 - € 6.70
child (up to 12 yrs)	€ 3.00 - € 5.10

Like its neighbouring province, Cantabria, Asturias also has a beautiful coastline, albeit more rugged and wild, with the Picos range separating them. In the south the Cantabrian mountains form a natural border between Asturias and Castilla-León.

THIS IS A ONE PROVINCE REGION

THE CAPITAL IS OVIEDO

Situated between the foothills of the Picos mountains and the coast is the seaside town of Llanes, in the east. It has several good beaches, beautiful coves and, given its location, is a good base for exploring the Picos del Europa. Along the coast towards Gijón are more seaside resorts including Ribadesella, with its fishing harbour and fine beach. The cities of Gijón and, in particular, Avilés are renowned for their carnival festivities, a national event which takes place in late February. This week-long party involves dancing, live music, fireworks and locals who dress up in elaborate costumes. South of here, towards the centre of the province, is the capital, Oviedo. The city boasts a pedestrian old quarter with numerous squares and narrow streets, a cathedral, palaces, a fine arts museum, an archaeological museum plus various remarkable churches that date from the ninth century. There are also plenty of sidrerías (cider houses). The west coast of Asturias is more rugged. One of the most attractive towns along here is Luarca, built around a cove surrounded by sheer cliffs. With a fishing harbour and an array of good restaurants and bars, the town's traditional character is reflected in its chigres – old Asturian taverns – where visitors learn the art of drinking cider.

Places of interest

Avilés: 14th- and 15th-century churches and palaces.

Cudillero: small, charming fishing port.

Gijón: 18th-century palace, beaches, museums.

Villahormes: seaside town with excellent swimming coves.

Villaviciosa: atmospheric old town, 13th-century church, cider factory.

Cuisine of the region

Local specialities include *fabada,* a type of stew made with haricot beans called *fabes*, *potes* (soups) and of course cider, which can be drunk in *sidrerías.* The customary way to serve cider is to pour it from a great height, a practice known as *escanciar*, into a wide-mouthed glass only just covering the *culín* or bottom. Rice pudding is the traditional dessert and *frixuelos* (crepe), *huesos de santo* (made from marzipan) and *tocinillo de cielo* (syrup pudding) are eaten during festivals.

Brazo de gitano: a type of Swiss roll.

Carne gobernada: beef in white wine with bacon, eggs, peppers and olives.

Fabada asturiana: haricot beans, chorizo, cabbage, cured pork shoulder and potatoes.

Pastel carbayón: almond pastry.

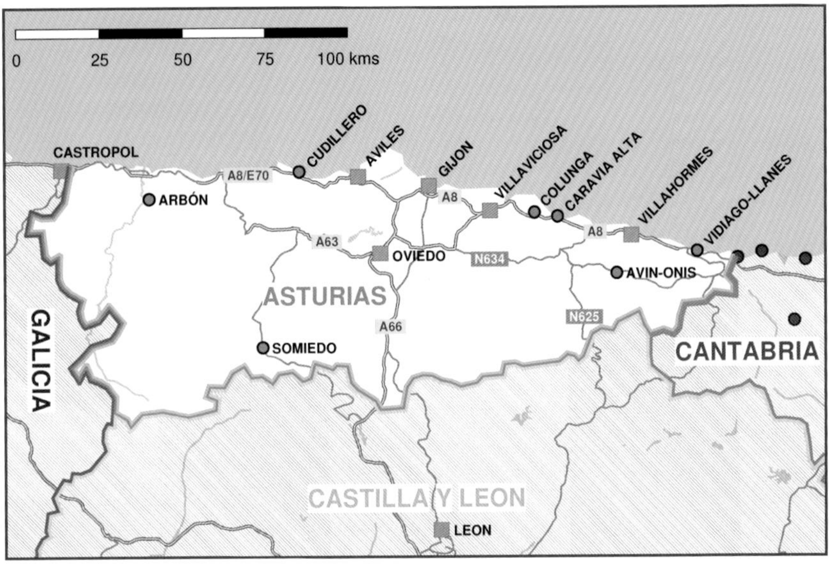

Arbón

Camping la Cascada

Arbón Villayón, E-33718 Arbón (Asturias) T: 985 625 081. E: campinglacascada@hotmail.com

alanrogers.com/ES89440

Located in a clearing of the attractive Arbon Valley this friendly, family run site offers the chance to experience the delights of rural Spain. There are 74 very small pitches (60 for touring units), all sited on gently sloping grass with electricity (4A), long leads are required. The beaches and small villages of the Costa Verde are only 12 km. away and the site has information about this spectacular region. Access to the site is not difficult but a 3,500 kg. weight restriction on the small bridge at the site entrance makes it unsuitable for larger units.

Facilities

Well maintained toilet block. No specific facilities for visitors with disabilities. No washing machine. Shop, bar and snacks (all season). Restaurant (July/Aug). Swimming pool with sun terrace (all season). Play area. Fishing. Covered communal barbecue area. WiFi in bar area.
Off site: Bicycle hire 500 m. Beaches 12 km.

Open: Easter - September.

Directions

From A8 (direction of La Coruna) take exit for Navia onto N634. Turn left, AS25 (Arbon). Site is 10 km. on right, well signed. Note: sign at site entrance refers to it as Camping Arbon/Camping la Cascada.
GPS: 43.47993, -6.70261

Charges guide

Per unit incl. 2 persons and electricity	€ 19.10
extra person	€ 3.80
child	€ 3.60

Avin-Onis

Camping Picos de Europa

E-33556 Avin-Onis (Asturias) T: 985 844 070. E: adrian@picos-europa.com

alanrogers.com/ES89650

This delightful site is, as its name suggests, an ideal spot from which to explore these dramatic limestone mountains on foot, by bicycle or on horseback. The site itself is continuously developing and the dynamic owner, José, and his nephew who helps out when he is away, are both very pleasant and nothing is too much trouble. The site is in a valley beside a pleasant, fast flowing river. The 160 marked pitches are of varying sizes and have been developed in three avenues, on level grass mostly backing on to hedging, with 6A electricity. An area for tents and apartments is over a bridge past the fairly small, but pleasant, round swimming pool.

Facilities

Toilet facilities include a new fully equipped block, along with new facilities for disabled visitors and babies. Pleasant room with tables and chairs for poor weather. Washing machine and dryer. Shop (July-Sept). Swimming pool (Feb-Sept). Bar and cafeteria style restaurant (all year) serves a good value 'menu del dia' and snacks. WiFi in restaurant area (free). Play area. Fishing. Torches necessary in the new tent area. Off site: Riding 12 km.

Open: All year.

Directions

From A8 (Santander-Oviedo) km. 326 exit take N634 northwest to Arriondas. Turn southeast on N625 to Cangas and join AS114 (Covodonga/Panes) bypassing Cangas. Site is beyond Avín after 16 km. marker. GPS: 43.3363, -4.94498

Charges guide

Per unit incl. 2 persons and electricity	€ 20.42 - € 26.06
extra person	€ 5.08 - € 5.40

Caravia Alta

Camping Caravaning Arenal de Moris

A8 Salida 337, E-33344 Caravia Alta (Asturias) T: 985 853 097. E: camoris@desdeasturias.com

alanrogers.com/ES89550

This smart, well run site is close to three fine sandy beaches so gets very busy at peak times. It has a backdrop of the mountains in the nature reserve known as the Sueve which is important for a breed of short Asturian horse, the Asturcone. The site has 330 grass pitches (269 for tourers) of 40-70 sq.m. and with 200 electricity connections available (10A). There are some shady, terraced pitches while others are on an open, slightly sloping field with limited views of the sea. The restaurant with a terrace serves local dishes and overlooks the pool with hills and woods beyond.

Facilities

Three sanitary blocks provide comfortable, controllable showers (no dividers) and vanity style washbasins, laundry facilities and external dishwashing (cold water). Supermarket. Bar/restaurant. Swimming pool. Tennis. Play area in lemon orchard. English is spoken. WiFi in the restaurant area. Off site: Beach and fishing 200 m. Bus 1 km. from gate. Bar and restaurants in village 2 km.

Open: 1 June - 17 September.

Directions

Leave A8 Santander-Oviedo motorway at km. 337 exit, turn left on N632 towards Colunga and site is signed to right in village, near 16 km. marker. GPS: 43.47248, -5.18332

Charges guide

Per person	€ 5.30 - € 6.20
pitch incl. car	€ 10.50 - € 14.50
electricity	€ 4.50 - € 4.90

Colunga

Camping Costa Verde

Playa de la Griega, E-33320 Colunga (Asturias) T: 985 856 373. E: info@campingcostaverde.com

alanrogers.com/ES89500

This uncomplicated coastal site has a marked Spanish flavour and is just 1.5 km. from the pleasant town of Colunga. Although little English is spoken, the cheerful owner and his helpful staff will make sure you get a warm welcome. The great advantage for many is that, 200 m. from the gate, is a spacious beach by a low tide lagoon with a recently constructed marine parade, ideal for younger children. Some of the 200 pitches are occupied on a seasonal basis, but there are 155 for touring units. These are flat but with little shade, and electricity (6A) is available (long leads needed in places). The site gets very busy in high season.

Facilities

The single toilet block is of a high standard with a mixture of British and Turkish style toilets (all British for ladies), large showers and free hot water throughout. Laundry. Well stocked shop. Bar/restaurant is traditional and friendly. Play area. Torches needed. Off site: Fishing in river alongside site. Nearby towns of Ribadesella, Gijón and Oviedo. Excellent beaches. Bicycle hire 2 km. Sailing 4 km. Golf and riding 18 km.

Open: Easter - 1 October.

Directions

Colunga is 45 km. east of Gijón. Leave the A8 Santander-Oviedo motorway at km. 345 exit and take N632 towards Colunga. In village, turn right on As257 towards Lastres; site is on right after 1 km. marker. GPS: 43.49662, -5.26447

Charges guide

Per person	€ 5.00
pitch incl. car	€ 8.50
electricity	€ 3.50

Cudillero

Camping l'Amuravela

El Pito, E-33150 Cudillero (Asturias) T: 985 590 995. E: camping@lamuravela.com

alanrogers.com/ES89480

This very well maintained, family run site, is close to the quaint old town of Cudillero and it is an ideal stopover when visiting 'green Spain'. Nearby is some of the most attractive mountain scenery in the region and if you stay here for one night it can easily extend to a much longer visit. There are 70 good sized touring pitches on level or gently sloping grass with easy access. Some pitches are able to accommodate large units. Mature trees give some shade and all pitches have 5A electricity. The excellent swimming pool provides an area for relaxation.

Facilities

One modern and very well maintained toilet block is close to all pitches and includes washbasins and shower cubicles. Facilities for visitors with disabilities. Washing machines and dryers. Well stocked shop. Café/bar and restaurant area (20/6-10/9). Swimming pool (June-Sept). Play area. Very little English is spoken. Off site: Fishing and beach 2 km. Golf 28 km.

Open: June - September.

Directions

From A8 take N632 towards Cudillero. After 120 km. marker turn right onto CU2 signed El Pito. Site is well signed on right in 2 km. On no account take caravans into Cudillero. GPS: 43.554391, -6.144581

Charges guide

Per unit incl. 2 persons and electricity	€ 22.45 - € 28.70
extra person	€ 4.90 - € 5.90

Somiedo

Camping Lagos de Somiedo

Valle de Lago, E-33840 Somiedo (Asturias) T: 985 763 776. E: campinglagosdesomiedo@hotmail.com

alanrogers.com/ES89450

This is a most unusual site in the Parque Natural de Somiedo. Winding narrow roads with challenging rock overhangs, hairpin bends and breathtaking views (for 8 km) finally bring you to the campsite at an elevation of 1,200 m. This is a site for 4x4s, powerful small campervans and cars – not for medium or large motorcaravans, and caravans are not accepted. It is not an approach for the faint hearted! The friendly Lana family make you welcome at their unique site, which is tailored for those who wish to explore the natural and cultural values of the park without the usual campsite amenities. There are 210 pitches (just four with electric hook-up), undefined in two open meadows.

Facilities

There are British style toilets and free hot water to clean hot showers and washbasins. Facilities for babies and children, and for disabled visitors. Washing machine. Combined reception, small restaurant with takeaway food, bar and reference section. Shop for bread, milk and other essentials, plus local produce and crafts. Horses for hire, trekking. Lectures on flora, fauna, history and culture. Fishing (licence required). Barbecue area. Small play area. Gas supplies. Traditional thatched cabins for hire.

Open: 1 April - 30 September.

Directions

From N634 via Oviedo turn left at 442 km. on AS-15 (Parque Natural de Somiedo). At 9 km. marker turn left on AS-227. At 38 km. marker, turn left into Pol de Somiedo (Centro Urbano). Follow signs for Valle de Lago; 8 km. of hairpin bends from Pola to the valley. Site is signed. GPS: 43.072018, -6.198885

Charges guide

Per unit incl. 2 persons and electricity	€ 25.00 - € 27.00
extra person	€ 5.50

Vidiago-Llanes

Camping la Paz

Ctra N634 Irun-Coruna km. 292, E-33597 Vidiago-Llanes (Asturias) T: 985 411 235.

E: delfin@campinglapaz.com **alanrogers.com/ES89600**

This site occupies a spectacular location. The reception building is opposite a solid rock face and many hundreds of feet below the site. The ascent to the upper part of the site is quite daunting, but staff will place your caravan for you, although motorcaravan drivers will have an exciting drive to the top, especially to the loftier pitches. Once there, the views are absolutely outstanding, both along the coast and inland to the Picos de Europa mountains. There are 434 pitches, 350 with 10/15A electricity. There is also a lower section in a shaded valley to which access is easier, if rather tight in places.

Facilities

Four good, modern toilet blocks are well equipped and include an interesting mix of electronic hot water and cold water from a tap for the showers. They are kept very clean even at peak times. Baby bath. Full laundry facilities. Motorcaravan services. Restaurant and bar/snack bar with small shop (all season). Watersports. Games room. Fishing. Torches useful in some areas. WiFi in restaurant. Off site: Shop, bar and restaurant in nearby village.

Open: Easter - 15 October.

Directions

Site is signed from A8/N634 Santander-Oviedo/Gijón road near km. 292 marker (on non-motorway section). Site approach road is just east of the village of Vidiago, marked by camping signs and flags. GPS: 43.39957, -4.65149

Charges guide

Per person	€ 6.95
child	€ 6.10
pitch incl. car	€ 14.50 - € 18.50
electricity	€ 4.90

The region of Cantabria in the north of Spain offers the best of both worlds. On the one hand there is the glorious coastline with beautiful beaches and pretty fishing villages; while inland there are several national parks including the mountainous, Picos de Europa.

CANTABRIA IS A ONE PROVINCE REGION

THE CAPITAL IS SANTANDER

The capital, Santander, is an elegant city which extends over a wide bay with views of the Cantabrian Sea. Its historic quarter is situated against a backdrop of sea and mountains, although the town is best known for its beaches; the Playa de la Magdalena, which has a summer windsurfing school, and the popular El Sardinero beach. There is also a Maritime Museum and Museum of Prehistory and Archaeology, plus a small zoo housed in the gardens of the old royal palace. A short distance from the city is the pretty medieval village of Santillana del Mar and the prehistoric caves of Altamira. The adjacent Altamira Museum houses a replica of these caves and their impressive prehistoric drawings. Also on the outskirts of the capital is the Cabárceno Nature Park with more protected areas scattered around the region, including those at Oyambre, Peña Cabarga and Saja-Besaya. The largest is the mountain range of Picos de Europa, a national park which shares its territory with Asturias and Castilla-León. With river gorges, valleys, woodlands and an abundance of wildlife, it is popular with walkers, trekkers and climbers.

Places of interest

Castro Urdiales: beaches, Gothic church, Roman bridge, old quarter.

Comillas: rural town, beaches, Gaudí-designed villa.

Laredo: lively seaside resort, 13th-century church, 5 km. long sandy beach.

Lienganes: 17th- and 18th-century architecture, spa.

Potes: on east side of Picos de Europa, mountain bike hire, paragliding available.

San Vicente de la Barquera: picturesque fishing port.

Cuisine of the region

Seafood is used a lot, including fresh shellfish, sardines, *rabas* (fried squid), *bocartes rebozados* (breaded whitebait). Cheese is produced throughout the region; *queso de nata* (cream cheese), *picón* from Treviso Bejes, and smoked cheeses from Áliva and Pido. A typical dish of the region is the Cantabrian stew, which contains haricot beans, cabbage, rice and sausage. Desserts include the traditional cheesecakes of the Pas Valley and pastries. The local tipple is *orujo*, a strong liquor.

Maganos encebollados: squid with onion.

Quesada: cheesecake.

Sobaos pasiegos: sponge cakes.

Sorropotún: type of fish stew.

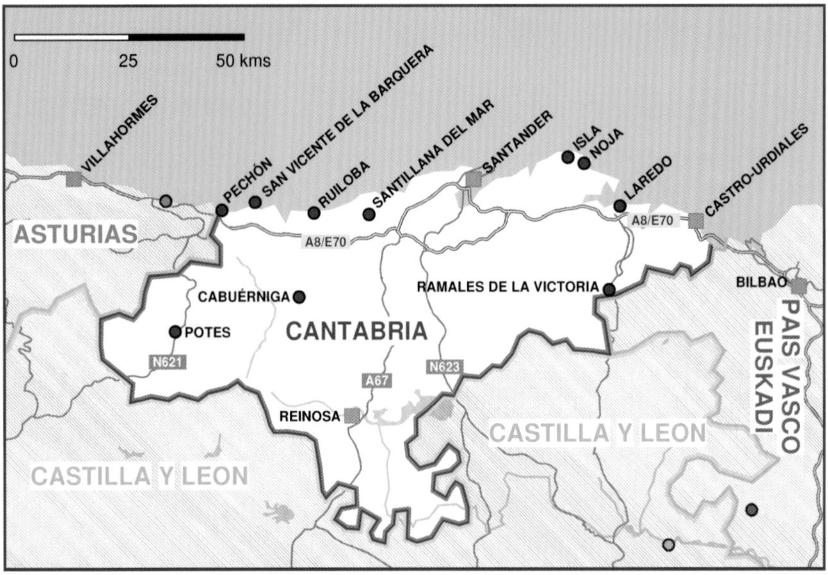

Cabuérniga

Camping El Molino de Cabuérniga

Sopeña de Cabuérniga, ctra C625 km. 42, E-39510 Cabuérniga (Cantabria) T: 942 706 259.

E: cmcabuerniga@campingcabuerniga.com **alanrogers.com/ES89640**

Located in a peaceful valley with magnificent views of the mountains, beside the Saja river and only a short walk from the picturesque and unspoiled village of Sopeña, this gem of a site is on an open, level, grassy meadow with trees. Wonderful stone buildings and artefacts are a feature of this unique site. There are 102 marked pitches, all with 6A electricity, although long leads may be needed in places. This comfortable site is very good value and ideal for a few nights (or you may well choose to stay longer once there) whilst you explore the Cabuérniga Valley which forms part of the Reserva Nacional del Saja.

Facilities

A superb, spotless sanitary block provides spacious, controllable showers and hot and cold water to washbasins. Washing machines and free ironing. Unit for disabled campers. Baby and toddler room. Bar serving breakfasts and 'bocadillos' (sandwiches) includes small shop section. Wonderful playground in rustic setting (supervision recommended). Fishing. Bicycle hire. Attractive stone cottages and apartments for rent.
Off site: Bus service 500 m. Restaurant in village 1 km. Riding and bicycle hire 3 km. Beach and golf 20 km. Skiing 50 km.

Open: All year.

Directions

From A8 (Santander-Oviedo) take km. 249 exit and join N634 to Cabezón de la Sal. Turn southwest on CA180 towards Reinosa for 11 km. to Sopeña (site signed to left). Turn into village (watch out for low eaves/gutters on buildings), continually bearing right following small site signs. GPS: 43.22594, -4.29034

Charges guide

Per unit incl. 2 persons and electricity	€ 27.00
extra person	€ 5.50
child	€ 5.00

Isla

Camping Playa de Isla

Ctra Arnadal no. 1, E-39195 Isla (Cantabria) T: 942 679 361. E: bernac@teleonica.net

alanrogers.com/ES89980

This well maintained site is set on a headland, overlooking the sea on one side and the village of Quejo on the other. The 200 well defined small pitches (100 for touring) with little shade are on two levels. All have 6A electricity and some have sea views. Large units may experience difficulty accessing some pitches. There is direct access via a short flight of steps to the superb beach with its golden sand and rocky pools. The site has an illuminated 500 m. footpath to the village where there are restaurants, shops and bars. Since its opening in 1979 this site has undergone continuous improvement and the owners are justifiably proud of the results.

Facilities

One modern spotless toilet block is centrally positioned. Family shower room. Washing machines and dryers. Well stocked shop (Easter-Sept). Café/bar (1/7-1/9), with terrace overlooking the sea. Play area. Fishing from adjacent beach. Dogs are not accepted. Off site: Boat launching 500 m. Golf and bicycle hire 5 km. Riding 6 km.

Open: Easter - 30 September.

Directions

From A8 (Santander-Bilbao) exit at 185 km. marker onto N634 (Beranga). Almost immediately turn right, CA147 (Noja). At roundabout turn left, CA141, towards Somo/Santander. Turn right, CA449 signed Isla. Site is 5 km. through village. Entrance road is very narrow in places. GPS: 43.5016, -3.54292

Charges guide

Per unit incl. 2 persons and electricity	€ 27.15 - € 30.35

Laredo

Camping Playa del Regaton

El Regaton 8, E-39770 Laredo (Cantabria) T: 942 606 995. E: recepcion@campingplayaregaton.com

alanrogers.com/ES89930

Situated a short distance from the bustling seaside town of Laredo and easily accessible from Santander and Bilbao, Camping Playa del Regaton is an ideal stopover for those en route to the ferries. The site has direct access to the beach and the estuary of the Ria del Ason and is an important marsh area for migrating birds. Of the 125 small pitches, 100 are for touring and have 6/10A electricity and a sink. All are on level grass, with mature trees providing separation and a degree of shade. The site is popular with Spanish holidaymakers. The owners and their staff are keen to ensure you enjoy your stay. Limited English is spoken outside high season.

Facilities

One dated but clean and heated toilet block. Baby bath. Facilities for disabled visitors. Washing machine and dryer. Small shop (1/4-25/9) sells most essentials. Café/bar (1/4-25/9) with snacks (1/7-31/8). Play area. Children's club in high season. Games room. Free WiFi throughout. Bicycle hire. Dogs are accepted if less than 12 kg. and only on certain pitches. Off site: Beaches nearby.

Open: 30 March - 30 September.

Directions

From the A8 (Santander-Bilbao) take exit 172 to Laredo. Straight on at roundabout signed hospital and beaches. Do not go into Laredo. At traffic lights turn left, site is well signed on left, 500 m. past hospital. GPS: 43.41319, -3.45039

Charges guide

Per unit incl. 2 persons and electricity	€ 18.70 - € 24.05

Noja

Camping Los Molinos

Ctra La Ria s/n, E-39180 Noja (Cantabria) T: 942 630 426. E: losmolinos@ceoecant.es

alanrogers.com/ES89950

Camping Los Molinos is close to the village of Noja, a seaside resort that gets very busy in high season. It is on the coast of Cantabria, a ten minute walk from the Playa del Ris beach which has fine sand and clear water. The site is divided into two main areas, both with a large number of permanent units, some of which look a little run down. There are 100 (60 sq.m) pitches for caravans and motorcaravans on level ground, but with little shade; 42 have 3A electricity. A separate large area without electricity is used for tents. All touring pitches are at the end of the site furthest from the entrance and therefore from the sea!

Facilities

Six fully equipped toilet blocks, two new and two recently refurbished, are kept clean. Facilities for disabled visitors. Washing machines. Supermarkets. Butcher. Restaurant (July/Aug). Bars and café bar serving tapas and pizzas. Swimming and paddling pools with lifeguard (20/6-7/9). Play area. ATM. Torch useful. WiFi (charged). Off site: Free bus hourly to beach and town (July/Aug). Beach 400 m.

Open: Easter, then 1 June - 30 September.

Directions

From A8 (Bilbao-Santander) exit at km. 185 and join N634 (Beranga) and immediately turn right on CA147 to Noja. In 10 km. turn left and go through town. At beach roundabout turn left, then left again before Camping Playa Joyel. GPS: 43.48516, -3.53807

Charges guide

Per unit incl. 2 persons and electricity	€ 22.60 - € 31.60

No credit cards.

Noja

Camping Playa Joyel

Playa de Ris, E-39180 Noja (Cantabria) T: 942 630 081. E: playajoyel@telefonica.net

alanrogers.com/ES90000

This very attractive holiday and touring site is some 40 kilometres from Santander and 80 km. from Bilbao. It is a busy, high quality, comprehensively equipped site by a superb beach providing 1,000 well shaded, marked and numbered pitches with 6A electricity available. These include 80 large pitches of 100 sq.m. Some 250 pitches are occupied by tour operators and seasonal units. This well managed site has a lot to offer for family holidays with much going on in high season when it gets crowded. The swimming pool complex (with lifeguard) is free to campers and the superb beaches are cleaned daily mid June to mid September.

Facilities

Six excellent, spacious and fully equipped toilet blocks include baby baths. Large laundry. Motorcaravan services. Gas supplies. Freezer service. Supermarket (all season). General shop. Kiosk. Restaurant and takeaway (1/7-31/8). Bar and snacks (all season). Swimming pools, bathing caps compulsory (20/5-15/9). Entertainment organised with a soundproofed pub/disco (July/Aug). Gym park. Tennis. Playground. Riding. Fishing. Nature animal park. Hairdresser (July/Aug). Medical centre. Torches necessary in some areas. Animals are not accepted. WiFi (charged). Off site: Bicycle hire and large sports complex with multiple facilities including an indoor pool 1 km. Sailing and boat launching 10 km. Riding and golf 20 km.

Open: 30 March - 30 September.

Directions

From A8 (Bilbao-Santander) take km. 185 exit and N634 towards Beranga. Almost immediately turn right on CA147 to Noja. In 10 km. turn left at multiple campsite signs and go through town. At beach follow signs to site. GPS: 43.48948, -3.53700

Charges guide

Per unit incl. 2 persons and electricity	€ 28.20 - € 47.40
extra person	€ 4.40 - € 6.70
child (3-9 yrs)	€ 3.10 - € 5.00

Pechón

Camping Las Arenas-Pechón

Ctra Pechón-Unquera km. 2, E-39594 Pechón (Cantabria) T: 942 717 188. E: info@campinglasarenas.com

alanrogers.com/ES89700

This site is in a very quiet, but rather spectacular location bordering the sea and the Tina Mayor estuary, with views to the mountains and access to an attractive little beach. Otherwise, enjoy the pleasant kidney shaped pool that also shares the views. Taking 350 units, half the site has grassy pitches (60 sq.m) in bays or on terraces with stunning sea and mountain views, with electricity available (5A) and connected by asphalted roads. There are some quite steep slopes to tackle – reception is at the top, as are the bar and restaurant; the latter has a terrace with fantastic views of the estuary and of the mountains beyond.

Facilities

Clean, well tiled sanitary facilities are in the older, simple style. Various blocks include showers (no divider; add hot water to the cold by pushing a switch). Washing machines. Well stocked supermarket. Restaurant/bar and snack bar (all season). Small playground. Riding arranged (collected from site). River and sea fishing. Torches helpful. English is spoken. Off site: Shops, bars and restaurants in Pechón, plus a disco/bar 1 km. Golf 28 km.

Open: 1 June - 30 September.

Directions

On A8 from Santander, take km. 272 exit for Unquera (N621) at end of motorway section. Take first exit CA380 signed Pechón and site is 2 km. on left. From Oviedo/Gijón on A8/N634 at km. 272 take N621 slip-road for Unquera (do not join motorway), then as above. GPS: 43.39093, -4.5106

Charges guide

Per person	€ 6.90
child	€ 6.00
pitch incl. car	€ 12.00 - € 16.60
electricity	€ 3.95

Potes

Camping la Isla Picos de Europa

Picos de Europa, E-39570 Potes-Turieno (Cantabria) T: 942 730 896. E: campicoseuropa@terra.es

alanrogers.com/ES89620

La Isla is beside the road from Potes to Fuente Dé, with many mature trees giving good shade and glimpses of the mountains above. Established for over 25 years, a warm welcome awaits you from the owners (who speak good English) and a most relaxed and peaceful atmosphere exists here. All the campers we spoke to were delighted with the family feeling of the site. The 106 unmarked pitches are arranged around an oval gravel track under a variety of fruit and ornamental trees. Electricity (6A) is available to all pitches, although some need long leads. A brilliant small bar and restaurant are located under dense trees where you can enjoy the relaxing sound of the river which runs through the site.

Facilities

Single, clean and smart sanitary block retains the style of the site. Washbasins with cold water. Washing machine. Gas supplies. Freezer service. Small shop. Restaurant/bar (1/4-30/9). Small swimming pool (caps compulsory; 1/5-30/9). Play area. Barbecue area. Fishing. Bicycle hire. Riding. WiFi. Off site: Bus from gate in high season. Potes 2.5 km. Riding 10 km. Fuente Dé and its spectacular cable car ride 18 km. Beach 40 km.

Open: 1 April - 15 October.

Directions

From A8/N634 (Santander-Oviedo) take km. 272 exit for Unquera (end of motorway section). Take N621 south to Panes and up gorge (take care if towing) to Potes. Take CA165 to Fuente Dé and site is on right, 2.5 km. beyond Potes. GPS: 43.14999, -4.69997

Charges guide

Per person	€ 4.15 - € 4.50
pitch	free - € 11.50
electricity	€ 3.60

Potes

Camping la Viorna

Ctra Santo Toribio, E-39570 Potes (Cantabria) T: 942 732 021. E: info@campinglaviorna.com

alanrogers.com/ES89630

The wonderful views of the valley below from the open terraces, with its spectacular backdrop of mountains, make this smart and sophisticated site an attractive base from which to tour this region or to relax by the excellent swimming pool. It is very popular with both families and couples. There are beds of flowers everywhere and the trees provide shade on many pitches. Access is good for all sizes of unit to the 115 pitches of around 70 sq.m, all of which have electricity (6A). In high season, however, tents may be placed on less accessible, steeply sloping areas. The cosy bar/restaurant (fixed menu and snacks) has a terrace overlooking the pools.

Facilities

Single, neat sanitary block of very high standard, clean and modern. Washbasins have cold water only. Facilities for disabled visitors double as unit for babies (key). Laundry facilities. Shop. Restaurant/bar with terrace (all season). Swimming pool (23x13 m) and paddling pool (25/6-30/9; caps compulsory). Play area. Games room. Many sporting activities can be arranged. WiFi. Off site: Bicycle hire 1 km. Potes 1.5 km.

Open: Easter/1 April - 31 October.

Directions

From A8/N634 (Santander-Oviedo) take km. 272 exit for Unquera (end of motorway section). Take N621 south to Panes and up gorge (take care if towing) to Potes. After town take left fork (Toribio de Liébana) to site on right in 800 m. GPS: 43.15435, -4.64348

Charges guide

Per person	€ 4.48 - € 5.07
pitch	€ 11.55 - € 13.28
electricity (3/6A)	€ 3.45 - € 3.73

Ramales de la Victoria

Camping la Barguilla

E-39800 Ramales de la Victoria (Cantabria) T: 942 646 586. E: info@campinglabarguilla.com

alanrogers.com/ES89910

Located in a rural setting on the outskirts of the small Spanish town of Ramales de la Victoria, this small site provides an opportunity to sample traditional Spanish life. Access to the town is via an easy 1 km. walk. There are 70 small pitches with 50 for touring, all with 3/6A electricity. Some pitches have shade, whilst others enjoy views of the nearby Sierra del Hornijo mountains. Facilities are minimal but the site is well maintained and you are sure of a comfortable stay. Advance booking in high season is recommended. Be sure to sample the on-site Periguena restaurant, which serves a variety of cuisine, popular with the locals.

Facilities

One heated toilet block provides WCs, washbasins and shower cubicles. No facilities for visitors with disabilities. Washing machines. Shop. Bar, cafeteria, restaurant (weekends only in low season). Fenced play area. Games room. Bicycle hire. Barbecues are not permitted. WiFi. Off site: Fishing 200 m. Riding 10 km. Golf 20 km.

Open: All year (except November).

Directions

From A8 exit 173 take N629 to R. de la Victoria. At entry to town, turn right (Arredondo). In 1.6 km, left over bridge (Parque Publico). Site behind Restaurant Perigena (sharp incline). GPS: 43.25918, -3.47151

Charges guide

Per unit incl. 2 persons and electricity	€ 22.50 - € 23.50

Ruiloba

Camping El Helguero

Ctra Santillana-Comillas, E-39527 Ruiloba (Cantabria) T: 942 722 124. E: reservas@campingelhelguero.com

alanrogers.com/ES89610

This site, in a peaceful location surrounded by tall trees and impressive towering rock formations, caters for 240 units (of which 100 are seasonal) on slightly sloping ground. There are many marked pitches on different levels, all with access to electricity (6A), but with varying amounts of shade. There are also attractive tent and small camper sections set close in to the rocks and 22 site owned chalets. The site gets very crowded in high season, so it is best to arrive early if you have not booked. The reasonably sized swimming pool and children's pool have access lifts for disabled campers.

Facilities

Three well placed toilet blocks, although old, are clean and all include controllable showers. Facilities for children and disabled visitors. Washing machines and dryers. Motorcaravan services. Small supermarket (July/Aug). Bar/snack bar plus separate more formal restaurant. Swimming pool (caps compulsory). Playground. Activities and entertainment (high season). ATM. Torches useful. WiFi (charged).

Open: 1 April - 30 September.

Directions

From A8 (Santander-Oviedo) take km. 249 exit (Cabezón and Comillas) and turn north on CA135 towards Comillas. At km. 7 turn right on CA359 to Ruilobuca and Barrio la Iglesia. After village turn right up hill on CA358 to site. GPS: 43.38288, -4.24800

Charges guide

Per unit incl. 2 persons and electricity	€ 24.10 - € 28.95

Camping Cheques accepted.

San Vicente de la Barquera

Camping Caravaning Playa de Oyambre

Finca Peña Guerra, E-39547 San Vicente de la Barquera (Cantabria) T: 942 711 461.

E: camping@oyambre.com **alanrogers.com/ES89710**

This exceptionally well managed site is ideally positioned to use as a base to visit the spectacular Picos de Europa or one of the many sandy beaches along this northern coast. Despite its name, it is a kilometre from the beach on foot. The 100 touring pitches all have 10A electricity (long leads needed in places), ten are fully serviced. The fairly flat central area is allocated to tents while caravans are mainly sited on wide terraces (access to some could be a little tight for larger units) and there is some shade. There may be some traffic noise on the lower terraces.

Facilities

Good, clean sanitary facilities are in one, well kept block. Showers are spacious but have a frustrating mixture of pushbutton hot and ordinary cold controls. Facilities for babies and disabled visitors. Washing machines. Motorcaravan services. Shop in bar (all season). Restaurant. Takeaway. Swimming pools with lifeguard (1/6-15/9). Playground. Bicycle hire. Free WiFi over site. Off site: Bus service at site entrance. Fishing and superb beach 1 km. Golf 2 km. Riding 5 km.

Open: 1 March - 28 September.

Directions

From A8 (Santander-Oviedo) take exit at km. 258 (Caviedes) and join N634. Turn towards San Vicente. Site is signed at junction to Comillas, at km. 265 on the E70, 5 km. east of San Vicente. The entrance is quite steep. Another Camping La Playa within 500 m. is not recommended. GPS: 43.385268, -4.33814

Charges guide

Per unit incl. 2 persons and electricity	€ 29.60 - € 32.65

No credit cards.

Santillana del Mar

Camping Santillana

Ctra de Comilias s/n, E-39330 Santillana del Mar (Cantabria) T: 942 818 250.

E: complejosantillana@cantabria.com **alanrogers.com/ES89730**

This is an attractive site on a hill above the charming medieval village of Santillana del Mar and five to ten kilometres from some of Costa Verde's good beaches. There are 400 pitches, all with access to electricity (5A), some primarily for tents, informally arranged on a slope, with others for caravans and motorcaravans on the lower part of the site. Where the pitches are numbered but unmarked some overcrowding may occur in high season, and those alongside the road will experience some noise as this is a busy route. There are 64 chalets and mobile homes for hire.

Facilities

Toilet blocks are modern, well placed (only one open in low season), fully equipped and with facilities for disabled campers. Washing machines and irons. Supermarket and souvenir shop. Bar/restaurant and self-service café. Swimming and paddling pools (1/5-30/9). Play areas. Minigolf. Games room. Tennis. Bicycle hire. Library. Security lockers. Entertainment in high season.

Open: All year.

Directions

From A8 (Santander-Oviedo) take km. 234 exit west of Torrelavega and follow CA133 north to Santillana. Turn left at T-junction (busy) towards Comillas and site is on right in 300 m. GPS: 43.39258, -4.11334

Charges guide

Per person	€ 5.00 - € 6.00
pitch incl. electricity	€ 10.00 - € 18.00

No credit cards.

Camping Cheques accepted.

Located in northern Spain, this is a region steeped in Basque traditions, which is reflected in the architecture, native language, local sports and cuisine.

THERE ARE THREE PROVINCES: ALAVA, GIPUZKOA AND BIZKAIA

THE REGIONAL CAPITAL IS VITORIA

The province of Gipuzkoa adjoins France in the east. Its capital, San Sebastián, is a bustling, picturesque seaside town with a strong Basque identity. Overlooking La Concha Bay and enclosed by rolling low hills, this popular resort boasts four good beaches, including the celebrated La Concha Beach. As cider production is one of the oldest traditions in Basque country there are also plenty of sidrerías (cider houses) to visit. Heading along the rocky fringe of Costa Vasca towards Bilbao in Bizkaia are more excellent beaches and pretty fishing villages including Orio, Zarautz and Getaria. The biggest attraction in Bilbao is the famous Guggenheim Museum. Opened in 1997 this spectacular building is completely covered with titanium sheets and houses a collection of modern and contemporary art from around the world. The city also boasts a beautiful old quarter with a Gothic cathedral, the Plaza Nueva and a museum. Further inland in Alava is Vitoria, the region's capital. Its medieval streets intermingle with Renaissance Palaces and fine churches and are lined with lively bars and tavernas. In the summer, the city plays host to a jazz festival. Elsewhere in the province are several nature reserves.

Places of interest

Encartanciones: one of the world's largest cave chambers Torca del Carlista, wildlife sanctuary.

Hondarribia: fishing port, beaches, charming walled old town.

Laguardia: old walled town with cobbled streets, historic buildings, in wine-growing district of Rioja Alavesa.

Oñati: Baroque architecture, old university.

Tolosa: impressive old town square, carnival in February.

Zarautz: seaside town, famous for production of *txakoli.*

Zumaia: beaches, good coastal walks, July fiesta with Basque sports, dancing and bull racing.

Cuisine of the region

Basque cuisine is considered to be the finest in Spain. Tapas or *pintxos* is readily available in bars, served with the local white wine *txakolí*. Fish is popular, especially *bacalao* (cod) and seafood is often used to make casseroles and sauces. Lots of milk based desserts. Founded in the 19th century, the tradition of dining clubs or *txokos* are unique to the Basque country.

Alubias pochas: white haricot bean stew.

Chipirones en su tinta: squid cooked in its ink.

Goxua: sponge cake with whipped cream and caramel.

Intxaursalsa: milk pudding with cinnamon and walnuts.

Marmitaco: fish and potato stew.

Pantxineta: custard slice.

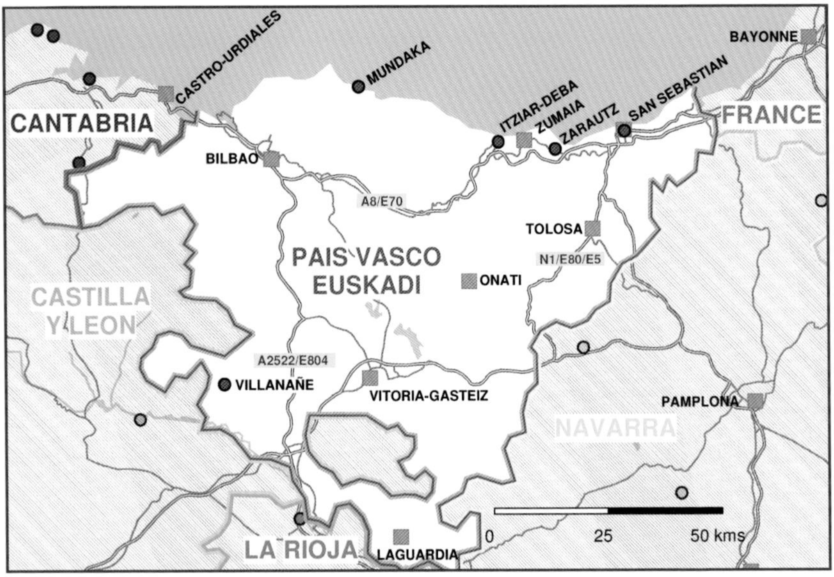

Itziar-Deba

Camping Itxaspe

Ctra Nacional 634 km. 38, E-20829 Itziar-Deba (Bizkaia) T: 943 199 377. E: itxaspe@hotmail.es

alanrogers.com/ES90380

Set on a hill, surrounded by farmland and with views of the mountains, this site is ideal for a stopover or a couple of days rest. A fifteen minute walk through the woods leads to a rocky beach and the sea. All of the 100 pitches are for touring units and are of medium size, flat and on grass. Seventy have electrical connections (6A, some Europlugs) and 40 are fully serviced. A comfortable bar, a restaurant and a swimming pool are open in July and August. Offering plenty of rural walks, this site will appeal to those wanting peace and quiet, but with little entertainment and some unfenced areas children will need supervision.

Facilities

The single traditional style sanitary block is basic but clean. Recently refurbished, new showers have been installed and more modernisation is gradually being undertaken. Facilities for disabled visitors. Washing machine. Well stocked shop. Restaurant and bar (July/Aug, weekends only in low season). Swimming pool (July/Aug). WiFi. Toddlers' play area. Barbecue and solarium area. Covered tables. Off site: Beach and fishing 1 km. Riding and bicycle hire 7 km. Surf school (discount for campers) 7 km. Golf 15 km.

Open: 1 April - 30 September.

Directions

From the A8 take exit 13 and follow signs for Itziar. At junction turn left. In 150 m. take right slip road for immediate turn left onto GI3291 (i.e. to cross main road). Site is signed and at end of road.
GPS: 43.29398, -2.32978

Charges guide

Per unit incl. 2 persons and electricity	€ 20.20 - € 34.30
extra person	€ 4.00 - € 5.60
child (under 10 yrs)	€ 3.50 - € 4.90

Mundaka

Camping Portuondo

Ctra Gernika-Bermeo, E-48360 Mundaka (Bizkaia) T: 946 877 701. E: recepcion@campingportuondo.com
alanrogers.com/ES90350

This site has an attractive restaurant, bar and terrace taking full advantage of the wonderful views across the ocean and estuary. Set amongst gardens, the 72 touring pitches are mainly for tents and small vans, but there are eight larger pitches at the lower levels for medium sized motorcaravans. Access to these is a little difficult as the road is very steep and there is no turning space. The site is mostly terraced, with tent pitches split, one section for your unit, the other for your car and there is some shade. Most are slightly sloping and all have 6A electricity (some may need long leads). In high season (July/August) it is essential to ring to book your space. English is spoken and the friendly owner, Imanol, and his staff are keen to help.

Facilities

Two toilet blocks include mostly British WCs and a baby room. One new block with facilities for disabled visitors. A reader reports poor cleaning and maintenance during their visit. Washing machines and dryers. Motorcaravan service point. Shop (22/6-8/9). Bar and two restaurants, open to public (28/1-15/12, closed Mon. in low season). Takeaway (22/6-8/9). Swimming pools (22/6-15/9). Free WiFi over part of site. Barbecue area. Torches may be useful. Off site: Fishing 100 m. Buses to Bilbao and Gernika (every 30 minutes) 300 m. Surfing on Mundaka beach 500 m. Boat launching and bicycle hire 1 km. Shops, bars and restaurants 2 km. Sailing 3 km. Riding 8 km. Golf 40 km.

Open: 23 January - 15 December.

Directions

Mundaka is 35 km. northeast of Bilbao. From A8 (San Sebastián-Bilbao) take exit 18 and follow signs for Gernika on BI635. Continue on BI2235 towards Bermeo. Site is on right approaching Mundaka. Take care as this is a sharp turn with a steep access. Road signs do not permit turning left to site.
GPS: 43.39918, -2.69610

Charges guide

Per unit incl. 2 persons and electricity	€ 30.05 - € 35.50
extra person	€ 6.35 - € 8.00
child (under 10 yrs)	€ 5.70 - € 7.25

From mid June to end August, one week min. reservation is required.

San Sebastián

Camping Igueldo

Paseo Padre Orkolaga no. 69, Barrio de Igueldo, E-20008 San Sebastián (Gipuzkoa) T: 943 214 502.
E: info@campingigueldo.com **alanrogers.com/ES90300**

A five kilometre drive from the city takes you to this terraced campsite, high above San Sebastián, between the mountains and the sea. It offers mostly level, shaded, small (max. 70 sq.m) grass pitches with electricity (5/10A) and drainage. Pitches are separated by neat, low hedging and some have excellent views. The restaurant and bar are open all year and a sun terrace looks toward the mountains. An excellent bus service to and from San Sebastián runs every 30 minutes. There are 25 attractive chalets to rent at the entrance to the site. These are often occupied by groups of younger visitors and can become lively at the weekends. English is spoken in reception.

Facilities

Three traditional toilet blocks are clean and bright with open style washbasins and controllable showers. Facilities for disabled visitors, children and babies (key). Laundry facilities. Motorcaravan service point. Shop for basics (all year). Bar/restaurant (all year, closed Wednesdays in low season). Fenced play area. Plans for a communal barbecue area. WiFi over site. Off site: The town of Igueldo within walking distance with shops, restaurants and bars. Bicycle hire, beach and fishing 5 km. Golf 9 km.

Open: All year.

Directions

From A8 take exit 9 for San Sebastián West (oeste). Head for Ondarreta. At Playa de Ondarreta, follow beach road on Avda de Satrustegui. At T-junction turn left. Keep right on Pase O De Igueldo. Continue up hill for 5 km. to site on left.
GPS: 43.304583, -2.045889

Charges guide

Per unit incl. 2 persons and electricity	€ 22.10 - € 33.20
extra person	€ 4.30 - € 5.40
child (3-10 yrs)	€ 3.00 - € 3.90

Special winter prices available.

Villanañe

Camping Angosto

Ctra Villanañe-Angosto no. 2, E-01425 Villanañe (Araba) T: 945 353 271. E: info@camping-angosto.com
alanrogers.com/ES90450

This is an eco-friendly site with basic facilities surrounded by wooded hills near the Valderejo National Park. Opened in 1999, the facilities are improving every year and a keen young team run things efficiently, gearing the site towards families. Most of the pitches are seasonal and in high season it is bustling and very Spanish! The limited number of touring pitches are flat and of average size. There is a large area for tents. Young trees have been planted around the site and are beginning to provide a little shade. The attractive new, heated pool has a sliding roof for inclement weather. A phone call before arriving is essential to establish availability.

Facilities

Adequate toilet block with facilities for disabled visitors. Washing machine and dryer. Good shop. Stylish bar with takeaway and separate restaurant (15/2-30/11; weekends only in low season). Indoor and outdoor swimming pools (1/4-30/11). Sauna. Small fenced play area close to entrance and grass toddler play area. Activities for children (high season). Mountain/electric bikes to hire. Fishing. Ice machine. Charcoal barbecues not permitted. WiFi. Off site: Many outdoor activities arranged locally. Riding 3 km. Bicycle hire 10 km. Sailing 40 km. Golf 45 km. Sea 60 km.

Open: Last weekend in February - 12 December.

Directions

From Miranda de Ebro, take A1 towards Burgos, leave at exit 5 and take A2122 to Puentelarrá and on to Espejo. From N1 Burgos-Victoria road, turn north on A2625 (west of Ameyugo) to Sta Gadea and Espejo. Site is just after village, clearly signed.
GPS: 42.84221, -3.06867

Charges guide

Per unit incl. 2 persons and electricity	€ 24.80 - € 29.60
extra person	€ 5.80
child (under 12 yrs)	€ 5.30

Zarautz

Gran Camping Zarautz

Monte Talai-Mendi, ctra N634 San Sebastián-Bilbao, E-20800 Zarautz (Gipuzkoa) T: 943 831 238.
E: info@grancampingzarautz.com **alanrogers.com/ES90390**

This friendly site sits high in the hills to the east of the Basque town of Zarautz and has commanding views over the bay and the island of Getaria. Of the 540 pitches, 440 are for touring units, with 6A electricity; ten also have water and drainage. The remaining pitches are for tents and seasonal caravans. The grass pitches are of average size, shaded by mature trees and those on the perimeter have superb sea views. A new footpath leads down to the ruins of a once busy iron ore works and a small exhibition. This path continues along the coastline for 1.5 km. into Zarautz, but does involve lots of steep steps.

Facilities

Three well equipped toilet blocks, one of which is new (plans to build a sauna, gym and spa area above this block). Separate facilities for children and four large toilet/shower rooms for disabled visitors. Laundry facilities. New motorcaravan sevices point. Well stocked shop. Restaurant with 'menu del día' and à la carte meals. Bar/snack bar with TV plus terrace. Communal barbecue area with picnic tables. Play area. WiFi (80% coverage). Off site: Beach, fishing and golf (9 holes) 1 km. Bicycle hire 2 km. Shops, restaurants, bars, indoor pool plus bus/train services in Zarautz 2 km. Boat launching 4 km.

Open: All year.

Directions

Zarautz is 20 km. west of San Sebastián. From A8 (San Sebastián-Bilbao) take exit 11 for Zarautz and straight on through two roundabouts and follow signs to site. If using the N634 coast road, site is signed near km. 17 marker.
GPS: 43.28958, -2.14603

Charges guide

Per unit incl. 2 persons and electricity	€ 28.65
extra person	€ 5.90
child (under 12 yrs)	€ 4.30

Camping Cheques accepted.

This small region located in the north eastern part of the country is the most outstanding wine growing area in Spain. Its production, Rioja wine, figures among the finest wines in the world.

THIS IS A ONE PROVINCE REGION

THE CAPITAL IS LOGROÑO

The capital of the region, Logroño, did not gain importance till the 11th century, when the rise in popularity of the Pilgrims' Route to Santiago de Compostela attracted people. Indeed the 12th-century Codex Calixtinus, the first guide to the route, mentions the city. And throughout the region, every town along the way has a church dedicated to the saint. Pilgrimages aside, La Rioja is best known for its wine. At the centre of the region's wine production is Haro, a stately town northwest of Logroño, and obviously a good place to stock up on a bottle or two! For those interested in the wine processes the Museum of Wine is worth a visit; admission includes cheese and wine tasting. During the last week of June the town comes alive with festivities. With free outdoor concerts, costumed characters on giant stilts, wine tastings and bargain buys, the climax of these fiestas is the Battle of the Wine, where thousands of people happily gather to be drenched in wine.

Places of interest

Calahorra: main town in Lower Rioja, Cathedral Museum.

Ezcaray: in the Sierra de la Demanda mountains, the surrounding area is made up of streams, forests and peaks over 2,000 metres high.

Nájera: monastery of Santa María la Real, built in 1032, History and Archaeological Museum.

San Millán de la Cogolla: traditional town, Monasteries of Suso and Yuso where the first texts written in Spanish are preserved.

Santo Domingo de la Calzada: last great staging post of the Pilgrims' Route in La Rioja, Cathedral of San Salvador.

Cuisines of the region

Asparagus, beans, peppers, garlic, artichokes and other vegetables and pulses are the basic ingredients of a long list of dishes such as vegetable stew, potatoes *a la riojana*, lamb cutlets with vine shoots or stuffed peppers. Traditional desserts include pears in wine, almond pastries from Arnedo and marzipan from Soto.

Camerano Cheese: cheese made from goat's milk, typical of La Rioja, usually eaten as a dessert with honey.

Fardelejo: pastry cake filled with marzipan.

Riojan-style potatoes: prepared with chorizo, peppers, garlic and lamp chops (optional).

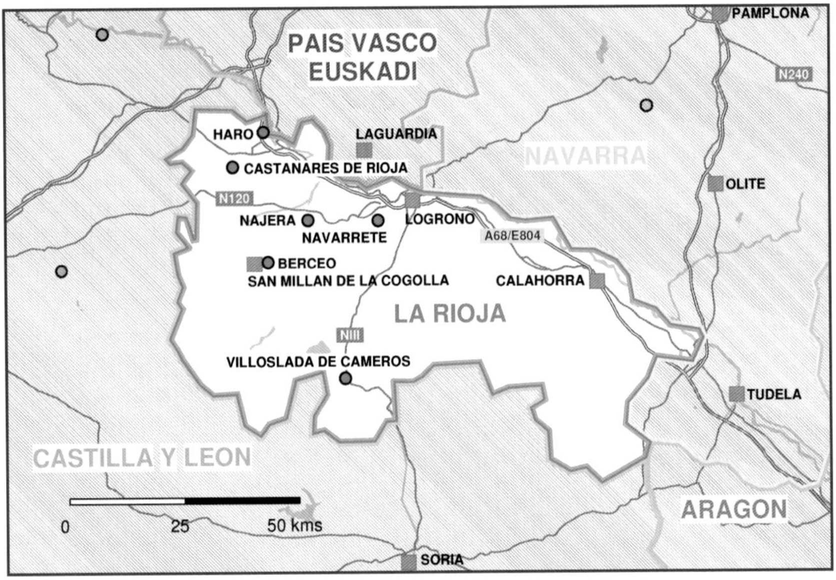

Berceo

Camping Berceo

Ctra de Nájera - Sto Domingo dir. San Millán, E-26227 Berceo (La Rioja) T: 941 373 227.

alanrogers.com/ES92280

Camping Berceo would ideally suit those looking for a quiet break at a site with limited facilities. It sits low in the San Millan valley in the heart of the Sierra de la Demanda and a steep walk of about 20 minutes will take you into the village. Here you will find several bars and restaurants, but little English is spoken. The 30 touring pitches are varied in size and separated by hedges. Some have shade and there are views of the green valley and mountains. Apart from the swimming pool which is open in peak season, there are few activities provided.

Facilities

One main toilet block providing sufficient facilities, but none for disabled visitors. Laundry area. Shop for basic supplies. Bar/restaurant. Takeaway on request. TV in bar and games area. Swimming and paddling pools. Play area. Off site: Berceo village 20 minute uphill walk. San Millan monasteries.

Open: All year.

Directions

From A68 head west until N120 exit. Turn left onto N120 signed Najera. Turn left onto LR113 (Bobadilla). Within 5 km. turn right onto 205 (Cárdenas) until Berceo village. In village centre follow site arrow down steep hill. Site is on left within 500 m. GPS: 42.33497, -2.85328

Charges guide

Per unit incl. 2 persons and electricity € 32.40 - € 42.10

Castanares de Rioja

Camping de La Rioja

Ctra de Haro - Sto Domingo de la Calzada, E-26240 Castanares de Rioja (La Rioja) T: 941 300 174.
E: info@campingdelarioja.com **alanrogers.com/ES92250**

This site is situated just beyond the town of Castanares de Rioja. This is a busy site during the peak season with many sporting activities taking place. In low season it becomes rather more quiet with limited facilities available. There are 30 level, grass touring pitches, out of a total of 250, and these are separated by hedges and trees allowing privacy. Each has their own water, drainage and electricity connection. To the rear of the site is the Oja river which is ideal for fishing and there are views of the Obarenes mountains in the distance. Some noise from the main road is possible.

Facilities

The central sanitary facilities are old and traditional in style but clean. Open style washbasins and controllable showers. Laundry facilities. Shop, bar, restaurant, takeaway (on request) all open 20/6-20/9. Outdoor swimming pool (20/6-20/9 supervised). Multisports court. Football. Tennis. River fishing. Riding. Children's cycle circuit. Play area. No individual barbecues.
Off site: Town centre 1.5 km. Guggenheim Museum.

Open: 1 January - 9 December.

Directions

Head west on N120. Turn right onto LR111 signed Castanares de Rioja. Continue through town towards Haro. Site is on left, 800 m. after leaving town speed restriction. GPS: 42.52911, -2.92243

Charges guide

Per person	€ 6.60 - € 7.48
child	€ 5.01 - € 5.90
pitch	€ 16.20
electricity	€ 4.67

Haro

Camping de Haro

Avenida Miranda 1, E-26200 Haro (La Rioja) T: 941 312 737. E: campingdeharo@fer.es
alanrogers.com/ES90400

This quiet riverside site is on the outskirts of Haro, the commercial centre for the renowned Rioja wines. It is a family run site with excellent pools. Staff in the modern reception are helpful and you may well get a cheery welcome from Carlos, the owner's son, who speaks excellent English. All 236 pitches are on level ground and of reasonable size. Approximately 50% are occupied on a seasonal basis. Many of the touring pitches have some shade, a few have a great deal. Electricity connections (6A) are provided, although long leads may be required on some pitches.

Facilities

Two toilet blocks, one heated in winter, the other with facilities for disabled campers. Laundry. Bar/snack bar with small counter selling basic provisions and adjacent swimming pool (15/6-15/9). Play area and entertainment for children in season. WiFi over part of site (charged). Torch useful. Charcoal barbecues are not permitted.
Off site: Large municipal pool complex nearby. Shops, bars, restaurants within walking distance. Bicycle hire 1 km. Boat launching 6 km. Riding 24 km. Golf 25 km.

Open: All year excl. 9 December - 19 January.

Directions

From AP68 (Bilbao-Logroño) take exit 9 to Haro. Keep to LR111 (Vitoria) bearing left, crossing lights and over river where site is signed to left. From N124 (Vitoria-Logroño) leave at exit north of Haro onto LR111 towards town and turn right before bridge (site signed). Avoid other turnings into town centre! GPS: 42.57894, -2.85157

Charges guide

Per unit incl. 2 persons and electricity	€ 21.35 - € 26.95
extra person	€ 4.30 - € 5.70

Najera

Camping El Ruedo

Paseo San Julián 24, E-26300 Najera (La Rioja) T: 941 360 102.
alanrogers.com/ES92290

Camping El Ruedo is situated 500 m. from the town of Najera and the River Rio Najerilla runs close by. There are numerous walks possible and seating provided along the riverbank. This is a small site with a total of 20 touring pitches on level ground, unmarked and with no separation. You can pitch at your own discretion. The traditional style sanitary block is kept clean and tidy with ample provision for the small amount of visitors. Extremely quiet and with very basic facilities, this site would suit those looking for peace and tranquillity. The site is not suitable for large units. No English is spoken.

Facilities

One immaculate toilet block with washbasins and showers. No facilities for disabled visitors. Washing machines (rather old). No shop, but provisions in town. Swings. No site lighting so torches useful. Off site: Town 500 m. (10 minutes' walk).

Open: 1 April - 10 September.

Directions

From Logroño head west on AP68 until sign for N120 Najera. Turn left onto LR113 signed Najera. At traffic lights turn sharp left immediately before cobbled bridge. Site on left within 500 m. It is poorly signed after the A12. GPS: 42.41068, -2.73284

Charges guide

Per unit incl. 2 persons	€ 21.00
extra person	€ 5.30

Navarrete

Camping Navarrete

Ctra de Entrena km. 1, E-26370 Navarrete (La Rioja) T: 941 440 169. E: campingnavarrete@fer.es

alanrogers.com/ES92270

Camping Navarrete is a spotlessly clean site in which the owners take great pride. Ideal as a base for exploring the surrounding countryside and sampling wonderful wines as it is located in the heart of La Rioja. Many of the 180 pitches are taken up by static caravans but a designated grassy area has been set aside for 40 unmarked, spacious touring pitches with 5A electricity. Some have shade and there are good views of the Rioja valley. Facilities on site are limited until the height of the season but the area is surrounded by many villages and places of artistic and historical importance. Noise is possible from the road.

Facilities

One modern central sanitary block with heating is clean and provides communal washbasins and separate shower cubicles. Facilities for disabled visitors, one unisex cabin. Laundry facilities. Motorcaravan services. Bar with mini-market, restaurant and takeaway (weekends only in low season). Outdoor swimming and paddling pools (15/6-15/9). Games machines. Tennis. Unfenced play area. Barbecues are allowed in special area of the campsite. WiFi (free). Off site: Riding 1 km. Bicycle hire 1.5 km. Golf 5 km. Large town of Logroño 10 km.

Open: 12 January - 10 December.

Directions

From Logroño proceed west along AP68. Take exit 11 signed Navarrete. At town centre turn left onto LR137 signed Entrena. Site is on the right in 800 m. GPS: 42.41614, -2.55172

Charges guide

Per unit incl. 2 persons and electricity	€ 22.50 - € 27.70
extra person	€ 4.75 - € 5.80
child (under 10 yrs)	€ 4.40 - € 5.20
dog	€ 2.00

Villoslada de Cameros

Camping Los Cameros

Ctra de la Virgen de Lomos de Orios km. 3, E-26125 Villoslada de Cameros (La Rioja) T: 941 747 021. E: info@camping-loscameros.com **alanrogers.com/ES92260**

Situated 3 km. from the small town of Villoslada de Cameros, this site is in a quiet location, in a valley surrounded by tree covered mountains. The area provides the opportunity for plenty of hill walking and a footpath from the site takes you into the town. Of the 173 pitches, 146 are available for touring. They are open with some shade and have 5/10A electricity. This is a simple site with limited facilities available but it is well kept and has character; ideal for relaxation. A large playing field allows children to play ball games and bicycles can be hired from reception.

Facilities

One heated sanitary block provides WCs, washbasins with cold water only (one with hot water) and cubicle showers. No facilities for disabled visitors. Cold water only for washing machine and dishwashing. Shop. Bar with games. Restaurant with comprehensive menu and takeaway to order. Playing field and play area. Picnic area. Only gas barbecues permitted. Off site: Town 3 km. with shops, bars and restaurants and swimming pool.

Open: 20 January - 20 December.

Directions

From Logroño (AP68) turn left onto N111 heading south towards Soria and Madrid. At sign for Villoslada de Cameros turn right, pass the centre and turn left by camping sign (LR448). Site on left in 3 km. Road bumpy and uneven, drive with care and watch for animals on road. GPS: 42.08068, -2.67723

Charges guide

Per unit incl. 2 persons and electricity	€ 22.80 - € 25.20
extra person	€ 4.30 - € 4.90
child (under 10 yrs)	€ 3.65 - € 4.15

The region of Navarra lies in the north of Spain, separated from France by the Pyrenees. With mountain retreats, beautiful valleys and an array of attractive towns and historic buildings, it is also popular for those wishing to follow the Pilgrims' Route to Santiago de Compostela.

THERE IS ONLY ONE PROVINCE ALSO KNOWN AS NAVARRA

THE CAPITAL IS PAMPLONA

Founded by the Roman general Pompey in 75 BC, the region's capital, Pamplona, is perhaps best known for the Fiestas de San Fermín (July), when the encierro takes place, a tradition which involves people running through the streets in front of bulls. The city also boasts its fair share of sights including the old town, with its ancient churches and elegant buildings. Outside the city is the Sierra de Aralar, with well marked paths of all grades. A wander through here will take you past waterfalls and caves and in Excelsis you'll come across Navarra's oldest church, the Sanctuario de San Miguel, a popular pilgrimage destination. In the south, the historic medieval town of Olite is home to an outstanding 15th-century castle, with turrets galore, and a Romanesque and Gothic church. To the west is the Urbasa and Andía Nature Reserve. Further north and in the east, the villages and valleys of the Pyrenees provide some of the most beautiful landscapes in the province and offer the perfect place to relax. Of particular note are the Valle de Baztán and the Valle de Salazar. For the more active, the Valle de Roncal is a good place to explore the mountains, as is the Pirenaico National Park.

Places of interest

Andía Nature Reserve: forests, ponds, wildlife including the golden eagle, wild boar and wildcat.

Camino de Santiago: ancient Pilgrims' route. There are variants but the most popular point of entry into Spain was the pass of Roncesvalles, in the Pyrenees. It then continues south through Navarra via Sangüesa, Puente La Reina and Estella, then west through the provinces of La Rioja and Castilla-León till it reaches Santiago in the Galicia province.

Orreaga-Roncesvalles: a town established as a sanctuary and hospital in 1132 and first staging post for pilgrims, museum with exhibition on the Pilgrims' Route.

Sangüesa: small town, 14th-century churches, medieval hospital.

Ujué: medieval defensive village, Romanesqe church.

Cuisine of the region

Typical products found in abundance in this area include asparagus grown on the river banks, small red peppers and artichokes from Tudela, pork from Estella, cherries from Ciriza, cheese made in the Roncal Valley and *chorizo* from Pamplona.

Ajoarriero: cod cooked with garlic, potato, 'choricero' peppers and tomatoes.

Canutillos de Sumbilla: sweet pastry made with aniseed, filled with lemon flavouring.

Chorizo: shaped like a candle, stuffed in thick tripe with pork and beef, seasoned with salt, paprika, garlic and sugars.

Cordero al chilindrón: lamb stew.

Cuajada: made from sheep's milk and natural curd, sweetened by honey or sugar.

Pacharán: traditional aniseed liquor.

Erratzu

Camping Baztan

Ctra Francia s/n, E-31714 Erratzu (Navarra) T: 948 453 133. E: campingbaztan@campingbaztan.com

alanrogers.com/ES90490

When driving through the small town of Erratzu, extreme caution is required due to the narrowness of the streets and it is not advised at all for large units. This site's rural setting and the mountain views make this a retreat for those who enjoy camping in quiet surroundings. It consists of a main building housing reception, a shop, a bar and a small restaurant beneath 14 tidy apartments. There are also ten timber cottages for rent. Tarmac roads lead to the grass touring pitches, which are supplied with water and electricity (10A). Shady and of a good size, most of the pitches are level. In early and late season, the campsite is open but a telephone call is necessary to gain access. You may be the only occupants.

Facilities

The single sanitary block is clean and has facilities for disabled visitors. Shop, bar and restaurant (weekends only outside 1/6-20/9). Swimming pool (1/6-20/9). Squash court. Only charcoal barbecues permitted. In April, May and 20/9-1/11 the site is only open at weekends. If you wish to stay on weekdays, entry can be obtained by dialling a number displayed at reception (sanitary block will be open). Off site: River fishing 50 m. Village (5 mins. walk) with a small supermarket, bars and restaurant. Riding 2 km. Excursions arranged to activity centre (riding, kayaking, rafting) 15 km. away. Buses run to Pamplona and San Sebastian (3 per day, all year). Bicycle hire 15 km. Golf (in France) 20 km.

Open: 10 March - 9 December.

Directions

From Hendaye head south on the N121A. Turn east on N121B. Continue north to the junction with NA2600. Turn right to Erratzu. Proceed through village, bear left at sign 'Francia NA2600' and site is on the right. GPS: 43.18067, -1.45139

Charges guide

Per unit incl. 2 persons and electricity	€ 24.50 - € 35.10

Espinal

Camping Urrobi

Ctra Pamplona-Valcarlos km. 42 N135, E-31694 Espinal (Navarra) T: 948 760 200.
E: info@campingurrobi.com **alanrogers.com/ES90480**

This large site is in a beautiful location with mountain views. At the entrance is a lively bar, a reasonably priced restaurant and a well stocked shop. The site is popular with Spanish families and there are many mobile homes, so it can be busy at holiday times and weekends. However, there is plenty of room on the 150 unmarked grass pitches. All have electricity points (6A) and there are plenty of water taps. Water activities of all types are catered for, with both a swimming pool and an area of the river sectioned off for safe bathing and paddling. This is a suitable site for families.

Facilities

Clean sanitary blocks include facilities for disabled visitors (key from reception). Laundry facilities. Motorcaravan service point. Shop, bar and restaurant (all season). Swimming pool. Games room with TV (Spanish). Internet access. Minigolf. Tennis. Playing field. Play area. WiFi (free). Off site: Village 1 km. with shops, restaurant and bars. Forest of Irati 15 minutes. Bicycle hire 15 km.

Open: 22 March - 3 November.

Directions

From Pamplona take N135 northeast for 42 km. After village of Auritzberri turn right onto NA172. Site is on the left. GPS: 42.97315, -1.351817

Charges guide

Per unit incl. 2 persons and electricity	€ 24.00 - € 25.50
extra person	€ 5.00

Etxarri-Aranatz

Camping Etxarri

Paraje Dambolintxulo s/n, E-31820 Etxarri-Aranatz (Navarra) T: 948 460 537. E: info@campingetxarri.com
alanrogers.com/ES90420

Situated in the Valle de la Burundi, this site is a peaceful oasis with superb views of the 1,300 m. high San-Donator Mountains. The approach to this improving site is via a road lined by huge 300-year-old oak trees, which are a feature of the site. Reception is housed in the main building beside the pool with a restaurant above (access also by lift). There are 108 pitches of average size on flat ground (50 for touring units) with 6A electricity to all and water to 25. The site is well placed for fascinating walks in unspoilt countryside and is close to three recognised nature walks. The site gets very crowded during the Fiestas de San Fermín (bull running) in Pamplona, early in July. It is essential to make a reservation if you wish to stay. A visit to Pamplona is recommended. Parking is difficult – try to the west of the bullring, then wander down to Plaza de Toros (renamed Plaza Hemingway), to savour the atmosphere. It is common to use dual naming of places and roads (one in the Spanish language, the other in Basque and it can be confusing) – ask for advice if in doubt.

Facilities

Toilet facilities are good and include a baby bath and facilities for disabled visitors. Laundry. Motorcaravan service point. Gas supplies. Essential supplies kept in high season. Bar (1/4-30/9). Restaurant and takeaway (1/6-15/9). Swimming and paddling pools (15/6-15/9) also open to the public and can get crowded. Bicycle hire. Minigolf. Play area. Entertainment for children in high season. WiFi (charged). Tennis. Squash. No charcoal barbecues. Off site: Bars, restaurants and shops 2 km. Golf, fishing and riding all 20 km. Pamplona 40 km.

Open: 1 March - 13 October.

Directions

Etxarri-Aranatz is 40 km. northwest of Pamplona. From A8 (San Sebastián-Bilbao) take A15 towards Pamplona, then 20 km. northwest of Pamplona, take A10 west towards Vitoria/Gasteix. At km. 19 take NA120 to and through town (site signed). Cross railway and turn left to site at end of road. GPS: 42.913031, -2.079924

Charges guide

Per unit incl. 2 persons and electricity	€ 29.50

FREE Alan Rogers Travel Card

Extra benefits and savings - see page 10

Mendigorría

Camping El Molino de Mendigorría

E-31150 Mendigorria (Navarra) T: 948 340 604. E: info@campingelmolino.com

alanrogers.com/ES90430

This is an extensive site set by an attractive weir near the town of Mendigorría, alongside the River Arga. It takes its name from an old disused water mill (molino) close by. The site is split into separate permanent and touring sections. The touring area is a new development with good sized flat pitches with electricity and water for touring units, and a separate area for tents. Many trees have been planted around the site but there is still only minimal shade. The friendly owner, Anna Beriain, will give you a warm welcome. The site has a sophisticated dock and boat launching facility and an ambitious watersports competition programme in season with a safety boat present at all times.

Facilities

The well equipped toilet block is very clean and well maintained, with cold water to washbasins. Facilities for disabled campers. Washing machine. Large restaurant, pleasant bar. Supermarket. Superb new swimming pools for adults and children (1/6-15/9). Bicycle hire. Riverside bar. Weekly entertainment programme (July/Aug) and many sporting activities. Squash courts. Internet access. River walk. Torches useful. Off site: Bus to Pamplona 500 m. Riding 15 km. Golf 35 km.

Open: All year (excl. 23 December - 4 January).

Directions

Mendigorría is 30 km. southwest of Pamplona. From A15 San Sebastián-Zaragoza motorway, leave Pamplona bypass on A12 towards Logon. Leave at km. 23 on NA601 to hilltop town of Mendigorría. At crossroads turn right towards Larraga and downhill to site. GPS: 42.62423, -1.84259

Charges guide

Per person	€ 4.70 - € 5.00
child	€ 3.95 - € 4.22
pitch incl. car and electricity	€ 12.90 - € 13.80

Discounts outside high season.

In the north eastern part of Spain, Aragón borders France with the Pyrenees lying between them. It is a region rich in folklore, with rural, mountainside villages renowned for their Romanesque architecture, beautiful valleys and awe-inspiring peaks.

ARAGÓN IS MADE UP OF THREE PROVINCES: HUESCA, ZARAGOZA AND TERUEL

THE CAPITAL OF THE REGION IS ZARAGOZA

The region can be separated into three different areas: the central area consisting of the Ebro basin, a vast flat lowland, the northern Pyrenees, and the area made up of the Iberian mountain range in the northwest and southeast of the region. The northern-most province of Huesca is located in the foothills of the Pyrenees mountains, a beautiful area with plenty of picturesque towns and villages to visit. It is also good walking country with numerous trails offering anything from short day-walks in the valleys to long-distance treks in the mountains. Skiing is popular too. Bordering Huesca, the province of Zaragoza is home to the region's capital, also of the same name. Zaragoza is a lively town with plenty of bars and restaurants, plus numerous museums and architectural treasures. Outside the capital you'll find more villages, countryside, and vineyards where the best of the region's wine is produced; the mapped out Ruta del Vino will take you through the area. The third province of Teruel is largely comprised of the Iberian mountain range, with attractive towns, medieval sights and more dramatic scenery to admire.

Places of interest

Aljafería Palace: spectacular Moorish monument.

Basílica de Nuestra Señora del Pilar: Baroque temple from the 17th and 18th centuries.

Benasque: attractive alpine town, gateway to the Pyrenees.

Casa-Museo de Goya: art museum, including engravings by Goya.

Jaca: home of the country's oldest Romanesque cathedral.

Monasterio de San Juan de la Peña: 17th-century Baroque monastery and 10th-century monastery in Romanesque style.

Parque Nacional de Ordesa y Monte Perdido: alpine national park.

Cuisine of the region

Specialities include lamb, locally produced ham and sausages; fruit is also used a lot in desserts.

Chilindrones: sauce of tomato and pepper.

Frutas de Aragón: sugar-candied fruits covered in chocolate.

Pollo al chilindrón: chicken (or lamb) stew with onions, tomatoes and red peppers.

Salmorrejos: cold soup.

Suspiros de amante: dessert with cheese and egg.

Ternasco: roast lamb.

Tortas de alma: dessert made with pumpkin, honey and sugar.

Trenza de Almudévar: dessert with nuts and raisins soaked in liqueur.

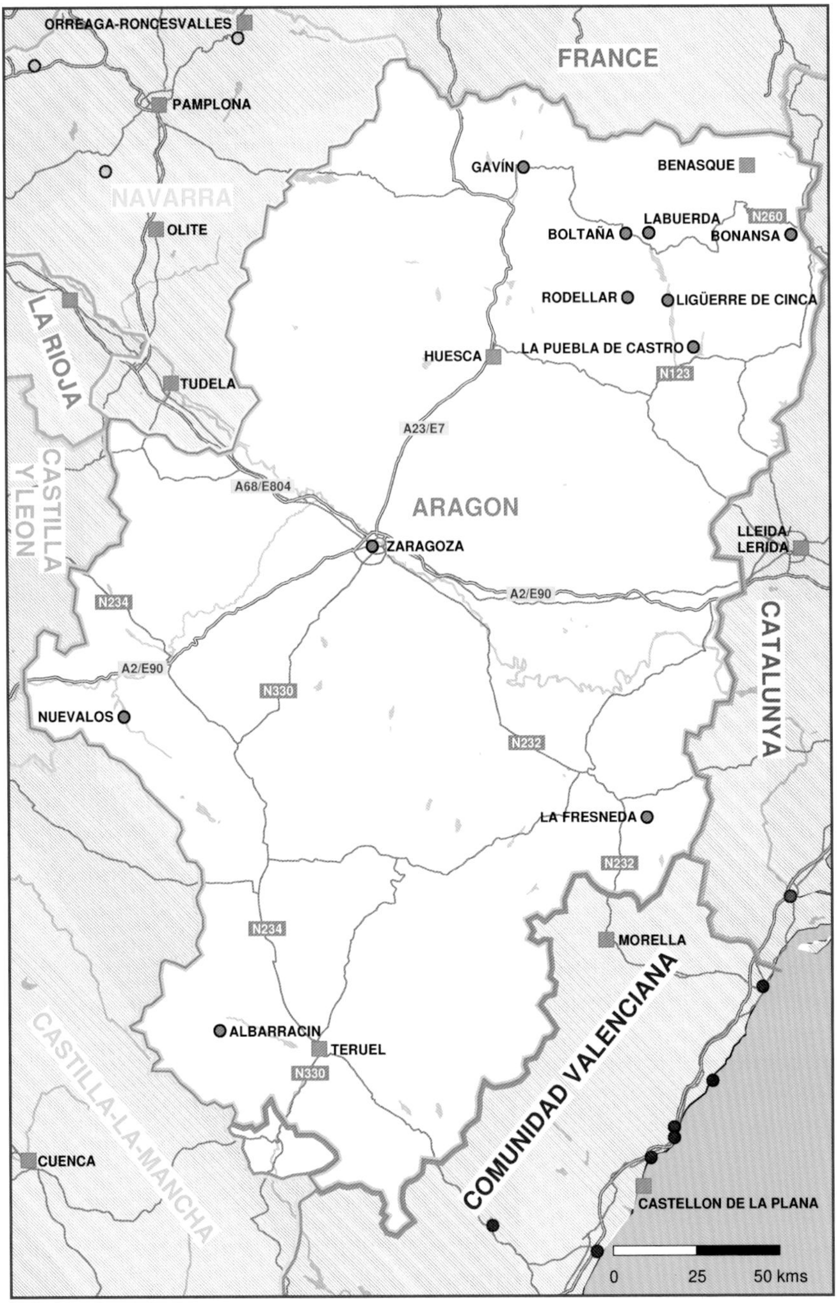
ORREAGA-RONCESVALLES
FRANCE
PAMPLONA
NAVARRA
OLITE
GAVÍN
BENASQUE
LABUERDA
N260
BOLTAÑA
BONANSA
LA RIOJA
RODELLAR
LIGÜERRE DE CINCA
HUESCA
LA PUEBLA DE CASTRO
N123
TUDELA
A23/E7
CASTILLA Y LEON
A68/E804
ARAGON
LLEIDA/ LERIDA
ZARAGOZA
A2/E90
N234
CATALUNYA
A2/E90
N330
NUEVALOS
N232
LA FRESNEDA
N232
MORELLA
N234
COMUNIDAD VALENCIANA
ALBARRACIN
TERUEL
N330
CASTILLA-LA-MANCHA
CUENCA
CASTELLON DE LA PLANA
0
25
50 kms

Albarracin

Camping Ciudad de Albarracin

Junto al Polideportivo, Camino de Gea, E-44100 Albarracin (Teruel) T: 978 710 197.
E: campingalbarracin5@hotmail.com **alanrogers.com/ES90950**

Albarracin, in southern Aragón, is set in the Reserva Nacional de los Montes Universales and is a much frequented, fascinating town with a Moorish castle. The old city walls towering above date from its days when it attempted to become a separate country within Spain. This neat and clean family site is set on three levels on a hillside behind the town, with a walk of 1 km. to the centre. It is very modern and has high quality facilities including a superb building for barbecuing. There are 140 pitches (70 for touring units), all with electricity and separated by trees. Some require cars to be parked separately.

Facilities

The two spotless, modern sanitary buildings provide British style WCs and quite large showers. Baby bath. Washing machines. Bar/restaurant. Essentials from bar. Special room for barbecues with fire and wood provided. Play area. Torches required in some areas. Off site: Municipal swimming pool 100 m. (high season). Town shops, bars and restaurants 500 m. Fishing 1 km.

Open: 1 March - 2 November.

Directions

From Teruel north on the N330 for 8 km. then west onto A1512 for 30 km. From the A23 use exit 124 then the A1512, from the N235 take exit for Albarracin and the A1512. Site is well signed in the town. GPS: 40.41655, -1.43332

Charges guide

Per unit incl. 2 persons and electricity	€ 19.35
extra person	€ 4.00

Boltaña

Camping Boltaña

Ctra N260 km. 442, E-22340 Boltaña (Huesca) T: 974 502 347. E: info@campingboltana.com
alanrogers.com/ES90620

Nestled in the Rio Ara valley, surrounded by the Pyrenees mountains and below a tiny but enchanting, historic, hilltop village, is the very pretty, thoughtfully planned Camping Boltaña. Generously sized, 190 grassy pitches (all with 10A electricity) have good shade from a variety of trees and a stream meanders through the campsite. The landscaping includes ten charming rocky water gardens and a covered pergola doubles as an eating and play area. Angel Moreno, the owner of the site, is a charming host and has tried to think of everything to make his guests comfortable.

Facilities

Two modern sanitary blocks include facilities for disabled visitors and laundry facilities. Supermarket. Bar, restaurant and takeaway (1/6-31/8). Swimming pools (15/6-15/9). Playground. Entertainment for children (high season). Pétanque. Guided tours, plus hiking, canyoning, rafting, climbing, mountain biking and caving. Bicycle hire. Fridge hire. WiFi. No charcoal barbecues. Torches useful in some parts. Off site: Local bus service. Fishing 1 km.

Open: All year.

Directions

South of the Park Nacional de Ordesa, site is 50 km. from Jaca near Ainsa. From Ainsa travel northwest on N260 toward Boltaña (near 443 km. marker) and 1 km. from Boltaña turn south toward Margudgued. Site is well signed and is 1 km. along this road. GPS: 42.43018, 0.07882

Charges guide

Per unit incl. 2 persons and electricity	€ 35.40
extra person	€ 6.50

Camping Cheques accepted.

Bonansa

Camping Baliera

Ctra N260 km. 355,5, E-22486 Bonansa (Huesca) T: 974 554 016. E: info@baliera.com
alanrogers.com/ES90580

With its wonderful location in a quiet river valley with views of the surrounding mountains, Camping Baliera is an excellent site for enjoying this beautiful area. Combining camping with timber chalets and apartments, the site has 133 well kept grass touring pitches (80-120 sq.m) all with electricity (5/7/10A). The pitches are mostly located close to the attractive, stone built reception building which also houses a comfortable bar and shop. The approach to this site is by narrow and winding mountain roads and it is 5 km. from the nearest village. However, for all but the largest units, the trip is well worth making.

Facilities

Two heated toilet blocks, one part of the apartment block near the entrance, the other in the reception building (closed in low season). They are good with well equipped showers and vanity style washbasins. Laundry room and drying room. Motorcaravan services. Shop (1/7-31/8). Bar (automatic). Takeaway (1/7-31/8). Swimming pool (1/6-15/9). Fitness equipment. Play area. Entertainment in high season. Communal barbecue. WiFi.

Open: 1 December - 31 October.

Directions

On N230, 34 km. south of Vielha, turn on N260 for 2-3 km, then onto A1605 signed Graus for 100 m. to site on left. Reception is 200 m. through the site. Approach roads are narrow and winding, but navigable. GPS: 42.43958, 0.69918

Charges guide

Per unit incl. 2 persons and electricity	€ 31.92 - € 38.40

Camping Cheques accepted.

Gavín

Camping Gavín

Ctra N260 km. 503, E-22639 Gavín (Huesca) T: 974 485 090. E: info@campinggavin.com

alanrogers.com/ES90640

Camping Gavín is set on a terraced, wooded hillside and you will find a friendly welcome. The site offers 150 pitches of 90 sq.m. in size and with electricity available to all (10A). In some areas the terracing means that some pitches are quite small. The main site buildings have been constructed using natural stone. There are also 13 bungalows and 11 superb, balconied apartments. At about 900 m. the site is surrounded by towering peaks at the portal of the Tena Valley. One can enjoy the natural beauty of the Pyrenees and venture near or far along the great Pyrenean footpaths.

Facilities

Excellent shower and toilet facilities in three main buildings with subtle, tasteful décor include facilities for babies and disabled visitors. Laundry facilities. Bar and snacks. Well stocked supermarket. Swimming pools (15/6-15/9). Paddling pools. Tennis. Playground. Barbecues are not permitted at some times of the year. Bicycle hire. Off site: Windsurfing, rafting, fishing, walking and climbing in the vicinity. Riding 6 km. Golf 15 km.

Open: All year.

Directions

Site is off the N260, 2 km. from Biescas at km. 503. GPS: 42.61940, -0.30408

Charges guide

Per unit incl. 2 persons and electricity	€ 29.92 - € 37.37
extra person	€ 4.60 - € 6.30

La Fresneda

Camping la Fresneda

Partida Vall del Pi, E-44596 La Fresneda (Teruel) T: 978 854 085. E: info@campinglafresneda.com

alanrogers.com/ES91100

La Fresneda is a great little campsite, situated on three terraces at the foot of a wooded escarpment and overlooking the huge valley of the National Reserve of Los Puertos de Beceite. Everything is in line with the natural beauty of the area and the very clean, very well equipped, toilet block is partly underground. There are 25 pitches with grass and gravel surfaces, all used for touring and with 6A electricity. The site is quite new and the enthusiastic Dutch owners, Jet Knijn and her partner, Joost Leeuwenberg, built it from scratch, recently adding a shady garden atrium with a terrace and plunge pool.

Facilities

Toilet block with hot water throughout. Washing machine. Bar with terrace where meals are served daily except Mondays. Fresh bread daily (except Sundays). Garden atrium with terrace and plunge pool. Information on walking and cycling routes. Pets are not accepted. WiFi throughout (charged). Off site: Baker, grocer, butcher and restaurants in the village. Supermarkets at Alcañiz 30 minutes drive. Bicycle hire and fishing 10 km.

Open: 1 April - 1 October.

Directions

From the N232 (Alcañiz-Vinaros/Castellón) turn off just east of Valdealgorfa (at Restaurant Las Ventas) onto A231 to Valjunquera/Valderrobres, then La Fresneda. GPS: 40.90695, 0.061667

Charges guide

Per unit incl. 2 persons and electricity	€ 24.50
extra person	€ 5.50
child (0-1 yrs)	free

La Puebla de Castro

Camping Barasona

Ctra N123a km. 25, E-22435 La Puebla de Castro (Huesca) T: 974 545 148. E: info@lagobarasona.com

alanrogers.com/ES91250

This site, alongside its associated ten room hotel, is beautifully positioned on terraces across a road from the shores of the Lago de Barasona (a large reservoir), with views of hills and the distant Pyrenees. The very friendly, English-speaking owner is keen to please and has applied very high standards throughout the site. The grassy, fairly level pitches are generally around 100 sq.m. with 35 high quality pitches of 110 sq.m. for larger units. All have electricity (6/10A), many are well shaded and some have great views of the lake and/or hills. This is a most pleasant and peaceful site in a lovely area and will suit families who wish for quality and choice in their camping. The views really are beautiful.

Facilities

Two toilet blocks in modern buildings have high standards and hot water throughout including cabins (3 for women, 1 for men). Bar/snack bar and two excellent restaurants (all season). Shop (1/4-30/9). Swimming pools (1/6-30/9). Tennis. Mountain bike hire. Canoe, windsurfing, motorboat and pedalo hire. Miniclub (high season). Lake swimming, fishing, canoeing, etc. Walking (maps provided). Money exchange. Mini-disco. WiFi. Wellness centre with sauna, jacuzzi and gym. Off site: Riding 4 km.

Open: All year.

Directions

Site is on the west bank of the lake, close to km. 25 on the N123A, 6 km. south of Graus (about 80 km. north of Lleida/Lerida). Travelling from the south, the site is on the left from a newly built roundabout and slip road. GPS: 42.14163, 0.31525

Charges guide

Per unit incl. 2 persons and electricity	€ 23.00 - € 36.80
extra person	€ 4.50 - € 6.90

Labuerda

Camping Peña Montañesa

Ctra Ainsa-Francia km 2, E-22360 Labuerda (Huesca) T: 974 500 032. E: info@penamontanesa.com
alanrogers.com/ES90600

A large site situated quite high up in the Pyrenees near the Ordesa National Park, Peña Montañesa is easily accessible from Ainsa or from France via the Bielsa Tunnel (steep sections on the French side). The site is essentially divided into three sections opening progressively throughout the season and all have shade. The 288 pitches on fairly level grass are of about 75 sq.m. and 10A electricity is available on virtually all. Grouped near the entrance are the facilities that make the site so attractive, including a fair sized outdoor pool and a glass-covered indoor pool with jacuzzi and sauna. The site is ideally situated for exploring the beautiful Pyrenees.

Facilities

A newer toilet block, heated when necessary, has free hot showers but cold water to open plan washbasins. Facilities for disabled visitors. Small baby room. An older block in the original area has similar provision. Washing machine and dryer. Bar, restaurant, takeaway and supermarket (all 1/1-31/12). Outdoor swimming pool (1/4-31/10). Indoor pool. Playground. Boules. Riding. Rafting. Bicycle hire. Gas barbecues only. Torches required in some areas. WiFi (free). Off site: Fishing 100 m. Skiing in season. Canoeing nearby.

Open: All year.

Directions

Site is 2 km. from Ainsa, on the road from Ainsa to France. GPS: 42.4352, 0.13618

Charges guide

Per unit incl. 2 persons and electricity	€ 25.25 - € 33.70

Ligüerre de Cinca

Camping Ligüerre de Cinca

Ctra A138 km. 28 de Barbastro a Ainsa, E-22393 Ligüerre de Cinca (Huesca) T: 974 500 800.
E: info@liguerredecinca.com **alanrogers.com/ES90610**

Ligüerre de Cinca, a medieval village abandoned when the El Grado reservoir was constructed, is now being regenerated for tourism. It is situated near the Ordesa National Park, in a beautiful region of the Pyrenees mountains and has the advantage of being open all year. Attractive traditional style buildings house the reception, bar, restaurant and takeaway. The swimming and paddling pools are surrounded by grass sunbathing areas with wonderful mountain views. There are 150 small, terraced, level pitches marked out and shaded by tall trees. These include 110 for touring units, all with 10A electricity. Access is easy for large outfits.

Facilities

Adequate central toilet block, heated in winter, with smaller one on periphery. No facilities for disabled campers. Shop (July/Aug). Bar, restaurant, takeaway. Swimming and paddling pools (July/Aug). Miniclub (July/Aug). Multisports court. Tennis. Boules. Playground. Fishing and watersports, boat storage. Organised watersports including courses. Internet access. ATM. Barbecues are not allowed. Off site: Bus to Huesca. Rafting, canyoning, climbing, biking, hiking. Ancient villages and wonderful area for lovers of mountains. Riding 18 km.

Open: All year.

Directions

Site is between El Grado and Ainsa on the N138. From the Tunnel de Bielsa at the French/Spanish border, go south on N138, through Ainsa. Site is on left in 20 km. GPS: 42.28111, 0.19638

Charges guide

Per person	€ 5.00
child (2-10 yrs)	€ 4.80
pitch	€ 5.75 - € 7.05

Low season and long stay discounts.

Nuevalos

Camping Lago Park

Ctra Alhama de Aragon-Nuevalos, E-50210 Nuevalos (Zaragoza) T: 976 849 038.

alanrogers.com/ES91050

Lago Park is situated in an attractive area which receives many visitors for the Monasterio de Piedra just 3 km. distant and it enjoys pleasant views of the surrounding mountains. This site is suitable for transit stops or if you wish to visit the monasterio, as it is the only one hereabouts and appears to make the most of that fact. It is not recommended for extended stays. Set on a steep hillside, the 280 pitches (260 for touring units) are on terraces. Only the lower rows are suitable for large caravans. These pitches are numbered and marked by trees, most having electricity (10A). The site's rather steep access and slopes probably make it unsuitable for disabled campers.

Facilities

The single very clean sanitary block has British style WCs, washbasins with hot water and controllable hot showers (no dividers). Restaurant/bar (June-Sept). Shop (all season). Swimming pool (late June-Sept). Play area. Gas supplies. Torches needed in some areas. Off site: Fishing 300 m. Riding 2 km.

Open: 1 April - 30 September.

Directions

From Zaragoza (120 km) take fast A2/N11/E90 road and turn onto C202 road beyond Calatayud to Nuévalos (25 km). From Madrid, exit A2 at Alhama de Aragón (13 km). Follow signs for Monasterio de Piedra from all directions. GPS: 41.21800, -1.792

Charges guide

Per unit incl. 2 persons and electricity	€ 23.05 - € 32.90
extra person	€ 4.60 - € 6.60

Rodellar

Camping El Puente

Ctra NZ40, E-22144 Rodellar (Huesca) T: 974 318 312. E: info@campingelpuente.com

alanrogers.com/ES90630

Situated in the world famous Parc de la Sierra y los Canyons de Guara in Aragon, this specialised site is a must for those who wish to experience canyoning and climbing. There are 78 rather dusty pitches, which are shaded by mature trees, just 12 with 6A electricity. The site is set on a hillside, although any views are restricted by trees. A pleasant restaurant serves excellent food at no-nonsense prices. A professional team of guides is here to hire, as is all the necessary equipment for you to experience the thrills of around 100 superb canyons in the area.

Facilities

One sanitary block has mature but clean facilities. Good hot showers. Cold water at washing sinks, hot for dishwashing. Motorcaravan service point. Washing machines. Well stocked shop. Excellent restaurant. Snack bar. Barbecue areas. River swimming. Fishing. Canyon guides and canyoning and climbing equipment for hire. Tourist information. Off site: Village of Rodella with all facilities 1 km. Adventurous sports.

Open: Easter - 1 November.

Directions

From the N240 (Lleida-Huesca), 15 km. west of Barbastro take A1229 (Abiego), then A1227 to Abiego and Bierge. Take the HU341 to Las Aluminas and continue to Rodellar. Site signed 1 km. before village. The village streets are unsuitable for caravans and motorcaravans. GPS: 42.274104, -0.073222

Charges guide

Per unit incl. 2 persons	€ 20.75 - € 22.80
extra person	€ 5.25 - € 5.90

Zaragoza

Camping Ciudad de Zaragoza

Ctra San Juan Bautista de la Salle s/n, E-50012 Zaragoza (Zaragoza) T: 876 241 495.

E: info@campingzaragoza.com **alanrogers.com/ES91040**

Zaragoza is a popular en route stop between the ports of Santander and Bilbao and the beaches of the Costa Brava. The city, however, has much more to offer as the former capital of Aragon and now Spain's fifth largest city. Primarily for short stay, transit visitors, this all-year site gives impressions of concrete, metal and plastic, although it will soften in time. There are 103 touring pitches with electricity and water, which are mostly of gravel and without shade as yet. A modern bar/restaurant serves good food at reasonable prices, there are good facilities for children and the very pleasant swimming and paddling pools are welcome as it gets very hot here.

Facilities

Modern toilet blocks include good facilities for disabled visitors. Motorcaravan services. Bar and restaurant. Swimming and paddling pools (30/5-30/9). Tennis. Pétanque. Multisports pitch. Play areas. Bungalows for rent. Hostel. Club and TV room. Internet access and free WiFi. Off site: Zaragoza city centre 4 km (regular bus service 100 m. from gate). Golf 5 km.

Open: All year.

Directions

Follow the Autovia del Nordeste (Zaragoza ring road) southwest to leave at the junction with the N11a. Follow signs to the city centre (Autovia de Madrid). Site is signed to the right. GPS: 41.63766, -0.94273

Charges guide

Per unit incl. 2 persons and electricity	€ 18.37 - € 25.90
extra person	€ 4.24 - € 5.30

Menorca, steeped in history and blanketed by mystery, is an enchanting island of roughly 270 square miles in area. The C721 highway provides the backbone to the island, connecting modest market towns to Mahon (the main town) in the east and Ciutadella in the west.

Mahon's classic Georgian-style buildings, complete with sash windows, will endear them to the British traveller. Its impressive harbour was captured by the British in 1708 during the Spanish War of Succession. In complete contrast, Ciutadella has a more Gothic feel to it. A labyrinth of tiny streets entwine the 'little city', most of which can only be accessed on foot. Monte Toro stands proudly at the centre of the island surveying all. To the south a greener lush terrain exists with long, luxurious beaches, while to the north a giant rockery erupts riddled with caves and prehistoric finds.

Alaior

Yelloh! Village Son Bou

Ctra de San Jaime km. 3,5, Apdo 85, Alaior, E-07730 Menorca (Menorca) T: 971 372 727.
E: info@campingsonbou.com **alanrogers.com/ES80000**

Camping Son Bou was opened in 1996 and has been purpose built in local style providing a large, irregular shaped pool with marvellous views across to Monte Toro, and overlooked by a shady, terraced bar and restaurant. The 255 large pitches, 143 for touring units with 10A electricity, are arranged in circles radiating out from the main facilities and clearly edged with stones. Natural pine tree shade covers most but the outer ring. Drinking water and refuse points are well placed. The ground is hard and devoid of grass except where sprinklers operate. The site gets very busy with Spanish people from the mainland in high season. Earlier in the year it is quieter and greener.

Facilities

Well designed toilet block of good quality, open plan in places. Some washbasins in cabins (cold water). Bathrooms and shower. Baby room. Facilities for disabled visitors. Service wash. Shop, bar, restaurant, takeaway and outdoor pool (all open all season). Tennis. Play area. Bicycle hire. Open-air cinema. Occasional barbecue with guitarist. Comprehensive activity programme. English spoken. Dogs are not accepted. Off site: Village and sandy beach 3 km. Riding 4 km.

Open: 11 April - 27 September.

Directions

From Mahon (Mao) follow main road to Ciutadella. Go past Alaior (bypassed) and watch for restaurant on left and sign for 3.5 km. Torre Soli Nou and campsite sign. GPS: 39.92199, 4.09114

Charges guide

Per unit incl. 2 persons and electricity	€ 29.10 - € 34.32
extra person	€ 6.56 - € 7.94
child (3-13 yrs)	€ 4.87 - € 5.34

Portugal is a relatively small country occupying the southwest corner of the Iberian peninsula, bordered by Spain in the north and east, with the Atlantic coast in the south and west. In spite of its size, the country offers a tremendous variety in both its way of life and traditions.

Tourist Office

Portuguese National Tourist Office
11 Belgrave Square
London SW1X 8PP

Tel: 020 7201 6666
Fax: 020 7201 6633
E-mail: info@visitportugal.com
Internet: www.visitportugal.com

Most visitors looking for a beach type holiday head for the busy Algarve, with its long stretches of sheltered sandy beaches, and warm, clear Atlantic waters, great for bathing and watersports. With its monuments and fertile rolling hills, central Portugal adjoins the beautiful Tagus river that winds its way through the capital city of Lisbon, on its way to the Atlantic Ocean.

Lisbon city itself has deep rooted, cultural traditions, coming alive at night with buzzing cafés, restaurants and discos. Moving southeast of Lisbon the land becomes rather impoverished, consisting of stretches of vast undulating plains, dominated by cork plantations. Most people head for the walled town of Evora, an area steeped in two thousand years of history. The Portuguese consider the Minho area in the north to be the most beautiful part of their country, with its wooded mountain and wild coastline, a rural and conservative region with picturesque towns.

Population

10.7 million

Capital

Lisbon

Climate

The country enjoys a maritime climate with hot summers and mild winters with comparatively low rainfall in the south, heavy rain in the north.

Language

Portuguese, but English is widely spoken in cities, towns and larger resorts. French can be useful.

Telephone

The country code is 00 351.

Currency

The Euro (€)

Banks

Mon-Fri 08.30-11.45 and 13.00-14.45. Some large city banks offer a currency exchange 18.30-23.00.

Shops

Mon-Fri 09.00-13.00 and 15.00-19.00. Sat 09.00-13.00.

Public Holidays

New Year; Carnival (Shrove Tues); Good Fri; Liberty Day 25 Apr; Labour Day; Corpus Christi; National Day 10 June; Saints Days; Assumption 15 Aug; Republic Day 5 Oct; All Saints 1 Nov; Immaculate Conception 8 Dec; Christmas 24-26 Dec.

The Algarve, Portugal's southernmost province, is a true sunseekers' paradise, offering all-year-round sunshine and over 150 miles of beautiful sandy beaches.

THE ALGARVE HAS ONE DISTRICT: FARO

The coast of the Algarve offers mile after mile of golden beaches and small sandy coves with interesting rock formations, interspersed with busy fishing ports. The capital, Faro, boasts excellent beaches, while the thriving fishing port and market centre of Lagos is one of the most popular destinations in the Algarve. Although the earthquake of 1755 caused great damage to Lagos, the streets and squares of the town have retained much of their charm. Within walking distance are some superb beaches, including Praia de Dona Ana, which is considered to be the most picturesque of all, and the smaller coves of Praia do Pinhão and Praia Camilo. Further inland and to the north, the hills mark the edge of a greener and more fertile region, brilliantly coloured by fig trees, orange groves and almond trees that come into blossom in the winter. Here you will also find a series of typical villages that have successfully preserved their ancestral traditions. The walled town of Silves has a Moorish fortress, 13th-century cathedral and archaeology museum. Nearby, the narrow streets of the old spa town of Monchique wind up a steep hillside, revealing magnificent views.

Places of interest

Albufeira: popular resort, daily market, good nightlife.

Cape São Vicente: south westernmost point of Europe.

Faro: monuments, churches, museums, Gothic cathedral, good shopping centre.

Sagres: 17th-century fortress.

Tavira: picturesque town, 17th- and 18th-century architecture.

Vilamoura: good sporting facilities including golf courses.

Cuisine of the region

Fresh fish and seafood are popular; the local speciality is *Ameijoas na Cataplana* (clams steamed in a copper pan). One of the most traditional dishes is *caldeiradas* (stew made with all kinds of different fish) and *sardinha assada* (grilled sardines). Given the abundance of trees in the region, figs and almonds are used a lot in desserts including *bolinhos de amêndoa* (small cakes made with almond paste), which are moulded into the shape of fruits and vegetables in all kinds of different sizes.

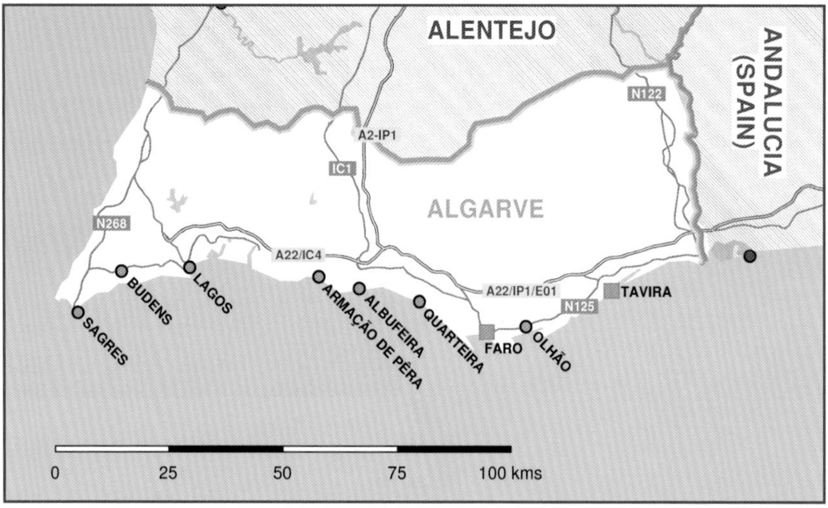

Albufeira

Camping Albufeira

Estrada Das Ferreiras, P-8200-555 Albufeira (Faro) T: 289 587 629. E: geral@campingalbufeira.net

alanrogers.com/PO8210

The spacious entrance to this site will accommodate the largest of units (watch for severe speed bumps at the barrier). One of the better sites on the Algarve, it has 1,500 touring pitches on fairly flat ground with some terracing, trees and shrubs giving reasonable shade in most parts. There are some marked and numbered pitches of 50-80 sq.m. Winter stays are encouraged with the main facilities remaining open, including a pool. An attractively designed complex of traditional Portuguese-style buildings on the hill, with an unusually shaped pool and two more for children, forms the central area of the site. It has large sunbathing terraces with pleasant views and is surrounded by a variety of flowers, shrubs and well watered lawns, complete with a fountain. The á la carte restaurant, impressive with its international cuisine, and the very pleasant self-service one, both have views across the three pools. A pizzeria, bars and a soundproofed disco are great for younger campers. In low season, services are limited to the bar, restaurant, supermarket and launderette.

Facilities

Very clean toilet blocks include hot showers. Launderette. Very large supermarket. Tabac (English papers). Waiter and self-service restaurants. Pizzeria. Bars. Swimming pools. Satellite TV. Soundproofed disco. Playground. Tennis. Bicycle hire. Free WiFi over part of site. First aid post with doctor nearby. Car wash. ATM. Car hire. Off site: Site bus service from gate to Albufeira every 45 minutes (2 km). Theme parks nearby. Beach and fishing 2 km. Golf 5 km. Riding and boat launching 10 km.

Open: All year.

Directions

From N125 coast road or N264 (from Lisbon) at new junctions follow N395 to Albufeira. Site is 2 km. on the left. GPS: 37.10639, -8.25361

Charges guide

Per unit incl. 2 persons	€ 23.50 - € 24.65
extra person	€ 5.50
child (4-10 yrs)	€ 2.70
electricity	€ 3.00

Discounts for stays over 30 days (October-May).

Armação de Pêra

Parque de Campismo de Armação de Pêra

P-8365 Armação de Pêra (Faro) T: 282 312 260. E: camping_arm_pera@hotmail.com

alanrogers.com/PO8410

A pleasant site with a wide attractive entrance and a large external parking area, the 1,200 pitches are in zones on level grassy sand. They are marked by trees that provide some shade, and are easily accessed from tarmac and gravel roads. Electricity is available for most pitches. The facilities are good and the self-service restaurant, bar and supermarket should cater for most needs. You can relax around the swimming pools. The disco near the entrance and café complex is soundproofed, which should ensure a peaceful night for non-revellers. The site is within easy reach of Albufeira and Portimão.

Facilities

Three modern sanitary blocks provide British and Turkish style WCs and showers with hot water (on payment). Facilities for disabled campers. A reader reports that maintenance can be variable. Laundry. Supermarket. Self-service restaurant. Three bars (one all year). Swimming and paddling pools (May-Sept; charged per day; no lifeguard). Games and TV rooms. Tennis. Play area. Internet access. Off site: Bus to town from gate. Fishing, bicycle hire and watersports nearby.

Open: All year.

Directions

Site is west of Albufeira. Turn off N125/IC4 road in Alcantarilha, taking the EN269-1 towards the coast. Site is the second 'campismo' left on the roundabout just before Armação de Pera. There are further sites with similar names in the area, so be sure to find the right one. GPS: 37.10947, -8.35329

Charges guide

Per unit incl. 2 persons and electricity	€ 16.50 - € 34.50

Min. stay 3 nights 1/6-31/8.

Budens

Parque de Campismo Quinta dos Carriços

Praia da Salema, Vila do Bispo, P-8650-196 Budens (Faro) T: 282 695 201. E: quintacarrico@gmal.com

alanrogers.com/PO8440

This is an attractive and peaceful valley site with a separate naturist area. A traditional tiled Portuguese-style entrance leads you down a steep incline into this excellent and well maintained site, which has a village atmosphere. With continuing improvements, the site has been developed over the years by the Dutch owner. It is spread over two valleys, with the 500 partially terraced pitches marked and divided by trees and shrubs. There are electricity connections (6/16A) to 270 pitches. A small stream (dry when seen) meanders through the site. The most remote part, 250 m. from the main site, is for naturists.

Facilities

Four modern, spacious sanitary blocks, well tiled with quality fittings, are spotlessly clean. Washbasins with cold water, hot showers on payment. Washing machine. Excellent facility for disabled campers. Gas supplies. Shop. Restaurant (1/3-15/10). Bar (daily in season, once weekly 1/3-15/10). TV (cable). Games room. WiFi over part of site (charged). Bicycle, scooter, moped and motorcycle hire. Off site: Fishing, golf and beach 1 km.

Open: All year.

Directions

Turn off RN125 (Lagos-Sagres) road at junction to Figuere and Salema (17 km. from Lagos). Site is signed. GPS: 37.075427, -8.831338

Charges guide

Per unit incl. 2 persons and electricity	€ 14.12 - € 29.50
extra person	€ 5.65 - € 5.85

Lagos

Orbitur Camping Valverde

Estrada da Praia da Luz, Valverde, P-8600-148 Lagos (Faro) T: 282 789 211. E: infovalverde@orbitur.pt

alanrogers.com/PO8200

A little over a kilometre from the village of Praia da Luz and its beach, and about 7 km. from Lagos, this large, well run site is certainly worth considering for your stay in the Algarve. It has 650 numbered pitches, of varying sizes, which are enclosed by hedges. All are on flat ground or broad terraces with good shade in most parts from established trees and shrubs. The site has a swimming pool with a long curling slide and a paddling pool (under tens free, adults charged). This is an excellent site with well maintained facilities and good security.

Facilities

Six large, clean, toilet blocks have some washbasins and sinks with cold water only, and hot showers. Units for disabled campers. Laundry. Motorcaravan services. Supermarket and shops (23/3-15/9). Restaurant and takeaway food (1/6-15/9). Coffee shop. Swimming pool (23/3-30/9) with paddling pool (June-Sept). Playground. Tennis. Satellite TV in bar. WiFi over part of site (free). Excursions. Off site: Beach and fishing 1.5 km.

Open: All year.

Directions

From Lagos on N125 road, after 7 km. turn south to Praia da Luz. At the town follow signs for 'campismo'. The beach road is narrow and cobbled and is very challenging in a large unit. GPS: 37.09973, -8.71744

Charges guide

Per person	€ 6.40
pitch incl. electricity	€ 25.50

Lagos

Yelloh! Village Turiscampo

EN125, Espiche, Luz, P-8600 Lagos (Faro) T: 282 789 265. E: info@turiscampo.com
alanrogers.com/PO8202

This good quality site has been thoughtfully refurbished and updated since it was purchased by the friendly Coll family, who are known to us from their previous Spanish site. The site provides 240 pitches (70 sq.m) for touring units, mainly in rows of terraces, all with electricity (6/10A) and some with shade. Thirty-six deluxe pitches have water and waste water. The upper areas of the site are mainly used for bungalow accommodation (and are generally separate from the touring areas). A new, elevated, Californian-style pool and a children's pool have been constructed. The supporting structure is a clever water cascade and surround, with a large sun lounger area on astroturf. One side of the pool area is open to the road. The restaurant/bar has been refurbished and Roberto and his staff are delighted to use their excellent English, providing good fare at most reasonable prices. The restaurant has two patios, one of which is used for live entertainment and discos in season, and the other for dining out. The sea is 2 km. away and the city of Lagos 4 km. with all the attractions of the Algarve within easy reach.

Facilities

Four toilet blocks are well located around the site. Two have been refurbished, two are new and contain modern facilities for disabled campers. Facilities for children. Washing machines. Shop. Gas supplies. Restaurant/bar. Swimming pool (Mar-Oct) with two terraces and new jacuzzi. Aqua gymnastics. New wellness facility (2012). Bicycle hire. Entertainment in high season on the bar terrace. Two children's playgrounds. Adult art workshops. Miniclub (5-12 yrs) in season. Boules. Archery. Sports field. Cable TV. Internet. WiFi on payment. Bungalows to rent. Off site: Fishing and beach 2 km. Golf 3 km. Sailing and boat launching 5 km. Riding 7 km.

Open: All year.

Directions

Take exit 1 from the N125 Lagos-Vila do Bispo. The impressive entrance is 3 km. on the right. GPS: 37.10111, -8.73278

Charges guide

Per unit incl. 2 persons and electricity	€ 17.00 - € 33.00
extra person	€ 4.00 - € 6.50
child (3-10 yrs)	free - € 3.50
dog	€ 5.00

Camping Cheques accepted.

Quarteira

Orbitur Camping Quarteira

Estrada da Fonte Santa, avenida Sá Cameiro, P-8125-618 Quarteira (Faro) T: 289 302 826.
E: infoquarteira@orbitur.pt **alanrogers.com/PO8220**

This is a large, busy, attractive site on undulating ground with some terracing, taking 795 units. On the outskirts of the popular Algarve resort of Quarteira, it is 600 m. from a sandy beach which stretches for a kilometre to the town centre. Many of the unmarked pitches have shade from tall trees and there are a few small individual pitches of 50 sq.m. with electricity and water. There are 659 electrical connections. Like others along this coast, the site encourages long winter stays.

Facilities

Five toilet blocks provide British and Turkish style toilets, washbasins with cold water, hot showers plus facilities for disabled visitors. Washing machines. Motorcaravan services. Supermarket. Self-service restaurant and separate takeaway (June-Sept). Swimming pools (23/3-30/9). General room with bar and TV. Free WiFi over part of site. Tennis. Open-air disco (high season).

Open: All year.

Directions

Turn off N125 for village of Almancil. In the village take road south to Quarteira. Site is on the left 1 km. after large, official town welcome sign. GPS: 37.06666, -8.08333

Charges guide

Per person	€ 6.50
pitch incl. electricity	€ 26.20

Olhão

Camping Olhão

Pinheiros de Marim, P-8700 Olhão (Faro) T: 289 700 300. E: parque.campismo@sbsi.pt

alanrogers.com/PO8230

This site, with around 800 pitches, is open all year. It has many mature trees providing good shade. The pitches are marked, numbered and in rows divided by shrubs, although levelling will be necessary and the trees make access tricky on some. There is electricity for 102 pitches (6A) and a separate area for tents. Permanent and long stay units take up one fifth of the pitches, the touring pitches filling up quickly in July and August, so arrive early. There is some noise nuisance from an adjacent railway. The site has a relaxed, casual atmosphere. Amenities include very pleasant swimming pools and tennis courts, a reasonable restaurant/bar and a café/bar with TV and games room. All are very popular with the local Portuguese who pay to use the facilities. The large, sandy beaches in this area are on offshore islands reached by ferry and are, as a result, relatively quiet; some are reserved for naturists. This site can get very busy in peak periods and maintenance can be variable. There was a large, low season British contingent when we visited, enjoying the low prices.

Facilities

Eleven sanitary blocks are adequate, clean when seen, and are specifically sited to be a maximum of 50 m. from any pitch. One block has facilities for disabled visitors. Laundry. Excellent supermarket. Kiosk. Restaurant/bar. Café and general room with cable TV. Playgrounds. Swimming pools (all year) and tennis courts (fees for both). Bicycle hire. Internet at reception. Off site: Bus service to the nearest ferry at Olhão 50 m. from site. Riding 1 km. Indoor pool, beach and fishing 2 km.

Open: All year.

Directions

Just over 1 km. east of Olhão, on EN125, take turn to Pinheiros de Marim. Site is back off the road on the left. Look for very large, white, triangular entry arch as the site name is different on the outside wall. GPS: 37.03528, -7.8225

Charges guide

Per person	€ 2.40 - € 4.20
pitch	€ 3.45 - € 12.80
electricity	€ 2.10

Sagres

Orbitur Camping Sagres

Cerro das Moitas, P-8650-998 Sagres (Faro) T: 282 624 371. E: infosagres@orbitur.pt

alanrogers.com/PO8430

Camping Sagres is a pleasant site at the western tip of the Algarve, not very far from a lighthouse in the relatively unspoilt southwest corner of Portugal. With 960 pitches for tents and 120 for tourers, the sandy pitches, some terraced, are located amongst pine trees that give good shade. There are some hardstandings for motorcaravans and electricity throughout. The fairly bland restaurant, bar and café/grill provide a range of reasonably priced meals. This is a reasonable site for those seeking winter sun, or as a base for exploring this 'Land's End' region of Portugal.

Facilities

Three spacious toilet blocks are showing some signs of wear but provide hot and cold showers and washbasins with cold water. Washing machines. Motorcaravan services. Supermarket (July/Aug). Bar (June-Sept). Restaurant (July/Aug). TV room. Satellite TV in restaurant. Bicycle hire. Barbecue area. Playground. Fishing. Medical post. Car wash. Free WiFi over part of site. Off site: Buses from village 1 km. Beach and fishing 2.5 km. Boat launching 8 km. Golf 12 km.

Open: All year.

Directions

From Sagres, turn off the N268 road west onto the EN268. After 2 km. the site is signed off to the right. GPS: 37.02278, -8.94583

Charges guide

Per person	€ 5.80
child (5-10 yrs)	€ 2.90
caravan and car	€ 8.00 - € 10.10
electricity (6A)	€ 3.50 - € 4.60

Camping Cheques accepted.

With huge, sparsely populated plains dominated by vast cork plantations, which provide nearly half of the world's cork, Alentejo's main attractions include the historic city of Évora and the coastal resorts with their fine, sandy beaches.

ALENTEJO IS MADE UP OF FOUR DISTRICTS: BEJA, ÉVORA, SETÚBAL AND PORTALEGRE

One of the most impressive cities in Portugal, Évora lies on a gently sloping hill rising out of the huge Alentejo plain. A city steeped in history, it was occupied by the Romans and Moors for centuries. With its narrow streets, of Moorish origin, and white-washed houses, it also boasts one of the best-preserved Roman temples in the country plus various palaces and monuments, the majority dating from the 14th-16th centuries. One of the more extraordinary sights can be found in the Capela dos Ossos in the church of São Francisco; adorning the walls and pillars of this chamber are the bones of more than 5,000 monks. On the Alentejo coast is the small, peaceful town of Santiago do Cacém, which has two of the best beaches in Portugal. The nearby archaeological site at Miróbriga includes ruins of a hippodrome, several houses (some of which have mural paintings) and a clearly defined acropolis. Further south along the coast is Porto Côvo and the larger, popular resort of Vila Nova de Milfontes, which has a little castle and ancient port.

Places of interest

Arraiolos: ancient town, 17th-century castle, famous for its carpets.

Beja: provincial town founded by Julius Caesar, 13th-century castle.

Borba: pretty town, noted for its marble and wine.

Elvas: ancient fortress town, 15th-century aqueduct.

Estremoz: market town, medieval castle.

Odemira: quiet, characterful country town.

Reguengos de Monsaraz: charming, unspoiled village with white-washed houses.

Vila Viçosa: attractive hillside town, 16th-century convent.

Cuisine of the region

Alentejo was traditionally an important wheat-growing region (it is frequently referred to as the 'granary of Portugal'). Local specialities include *sopa de cação* (skate soup), made from fish and bread, and *ensopado de borrego* (lamb stew). Cheeses of the region include *queijo de Serpa* and *queijos de Niza*, made from goats' milk. The *queijos de Évora*, made from ewes' milk, is smaller in size with a strong, spicy flavour. *Arroz Doce* (rice pudding topped with cinnamon) is the traditional dessert for festivals and parties and is to be found all over the country.

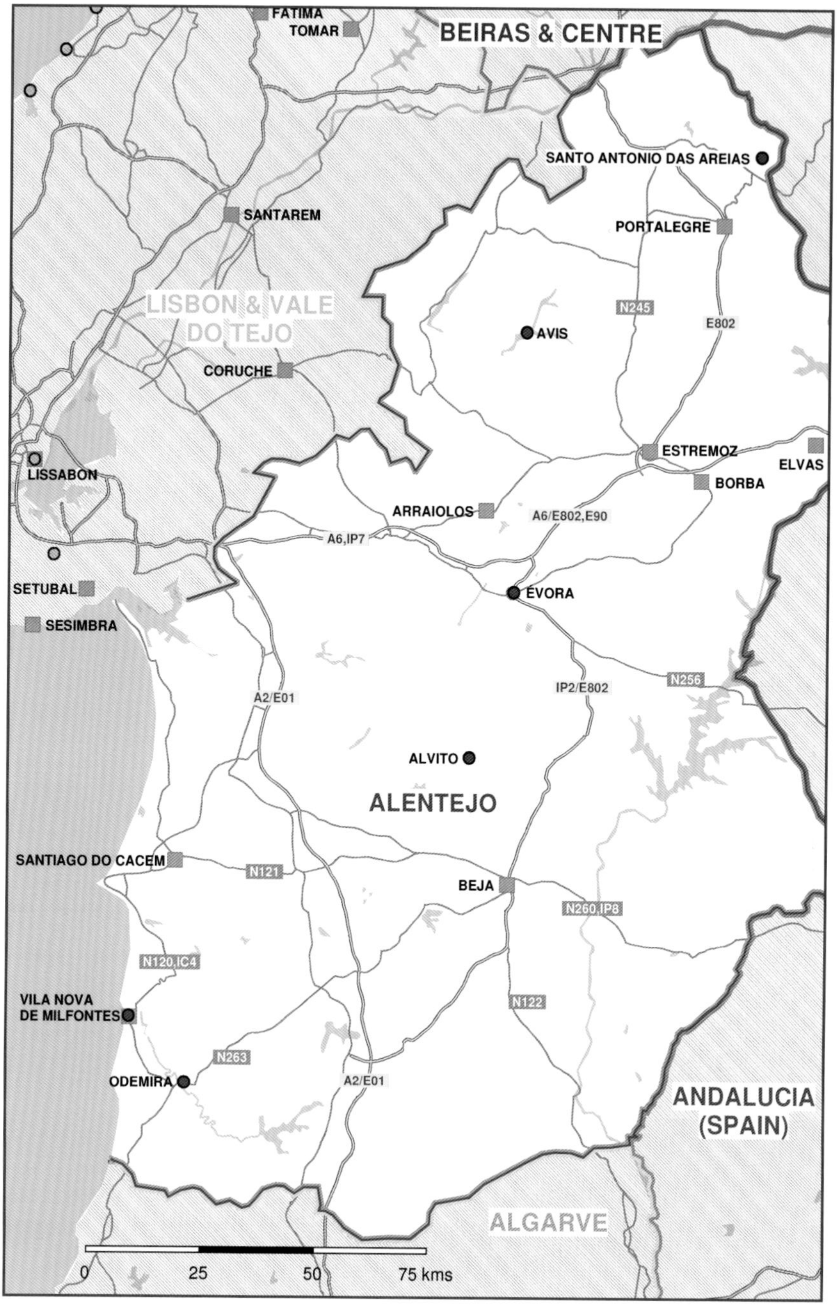
FATIMA
TOMAR
BEIRAS & CENTRE
SANTO ANTONIO DAS AREIAS
SANTAREM
PORTALEGRE
LISBON & VALE DO TEJO
N245
E802
AVIS
CORUCHE
ESTREMOZ
ELVAS
LISSABON
BORBA
ARRAIOLOS
A6/E802,E90
A6,IP7
SETUBAL
EVORA
SESIMBRA
N256
A2/E01
IP2/E802
ALVITO
ALENTEJO
SANTIAGO DO CACEM
N121
BEJA
N260,IP8
N120,IC4
VILA NOVA DE MILFONTES
N122
N263
ODEMIRA
A2/E01
ANDALUCIA (SPAIN)
ALGARVE
0
25
50
75 kms

Alvito

Camping Markádia

Barragem de Odivelas, Apdo 17, P-7920-999 Alvito (Beja) T: 284 763 141. E: markadia@hotmail.com

alanrogers.com/PO8350

A tranquil, lakeside site in an unspoilt setting, this will appeal most to those nature lovers who want to 'get away from it all' and to those who enjoy country pursuits such as walking, fishing and riding. There are 130 casual unmarked pitches on undulating grass and sand with ample electricity connections (16A). The site is lit but a torch is required. The friendly Dutch owner has carefully planned the site so each pitch has its own oak tree to provide shade. The open countryside and lake provide excellent views and a very pleasant environment. The lake is in fact a 1,000-hectare reservoir, and more than 150 species of birds can be found in the area.

Facilities

Four modern, very clean and well equipped toilet blocks are built in traditional Portuguese style with hot water throughout. Washing machines. Motorcaravan services. Bar and restaurant (1/4-30/9). Shop (bread to order). Lounge. Playground. Fishing. Boat hire. Tennis. Riding. Medical post. Car wash. No dogs in July/Aug. Facilities and amenities may be reduced outside the main season. Off site: Swimming and boating in the lake.

Open: All year.

Directions

From A2 between Setubal and the Algarve take exit 10 on IP8 (Ferreira and Beja). Take road to Torrao and 13 km. later, 1 km. north of Odivelas, turn right (Barragem) and site is 3 km. after crossing head of reservoir following signs. GPS: 38.1812, -8.10293

Charges guide

Per unit incl. 2 persons and electricity	€ 27.00

No credit cards.

Avis

Parque de Campismo da Albufeira do Maranhão

P-7480 Avis (Portalegre) T: 242 412 452. E: parque_campismo@cm-avis.pt

alanrogers.com/PO8353

Campismo da Albufeira is a medium size campsite in central Portugal, forming part of a larger entertainment park, the Avis Nautical Club. The campsite is within easy waking distance of a multitude of water based sports and beaches on the large Maranhão, or reservoir. The nautical complex provides a great variety of dining options, from full restaurants to takeaway outlets along with swimming pools and playgrounds (charged). Camping pitches are mostly well shaded and have electricity. Shower blocks are well maintained and have modern fittings. A range of chalets are available, sleeping from two to six persons. Situated in the heart of the Portuguese countryside, this campsite offers plenty of sporting facilities together with tranquillity once out on the plentiful hiking trails. The site is committed to environmental conservation with solar power being used whenever possible. The nearby historic town of Avis with its castle and views over the surrounding area is recommended to all for shopping and cultural experiences. The local festivals, fairs and many exhibitions extend to cover the entire holiday season with something for all ages.

Facilities

Modern shower blocks. Bar. Choice of restaurants. Swimming pool. Children's pool. Nautical complex. Tourist information. Caravans and chalets for rent. Direct beach access. WiFi. Off site: Walking and cycle tracks. Riding. Fishing. Historic town of Avis.

Open: All year.

Directions

Campismo da Albufeira is 110 km. east of Lisbon. From junction 10 of E806 take N2 south to Ponte de Sor. Follow signs to Avis N224. At Avis turn right. Follow site signs. GPS: 39.05683, -7.9115

Charges guide

Per unit incl. 2 persons and electricity	€ 10.60 - € 16.60
extra person	€ 2.00 - € 3.50

Évora

Orbitur Camping Évora

Estrada de Alca Covas, Herdade Esphrragosa, P-700-703 Évora (Evora) T: 266 705 190.
E: infoevora@orbitur.pt **alanrogers.com/PO8340**

Situated some 1.5 km. from the historic former provincial capital, this site is well located for an overnight stop. There is a small swimming pool and a simple small bar where snacks may be served. Most of the 285 sandy and good sized touring pitches have 15A electricity and those in the older part of the site have well developed shade. The ground is probably not suitable for visitors using wheelchairs. The historic walled town and its castle (on the World Heritage list), and the surrounding area with its megalithic monuments, are well worth visiting.

Facilities

Two toilet blocks are just acceptable. Free hot showers and British style WCs. Facilities for disabled visitors. Laundry. Motorcaravan services. Gas supplies. Bar (1/6-15/9). Bread to order (July/Aug). Swimming pool (23/3-23/9). Tennis. Mature play area (supervision necessary). Free WiFi over part of site. Off site: Bicycle hire 2 km. Supermarkets in the town.

Open: All year.

Directions

Site is 1.5 km. southwest of the town on the N380 road to Alcáçovas. GPS: 38.557294, -7.925863

Charges guide

Per person	€ 3.50 - € 5.80
child (5-10 yrs)	€ 1.70 - € 2.90
pitch	€ 4.80 - € 13.50
electricity	€ 3.50

Odemira

Parque de Campismo São Miguel

São Miguel, Odeceixe, P-7630-592 Odemira (Beja) T: 282 947 145. E: camping.sao.miguel@mail.telepac.pt
alanrogers.com/PO8170

Nestled in green hills near two pretty white villages, 4 km. from the beautiful Praia Odeceixe (beach) is the attractive camping park São Miguel. Unusually, the site works on a maximum number of 700 campers, you find your own place (there are no defined pitches) under the tall trees, there are ample electrical points, and the land slopes away gently. Wooden chalet-style accommodation to rent is in a separate area, but some mobile homes share the two traditional older style but clean sanitary blocks. The main building with its Portuguese architecture is built around two sides of a large grassy square.

Facilities

Two older style toilet blocks with British style WCs and free hot showers. Washing machines. Toilets and basins for disabled campers but no shower. Shop (June-Sept). Self-service restaurant (Mar-Oct). Bar, snacks and pizzeria (June-Sept). Satellite TV. Playground. Tennis (charged). Swimming pool (charged). Dogs are not accepted. Torches useful. Off site: Bus service from gate. Historic village of Odeceixe 2 km. Beach, fishing and sailing 4 km. Riding 20 km. Site is inside the Alentejo nature park.

Open: All year.

Directions

Between Odemira and Lagos on the N120 just before the village of Odeceixe on the main road well signed. GPS: 37.43868, -8.75568

Charges guide

Per unit incl. 2 persons and electricity	€ 17.40 - € 27.40
extra person	€ 4.20 - € 6.40
child (5-10 yrs)	€ 2.50 - € 3.70

Odemira

Zmar-Eco Camping Resort

Herdade A de Mateus EN393/1, San Salvador, P-7630 Odemira (Beja) T: 707 200 626. E: info@zmar.eu
alanrogers.com/PO8175

Zmar is an exciting new project which should be fully open this year. The site is located near Zambujeira do Mar, on the Alentejo coast. This is a highly ambitious initiative which has been developed along strict environmental lines. For example, renewable resources such as locally harvested timber and recycled plastic are used wherever possible and solar energy is used whenever practicable. Public indoor spaces have no air conditioning, but there is adequate cooling through underfloor ventilation and electric fans where possible. Pitches are 100 sq.m. and benefit from artificial shade. Accommodation available for rent.

Facilities

Eight toilet blocks provide comprehensive facilities, including those for children and disabled visitors. Bar. Restaurant. Crêperie. Takeaway. Large supermarket. Swimming pool. Covered pool. Wellness centre. Sports field. Games room. Play area, farm and play house. Tennis. Bicycle hire. Activity and entertainment programme. Mobile homes and caravans for rent. Caravan repair and servicing. The site's own debit card system is used for payment at all facilities.

Open: All year.

Directions

From the N120 from Odemira to Lagos, at roundabout in the centre of Portas de Transval turn towards Milfontes. Take turn to Cabo Sardão and then Zambujeira do Mar. Site is on the left. GPS: 37.60422, -8.73142

Charges guide

Per unit incl. up to 4 persons and electricity	€ 20.00 - € 37.00
extra person	€ 5.00 - € 10.00

Camping Cheques accepted.

Santo Antonio das Areias

Camping Asseiceira

Caixa Postal 2, Santo António Das Areias, 7330-204 Marvão (Portalegre) T: 245 992 940.

E: gary-campingasseiceira@hotmail.com **alanrogers.com/PO8355**

Set amongst unspoilt mountain scenery in the spectacular Serra de São Mamede National Park, Camping Asseiceira is a British-owned site offering visitors a warm welcome. The Spanish border is just 8 km. away. Arranged in a small olive grove are 20 pitches with views rising up to the spectacular medieval castle and town of Marvão. This is a small, pleasant, well cared for site with few facilities, although the village of Santo António das Areias is only a few minutes walk with shops, restaurants and a bank. Access to the site is from a tarmac road suitable for most units. The site has a small swimming pool with a bar service. The British owner, Gary Chuwen, oversees every aspect of the site personally.

Facilities

The shower block has recently been re-built to a high standard, using locally sourced materials and has hot water throughout. Small swimming pool with adjacent bar and terrace (June-Oct). WiFi (free). Off site: Village with shops, restaurants and bank 2 km. Daily bus to Lisbon. Riding 2 km. Golf and bicycle hire 8 km. Fishing 13 km.

Open: 1 January - 31 October.

Directions

From IP1 take exit 7 onto A6/IP7 towards Estremoz, then IP2/E802 towards Portalegre. Continue past Portalegre to right turn for Marvão and Spain. Follow signs for Marvão and after roundabout at Portagem take first right (towards Ponte Velha) and follow road to Santo António das Areias. At petrol station turn right down hill and site is 400 m. on left.
GPS: 39.410007, -7.340736

Charges guide

Per unit incl. 2 persons and electricity	€ 18.00 - € 19.00
extra person	€ 5.00
child (under 10 yrs)	€ 2.00
dog	free

Vila Nova de Milfontes

Orbitur Camping Sitava Milfontes

Sitava Turismo, Brejo de Zimbreira, P-7645-017 Vila Nova de Milfontes (Beja) T: 283 890 100.

E: infositava@orbitur.pt **alanrogers.com/PO8190**

With a huge entrance off the road, then a 500 m. drive through a pine forest to the camping area, this is a very large site (27 hectares) complete with beach access. It has good sized, level pitches, although the numerous tall pines concentrate the mind when manoeuvring – on the other hand they provide shade. There are two large buildings, one housing the well stocked mini supermarket, while the other has a bar, restaurant, games room and large courtyard terrace. An attractive feature is a fountain in a circle of lawn, that in turn is in the centre of a covered walkway supporting blooms of vivid colours, ideal for sitting and relaxing. The beaches are 600 m. away through a gated entrance.

Facilities

The two original toilet blocks are rather dated and are supplemented by a further two blocks, which are well designed with tiling throughout, and offer superb facilities including a separate baby changing room, disabled cubicle, hot showers, hot and cold 'set in' sinks with full wall mirrors. Large restaurant and bar (all year). Small supermarket (1/6-30/9). Large swimming pool with adjacent toddler pool (1/6-30/9). Large play area. TV room with games area - darts, pool and electronic games. Multisports pitch. Tennis. Dogs are not accepted. Torches needed on some pitches. Off site: Fishing and beach 600 m. Minimal bus service in high season, reduced to two a day in low season. Lisbon (with changes) and Algarve (with changes) both 2 hrs. plus.

Open: All year.

Directions

From E201-1 Cercal-Sines road (E120 at Tanganheira), take the left (southwest) to Porto Covo and follow signs (south) to Vila Nova de Milfontes. Site is well signed on the right.
GPS: 37.77989, -8.783725

Charges guide

Per unit incl. 2 persons and electricity	€ 8.77 - € 18.00
extra person	€ 1.95 - € 5.10
child (6-11 yrs)	€ 0.98 - € 2.50

Reductions in low season.

Camping Cheques accepted.

Vila Nova de Milfontes

Camping Milfontes

P-7645-300 Vila Nova de Milfontes (Beja) T: 283 996 140. E: geral@parquemilfontes.com

alanrogers.com/PO8180

This popular site with good facilities has the advantage of being open all year and is within walking distance of the town and beach. As such, it makes a perfect base for those visiting out of main season, or for long winter stays when fees are heavily discounted. Well lit and fenced, it has around 500 shady pitches for touring units on sandy terrain, marked out and divided by hedges and nicely paved paths. Some pitches may be too small for caravan and car, so cars may have to be parked in an internal car park. Electricity (6A) is available throughout. The site also has a restaurant and bar complex and a well stocked supermarket. There are opportunities for watersports, fishing, canoeing and swimming from the resort beaches.

Facilities

The four toilet blocks are clean and well maintained. Two have complete suites for disabled visitors with ramped entrances. Mainly British style WCs, bidets, washbasins (some with hot water), hot and cold showers, footbaths and some children's facilities, in a mix of combinations and styles. Motorcaravan services. Outdoor pool, supermarket, bar, snacks and takeaway (all 15/4-30/9). Laundry. TV room. Playground. Car wash. Gas supplies. Off site: Fishing and bicycle hire 1 km. Riding 15 km. Golf 20 km.

Open: All year.

Directions

From N120 coast road at Cercal, turn on E390 and continue into Vila Nova de Milfontes. Turn right in town and follow site signs. Site is on right-hand side at end of no through road. Do not confuse it with another site on left just before the entrance to Milfontes. GPS: 37.7319, -8.78301

Charges guide

Per unit incl. 2 persons and electricity	€ 14.30 - € 23.20
extra person	€ 3.00 - € 4.40
child (5-10 yrs)	€ 1.60 - € 2.30
dog	free

With its deep-rooted cultural traditions, range of leisure activities, year-round sunshine, sandy beaches, historic towns and villages, Lisbon and Vale do Tejo has something for everyone. It is also the centre of Fado, the traditional haunting folk song of Portugal.

THIS REGION IS DIVIDED INTO FOUR DISTRICTS: LEIRIA, LISBON, SANTARÉM AND SETÚBAL

(PART OF SETÚBAL ALSO FEATURES IN THE ALENTEJO REGION)

Standing on the banks of the Tagus river, Lisbon has been the capital of Portugal since 1255. Places of interest in the city include the medieval quarters of Alfama and Mouraria, with their cobbled streets and alleys, colourful buildings, markets and castles, and Belém, with its tower and the 16th-century Jerónimos monastery. Lisbon also boasts an assortment of museums. Not far from the capital lies the romantic town of Sintra, which has an array of cottages, manor houses and palaces. Its mountains also form part of the Sintra-Cascais Natural Park. Along the Atlantic coast, high sweeping cliffs lead down to white sandy beaches, backed by lagoons. Europe's westernmost point, Cabo da Roca, is found here as are plenty of coastal towns and villages including Peniche, Nazaré and Óbidos, a small medieval walled town with cobbled streets, tiny white-washed houses and balconies brimming with flowers. Further inland, at Alcobaça, Tomar and Batalha, are ancient monasteries, with castles in Leiria, Tomar and Santarém. Recreational pursuits include watersports, fishing and golf. In summer there are open-air music festivals.

Places of interest

Estoril: casino, golf course and racing track.

Fátima: one of the most important centres of pilgrimage in the Catholic world.

Leiria: medieval royal castle, 16th-century cathedral, Romanesque church.

Mafra: 18th-century Palace-Convent, the largest Portuguese religious monument.

Santarém: castle, archaeology museum, Gothic convent and churches.

Sesimbra: picturesque small fishing town, medieval castle, the Lagoa de Albufeira is a favourite spot for windsurfers.

Setúbal: nature reserve, beaches, golf courses.

Tomar: 12th-century Templars' Castle, Gothic and Renaissance churches, 15th-century synagogue.

Cuisine of the region

Fish soups, stews and seafood are popular, including *sardinha assada* (grilled sardines) and *Bifes de Espardarte* (swordfish steaks). Sintra is famed for its cheesecakes which, according to ancient documents, were already being made in the 12th century and were part of the rent payments. Wine-producing regions include Azeitão, Bucelas, Carcavelos and Colares.

Caldeiradas: fish stews.

Queijadas: cheese tarts.

Pastéis de Belém: custard tarts.

Travesseiros: puff pastries stuffed with a sweet eggy mixture.

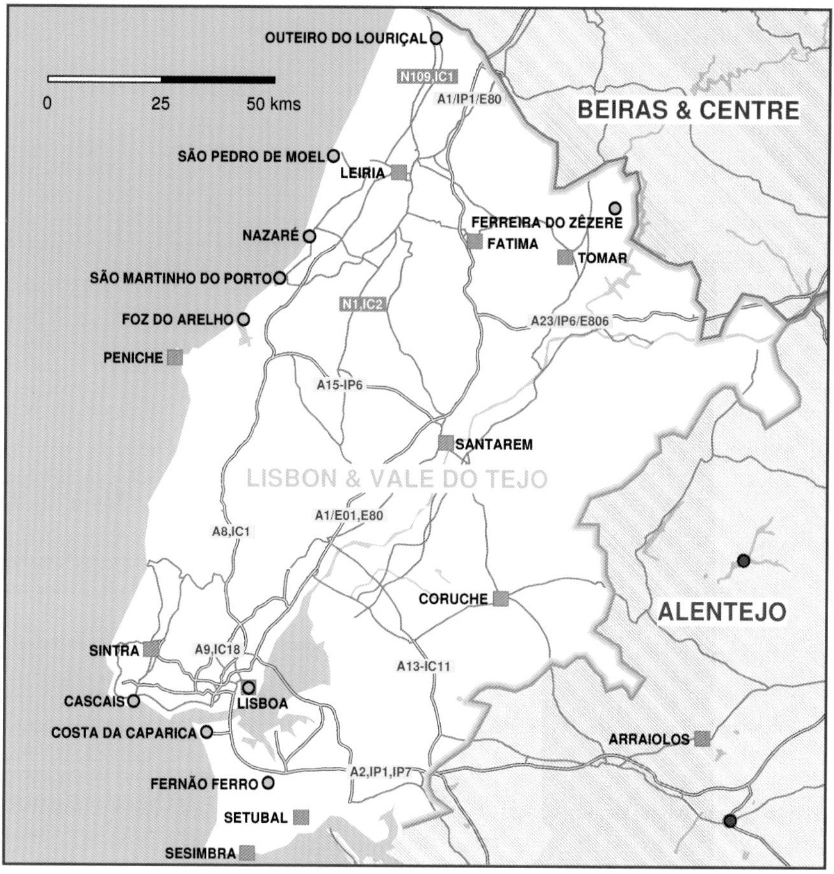

Cascais

Orbitur Camping Guincho

EN247, Lugar da Areia - Guincho, P-2750-053 Cascais (Lisbon) T: 214 870 450. E: infoguincho@orbitur.pt

alanrogers.com/PO8130

Although this is a popular site for permanent Portuguese units with 1,295 pitches, it is nevertheless quite attractively laid out among low pine trees and with the A5 autostrada connection to Lisbon (30 km), it provides a useful alternative to sites nearer the city. This is viewed as an alternative for visiting Lisbon, not a holiday site. There is a choice of pitches (small – mainly about 50 sq.m), mostly with electricity, although siting amongst the trees may be tricky, particularly when the site is full. Located behind sand dunes and a wide, sandy beach, the site offers a wide range of facilities.

Facilities

Three sanitary blocks, one refurbished, are in the older style but are clean and tidy. Washbasins with cold water but hot showers. Facilities for disabled visitors. Washing machines and dryers. Motorcaravan services. Gas. Supermarket. Restaurant, bar and terrace. Swimming pool (23/3-30/9). General room with TV. Tennis. Playground. Entertainment in summer. WiFi. Chalets to rent. Off site: Bus service from gate. Excursions. Riding 500 m. Beach 800 m. Fishing 1 km. Golf 3 km.

Open: All year.

Directions

Approach from either direction on N247. Turn inland 6.5 km. west of Cascais at site sign. Travelling direct from Lisbon, the site is well signed as you leave the A5 at exit 12 and follow directions for Birre. GPS: 38.72117, -9.46667

Charges guide

Per person	€ 3.90 - € 6.50
child (5-10 yrs)	€ 2.00 - € 3.30
pitch	€ 9.20 - € 15.40
electricity	€ 3.50

Costa da Caparica

Orbitur Camping Costa da Caparica

Avenida Alfonso de Albuquerque, Quinta de Ste Antonio, P-2825-450 Costa da Caparica (Setubal)
T: 212 901 366. E: infocaparica@orbitur.pt **alanrogers.com/PO8150**

This site has relatively easy access to Lisbon (just under 20 km) via the motorway, by bus or even by bus and ferry if you wish. It is situated near a small resort, favoured by the Portuguese themselves, which has all the usual amenities plus a good sandy beach (200 m. from the site) and promenade walks. An area for touring units includes some larger pitches for motorcaravans. There are 240 pitches with electricity connections (long electricity leads may be needed). In addition, there are 140 permanent caravans. We see this very much as a site to visit Lisbon rather than for prolonged stays.

Facilities

The three toilet blocks have mostly British style toilets, washbasins with cold water and some hot showers – they come under pressure when the site is full. Facilities for disabled visitors. Washing machine. Motorcaravan services. Supermarket. Large bar/restaurant (not Nov). TV room (satellite). Playground. Gas supplies. Free WiFi over part of site. Off site: Bus service from site gate. Fishing 1 km. Riding 4 km. Golf 5 km.

Open: All year.

Directions

Cross the Tagus bridge (toll) on A2 motorway going south from Lisbon, immediately take the turning for Caparica and Trafaria. At 7 km. marker on IC20 turn right (no sign) – the site is at the second roundabout. GPS: 38.65595, -9.24107

Charges guide

Per person	€ 6.40
pitch	€ 10.90 - € 11.90
electricity	€ 3.50 - € 4.60

Camping Cheques accepted.

Fernão Ferro

Camping Parque Verde

Avenida do Casal Sapo, Fontainhas, P-2685-065 Fernão Ferro (Setubal) T: 212 108 999.
E: info@parqueverde.pt **alanrogers.com/PO8155**

This is very much a site for 812 permanent caravans but it has relatively easy access to Lisbon (just under 20 km) via the motorway and the impressive bridge. It is very much favoured by the Portuguese themselves. The site has all the usual amenities and a village-like central bar and restaurant complex. Most of the amenities are open all year round. There is a small area for touring units containing about 18 pitches and some larger pitches for motorcaravans. There are 20 mobile homes for rent. We see this site as useful for visiting Lisbon rather than for prolonged stays.

Facilities

The single toilet block for the touring units provides acceptable facilities. Washing machines. Supermarket. Bar, restaurants and snack bar (all year). Swimming pool and children's pool (1/5-30/9). Fitness facilities. Play area. Disco and other entertainment. Off site: Trains for Lisbon 4 km. Golf 5 km. Riding 12 km. Fishing 15 km.

Open: All year.

Directions

From the A2 toll road take exit 2 onto the N378 (Sesimbra). Pass through Fernão Ferro and at roundabout follow for Coina into Fontainhas. Stay on tarred road meandering through Fontainhas (rua 25 de Abril). Site on right. GPS: 38.55056, -9.07167

Charges guide

Per unit incl. 2 persons and electricity	€ 20.00
extra person	€ 2.00 - € 3.00

Ferreira do Zêzere

Camping Quinta da Cerejeira

Rua D. Maria Fernanda da Mota Cardoso 902, P-2240-333 Ferreira do Zêzere (Santarem) T: 249 361 756.
E: info@cerejeira.com **alanrogers.com/PO8550**

This is a delightful, small, family owned venture run by Gert and Teunie Verheij. It is a converted farm (quinta) and has been coaxed into a very special campsite. The pitches are on flat grass or on long terraces under fruit and olive trees. There are 25 pitches of which 18 have access to 6A electricity (long leads may be needed). There is some shade and the site is full of rustic charm and craft works. It is very peaceful with views of the surrounding green hills from the charming vine-covered patio above a small swimming pool. You will notice the working well, no longer powered by a donkey but you can see where he used to circle to pump water.

Facilities

The single rustic sanitary building has British style WCs with hot showers. It could be busy at peak periods. Washing machine. No facilities for disabled campers. No shop but just ask and the baker calls daily. Self-service bar with WiFi and library. Restaurant. Separate games and rest room with satellite TV. Artistic workshops. Swimming pool. Off site: Town with shops, bars and restaurants and bus service 1 km. Fishing and watersports 5 km.

Open: 1 February - 30 November.

Directions

From Lisbon take A1/A23 to Torres Novas then IC3 to Tomar and N238 to Ferreira do Zêzere. Take N348 to Vila de Rei and site is 1 km. from Ferreira do Zêzere to eastern side of town (do not enter town). From Coimbra use N238 road at an earlier exit. GPS: 39.70075, -8.2782

Charges guide

Per unit incl. 2 persons and electricity	€ 16.25 - € 18.25

Foz do Arelho

Orbitur Camping Foz do Arelho

Rua Maldonado Freitas, P-2500-516 Foz do Arelho (Leiria) T: 262 978 683. E: infofozarelho@orbitur.pt

alanrogers.com/PO8480

This is a large and roomy ex-municipal site and improvements are still taking place. It is 2 km. from the beach and has a new central complex with a most impressive swimming pool and separated children's pool with lifeguard. Pitches are generally sandy with some hardstandings. They vary in size and are unmarked on two main levels with wide tarmac roads. There is some shade and all touring pitches have electricity (5/15A). The large two storey, brick-faced building contains all the site's leisure facilities but has no ramped access. This is a pleasant site with sound facilities for all. Some permanent Portuguese units are occupied in high season and weekends at other times.

Facilities

Four identical modern sanitary buildings (solar heating) with seatless British and Turkish style WCs and free showers. Washing machine in one. Facilities for disabled campers at the block near reception. Supermarket, bar/snacks and restaurant, bread to order (all 1/6-15/9). Swimming pool (1/6-30/9). Children's club. Games room. Small new amphitheatre. Playground – supervision needed. Bus service. Doctor's room. Free WiFi over part of site. Torches useful. Off site: Bus 500 m. Seaside town and fishing 3 km. Three supermarkets in Foz do Arelho.

Open: All year.

Directions

Site is north of Lisbon and west of Caldos la Rainha. From the A8 take N360 to Foz do Arelho. Site is well signed. GPS: 39.43067, -9.20083

Charges guide

Per person	€ 5.80
child (5-10 yrs)	€ 2.90
pitch	€ 19.90
electricity	€ 3.50

Lisboa

Lisboa Camping & Bungalows-Parque Municipal de Monsanto

Estrada da Circunvalacao, P-1400-061 Lisboa (Lisbon) T: 217 628 200. E: info@lisboacamping.com

alanrogers.com/PO8140

This very large site is professionally operated by many uniformed staff, providing a quality service at a good price. The wide entrance with its ponds and fountains, and the trees, lawns and flowering shrubs leading up to the two swimming pools, is a most attractive feature. On sloping ground, the site's many terraces are well shaded by trees and shrubs. The 400 good pitches (all with 6/16A electricity) include 171 serviced pitches on concrete hardstandings. There is a huge separate area for tents, and 70 chalet-style bungalows are for hire. Central Lisbon is 8 km. away with two bus routes giving a regular service from the gate. This is a most pleasant site for visiting Lisbon.

Facilities

Eight solar-powered toilet blocks contain quality facilities, including those for disabled visitors. Launderette. Motorcaravan service point. Shops, bar and restaurants. Two swimming pools (with lifeguard; May-Sept). Tennis. Minigolf. Sports field. Playgrounds. Roman theatre. Entertainment in high season. General and TV (cable) rooms. Bicycle hire. Minigolf. Free WiFi over part of site. Organised excursions. Off site: Excellent bus service from site gate. Lisbon city. Riding 7 km. Golf 8 km. Beaches 11 km.

Open: All year.

Directions

From Lisbon take A5 motorway towards Estoril and site is signed from exit 4 onto the IC17 (huge site signs at first exit to Buraca). The site is immediately on the right. Enter to the right of the fountain on the tiled road. GPS: 38.72477, -9.20737

Charges guide

Per unit incl. 2 persons and electricity	€ 22.00 - € 32.20
extra person	€ 5.95 - € 7.50
child (6-11 yrs)	€ 2.70 - € 3.80

Electricity included.

Camping Cheques accepted.

Nazaré

Orbitur Camping Valado

Rua dos Combatentes do Ultramar 2, Valado, P-2450-148 Nazaré (Leiria) T: 262 561 111.
E: infovalado@orbitur.pt **alanrogers.com/PO8110**

This popular site is close to the old, traditional fishing port of Nazaré which has now become something of a holiday resort and is popular with coach parties. The large sandy beach in the town (about 2 km. steeply downhill from the site) is sheltered by headlands and provides good swimming. The campsite is on undulating ground under tall pine trees. There are said to be 503 pitches and, although some smallish individual pitches with electricity and water can be reserved, the bulk of the site is not marked out and units are close together during July/August. About 420 electrical connections are available.

Facilities

The three toilet blocks have British and Turkish style WCs, washbasins (some cold water) and 17 hot showers, all very clean when inspected. Laundry. Motorcaravan services. Gas supplies. Supermarket (July/Aug). Bar (July/Aug). Swimming pool (1/6-30/9). TV/general room. Playground. Tennis. Free WiFi over part of site. Off site: Bus service 20 m. Fishing and bicycle hire 2 km.

Open: All year.

Directions

Site is on the Nazaré-Alcobaca N8-5 road, 2 km. east of Nazaré. GPS: 39.5934, -9.02783

Charges guide

Per person	€ 3.50 - € 5.80
pitch	€ 8.10 - € 13.50
electricity	€ 3.50

Camping Cheques accepted.

Nazaré

Camping Caravaning Vale Paraiso

EN242, P-2450-138 Nazaré (Leiria) T: 262 561 800. E: info@valeparaiso.com
alanrogers.com/PO8460

A pleasant, well managed site, Vale Paraiso improves every year, with the latest additions being new reception buildings and pool areas. The owners are keen to welcome British visitors and English is spoken. The site is by the main N242 road in eight hectares of undulating pine woods. There are 650 shady pitches, many on sandy ground only suitable for tents. For other units there are around 190 individual pitches of varying size on harder ground with electricity available. A large range of sporting and leisure activities includes an excellent outdoor pool and paddling pool with sunbathing areas.

Facilities

Spotless sanitary facilities with mainly British style WCs. Modern facilities for disabled visitors. Baby baths. Laundry facilities. Motorcaravan services. Supermarket (1/5-30/9). Restaurant (15/5-15/9). Café/bar with satellite TV. Takeaway. Tabac. Swimming and paddling pools (Mar-Sept; free for under 11s). Pétanque. Leisure games. Amusement hall. Safety deposit. Gas supplies. Email and fax facilities. Free WiFi. Apartments, tents and mobile homes to rent. Off site: Fishing 2 km. Riding 6 km. Golf 40 km.

Open: All year except 16-26 December.

Directions

Site is 2 km. north of Nazaré on the EN242 Marinha Grande road. GPS: 39.62028, -9.05639

Charges guide

Per unit incl. 2 persons and electricity (6A)	€ 16.50 - € 27.20
extra person	€ 3.25 - € 4.85
child (3-10 yrs)	€ 1.60 - € 2.40

Credit cards accepted for amounts over € 150.

Camping Cheques accepted.

Outeiro do Louriçal

Campismo O Tamanco

Rua do Louriçal 11, Casas Brancas, P-3105-158 Outeiro do Louriçal (Leiria) T: 236 952 551.
E: tamanco@me.com **alanrogers.com/PO8400**

O Tamanco is a peaceful countryside site, with a homely almost farmstead atmosphere; you will have chickens and ducks wandering around and there is a Burro here. The young Dutch owners, Irene and Hans, are sure to give you a warm welcome at this delightful little site. The 65 good sized pitches are separated by cordons of all manner of fruit trees, ornamental trees and flowering shrubs, on level grassy ground. There is electricity (6/16A) to all the pitches and 5 pitches are suitable for large motorcaravans. The site is lit and there is nearly always space available.

Facilities

The single toilet block provides very clean and generously sized facilities including washbasins in cabins. No easy access for disabled visitors. As facilities are limited they may be busy in peak periods. Hot water throughout. Washing machine. Bar/restaurant. Roofed patio with fireplace. TV room/lounge (satellite). Internet access. Swimming pool. Yurts for hire. Off site: Bus service 1 km. Lake 2 km. Beach 11 km. Lake 12 km.

Open: All year.

Directions

From the A17 (Lisboa-Porto), take exit 5 for Carrico, turn right at the roundabout and O Tamanco is on the left. GPS: 39.99455, -8.78584

Charges guide

Per unit incl. 2 persons and electricity	€ 18.55
extra person	€ 4.20
child (up to 10 yrs)	€ 2.30
dog	€ 1.00

No credit cards.

São Martinho do Porto

Parque de Campismo Colina do Sol

Serra dos Mangues, P-2460-697 São Martinho do Porto (Leiria) T: 262 989 764. E: geral@colinadosol.net

alanrogers.com/PO8450

Colina do Sol is a well appointed site with its own swimming pool and close to the beach. Only 2 km. from the small town of São Martinho do Porto, it has around 350 pitches marked by fruit and ornamental trees on grassy terraces. Electricity (6A) is available. The attractive entrance with its beds of bright flowers, is wide enough for even the largest of outfits, and the surfaced roads are very pleasant for manoeuvring. There is a warm welcome and good English is spoken. The beach is at the rear of the site, with access via a gate which is locked at night. We are told that swimming in the sea requires great care when there are large waves – there is no lifeguard.

Facilities

Two large, clean and modern toilet blocks provide British style WCs (some with bidets), washbasins, some with hot water. Motorcaravan services. Supermarket. Bar and restaurant (1/7-31/8). Satellite TV. Swimming pool (1/7-10/9). WiFi (free). Off site: Bus from the gate to nearby towns. Shop, restaurant and bar within 200 m. Beach (no lifeguard).

Open: All year excl. 25 December.

Directions

Turn from EN242 (Caldas-Nazaré) road northeast of São Martinho do Porto. Site is clearly signed. GPS: 39.52283, -9.123

Charges guide

Per unit incl. 2 persons and electricity	€ 14.00 - € 18.50
extra person	€ 3.50 - € 5.00
child (4-10 yrs)	€ 1.75 - € 2.50

Less in low seasons.

São Pedro de Moel

Orbitur Camping São Pedro de Moel

alan rogers Runner up 2013 Awards

Rua Volta do Sete, P-2430 São Pedro de Moel (Leiria) T: 244 599 168. E: infospedro@orbitur.pt

alanrogers.com/PO8100

This quiet and very attractive site is situated under tall pines, on the edge of the rather select small resort of São Pedro de Moel. This is a shady site which can be crowded in July and August. The 525 pitches are in blocks and unmarked (cars may be parked separately) with 404 electrical connections. A few pitches are used for permanent units. Although there are areas of soft sand, there should be no problem in finding a firm place. The large restaurant and bar are modern as is the superb swimming pool, paddling pool and flume (there is a lifeguard). The attractive, sandy beach is a 600 m. walk downhill from the site and is sheltered from the wind by low cliffs.

Facilities

Four clean toilet blocks have mainly British style toilets (some with bidets), some washbasins with hot water. Hot showers are mostly in one unisex block. Laundry. Motorcaravan services. Gas supplies. Supermarket (1/6-15/9). Large restaurant and bar with terrace (1/6-15/9). Swimming pools (1/6-30/9). Satellite TV. Games room. Playground. Tennis. Free WiFi over part of site. Off site: Beach 500 m. Fishing 1 km.

Open: All year.

Directions

Site is 9 km. west of Marinha Grande, on the right as you enter São Pedro de Moel. GPS: 39.75883, -9.02229

Charges guide

Per person	€ 3.80 - € 6.40
child (5-10 yrs)	€ 1.90 - € 3.20
pitch	€ 8.50 - € 14.30
electricity	€ 3.50

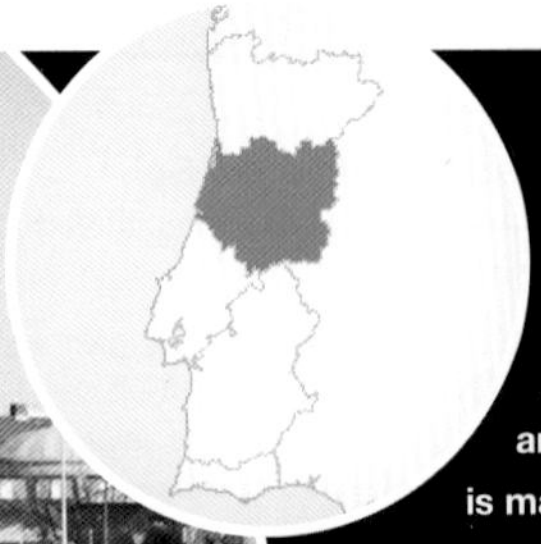

Beiras is the traditional name for the strip of land flanked by Portugal's two main rivers – the Douro and the Tagus. This region is made up of two contrasting areas: white sandy beaches, fishing villages and pine forests lie along the coast, while inland the mountains dominate the landscape.

BEIRAS HAS FIVE DISTRICTS: AVEIRO, COIMBRA, CASTELO BRANCO, GUARDA AND VISEU

One of Europe's oldest university towns, Coimbra was Portugal's capital from 1143 to 1255. The university, founded in 1290, has kept its academic traditions, as seen in the black-capped students, in the soulful tones of the fado de Coimbra (a traditional song sung to the sound of guitars by the students) and in the Queima das Fitas (Burning of the Ribbons), a boisterous celebration of graduating students. Coimbra also boasts a Romanesque cathedral, and south of the town lies Conímbriga, with the most important Roman remains in Portugal. Surrounded by the original walls, the archaeological site features an early Christian burial ground, hot springs and a museum. Further north lies Aveiro. Famous for its lagoon, the town is criss-crossed by canals where colourfully-painted moliceiro boats sail. To the east lies the Serra de Estrela, the highest mountain range in the country. It is home to the textile town of Covilha, attractive villages including Gouveia, Manteigas and Seia, plus the mountain resort of Guarda. Along the coast, the pretty seaside resorts of São Martinho do Porto, Nazaré and Figueira da Foz offer fine sandy beaches, good seafood restaurants and watersports facilities.

Places of interest

Belmonte: hilltop town, castle, Romanesque-Gothic church.

Bussaco: national park founded by monks in the 6th century.

Castelo Branco: 13th-century castle, medieval quarter, 16th- and 18th-century churches.

Curia and *Luso:* spa towns.

Monsanto: historic village, 12th-century castle, 18th-century manor houses.

Viseu: remains of Gothic walls, cathedral.

Cuisine of the region

Roast pork, lamb stew, seafood and fresh fish are popular, including *truta* (trout) from the mountains of Serra da Estrela. The famous ewes' milk cheese *Queijo da Serra*, is also produced in the mountains, and can be bought at cheese fairs held in villages and towns throughout the region during February and March. Regional desserts include hard and sweet biscuits, pancakes and sponge cake (*ovos-moles*, *pão-de-ló*).

Chanfana: lamb stewed in red wine.

Leitão assado da Bairrada: roast pork.

Arganil

Camping Municipal Arganil

EN17 km. 5, Sarzedo, P-3300 Arganil (Coimbra) T: 235 205 706. E: camping@cm-arganil.pt

alanrogers.com/PO8330

This peaceful, inland site, attractively located in the hamlet of Sarzedo, some 2 km. from the town of Arganil, is among pine trees above the River Alva where one can swim, fish or canoe. A spacious and well planned site, it is high quality for a municipal and prices are very reasonable! The 150 pitches, most with electricity (15A), are of a reasonable size, mainly on flat sandy grass terraces and most shaded by tall trees. The site is kept beautifully clean and neat and access roads are tarmac. An excellent, small restaurant has an unusual attached bar with terrace.

Facilities

Sanitary facilities are clean and well maintained, with Turkish and British style WCs, controllable hot showers, washbasins in semi-private partitioned cabins and a hairdressing area. Ramped entrances make it suitable for disabled visitors. Washing machines. Bar, restaurant and snacks. Shop (July-Sept). TV room. Tennis. Free WiFi over part of site. Off site: Swimming pool in nearby Arganil. Golf 25 km. Bus service 50 m. River beach and fishing 100 m. Watersports 200 m.

Open: All year.

Directions

From Coimbra on IC2 take exit 8 onto IP3 towards Viseu. Take exit 13 onto IP6 (N17) towards Arganil and onto N324-4 to Sarzedo (site signed). Ignore first site sign in Avelar as there is better access 500 m. further along on right, also signed.
GPS: 40.23333, -8.08333

Charges guide

Per unit incl. 2 persons and electricity	€ 8.30 - € 13.00
extra person	€ 1.60 - € 1.80
child (5-10 yrs)	€ 1.10 - € 1.30
electricity	€ 2.00 - € 2.40

Aveiro

Orbitur Camping São Jacinto

EN327 km. 20, São Jacinto, P-3800-909 Aveiro (Aveiro) T: 234 838 284. E: infosjacinto@orbitur.pt

alanrogers.com/PO8050

This small site is in the São Jacinto Nature Reserve, on a peninsula between the Atlantic and the Barrinha, with views to the mountains beyond. The area is a weekend resort for locals and can be crowded in high season – it may therefore be difficult to find space in July and August, particularly for larger units. This is not a large site, taking 169 units on unmarked pitches, but in most places trees provide natural limits and shade. Swimming and fishing are both possible in the adjacent Ria, or the sea, a 20 minute walk from a guarded back gate. A deep borehole supplies the site with drinking water.

Facilities

Two toilet blocks, very clean when inspected, contain the usual facilities. Washing machine and ironing board in a separate part of the toilet block. Motorcaravan services. Shop. Restaurant, bar and snack bar. Attractive new playground. Five bungalows to rent. Off site: Bus service 20 m. Fishing 200 m. Bicycle hire 10 km.

Open: 1 June - 30 September.

Directions

Turn off N109 at Estarreja to N109-5 to cross bridge over Ria da Gosta Nova and on to Torreira and São Jacinto. From Porto go south N1/09, turn for Ovar on the N327 which leads to São Jacinto.
GPS: 40.67497, -8.72295

Charges guide

Per person	€ 4.30 - € 5.10
pitch	€ 11.40 - € 16.00
electricity	€ 2.90 - € 3.50

Figueira da Foz

Orbitur Camping Gala

EN109 km. 4, Gala, P-3090-458 Figueira da Foz (Coimbra) T: 233 431 492. E: infogala@orbitur.pt

alanrogers.com/PO8090

One of the best Orbitur sites, Gala has around 450 pitches on sandy terrain under a canopy of pine trees and is well cared for. Some pitches near the road are rather noisy. One can drive or walk the 300 m. from the back of the site to a private beach; you should swim with caution when it is windy – the warden will advise. The site fills up in July/August and units may be very close together, but there should be plenty of room at other times. Besides the beach, Coimbra and the nearby Roman remains are worth visiting.

Facilities

The three toilet blocks have British and Turkish style toilets, individual basins (some with hot water) and free hot showers. Laundry. Motorcaravan services. Gas supplies. Supermarket and bar/restaurant with terrace. Lounge. Open-air pool (March-Sept). Playground. Tennis. TV. WiFi throughout. Doctor visits in season. Car wash area. Off site: Beach 300 m. Fishing and bicycle hire 2 km.

Open: All year.

Directions

Coming from the north, the site is 4 km. south of Figueira da Foz beyond the two rivers; turn off N109 1 km. from bridge on southern edge of Gala, look for Orbitur sign on roundabout, it is then 600 m. to site.
GPS: 40.11850, -8.85683

Charges guide

Per unit incl. 2 persons and electricity	€ 22.70 - € 37.90
extra person	€ 3.80 - € 6.40
child (5-10 yrs)	€ 1.90 - € 3.20
dog	€ 1.10 - € 2.20

Camping Cheques accepted.

Ilhavo

Camping Costa Nova

Quinta dos Patos, Gafanha da Encarnação, P-3830 Ilhavo (Aveiro) T: 234 393 220.
E: info@campingcostanova.com **alanrogers.com/PO8060**

Camping Costa Nova lies between a river (Ria de Aveiro) and the sea in a protected natural reserve. There is direct access to a large sandy beach via a wooden walkway across the dunes. The 300 grassy pitches are provided with electricity hook-ups (10A). This site is ideal for those who enjoy watersports and the surroundings offer plenty of sites of interest for exploration. The site boasts a large bar and restaurant, and a café with TV and Internet access. English speaking visitors are welcomed and this sheltered site also attracts many for winter stays. Apartments are available for let.

Facilities

Three toilet blocks are well spaced around the site and offer adequate facilities with free hot water. Laundry room. Supermarket. Bar (all season). Restaurant (1/7-31/8). Takeaway. Snack bar. Shop. Games room. Disco. TV. Play area. Football field. Internet access. Off site: Beach 500 m. Fishing. Golf 600 m.

Open: 2 February - 31 December.

Directions

On the IP5 travelling from Aveiro east towards Barra, cross the bridge. At roundabout take third exit and site is well signed. GPS: 40.59972, -8.75139

Charges guide

Per unit incl. 2 persons and electricity	€ 12.70 - € 16.40
extra person	€ 3.00 - € 4.30
child (5-10 yrs)	€ 1.50 - € 2.15
dog	€ 1.50 - € 1.70

Praia de Mira

Orbitur Camping Mira

Estrada Florestal no. 1 km. 2, Dunas de Mira, P-3070-792 Praia de Mira (Coimbra) T: 231 471 234.
E: infomira@orbitur.pt **alanrogers.com/PO8070**

A small, peaceful seaside site set in pinewoods, Orbitur Camping Mira is situated to the south of Aveiro and Vagos, in a quieter and less crowded area. It fronts onto a lake at the head of the Ria de Mira, which eventually runs into the Aveiro Ria. A back gate leads directly to the sea and a wide quiet beach 300 m. away. A road runs alongside the site boundary where the restaurant complex is situated resulting in some road noise. The site has around 225 pitches on sand, which are not marked but have trees creating natural divisions. Electricity and water points are plentiful.

Facilities

The modern toilet blocks are clean, with 14 free hot showers and washing machines. Facilities for disabled visitors. Motorcaravan services. Gas supplies. Shop. Bar. Restaurant and takeaway (1/6-15/9). TV room. Play area. Bicycle hire. Free WiFi at the bar. Bungalows (7) to rent. Off site: Bus service 150 m. (summer only). Fishing and beach 200 m. Indoor pool, lake swimming and riding at Mira 7 km.

Open: 23 March - 30 September.

Directions

Take the IP5 (A25) southwest to Aveiro then the A17 south to Figuera da Foz. Then take the N109 north to Mira and follow signs west to Praia (beach) de Mira. GPS: 40.4533, -8.79902

Charges guide

Per person	€ 5.80
child (5-10 yrs)	€ 2.90
pitch	€ 8.60 - € 11.90
electricity	€ 3.50 - € 4.60

Sátão

Camping Quinta Chave Grande

Casfreires, Ferreira d'Aves, P-3560-043 Sátão (Viseu) T: 232 665 552. E: info@chavegrande.com
alanrogers.com/PO8335

Quinta Chave Grande is a good quality campsite with friendly Dutch owners. It is set in a rural valley, close to many charming old villages, yet also only 25 km. from the provincial capital of Viseu, with its museums, churches and beautiful old town centre. The site occupies a large area and there are 150 unmarked touring pitches, although some are defined by trees. Electricity (6A) is available to all but long leads may be required. Larger units can be accommodated and there is a separate terraced area for tents. Torches are essential. For those who enjoy walking there are eight marked walking tours starting from the campsite.

Facilities

Three modern toilet blocks, one with private en-suite cubicles for use by families and for visitors with disabilities. Service wash available. No shop but local tradesmen visit the site. Bar (all season). Swimming pool and children's pool (15/5-1/10). Fenced play area. Organised events for children and teenagers in July/Aug. Tennis. Boules. Off site: Fishing and bicycle hire 4 km. Riding 25 km.

Open: 1 April - 15 October.

Directions

From A25 Guarda-Viseu road take exit 19, than at the IP5 take exit 17 to Sátão. Take the N229 northeast to Sátão. Site is very well signed along road and is 12 km. northeast of Sátão.
GPS: 40.8227, -7.69609

Charges guide

Per unit incl. 2 persons and electricity	€ 22.50
extra person	€ 5.00

Vagos

Orbitur Camping Vagueira

Gafanha da Vagueira, Gafanha da Boa Hora, P-3840-254 Vagos (Aveiro) T: 234 797 526.
E: infovagueira@orbitur.pt **alanrogers.com/PO8040**

This is a large site set 1.5 km. from the beach and 500 m. from the Ria da Gosta Nova river. It is shaded under tall pine trees and has comprehensive facilities and reasonable prices. The 800 pitches are unmarked, on sand and pine needles, with a large number of permanent Portuguese units, which are here in high season and weekends at other times. Groups are taken in high season. All touring pitches have electricity (6A). In sympathy with the surroundings, the modern buildings have clean lines and include a restaurant and bar with a disco area outside where music is played at weekends.

Facilities

Seven modern sanitary buildings with British and Turkish style WCs and free showers. Facilities for disabled campers (unlocked). Washing machines. Bar/snacks and separate restaurant (June-Sept). No shop but some groceries available from reception. Outdoor disco. Games room. Playground. Tennis (charge). Satellite TV. Free WiFi over part of site. Torches useful. Off site: Seaside town has shops, bars and restaurants. Bus 500 m. Golf 1 km.

Open: All year.

Directions

Site is south of Aveiro. Take N109 south from Aveiro towards Mira. At Vagos take the N333 right turn towards Vagueira. Site is well signed at this turn and is just off the roundabout you arrive at on the beach road. GPS: 40.55792, -8.74517

Charges guide

Per person	€ 2.90 - € 5.10
pitch and car	€ 6.40 - € 10.80
electricity	€ 3.50

Camping Cheques accepted.

Originally inhabited by Celtics, Romans and Moors, the North is a region steeped in history. Renowned for its beautiful countryside, the River Douro winds its way past mountains, valleys, vineyards and cliffs until it reaches the sandy beaches of the Atlantic coast near the city of Porto.

THE REGION COMPRISES FIVE DISTRICTS: BRAGA, BRAGANÇA, PORTO, VIANA DO CASTELO AND VILA REAL

Situated in the north western corner of Portugal, the Costa Verde boasts lush green pine forests and unspoilt sandy beaches, dotted with picturesque seaside villages, including Caminha and Vila Nova de Cerveira. It is also renowned for its wine, being the home of Port and Vinho Verdo. Located on the banks of the River Douro, the attractive city of Porto is the centre of the Port wine trade – free tastings are offered at the wine cellars in Vila Nova de Gaia – and terraced vineyards can be found across the Douro Valley. The region is also a perfect place for walking, mountain trekking, canoeing or simply relaxing in the spa towns of Carvalhelhos, Chaves and Pedras Salgadas. Vidago has a magnificent park with swimming pools and a golf course, while the mountains of Peneda, Soajo and Gerês form the Peneda Geres National Park, an area covering 170,000 acres, with an abundance of wildlife. Vila Nova de Foz is the centre for visits to the Côa Archaeological Park, which houses one of the world's largest collections of outdoor Palaeolithic rock art, dating back 22,000 years.

Places of interest

Barcelos: medieval walled town with dungeon, ceramics museum, archaeology museum.

Bragança: medieval castle and walls, 16th-century cathedral, railway museum with 19th-century locomotives and carriages.

Chaves: Roman bridge, 14th-century castle with Archaeology and Epigraphy Museum.

Guimarães: medieval castle and walls, palace.

Lamego: medieval castle, 12th-century fortress.

Ponte de Lima: beautiful small town, Roman bridge, medieval towers, manor houses.

Viana do Castelo: town famous for its handicrafts and colourful regional costumes.

Vila do Conde: ancient medieval shipyard, famous for its manufactured lace.

Cuisine of the region

Typical dishes include *bacalhau* (dried and salted cod), *rabanadas*, *papos-de-anjo* and *barrigas-de-freiras* (sweetmeats). Porto has its own tripe dish, *Tripas à moda do Porto*. The Minho region is renowned for its *Vinhos Verdes*, whose vines are grown on trellises (suspended high in the air on special frames). In the Douro region, the vines are grown on terraces, giving the impression of huge, natural staircases leading down to the banks of the river. Both red and white wines are produced here including the famous *Vinho do Porto* (Port wine).

Caldo verde: thick soup made with green cabbage, potatoes and spicy sausage.

Feijoada à transmontana: bean stew.

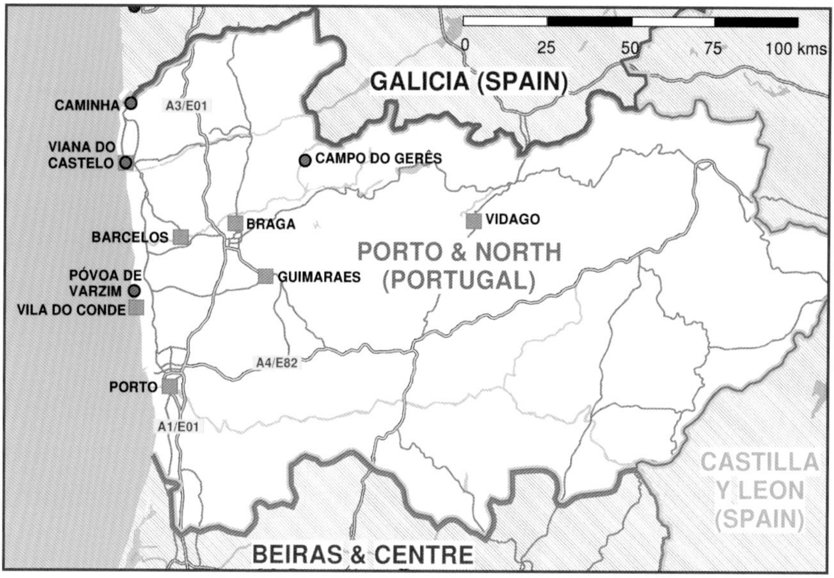

Caminha

Orbitur Camping Caminha

EN13 km. 90, Mata do Camarido, P-4910-180 Caminha (Viana do Costelo) T: 258 921 295.
E: infocaminha@orbitur.pt **alanrogers.com/PO8010**

In northern Portugal, close to the Spanish border, this pleasant site is just 200 m. from the beach. It has an attractive and peaceful setting in woods alongside the river estuary that marks the border with Spain and on the edge of the little town of Caminha. Of the 262 pitches, just 25 are available for touring with electricity (5/15A Europlug), the remainder are occupied by permanent units and chalets for rent. The site is shaded by tall pines with other small trees planted to mark large sandy pitches. The main site road is surfaced but elsewhere take care not to get trapped in soft sand. Pitching and parking can be haphazard. Static units are grouped together on one side of the site.

Facilities

The clean, well maintained toilet block is modern with British style toilets, open style washbasins and hot showers, plus beach showers. Facilities for disabled visitors and babies. Laundry facilities. Motorcaravan services. Supermarket, bar with satellite TV (1/6-30/9). Restaurant and takeaway (1/6-15/9). Bicycle hire. Entertainment in high season. Charcoal barbecues are permitted. Off site: Beach and fishing 100 m. Bus service 800 m. Kayak excursions. Birdwatching.

Open: All year.

Directions

From the north, turn off the main coast road (N13-E50) just after the camping sign at the end of the embankment alongside estuary, 1.5 km. south of ferry. From the south on N13 turn left at Hotel Faz de Minho at start of estuary and follow for 1 km. through woods to site. GPS: 41.86635, -8.85844

Charges guide

Per unit incl. 2 persons and electricity	€ 15.00 - € 31.30
extra person	€ 3.40 - € 5.70
child (5-10 yrs)	€ 1.70 - € 2.90
dog	€ 1.00 - € 2.00

Camping Cheques accepted.

Campo do Gerês

Parque de Campismo de Cerdeira

Rua de Cerdeira 400, P-4840 030 Campo do Gerês (Braga) T: 253 351 005. E: info@parquecerdeira.com

alanrogers.com/PO8370

Located in the Peneda-Gerês National Park, amidst spectacular mountain scenery, this excellent site offers modern facilities in a truly natural area. The national park is home to all manner of flora, fauna and wildlife, including the roebuck, wolf and wild boar. The well fenced, professional and peaceful site offers 600 good sized, unmarked, mostly level, grassy pitches in a shady woodland setting. Electricity (5/10A) is available for 200 of the 550 touring pitches, though some long leads may be required. A very large timber complex, tastefully designed with the use of noble materials – granite and wood – provides a superb restaurant with a comprehensive menu.

Facilities

Three very clean sanitary blocks provide mixed style WCs, controllable showers and hot water. Good facilities for disabled visitors. Laundry. Gas supplies. Shop. Restaurant/bar. Outdoor pool (June-Sept). Playground. TV room (satellite). Medical post. Good tennis courts. Minigolf. Adventure park. Car wash. Barbecue areas. Torches useful. English spoken. Attractive bungalows to rent. WiFi in reception/bar area.

Open: All year.

Directions

From north, N103 (Braga-Chaves), turn left at N205 (7.5 km. north of Braga). Follow N205 to Caldelas Terras de Bouro and Covide where site is signed to Campo do Gerês. An eastern approach from N103 is for the adventurous but with magnificent views over mountains and lakes. GPS: 41.7631, -8.1905

Charges guide

Per unit incl. 2 persons and electricity € 13.60 - € 28.60

Viana do Castelo

Orbitur Camping Viana do Castelo

Rua Diogo Alvares, Cabedelo, P-4900-161 Viana do Castelo (Viana do Costelo) T: 258 322 167.

E: infoviana@orbitur.pt **alanrogers.com/PO8020**

This site in northern Portugal is worth considering as it has the advantage of direct access, via a gate in the fence (locked at night), to a large and excellent soft sand beach (200 m) which is popular for windsurfing. There are 225 pitches on three wide terraces with easy access, 150 of these with electricity (long leads may be needed). Some flat, good sized pitches are numbered and reserved for caravans and motorcaravans but with little shade. The large grass area for tents has more shade. It could become crowded in July/August. A pleasant restaurant terrace overlooks the pool.

Facilities

Toilet facilities are in two blocks, both with open style washbasins and hot showers. Facilities for disabled visitors. Baby changing. Laundry. Motorcaravan services. Gas supplies. Supermarket and bar (23/3-15/9). Small restaurant with terrace and takeaway (1/6-15/9). Open-air pool (23/3-30/9). Reading room with TV, video and fireplace. Playground. Children's club (July/Aug). First-aid post. WiFi in bar. Off site: Beach 200 m. Fishing 500 m.

Open: 23 March - 30 September.

Directions

On N13 coast road driving north to south drive through Viana do Castelo and over estuary bridge. Turn immediately right off N13 towards Cabedelo and the sea. Site is the third campsite signed, the other two are not recommended.
GPS: 41.67866, -8.82637

Charges guide

Per unit incl. 2 persons and electricity € 15.80 - € 33.70

Póvoa de Varzim

Orbitur Camping Rio Alto

EN13 km. 13 Rio Alto-Est, Estela, P-4570-275 Póvoa de Varzim (Porto) T: 252 615 699.

E: inforioalto@orbitur.pt **alanrogers.com/PO8030**

This site makes an excellent base for visiting Porto which is some 35 km. south of Estela. It has around 700 pitches on sandy terrain and is next to a virtually private beach. There are some hardstandings for caravans and motorcaravans and electrical connections to most pitches (5/15A long leads may be required). The area for tents is furthest from the beach and windswept, stunted pines give some shade. There are arrangements for car parking away from camping areas in peak season. There is a quality restaurant, a snack bar and a large swimming pool across the road from reception.

Facilities

Four refurbished and well equipped toilet blocks have hot water. Laundry facilities. Facilities for disabled visitors. Gas supplies. Motorcaravan service point. Shop (1/6-15/9). Restaurant (1/6-15/9). Bar, snack bar (all year). Swimming pool (1/6-30/9). Tennis. Play area. Games room. Surfing. TV. First-aid post. Car wash. Evening entertainment twice weekly in season. Bicycle hire arranged at reception. WiFi. Off site: Fishing 200 m. Golf 700 m. Riding 8 km.

Open: All year.

Directions

From A28 in direction of Porto, leave at exit 18 signed Fao/Apuila. At roundabout take third exit, N13 in direction of Pavoa de Varzim for 2.5 km. At Hotel Contriz, turn right onto narrow cobbled road. Site well signed in 2 km. GPS: 41.44504, -8.75767

Charges guide

Per unit incl. 2 persons and electricity € 19.30 - € 28.50

Camping Cheques accepted.

Accommodation

Over recent years many of the campsites featured in this guide have added large numbers of high quality mobile homes and chalets. Many site owners believe that some former caravanners and motorcaravanners have been enticed by the extra comfort they can now provide, and that maybe this is the ideal solution to combine the freedom of camping with all the comforts of home.

Quality is consistently high and, although the exact size and inventory may vary from site to site, if you choose any of the sites detailed here, you can be sure that you're staying in some of the best quality and best value mobile homes available.

Home comforts are provided and typically these include a fridge with freezer compartment, gas hob, proper shower – often a microwave and radio/cassette hi-fi too, but do check for details. All mobile homes and chalets come fully equipped with a good range of kitchen utensils, pots and pans, crockery, cutlery and outdoor furniture. Some even have an attractive wooden sundeck or paved terrace – a perfect spot for outdoors eating or relaxing with a book and watching the world go by.

Regardless of model, colourful soft furnishings are the norm and a generally breezy décor helps to provide a real holiday feel.

Although some sites may have a large number of different accommodation types, we have restricted our choice to one or two of the most popular accommodation units (either mobile homes or chalets) for each of the sites listed.

The mobile homes here will be of modern design, and recent innovations, for example, often include pitched roofs which substantially improve their appearance.

Design will invariably include clever use of space and fittings/furniture to provide for comfortable holidays – usually light and airy, with big windows and patio-style doors, fully equipped kitchen areas, a shower room with shower, washbasin and WC, cleverly designed bedrooms and a comfortable lounge/dining area (often incorporating a sofa bed).

In general, modern campsite chalets incorporate all the best features of mobile homes in a more traditional structure, sometimes with the advantage of an upper mezzanine floor for an additional bedroom.

Our selected campsites offer a massive range of different types of mobile home and chalet, and it would be impractical to inspect every single accommodation unit. Our selection criteria, therefore, primarily takes account of the quality standards of the campsite itself.

However, there are a couple of important ground rules:

- Featured mobile homes must be no more than five years old
- Chalets no more than ten years old
- All listed accommodation must, of course, fully conform with all applicable local, national and European safety legislation.

For each campsite we have given details of the type, or types, of accommodation available to rent, but these details are necessarily quite brief. Sometimes internal layouts can differ quite substantially, particularly with regard to sleeping arrangements, where these include the flexible provision for 'extra persons' on sofa beds located in the living area. These arrangements may vary from accommodation to accommodation, and if you're planning a holiday which includes more people than are catered for by the main bedrooms you should check exactly how the extra sleeping arrangements are to be provided!

Charges

An indication of the tariff for each type of accommodation featured is also included, indicating the variance between the low and high season tariffs. However, given that many campsites have a large and often complex range of pricing options, incorporating special deals and various discounts, the charges we mention should be taken to be just an indication. We strongly recommend therefore that you confirm the actual cost when making a booking.

We also strongly recommend that you check with the campsite, when booking, what (if anything) will be provided by way of bed linen, blankets, pillows etc. Again, in our experience, this can vary widely from site to site.

On every campsite a fully refundable deposit (usually between 150 and 300 euros) is payable on arrival. There may also be an optional cleaning service for which a further charge is made. Other options may include sheet hire (typically 30 euros per unit) or baby pack hire (cot and high chair).

Low Cost Flights

An Inexpensive Way To Arrive At Your Campsite

Many campsites are conveniently served by a wide choice of low cost airlines. Cheap flights can be very easy to find and travellers increasingly find the regional airports often used to be smaller, quieter and generally a calmer, more pleasurable experience.

Low cost flights can make campsites in more distant regions a much more attractive option: quicker to reach, inexpensive flights, and simply more convenient.

Many campsites are seeing increased visitors using the low cost flights and are adapting their services to suit this clientele. An airport shuttle service is not uncommon, meaning you can take advantage of that cheap flight knowing you will be met at the other end and whisked to your campsite. No taxi queues or multiple drop-offs.

Obviously, these low cost flights are impractical when taking all your own camping gear but they do make a holiday in campsite owned accommodation much more straightforward. The low cost airline option makes mobile home holidays especially attractive: pack a suitcase and use bed linen and towels provided (which you will generally need to pre-book).

Pricing Tips

- Low cost airlines promote cheap flights but only a small percentage of seats are priced at the cheapest price. Book early for the best prices (and of course you also get a better choice of campsite or mobile home)
- Child seats are usually the same costs as adults
- Full payment is required at the time of booking
- Changes and amendments can be costly with low cost airlines
- Peak dates can be expensive compared to other carriers

Car Hire

For maximum flexibility you will probably hire a car from a car rental agency.
Car hire provides convenience but also will allow you access to off-site shops, beaches and tourist sights.

ES85400 Camping La Torre del Sol

see report page 44

Ctra N340 km. 1136, E-43300 Montroig

AR1 – PAGAN – Bungalow Tent

Sleeping: 2 bedrooms, sleeps 5: 3 singles, bunk bed, pillows and blankets provided

Living: shower, WC, separate WC

Eating: fitted kitchen with hob, coffee maker, fridge

Outside: table & chairs, parasol, 2 sun loungers

Pets: not accepted

Open: 15 March - 31 October

Weekly Charge	AR1
Low Season **(from)**	€ 162
High Season **(from)**	€ 587

ES84700 La Siesta Salou Camping Resort

see report page 54

Calle Norte 37, E-43840 Salou

AR1 – EDEN – Bungalow

Sleeping: 3 bedrooms, sleeps 6: 1 double, 4 singles, bunk bed

Living: heating, TV, air conditioning, shower, WC, separate WC

Eating: fitted kitchen with hob, microwave, grill, coffee maker, fridge, freezer

Outside: table & chairs

Pets: not accepted

AR2 – BAHIA – Bungalow

Sleeping: 2 bedrooms, sleeps 4: 1 double, 2 singles

Living: heating, TV, air conditioning, shower, WC, separate WC

Eating: fitted kitchen with hob, microwave, grill, coffee maker, fridge, freezer

Outside: table & chairs

Pets: not accepted

Other (AR1 and AR2): bed linen to hire

Open: 1 April - 10 October

Weekly Charge	AR1	AR2
Low Season **(from)**	€ 665	€ 616
High Season **(from)**	€ 1645	€ 1182

Travelling in Europe

When taking your car (and caravan, tent or trailer tent) or motorcaravan to the continent you do need to plan in advance and to find out as much as possible about driving in the countries you plan to visit. Whilst European harmonisation has eliminated many of the differences between one country and another, it is well worth reading the short notes we provide in the introduction to each country in this guide in addition to this more general summary.

Of course, the main difference from driving in the UK is that in mainland Europe you will need to drive on the right. Without taking extra time and care, especially at busy junctions and conversely when roads are empty, it is easy to forget to drive on the right. Remember that traffic approaching from the right usually has priority unless otherwise indicated by road markings and signs. Harmonisation also means that most (but not all) common road signs are the same in all countries.

Your vehicle

Book your vehicle in for a good service well before your intended departure date. This will lessen the chance of an expensive breakdown. Make sure your brakes are working efficiently and that your tyres have plenty of tread (3 mm. is recommended, particularly if you are undertaking a long journey).

Also make sure that your caravan or trailer is roadworthy and that its tyres are in good order and correctly inflated. Plan your packing and be careful not to overload your vehicle, caravan and trailer – this is unsafe and may well invalidate your insurance cover (it must not be more fully loaded than the kerb weight of the insured vehicle).

There are a number of countries that have introduced low emission zones in towns and cities, including Germany, Czech Republic, Denmark, Italy and Sweden. For up-to-date-details on low emission zones and requirements please see: www.lowemissionzones.eu

CHECK ALL THE FOLLOWING:

- GB sticker. If you do not display a sticker, you may risk an on-the-spot fine as this identifier is compulsory in all countries. Euro-plates are an acceptable alternative within the EU (but not outside). Remember to attach another sticker (or Euro-plate) to caravans and trailers. Only GB stickers (not England, Scotland, Wales or N. Ireland) are valid in the EU.
- Headlights. As you will be driving on the right you must adjust your headlights so that the dipped beam does not dazzle oncoming drivers. Converter kits are readily available for most vehicles, although if your car is fitted with high intensity headlights, you should check with your motor dealer. Check that any planned extra loading does not affect the beam height.
- Seatbelts. Rules for the fitting and wearing of seatbelts throughout Europe are similar to those in the UK, but it is worth checking before you go. Rules for carrying children in the front of vehicles vary from country to country. It is best to plan not to do this if possible.
- Door/wing mirrors. To help with driving on the right, if your vehicle is not fitted with a mirror on the left hand side, we recommend you have one fitted.
- Fuel. Leaded and Lead Replacement petrol is increasingly difficult to find in Northern Europe.

Compulsory additional equipment

The driving laws of the countries of Europe still vary in what you are required to carry in your vehicle, although the consequences of not carrying a required piece of equipment are almost always an on-the-spot fine.

To meet these requirements we suggest that you carry the following:

- FIRE EXTINGUISHER
- BASIC TOOL KIT
- FIRST AID KIT
- SPARE BULBS
- TWO WARNING TRIANGLES – two are required in some countries at all times, and are compulsory in most countries when towing.
- HIGH VISIBILITY VEST – now compulsory in France, Spain, Italy and Austria (and likely to become compulsory throughout the EU) in case you need to walk on a motorway.
- BREATHALYSERS – now compulsory in France. Only breathalysers that are NF-approved will meet the legal requirement. French law states that one breathalyser must be produced, but it is recommended you carry two in case you use or break one.

Insurance and Motoring Documents

Vehicle insurance

Contact your insurer well before you depart to check that your car insurance policy covers driving outside the UK. Most do, but many policies only provide minimum cover (so if you have an accident your insurance may only cover the cost of damage to the other person's property, with no cover for fire and theft).

To maintain the same level of cover abroad as you enjoy at home you need to tell your vehicle insurer. Some will automatically cover you abroad with no extra cost and no extra paperwork. Some will say you need a Green Card (which is neither green nor on card) but won't charge for it. Some will charge extra for the Green Card. Ideally you should contact your vehicle insurer 3-4 weeks before you set off, and confirm your conversation with them in writing.

Breakdown insurance

Arrange breakdown cover for your trip in good time so that if your vehicle breaks down or is involved in an accident it (and your caravan or trailer) can be repaired or returned to this country. This cover can usually be arranged as part of your travel insurance policy (see below).

Documents you must take with you

You may be asked to show your documents at any time so make sure that they are in order, up-to-date and easily accessible while you travel.

These are what you need to take:

- Passports (you may also need a visa in some countries if you hold either a UK passport not issued in the UK or a passport that was issued outside the EU).
- Motor Insurance Certificate, including Green Card (or Continental Cover clause)
- DVLA Vehicle Registration Document plus, if not your own vehicle, the owner's written authority to drive.
- A full valid Driving Licence (not provisional) The new photo style licence is now mandatory in most European countries.

Personal Holiday insurance

Even though you are just travelling within Europe you must take out travel insurance. Few EU countries pay the full cost of medical treatment even under reciprocal health service arrangements. The first part of a holiday insurance policy covers people. It will include the cost of doctor, ambulance and hospital treatment if needed. If needed the better companies will even pay for English language speaking doctors and nurses and will bring a sick or injured holidaymaker home by air ambulance.

Personal Holiday insurance (continued)

An important part of the insurance, often ignored, is cancellation (and curtailment) cover. Few things are as heartbreaking as having to cancel a holiday because a member of the family falls ill. Cancellation insurance can't take away the disappointment, but it makes sure you don't suffer financially as well. For this reason you should arrange your holiday insurance at least eight weeks before you set off.

Whichever insurance you choose we would advise reading very carefully the policies sold by the High Street travel trade. Whilst they may be good, they may not cover the specific needs of campers, caravanners and motorcaravanners.

Telephone **01580 214000** for a quote for our Camping Travel Insurance with cover arranged through leading leisure insurance providers.
Alternatively visit our website at: **alanrogers.com/insurance**

European Health Insurance Card (EHIC)

Make sure you apply for your EHIC before travelling in Europe. Eligible travellers from the UK are entitled to receive free or reduced-cost medical care in many European countries on production of an EHIC. This free card is available by completing a form in the booklet 'Health Advice for Travellers' from local Post Offices. One should be completed for each family member. Alternatively visit **www.ehic.org.uk** and apply on-line. Please allow time to send your application off and have the EHIC returned to you.

The EHIC is valid in all European Community countries plus Iceland, Liechtenstein, Switzerland and Norway. If you or any of your dependants are suddenly taken ill or have an accident during a visit to any of these countries, free or reduced-cost emergency treatment is available – in most cases on production of a valid EHIC.

Only state-provided emergency treatment is covered, and you will receive treatment on the same terms as nationals of the country you are visiting. Private treatment is generally not covered, and state-provided treatment may not cover all of the things that you would expect to receive free of charge from the NHS.

Remember an EHIC does not cover you for all the medical costs that you can incur or for repatriation - it is not an alternative to travel insurance. You will still need appropriate insurance to ensure you are fully covered for all eventualities.

Travelling with children

Most countries in Europe are enforcing strict guidelines when you are travelling with children who are not your own. A minor (under the age of 18) must be accompanied by a parent or legal guardian or must carry a letter of authorisation from a parent or guardian. The letter should name the adult responsible for the minor during his or her stay. Similarly, a minor travelling with just one of his/her parents, must have a letter of authority to leave their home country from the parent staying behind. Full information is available at **www.fco.gov.uk**

Travelling with dogs

Many British campers and caravanners prefer to take their pets with them on holiday. However, pet travel rules changed on 1 January 2012 when the UK brought its procedures into line with the European Union. From this date all pets can enter or re-enter the UK from any country in the world without quarantine provided they meet the rules of the scheme, which will be different depending on the country or territory the pet is coming from. Please refer to the following website for full details: **www.gov.uk/take-pet-abroad**

Open All Year

The following sites are understood to accept caravanners and campers all year round. It is always wise to phone the site to check as the facilities available, for example, may be reduced.

SPAIN

Cataluña-Catalunya

ES85360	Ametlla	23
ES82280	Blanes	26
ES82350	Bon Repos	61
ES85350	Cala d'Oques	37
ES81300	Calonge	28
ES80360	Esponellà	35
ES84770	Llosa	29
ES80720	Medes	39
ES80240	Pedres	31
ES84820	Pineda de Salou	40
ES85080	Poboleda	50
ES85060	Serra de Prades	64
ES91225	Vall de Camprodon	30
ES83900	Vilanova Park	65

Comunidad Valenciana

ES86200	Alqueria	74
ES85850	Altomira	77
ES86830	Benisol	71
ES85800	Bonterra	70
ES86900	Costa Blanca	74
ES85790	Didota	80
ES86850	El Raco	71
ES86120	Euro (Oliva)	79
ES87410	Florantilles	80
ES87540	Javea	75
ES86150	Kiko	79
ES86250	Kiko Rural	81
ES87420	Marina	76
ES86450	Mariola	72
ES87435	Marjal Costa Blanca	73
ES87430	Marjal Resort	75
ES85900	Monmar	77
ES87550	Moraira	77
ES86130	Olé	78
ES85600	Playa Tropicana	69
ES85610	Ribamar	69
ES85700	Torre la Sal 2	80
ES86750	Vall de Laguar	72
ES86820	Villamar	71
ES86810	Villasol	70
ES85580	Vinaros	81

Murcia

ES87520	El Portus (Naturist)	85
ES87450	Fuente	84
ES87480	Madriles	85
ES87530	Manga	86
ES87440	Puerta	86

Andalucia

ES88730	Aldea	90
ES87830	Almanat (Naturist)	89
ES88100	Bella Vista	96
ES88030	Buganvilla	97
ES87630	Cabo de Gata	91
ES88020	Cabopino	97
ES90840	Campiña	102
ES90850	Carlos III	95
ES87560	Cueva Negra	98
ES87510	Cuevas Mar	100
ES90890	Despeñaperros	102
ES92950	Don Cactus	99
ES92900	El Balcon	100
ES90800	El Brillante	92
ES87810	El Pino	104
ES88090	El Sur	101
ES87620	Escullos	99
ES87900	Fuente de Piedra	93
ES87650	Garrofa	89
ES88900	Gazules	89
ES88710	Giralda	95
ES87820	Laguna Playa	103
ES92850	Lomas	94
ES88000	Marbella Playa	97
ES92930	Orgiva	100
ES88500	Paloma	103
ES88570	Pinar San José	90
ES88650	Playa Las Dunas	93
ES92920	Puerta la Alpujarra	99
ES92760	Reina Isabel	96
ES88590	Roche	91
ES87680	Roquetas	101
ES88580	Rosaleda	92
ES87850	Rural Iznate	95
ES87905	Sierrecilla	94
ES87490	Sopalmo	98
ES92700	Suspiro-Moro	93
ES92890	Trevélez	104

Extremadura

ES90870	Merida	108
ES90270	Monfrague	108

Castilla-La Mancha

ES90970	Batanes	112
ES90900	El Greco	112
ES90960	Mirador	111

Madrid

ES90910	Aranjuez	115
ES92000	El Escorial	116
ES92120	Monte Holiday	115
ES92100	Pico-Miel	116

Castilla y León

ES92500	Costajan	119
ES90210	Fuentes Blancas	119
ES90250	Regio	121
ES90245	Riaza	120

Galicia

ES90240	As Cancelas	126
ES89360	Bayona Playa	124

Asturias

ES89650	Picos-Europa	129

Cantabria

ES89640	Molino	132
ES89730	Santillana	136

Pais Vasco-Euskadi

ES90390	Gran Zarautz	140
ES90300	Igueldo	139

La Rioja

ES92280	Berceo	142

Aragón

ES90620	Boltana	151
ES91040	Ciudad de Zaragoza	154
ES90640	Gavín	152
ES91250	Lago Barasona	152
ES90610	Ligüerre de Cinca	153
ES90600	Peña Montañesa	153

PORTUGAL

Algarve

PO8210	Albufeira	158
PO8410	Armacao-Pêra	159
PO8230	Olhão	161
PO8220	Quarteira	160
PO8440	Quinta	159
PO8430	Sagres	161
PO8202	Turiscampo	160
PO8200	Valverde	159

Alentejo

PO8353	Albufeira do Maranhão	164
PO8340	Évora	165
PO8350	Markádia	164
PO8180	Milfontes	167
PO8170	São Miguel	165
PO8190	Sitava Milfontes	166
PO8175	Zmar	165

Lisbon & Vale do Tejo

PO8150	Caparica	170
PO8480	Foz do Arelho	171
PO8130	Guincho	169
PO8140	Monsanto	171
PO8400	O Tamanco	172
PO8155	Parque Verde	170
PO8100	São Pedro-Moel	173
PO8110	Valado	172

Beiras & Centre

PO8330	Arganil	175
PO8090	Gala	176
PO8040	Vagueira	177

Porto & North

PO8010	Caminha	179
PO8370	Cerdeira	180
PO8030	Rio Alto	180

Dogs

Please refer to the 'Travelling with dogs' notes on page 189.

For the benefit of those who want to take their dogs with them or for people who do not like dogs at the sites they visit, we list here the sites that have indicated to us that they do not accept dogs. If you are, however, planning to take your dog we do advise you to contact them first to check – there may be limits on numbers, breeds, etc. or times of the year when they are excluded.

Never – these sites do not accept dogs at any time

SPAIN

Cataluña-Catalunya

ES80900	Cypsela	48
ES81030	El Maset	24
ES80700	Escala	38
ES91430	Pirineus	37
ES81010	Playa Brava	49
ES85300	Playa Montroig	46
ES84200	Stel (Roda)	50
ES85370	Templo del Sol (Naturist)	37
ES85400	Torre del Sol	44
ES81400	Treumal	29

Comunidad Valenciana

ES85900	Monmar	77
ES86820	Villamar	71
ES86810	Villasol	70

Murcia

ES87480	Madriles	85

Andalucia

ES88550	Tarifa	103
ES87580	Tau de San José	101

Castilla y León

ES92540	Demanda	122
ES92510	Rio Lobos	122

Cantabria

ES89980	Playa de Isla	133
ES90000	Playa Joyel	134

Aragón

ES91100	Fresneda	152

Balears

ES80000	Son Bou	155

PORTUGAL

Alentejo

PO8170	São Miguel	165
PO8190	Sitava Milfontes	166

Maybe – at cerain times or with other conditions.

SPAIN

Cataluña-Catalunya

ES81600	Cala Gogo	28
ES80800	Delfin Verde	63
ES80720	Medes	39
ES84820	Pineda de Salou	40
ES80090	Salatà	51

Comunidad Valenciana

ES85800	Bonterra	70

Andalucia

ES88030	Buganvilla	97
ES88500	Paloma	103
ES88570	Pinar San José	90
ES88580	Rosaleda	92

PORTUGAL

Alentejo

PO8350	Markádia	164

Fishing

We are pleased to include details of sites which provide facilities for fishing on site. However, it is always best to contact sites directly to check that they provide for your individual requirements.

SPAIN

Cataluña-Catalunya

ES85360	Ametlla	23
ES80350	Amfora	59
ES80500	Aquarius	60
ES80600	Ballena Alegre	61
ES82320	Bella Terra	26
ES82280	Blanes	26
ES82350	Bon Repos	61
ES82380	Caballo de Mar	46
ES85350	Cala d'Oques	37
ES81600	Cala Gogo	28
ES82000	Cala Llevadó	64
ES80100	Castell Mar	31
ES82340	Del Mar	42
ES80800	Delfin Verde	63
ES80400	Dunas	56
ES82300	El Pinar	26
ES85330	Els Prats Village	43
ES80310	Gaviota	55
ES84780	Joan	30
ES80150	Laguna	34
ES84770	Llosa	29
ES80650	Maçanet de Cabrenys	41
ES80300	Nautic Almata	32
ES84850	Palmeras	62
ES85300	Playa Montroig	46
ES80320	Riu	56
ES91420	Solana del Segre	25
ES84200	Stel (Roda)	50
ES84830	Tamarit	62
ES85370	Templo del Sol (Naturist)	37
ES82330	Tordera	42
ES84860	Torre de la Mora	63
ES85400	Torre del Sol	44
ES81400	Treumal	29
ES91225	Vall de Camprodon	30

Fishing continued

Comunidad Valenciana

ES86115	Azul	78
ES85790	Didota	80
ES86120	Euro (Oliva)	79
ES86150	Kiko	79
ES86130	Olé	78
ES86880	Playa Paraiso	81
ES85600	Playa Tropicana	69
ES85610	Ribamar	69
ES85700	Torre la Sal 2	80

Murcia

ES87520	El Portus (Naturist)	85
ES87530	Manga	86
ES87440	Puerta	86

Andalucia

ES87830	Almanat (Naturist)	89
ES92950	Don Cactus	99
ES87650	Garrofa	89
ES87820	Laguna Playa	103

Castilla-La Mancha

ES90900	El Greco	112
ES90980	Rio Mundo	111

Madrid

ES90910	Aranjuez	115

Castilla y León

ES92570	Frias	120
ES92510	Rio Lobos	122

Galicia

ES89360	Bayona Playa	124
ES89380	Paxarinas	125

Asturias

ES89440	Cascada	128
ES89500	Costa Verde	129
ES89450	Lagos-Somiedo	130
ES89600	Paz	130
ES89650	Picos-Europa	129

Cantabria

ES89700	Arenas-Pechón	134
ES89910	Barguilla	135
ES89620	Isla	135
ES89640	Molino	132
ES89980	Playa de Isla	133
ES89930	Playa del Regaton	133
ES90000	Playa Joyel	134

Pais Vasco-Euskadi

ES90450	Angosto	140
ES90350	Portuondo	139

La Rioja

ES92260	Cameros	144
ES92250	Rioja	143

Navarra

ES90420	Etxarri	147
ES90430	Molino Mendigorria	148
ES90480	Urrobi	147

Aragón

ES90580	Baliera	151
ES90610	Ligüerre de Cinca	153
ES90600	Peña Montañesa	153
ES90630	Puente	154

PORTUGAL

Alentejo

PO8350	Markádia	164

Beiras & Centre

PO8060	Costa Nova	176
PO8070	Mira	177

Horse Riding

We understand that the following sites have horse riding stables on site. Where facilities are within easy reach and we have been given details, we have included this information in the individual site reports. However, we recommend that you contact the site to check that they meet your requirements.

SPAIN

Cataluña-Catalunya

ES80150	Laguna	34
ES80300	Nautic Almata	32
ES85060	Serra de Prades	64
ES91420	Solana del Segre	25
ES91225	Vall de Camprodon	30

Comunidad Valenciana

ES85790	Didota	80

Andalucia

ES88900	Gazules	89

Asturias

ES89450	Lagos-Somiedo	130

Cantabria

ES89700	Arenas-Pechón	134
ES89620	Isla	135

La Rioja

ES92250	Rioja	143

Aragón

ES90600	Peña Montañesa	153
ES90630	Puente	154

PORTUGAL

Alentejo

PO8350	Markádia	164

Benefits that add up

- Offers and benefits on many Alan Rogers campsites across Europe
- Save up to 60% in low season on over 600 campsites

Camping Cheque

- Free cardholders' magazine
- Big savings on rented accommodation and hotels at 400 locations

HOLIDAY CHEQUE

- Discounted ferries
- Savings on Alan Rogers guides
- Vote for your favourite campsite in the Alan Rogers Awards

Register today... and start saving

Carry the Alan Rogers Travel Card on your travels through Europe and save money all the way.

You'll enjoy exclusive deals with ferry operators, continental partners, tourist attractions and more. Even hotels, apartments, mobile homes and other campsite accommodation.

We've teamed up with Camping Cheque, the leading low season discount scheme, to offer you the widest choice of quality campsites at unbelievable prices. Simply load your card with Cheques before you travel.

Step 1

Register at **www.alanrogers.com/travelcard**

Step 2

You'll receive your activated card, along with a Welcome email containing useful links and information.

Step 3

Start using your card to save money or to redeem benefits during your holiday.

alanrogers.com/travelcard

essentials

Any experienced camper or caravanner knows that family camping trips take a lot of organisation. There's the equipment to check, the campsite to choose, the pitch to book, the ferry crossing to arrange – and that's before you've taken the kids shopping for summer clothes.

Getting the most from **off peak touring**

There are many reasons to avoid high season, if you can. Queues are shorter, there's less traffic, a calmer atmosphere and prices are cheaper. And it's usually still nice and sunny!

And when you use Camping Cheques you'll find great quality facilities that are actually open and a welcoming conviviality.

Did you know?

Camping Cheques can be used right into mid-July and from late August on many sites. Over 90 campsites in France alone accept Camping Cheques from 20th August.

Camping Cheque

Save up to 60% with Camping Cheques

Camping Cheque is a fixed price scheme allowing you to go as you please, staying on over 600 campsites across Europe, always paying the same rate and saving you up to 60% on regular pitch fees. One Cheque gives you one night for 2 people + unit on a standard pitch, with electricity. It's as simple as that.

Special offers mean you can stay extra nights free (eg 7 nights for 6 Cheques) or even a month free for a month paid! Especially popular in Spain during the winter, these longer-term offers can effectively halve the nightly rate. See Site Directory for details.

Check out our amazing Ferry Deals!

Why should I use Camping Cheques?

- It's a proven system, recognised by all 600+ participating campsites - so no nasty surprises.
- It's flexible, allowing you to travel between campsites, and also countries, on a whim - so no need to pre-book. (It's low season, so campsites are rarely full, though advance bookings can be made).
- Stay as long as you like, where you like - so you travel in complete freedom.
- Camping Cheques are valid at least 2 years - so no pressure to use them up. (If you have a couple left over after your trip, simply keep them for the following year, or use them up in the UK).

Tell me more... (but keep it brief!)

Camping Cheques was started in 1999 and has since grown in popularity each year (nearly 2 million were used last year). That should speak for itself. There are 'copycat' schemes, but none has the same range of quality campsites that save you up to 60%.

Ask for your **FREE** continental road map, which explains how Camping Cheque works

01580 214002

FREE

downloadable Site Directory

alanrogers.com/directory

campingcheque.co.uk

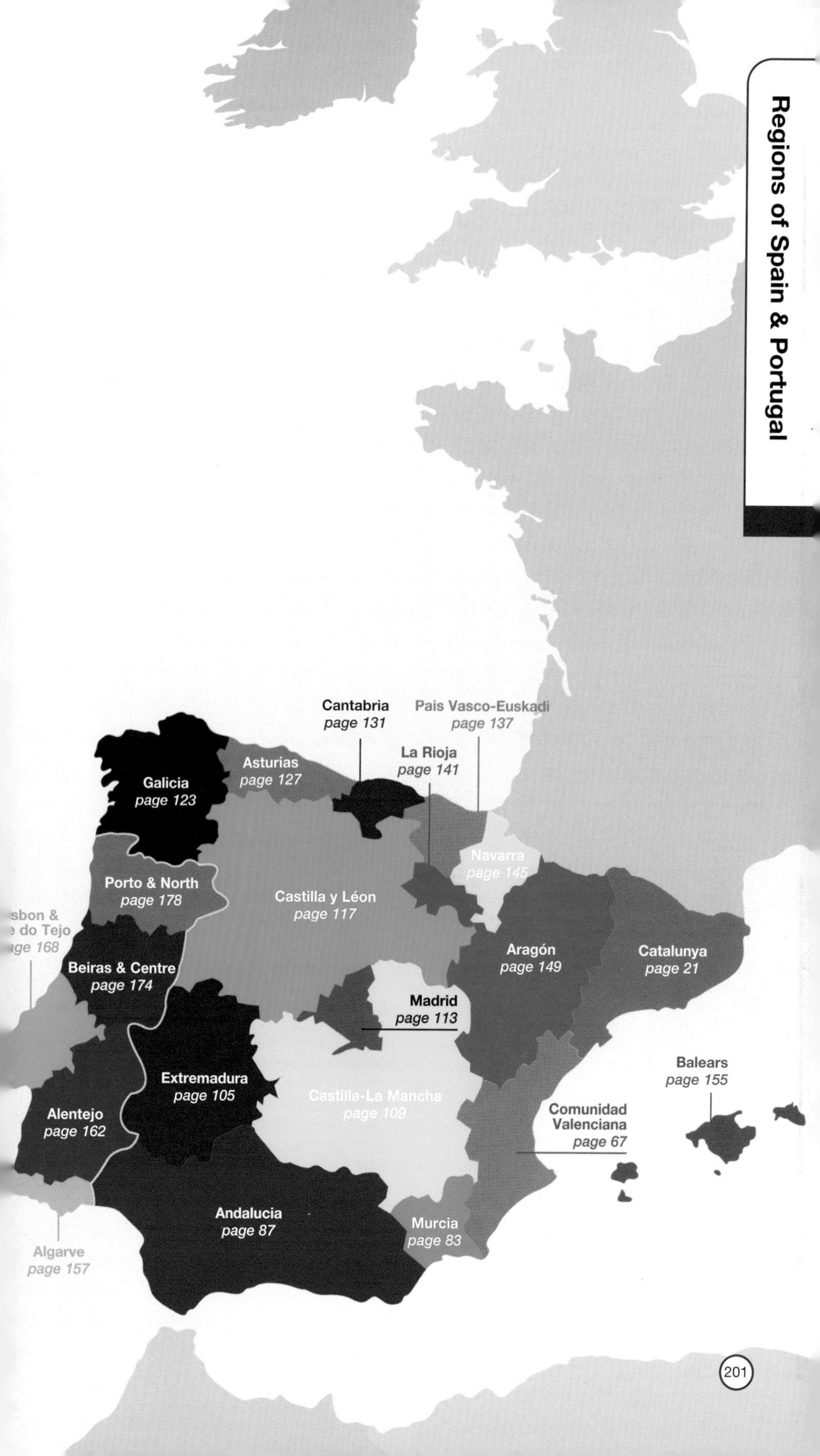

Cantabria
page 131
Pais Vasco-Euskadi
page 137
La Rioja
page 141
Asturias
page 127
Galicia
page 123
Navarra
page 145
Porto & North
page 178
Castilla y Léon
page 117
sbon &
do Tejo
ge 168
Aragón
page 149
Catalunya
page 21
Beiras & Centre
page 174
Madrid
page 113
Balears
page 155
Extremadura
page 105
Castilla-La Mancha
page 109
Comunidad
Valenciana
page 67
Alentejo
page 162
Andalucia
page 87
Murcia
page 83
Algarve
page 157

Town & Village Index

SPAIN

Town & Village Index continued

Index by Campsite Number

Index by Campsite Number continued

PORTUGAL

Index by Campsite Region & Name

SPAIN

Cataluña-Catalunya

Comunidad Valenciana

Murcia

Index by Campsite Region & Name continued